ENCYCLOPEDIC HANDBOOK
OF CULTS IN AMERICA
REVISED AND UPDATED
EDITION

Garland Reference Library of Social Science (Vol. 797)

Religious Information Systems Series, Vol. 7

Religious Information Systems
J. Gordon Melton
General Editor

Religious Bodies in the United States:
A Directory
by J. Gordon Melton

Religious Information Sources:
A Worldwide Guide
by J. Gordon Melton and Michael A. Köszegi

Magic, Witchcraft, and Paganism in America:
A Bibliography
Second Edition
by J. Gordon Melton and Isotta Poggi

The African-American Holiness Pentecostal Movement:
An Annotated Bibliography
by Sherry Sherrod DuPree

Holy Ground:
A Study of the American Camp Meeting
by Kenneth O. Brown

The Cult Controversy:
A Guide to Sources
by J. Gordon Melton

Islam in North America:
A Sourcebook
by Michael A. Köszegi and J. Gordon Melton

ENCYCLOPEDIC HANDBOOK OF CULTS IN AMERICA
REVISED AND UPDATED EDITION

by
J. Gordon Melton

RELIGIOUS INFORMATION SYSTEMS

Garland Publishing, Inc.
New York & London
1992

This is a revised and updated edition of *Encyclopedic Handbook of Cults in America* by J. Gordon Melton (Garland Publishing, 1986).

Library of Congress Cataloging-in-Publication Data

Melton, J. Gordon.
    Encyclopedic handbook of cults in America / by J. Gordon Melton —
revised and updated ed.
        p.   cm. — (Religious information systems series; vol. 7)
(Garland reference library of social science; v. 797)
        Includes index.
        ISBN 0-8153-0502-8. — ISBN 0-8153-1140-0 (pbk.)
        1. Cults—United States. 2. Sects—United States. 3. United
States—Religion. 4. Cults—Controversial literature—History
and criticism. I. Title. II. Series. III. Series: Garland reference
library of social science; v. 797.
BL2525.M45   1992
291'.0973—dc20
                                            92-11540
                                                CIP

Printed on acid-free, 250-year-life paper
Manufactured in the United States of America

CONTENTS

86948

INTRODUCTION
TO THE FIRST EDITION

There has been a growing need in the past several years for a concise summary of the most accurate information available on the more important of the alternative and nonconventional religious movements. As the cult wars of the 1970s have waned, the groups which had been the object of so much controversy remain. They have settled into the American religious landscape and show every sign of staying in place for the foreseeable future. For that reason alone, a guide to the more prominent of the 500 plus alternatives to the more familiar churches is necessary. The controversy which surrounds each of the groups considered here reinforces that observation.

The volume is divided into six sections. Section I surveys the broad range of issues surrounding the topic of "cults," the popular label given alternative religion, and attempts to summarize the present state of knowledge. Because of the nature of the controversies concerning the cults, a number of false stereotypes exist about them. These are discussed in the appropriate succeeding chapters.

Section II discusses approximately twenty of the older, more established nonconventional religions, all of which have their origin in the nineteenth or early twentieth century. Out of the many which could have been discussed, those chosen were selected primarily on the basis of size (a major criterion of success) and the presence of continuing controversy about them. As a whole, their main opponents have been the evangelical Christian counter-cult ministries who oppose these groups for deviating in their teachings from orthodox Christianity. Several of these groups, among them the "I AM" Activity and the Universal Peace Mission Movement, were selected as examples of still-vital movements which were at one time widely discussed but which have in recent years been forgotten.

Section III gives an in-depth treatment of the prominent and growing New Age Movement, about which very little descriptive literature exists. It has been a difficult movement to grasp because it is so decentralized and diverse. To aid readers in further research and understanding, a lengthy bibliography of New Age literature has been appended to the description.

Section IV is the heart of the volume. It discusses sixteen of the most significant "new" religions which have either emerged in America or been transported to its shores in the past few decades. For each group, as with the older cults, an attempt has been made to highlight basic data about the group's history, founder(s), beliefs and practices, and organization. An estimate of current strength is given and the recent controversies summarized.

Section V will be especially helpful to the neophyte to the cult controversies. It discusses the two main groups opposing nonconventional religions. The secular anti-cult movement appeared in the 1970s and has concentrated its attack primarily on the groups discussed in Section IV. Christian ministries, responding from an Evangelical perspective to the growing pluralism in American society, appeared earlier, after World War II. They speak to the issue of cults from a Christian theological stance. Up to now there has been little effort to compile the story of the development of this particular mission thrust and to see it as a distinct evangelical enterprise. In its developing years, the Christian ministries directed most of their energy to the older and larger groups, such as the Jehovah's Witnesses and the Mormons. Recently there has been a shift of considerable time and effort to the newer Eastern religions. In the final section a single important issue is raised for more substantial consideration: violence. The section discusses violence inflicted upon cult groups and members as well as that initiated within a cult body. Suggestions on reducing and eliminating cult-related violence are offered.

This book is by no means the final word. A separate chapter on legal matters, from lawsuits to nonviolent crime, should possibly have been included, but not feeling sufficiently versed to offer an adequate survey, I limited my remarks to those several cases discussed in the chapters on the specific group involved. It is my hope that such a survey can be accomplished in the near future.

The information contained in these chapters is as accurate as possible. Members and leaders of the groups discussed have been contacted, as have their critics. It has not always been possible to reach an agreement on matters of fact, and I am quite sure that people will disagree with interpretations placed upon data. I welcome additional information that will correct any errors in this volume or provide important but overlooked information which should be taken into account in making an informed evaluation.

A Word About Approaching the Cults

I have been studying nonconventional religion in America for over twenty years and writing about it for over a decade. I have worked as a professional church historian while wearing a second hat as a United Methodist minister with a distinct commitment to a conservative evangelical Wesleyan Christian faith. As a youth, I became both concerned about and fascinated by the multitudinous splinters of Christianity and then intrigued with the growing presence of so many non-Christian groups. During the 1960s, while still in seminary, I became convinced that the heterodox Christian groups and the non-Christian groups represented a phenomenon which was inadequately understood by my colleagues in church history and which was destined soon to play a much more important role in American life than any had anticipated. The cult wars and the spread of Asian religion in America in the last decade have proved my premonition correct.

However, in the 1960s, I set out to document and build a library of materials about the smaller and more nonconventional religions in America, and in 1969, with the aid of some fellow students at Garrett Theological Seminary, I founded the Institute for the Study of American Religion as an independent research facility concerned with America's less-documented religions. It began and has continued as a scholarly pursuit, and other researchers around the country have contributed their time and talent to make it the success it has been. It has deliberately remained neutral in the cult wars, though I as its director have occasionally fought a battle or two. Furthermore, it was not turned into a ministry with a prime task of evangelizing non-Christians, though this has on occasion been a by-product of counseling individuals who turned to the institute staff for assistance. Rather, the institute's role has been one of providing a resource for the church and the public from which both could draw accurate information upon which policy decisions about ministry to and relationships with the new religions could be made.

Because of the different approach that the institute took, and because for many years I did little but gather information, attend meetings of different religions, and read document after document, I have reached a somewhat different position from that of some of my evangelical Christian colleagues who helped pioneer the church's response to the cults. In particular, I feel that the church must make a much more positive approach to the presence of so many non-Christians now in our midst. Rather than simply opposing cults, I strongly believe that the church must build a widespread, loving, and evangelical ministry to non-Christians. That ministry must honor the sincerity and integrity of people who are and who will continue to be non-Christians. It should include, along with the presentation of the Christian message, time to listen and try to understand the position of those to whom the Gospel is directed. It should, in its attempt to inform church members of the nature of alternative religions, strive to present the account of their beliefs and practices with the same care that it would that of a different denomination. In that understanding, this volume is offered to the church as a tool to assist in its development of its ministry.

From this perspective, it is also felt that at least one group should not have been included in this volume. The Local Church is included because in the past few years it has fought a head-on battle with a prominent evangelical Christian anti-cult writer and most recently pursued a lawsuit which sent a well-known Christian ministry, the Spiritual Counterfeits Project, into bankruptcy. SCP had been recognized by many in this field, this author included, as the most scholarly and research-oriented of the several hundred counter-cult ministries. It played an important role in the late 1970s in opposing the use of state funds to support Transcendental Meditation programs in public schools and the Army.

This author has also undertaken a lengthy study of the Local Church and the writings of its leaders, Watchman Nee and Witness Lee. I have observed the group from time to time for a decade. I have found no evidence that it is anything but an orthodox Christian body, even though it has some unusual and unfamiliar practices, none of which detract from its Christian faith. For whatever reason, the Local Church has been branded a heretical group by, I believe, colleagues in ministry, who have misunderstood its theology. It was included in this volume only because of the controversy surrounding it and to set the record straight.

Finally, I want to thank all who assisted in the preparation of this volume and ask that I be forgiven for not mentioning each by name. There have been so many. I am truly grateful for their assistance in providing information and checking various sections of this volume before it went to press.

I invite their continued assistance and especially invite any readers who have additional information of interest and importance to contact me through the institute.

J. GORDON MELTON

INTRODUCTION
TO THE REVISED AND UPDATED EDITION

Characteristic of new religions is rapid change. During its first generation, any religion which hopes to survive in the modern West must develop a believable sophisticated theology out of the vision which gave it birth. The change which we would normally expect has been accelerated by the pressurized atmosphere created by the existence of a reactionary milieu strongly opposed to the new religions, a symbol of the opposition in society to the growing pluralism in Western culture.

The rapid change undergone by new religions quickly dates descriptive literature on the "cults," as those which have provoked the greatest interest in recent years are living out their first generations in the West. Their teachings remain in flux; organizational structures are not yet entrenched and can still be rather easily altered; and as old controversies are settled, new ones arise. In spite of some understanding of the continuing transformation new religions undergo, I was still surprised by the amount of change in the period since the first edition of this *Handbook*. Several groups had undergone significant reorganization (Unification Church, Church of Scientology). The New Age Movement, about which scant literature then existed, has become the object of detailed scrutiny. The Satanism controversy largely overwhelmed and pushed aside the issues of new religions, at least for the media.

If any trend has been evident it is the gradual demise of new religions as an issue of public controversy. The various programs devised by the anti-cult movement to fight new religions have largely proven ineffective. Civil suits, the last major weapon in the anti-cult arsenal, seems to have now been taken away by the action of the American

Psychological Association in refusing to recognize the existence of "brainwashing" in new religions. With the demise of the civil suits, the cult controversies seem to be settling down to a war of words and an attack upon members and leaders of religious groups who actually overstep the boundaries of the law. Certainly deprogrammings continue, in spite of the denials of the Cult Awareness Network, which also continues to talk of brainwashing, but neither remains a factor to which new religions have to budget significant time and resources. Actually, as the Cult Awareness Network assumes the role of a consumer watchdog group and withdraws from the activities which its critics found so objectionable on constitutional grounds, it may find a new set of allies. There are many who oppose the new religions but insist upon fighting them fairly.

Documenting Change

This new edition of the *Handbook* is a thorough revision and complete updating of the earlier volume. It also adds material on a number of groups not previously covered. One, the International Society for Krishna Consciousness of West Virginia, came into existence as a separate body just a few years ago. Others, such as the Movement of Spiritual Inner Awareness, became the center of intense controversy.

For each group covered basic data about the history, beliefs, practices, and organization are given, along with the latest statistics on membership. The heart of each chapter remains the discussion of the controversy, above and beyond the standard anti-cult rhetoric about brainwashing, which has surrounded it. For many, individual controversies pushed the groups into the spotlight for a period of time; for others their history has been a history of controversy as they have tried to make a place for themselves in the culture.

While groups have changed, theoretical perspectives on new religions continue to mature, undergirded by a decade of intense study. For example, over the last decade a number of prominent founders/ leaders of new religions died: L. Ron Hubbard, Herbert W. Armstrong, Victor Paul Wierwille, Chogyam Trungpa Rinpoche. The fact, that after a brief pause for mourning, the group continued on as it had previously, further called into question the group's reliance on the founding charismatic leader. Further, the rate of appearance of new religions has been fairly steady for over a generation thus providing some disconformation of theories which tied their appearance to the social unrest of the 1960s. The rate of appearance in Europe has also equaled and in many cases surpassed that of the United States, indicating that the growth of religious pluralism is not simply an American phenomenon, but is a major trend in Western society.

In the end, the problem of new religions, i.e., cults, is but a phase of the larger transformation of world culture in the destruction of religious hegemonies and the emergence of religiously cosmopolitan countries and urban center communities in which no one religious group retains cultural dominance. In such a setting, a secular government provides a rule book within which different groups can function and each make their contribution to the whole society.

This book has been written out of an underlying assumption that such a religiously pluralistic society is now being created. To ease the tension and prevent further rifts in the social order, a new degree of literacy and understanding between people of different faiths is imperative. When approaching groups which have been involved in controversy, special attention needs to be exercised in the elimination of negative stereotypes and dehumanizing of both leaders and members of new religions. It is hoped that this *Handbook* will continue to contribute to such understanding.

Finally, I invite readers of the *Handbook* to assist in its further improvement. While I cannot answer every bit of correspondence, I am eager to have comments about corrections, omissions and/or suggestions for making the *Handbook* a more useful volume. Please write:

J. Gordon Melton, Director
Institute for the Study of American Religion
Box 90709
Santa Barbara, CA 93190-0709

I.

What Is a Cult?

WHAT IS A CULT?

The term "cult" is a pejorative label used to describe certain religious groups outside of the mainstream of Western religion. Exactly which groups should be considered cults is a matter of disagreement among researchers in the cult phenomena, and considerable confusion exists. However, three definitions dominate the writings of social scientists, Christian counter-cult ministries, and secular anti-cultists.

Social scientists tend to be the least pejorative in their use of the term. They divide religious groups into three categories: churches, sects, and cults. "Churches" are the large denominations characterized by their inclusive approach to life and their identification with the prevailing culture. In the United States, the churchly denominations would include such groups as the Roman Catholic Church, the United Methodist Church, the American Baptist Church, the United Church of Christ, and the Protestant Episcopal Church. Groups that have broken away from the churchly denominations are termed "sects." They tend to follow the denominations in most patterns but are more strict in doctrine and behavioral demands placed upon members and emphasize their separation and distinctiveness from the larger culture (frequently spoken of as a "rejection of worldliness"). Typical sects have disavowed war (Quakers and Mennonites), championed controversial religious experiences (Pentecostals), and demanded conformity to detailed codes of dress, personal piety, and moral conduct (the holiness churches). Sects such as the fundamentalist Christian groups have argued for a stringent orthodoxy in the face of the doctrinal latitude allowed in most larger church bodies. More extreme sect bodies have developed patterns and practices which have largely isolated them from even their closest religious neighbors—snake-handling, drinking poison, alternative sexual relationships, nonconventional forms of dress.

While most sects follow familiar cultural patterns to a large extent, "cults" follow an altogether different religious structure, one foreign and alien to the prevalent religious communities. Cults represent a force of religious innovation within a culture. In most cases that innovation comes about by the transplantation of a religion from a different culture by the immigration of some of its members and leaders. Thus during the twentieth century, Hinduism and Buddhism have been transplanted to America. In sociological terms, Hindu and Buddhist groups are, in America, cults. Cults may also come about through religious innovation from within the culture. The Church of Christ, Scientist, and the Church of Scientology are new religious structures which emerged in American society without any direct foreign antecedents.

When social scientists began their discussion of cults in the 1920s, they were aware of only a few cult groups, well-known groups which they could not fit into their more crucial debates about churches versus sects—theosophy, Christian Science, spiritualism, and the two large Hindu groups: the Vedanta Society and the Self-Realization Fellowship. Elmer Clark's pioneering survey of *The Small Sects in America* (1949) listed fourteen New Thought bodies and thirteen Esoteric bodies, showing an awareness of some twenty-seven cults (plus a few others such as the black Jews considered in the body of his text).

A second definition of cult arose among Christian polemicists. In the early twentieth century several conservative Evangelical Protestant writers, concerned about the growth of different religions in America, attacked these religions for their deviation from Christian orthodox faith. These writers assumed that Christian faith provided a norm for religious truth and that the United States was meant to be a Christian country. Among the first of the prominent Christian writers on the subject of cults, Jan Karel Van Baalen described cults as non-Christian religions but included those groups which had their roots in Christianity while denying what he considered its essential teaching. According to Van Baalen, all religions could be divided into two groups, those which ascribe to humans the ability to accomplish their own salvation and those which ascribe that ability to God. The latter group is called Christianity. All other religion fits into the first group. In *The Chaos of Cults*, which has gone through numerous editions from its first appearance in 1938, Van Baalen analyzed various non-Christian religions in the light of Christian teachings.

With little change, contemporary Christian counter-cult spokespersons have followed Van Baalen's lead. Cults follow another gospel (Gal. 1:16). They are heretical. They set up their own beliefs in opposition to orthodox faith. As Josh McDowell and Don Stewart, two popular Evangelical writers assert, "A cult is a perversion, a distortion of biblical Christianity, and, as such, rejects the historical teachings of the Christian Church."

The Evangelical Christian approach to cults would include every group which has departed from orthodox Christianity (such as the Church of Christ, Scientist, the Latter Day Saints, and the Jehovah's Witnesses) as well as those groups which have never made any claim to be Christian. Individual writers disagree over the cultic nature of such groups as the Roman Catholic Church (included and then dropped by Van Baalen) or the Unitarian-Universalist Church. Only recently has consideration been given to non-Trinitarian Pentecostal groups.

The third definition, the one which became the dominant force in the public debates on cults in the 1970s, developed within the secular anti-cult movement. The definition has shifted and changed over the last decade. It did not develop out of any objective research on alternative religions, rather it emerged in the intense polemics of parents who had been disturbed by changes observed in their sons and daughters who had joined particular religious groups. These "cults"—predominantly the Children of God (Family of Love), the Church of Armageddon (Love Israel Family), the Unification Church, the International Society for Krishna Consciousness, The Way International, and the Church of Scientology—had, they charged, radically altered the personality traits of their children.

Anti-cultists began to speak of "destructive cults," groups which hypnotized or brainwashed recruits, destroyed their ability to make rational judgments and turned them into slaves of the group's leader. While drawing upon Christian counter-cult literature in the beginning, the secular anti-cultists gradually discarded any overtly religious language as a means of designating cults in order to appeal to government authorities and avoid any seeming attack upon religious liberties. Thus, "cults" have come to be seen as groups that share a variety of generally destructive characteristics. While no one group may embody all of them, any "cult" will possess a majority. Marcia Rudin, a popular anti-cult writer, listed fourteen commonly accepted characteristics of a cult:

1. Members swear total allegiance to an all-powerful leader whom they believe to be the Messiah.
2. Rational thought is discouraged or forbidden.
3. The cult's recruitment techniques are often deceptive.
4. The cult weakens the follower psychologically by making him/her depend upon the group to solve his/her problems.
5. The cults manipulate guilt to their advantage.
6. The cult leader makes all the career and life decisions of the members.
7. Cults exist only for their own material survival and make false promises to work to improve society.
8. Cult members often work fulltime for the group for little or no pay.
9. Cult members are isolated from the outside world and any reality testing it could provide.
10. Cults are antiwoman, antichild, and antifamily.
11. Cults are apocalyptic and believe themselves to be the remnant who will survive the soon-approaching end of the world.
12. Many cults follow an "ends justify the means" philosophy.
13. Cults, particularly in regard to their finances, are shrouded in secrecy.
14. There is frequently an aura of or potential for violence around cults.

Anti-cultists suggest that, as of the early 1980s, 3,000 to 5,000 destructive cults operated in the United States. However, no evidence of the existence of such a large number of religious groups, either cultic or otherwise, has been produced. Anti-cult literature reflects a great concern with approximately 15 groups, though as many as 75 to 100 have received passing mention. Only five groups—the Unification Church, the Children of God, the Church of Scientology, the International Society for Krishna Consciousness, and The Way International—have received consistent coverage over the years of the anti-cult movement's existence.

The discussion of cults by social scientists, Christian counter-cult ministries, and secular anti-cultists has singled out a number of groups for attention as prominent or typical examples of cults. Among these groups, some became controversial because of their divergent behavioral norms (polygamy, a leader's claim to divinity, exotic rituals, communalism). Others came into open conflict with the authorities because of violence (the black Muslims). Many groups recruited single young adults and moved them into intense religious communities against the wishes of their parents. Such groups have received the most attention in the last decade.

This handbook includes the most prominent "cults" for analysis and discussion. It is designed to provide a concise overview of each group and a summary of the controversy surrounding it. Along with the "cult," the secular anti-cult and Christian counter-cult movements are also given treatment, as they are a very active element in the contemporary milieu. This volume will cover most groups which one is likely to encounter; however, for a more complete listing of all the individual religious groups currently functioning in the United States, including a brief descriptive statement of each, the reader is referred to the third edition of the author's *Encyclopedia of American Religion*, which can be found in the reference section of most libraries.

It should be noted that most writers, except for the harshest of anti-cult polemicists, have moved away from the term "cult" and now use the less pejorative term "new religion" to designate the more non-conventional religious groups in Western society. From this point, in spite of the problems inherent in the term "new religions," we shall increasingly use it to designate the groups under discussion.

The Flowering of the Cults in the Twentieth Century

Numbers. Everyone who has looked at the cult phenomenon has agreed that the number of alternative new religious groups has grown significantly during the twentieth century, particularly since World War II. Using the broad definition of the social scientists, one can find some 500 to 600 cults or alternative religions in the United States. Of these, over 100 are primarily ethnic bodies confined to first and second generation immigrant communities. These ethnic religions do no recruiting beyond their ethnic base and often use the language of their home country, a significant barrier to their spread into the general population.

Beyond the cults, however, numerous sect groups have splintered from the large mainline denominations, although they resemble each other in most ways. They affirm the Western Christian tradition but dissent on one or more significant points. When their dissent becomes extreme or centers upon some key issues of doctrine, the label "cult" is frequently applied to these groups as well. Among the sects, for example, the Jehovah's Witnesses disagree with the Christian tradition by their denial of a number of central affirmations of orthodox Christian faith—the Trinity, hell, salvation by grace alone—not to mention a number of lesser beliefs. The Witnesses placed great importance upon their predictions of the exact date of the end of the world, and they have tended to draw their members into a closed social circle. Other sects deviated by their acceptance of faith healing or glossolalia or other nonconventional behavioral patterns and thus earned the designation "cult," particularly from Christian writers. If one adds the Christian groups which have strongly dissented from the doctrinal norms of the Western Christian tradition, several hundred more groups join the list of cultic groups. Such groups deserve attention in any survey of the "cultic milieu" in America as they have tended to become separatist and develop alternative social structures which become the focus of their members' daily lives. Also, the more extreme sects occasionally have developed corrupt, rigid, authoritarian leadership structures. Unhampered by normal societal checks, such corrupt leadership has led to disastrous results, amply illustrated, for example, in the murders and crimes perpetrated by the members of the Church of the Lamb of God. Anti-cultists draw their image of destructive cults from extreme sects as well as from those groups more normally labeled cults.

Just as there are not really so many cult groups as are frequently reported in the press, cults also lack the huge membership often credited to them. If such alleged membership, reportedly in the millions, existed, every neighborhood would have visible cult centers. Only a few of the older cults—the Jehovah's Witnesses, the Church of Jesus Christ of Latter Day Saints—have attained a broad membership throughout the nation. Of those groups formed in the twentieth century, only a few, such as the black Muslims (founded in 1930), can count their membership in the tens of thousands. The more famous of the contemporary cults, such as the Unification Church (with 5,000 to 7,000 members) or the Hare Krishna (with approximately 2,500 initiated members), can count their membership in the thousands. Most cults have only a few hundred members and spend most of their energy just surviving. Thus, a more reasonable total membership estimate for the several hundred prominent new religions of the last decades would be 150,000 to 200,000.

One cannot, however, measure cult statistics solely by membership. It must be noted that many times the number of members have had only a brief period of cult involvement. Over ninety percent of those who join an alternative religion leave it within a few years. Even larger numbers of individuals, in the process of examining a religious group, participate in some activity but never join. Over one million people took the basic course in Transcendental Meditation, but only a minority joined the TM organization, and the total American membership remains in the 10,000 to 20,000 range. Similarly, only a few of the many thousands who were initiated into the Divine Light Mission became "premies." Between thirty and forty thousand of the several hundred thousand who have taken the basic weekend introduction to the Unification Church eventually joined the organization. Of that number fewer than 6,000 remain as members as of 1990. While the cults grew appreciably during the 1970s, they still constitute a numerically small part of the American religious scene.

The Course of Growth. While the growth of cults has not been alarming, it has been noticeable and raised questions of its causes. Why has the United States experienced this sudden burst of new alternative religions with its element of Oriental religions and Christian groups which originated in the Orient (such as the Local Church)? Some researchers have pointed to the social unrest of the 1960s and the pattern of emergent religions arising in times of social upheaval. However, while this observation provided some helpful reflection on the patterns of religious diversification, it did little to explain the spread of the new religions. New religions began their rise in the conservative 1950s and after 1965 began a new phase of growth that has continued unabated through the 1980s and shows no signs of slowing through the next decades. Social unrest theories also did very little to explain the different responses in Europe and Japan following the extreme social disintegration experienced by each after World War II. The former experienced no reported sudden rise in new religions, while the phenomena in Japan startled longtime observers of the religious scene.

Other students, primarily critics of the new religions, claim the growth of the new religions to be a result of their use of new manipulative psychological techniques which attract and control (i.e., brainwash) youthful followers, many of whom join during the crises of adolescence. This explanation suffers from its lack of any empirical base demonstrating the mechanisms of the process and its inability to describe any demonstrably new and distinct element in the cultic conversion techniques which have not been used by Evangelical Christians for generations, in spite of the development of modern psychological terminology in discussions of conversion events. Finally, one group of observers of the milieu of the new religions, their supporters, sees these groups as the visible expression of a new religious consciousness.

More detailed and dispassionate observation has suggested that several mundane causes may underlie the recent flowering of the new religions. Most importantly, it has been noted, the contemporary burst of alternative religions continues a long history of growth in metaphysical, occult, and Eastern religion which can, at the very least, be dated to the magnetist movement in the nineteenth century. Asian religion entered the United States in the early 1800s but had found an earlier expression in the Transcendentalist Movement in New England. The large immigration of Asians in the last half of the nineteenth century brought the first Buddhist and Hindu teachers to the United States and threatened many West Coast residents. California could have become like Hawaii, which is one third Buddhist, during the first decades of this century, had legislators not passed a series of Asian exclusion acts which slowed the flow of immigrants from India, Japan, and Southeast Asia to a trickle. The natural growth of Asian religion was thus effectively stunted. Then in 1965, President Lyndon Johnson rescinded the Asian exclusion laws and raised Asian immigration quotas to a par with those of other nations. As a result, Asians have come to the United States in the hundreds of thousands and are currently reshaping urban centers by their presence. For example, census records show that fewer than 12,000 Indians were admitted to the United States prior to 1960 (though many more than that came into the country illegally). Most lived in California. By 1980 over 380,000 had been admitted. 84,000 live in New York City, 34,000 in Chicago, and 60,000 in California. Equally dramatic figures could be cited for Japanese, Koreans, and other Asians.

The Asians brought with them their teachers—swamis, Zen masters, gurus—and a zeal to spread their religions among Americans. The new availability of Asian teachers has been the major factor in the growth of alternative religions in the last generation. For the first time Asian faiths become a genuine option for religious seekers in the West. And the role played by Asians in the religious culture of the United States is very much on the rise. In 1990, a new immigration act was passed by Congress and signed into law. It raises the immigration quotas from

Asian countries (predominantly Buddhist and Hindu) by 60 percent. Thus the upward trend of Eastern religion practice in the United States should take another dramatic upswing during this last decade of the twentieth century.

As the Asian missionaries arrived, they found a West prepared by recent cultural events and scientific developments to receive them. Within the occult and metaphysical communities, which had grown steadily through the century, the gurus found a welcome image of the East as the fountainhead of pure wisdom. Occult/metaphysical groups, which had previously been the primary conduit for Eastern teachings, had, as a result, built a hunger for unmediated experiences under a Hindu swami or a Japanese Zen master. Such a desire for firsthand acquaintance with Eastern religion had also been created within the colleges that were offering a growing number of courses in Eastern faiths. Many students desired to go beyond their academic experience.

Three significant developments within the large scientific community also prepared the West for the growth of the new religions. (1) The emergence of parapsychology out of the older field of psychical research, (2) the discovery and spread of LSD and other mind-altering drugs, and (3) the rise of alternative branches of the psychological disciplines (most notably humanistic psychology, and its stepchild, transpersonal psychology, and Jungian psychotherapy) established a "scientific" basis for the introspective search which Eastern and occult religions claimed as their special expertise. In their own differing ways, parapsychology, hallucinogenics, and the new psychologies became the legitimizing agents for mystical occultism and Eastern spiritual disciplines.

The flowering of the cults in the last two decades is best seen as the convergence and maturation of several trends which had been developing in North America for many decades. Unleashed by the demise of Asian immigration restrictions, these trends flowed into a new permissive environment. Without the many years of effort by members of alternative religions prior to 1965 and the development of the culture to receive the Eastern gospel, there would have been little response to the Eastern teachers when they finally did arrive.

Who Joins? Since World War II, America has experienced two periods of national religious revival, first in the early 1950s and again in the

1970s. In both of them, millions of Americans attained a new religious appreciation and joined a church or some religious organization. While thousands were joining alternative religions, hundreds of thousands were joining conservative Protestant Evangelical churches, especially the pentecostal ones. Many thousands of members of mainline churches formed pentecostal groups without leaving their primary affiliation. Many blacks were attracted to Muslim organizations, while many poorer whites moved to new sectarian churches. Older "cults"—Mormons, Jehovah's Witnesses—grew among broad segments of the population.

The new cults, those which experienced their first real growth in the 1970s, and many of which had an Eastern or occult orientation, grew among a very narrow segment of the population. They primarily attracted single young adults (age 18-25). The new recruits were generally drawn from the upper half of the population economically and educationally. University campuses have continued to be a favorite recruiting ground.

Members of the new cults have been drawn equally from all segments of the established religious population though some groups show a marked individual variance. Like the population, about half of the new members have a Protestant-Free Church background and another fourth are Roman Catholic. The Jewish community is the exception, being overrepresented. Nonconventional religions tend to draw a much higher percentage of their membership, particularly their leadership, from among the Jewish segment of the population than national percentages would lead one to expect. This overrepresentation of Jews in some new religions has become a matter of legitimate concern for some Jewish religious leaders though no consensus of opinion on a single method of response has emerged. Some have become leaders in the anti-cult movement while others, noting that while percentages are very high, actual numbers are very low, have become equally vocal in defending the cults from what they feel are unjustified attacks by anti-cultists.

Though the great majority of people who join nonconventional religions could easily adopt the religion of their parents, only a minority are ever active in a church or synagogue as a teenager. The weak tie to the parental religion often proves unable to hold in the face of the young adults reading books about and then visiting different religious groups available in the community. For example, the great majority of people who joined the Hare Krishna movement had done some reading in Eastern religion and had adopted vegetarianism prior to any firsthand contact with group members. Members of many new religions had participated in the drug culture and were drawn to a religious group which promised a chemical-free alternative to the psychedelic experience which they had previously experienced.

Thus, while some groups have been actively recruiting members, potential converts have also been actively searching for a group that can meet their specific needs and desires (both religious and otherwise). They will test and reject groups until they find the right one and will leave that group if it no longer fulfills their expectations.

The nonconventional religions also vary widely in their recruitment processes. Some, particularly those with Evangelical Christian roots (and a few which are Eastern, but reacting to Christian missionary activity) have an aggressive program of membership enlistment. Most others rely upon the distribution of literature or the sponsoring of introductory classes to which a potential convert must make the initial effort and attend. Many Hindu groups offer hatha yoga exercise classes out of which they recruit individuals who show an interest in more religious forms of yoga (bhakti, raja, or japa). Some of the groups that lead a more austere and demanding life put prospective members through a testing period (similar to a monastic novitiate) before initiating them. A few, such as the Pagan and magickal groups, do not recruit at all, and prospective members must take all the initiative in locating a group (frequently a difficult process).

In return, nonconventional religions reap a small harvest from those with whom they come in contact. Of those who attend an initial recruitment event—an introductory TM lecture, a weekend on Unification theology, a Scientology personality test, a five-week hatha yoga class—less than 10% will join. Of those who do join, the overwhelming majority will stay with the group for less than two years. For example, during its first decade (1965-74), the International Society for Krishna Consciousness (the Hare Krishnas) initiated 5,000 members. An additional 2,500 were initiated between 1975 and 1983. Of the 7,500, only 2,500 remained active in 1984. Only a handful were deprogrammed; the rest simply walked away, either to a new religion or remaining loosely affiliated. Most return to the religion in which they were raised.

Nonconventional religions, particularly those singled out as "destructive cults," have frequently been accused of engaging in deceptive recruitment practices. These charges developed from the peculiar situation at the end of the 1960s in California with the emergence of the street people subculture. That subculture was radically expanded each summer as thousands of college students traveled West to join the post-hippie world for a few months with the intention of returning to school in the fall. During their sojourn on the streets of Berkeley or Hollywood, some of these vacationers found themselves attracted to one of the new youth-oriented religions such as the Christian Foundation, the Children of God, the Unification Church, or the Hare Krishna. They found a new life in the groups and at the end of the summer simply stayed in California. Some had broken contact with families and emerged at Thanksgiving or Christmas ready to tell the family of their conversion.

Many parents were startled at the seeming radical change of values and offended by the decision to drop out of college and not pursue professional careers. They charged the new religions with distorting a lifetime of planning.

In Northern California, the charges of deception centered upon the Oakland Family, a local center of the Unification Church headed by Rev. Sun Myung Moon. The Family operated several structures which were not openly identified with the controversial Church and distributed literature which made no reference to the Church as its sponsor. Some people who eventually became members of the Church for a short period claimed that they became active in the life of the Church before realizing that it was the Unification Church with which they had affiliated. Most serious charges about deceptive elements in the recruiting process have stemmed from the Oakland Family in the 1970s. In Southern California, the Christian Foundation (founded by Susan and Tony Alamo) became a target for charges of deceptive recruitment practices because of their habit of busing potential recruits from the streets of Hollywood to their center in the desert north of town for an evening of high pressure evangelism.

Complaints about deceptive recruiting have been little heard in recent years except in the most general checklists of cult practices published by anti-cult organizations. It is very hard for someone to join most new religions, given their peculiar dress and worship practices, without knowing immediately its religious nature. The practices decried as deceptive seem to have been a product of the street people culture and died with it.

Overwhelmingly new religions are and have been quite open about and proud of their organization, and many, particularly those whose members adopt distinctive dress, would have a next to impossible task concealing their identity. No adult would have any question about whom they were dealing with when they met a Krishna devotee on the street or visited a Krishna temple. The Church of Scientology has had a long-standing policy of having prospective members fill out a form in which they acknowledge their awareness that they are about to participate in a Scientology event. While new members may not be aware of all of the implications of joining a distinctively different religion, they do understand the basic beliefs and requirements and the identity of the group they are joining.

Life in a New Religion

Once a person joins what to them is a new or nonconventional religious group, he or she must begin to adapt to group life. New recruits will go through a program of education in group beliefs and training in group practices. Frequently, they will begin to master a spiritual discipline and, most perturbing to former acquaintances, they will begin to change their behavior patterns to conform to group demands.

Indoctrination. Most new religions develop a more or less standard program through which they process new members. The smaller and newer the group, the more informal the induction process will be. It will involve attendance at various classes and mastering of a body of information about group beliefs. Over a period of time, the classes may become quite standardized. In some occult groups, advancement in the group is through a system of degrees. All members must master a set of studies and become accomplished in the practical use of the teachings at one level before receiving the information concerning the next.

Whatever the methods used, most groups adopted an amateurish approach to training new members. Average recruit trainers receive no teacher training to assist them in the presentation of materials. Their only asset is usually a winsome personality.

Cults expend a considerable amount of time educating new members in the ways of the group. While the average new member knows some of the teachings, especially those which proved most influential in his or her decision to join, a lengthy indoctrination by the group is frequently necessary. Unlike a person moving between Christian denominations, where much of the doctrine and practice are the same, a new cult member has to learn a totally new way to be religious and to master a different religious tradition from scratch. At the very least, if a nominal Christian joined an intense Christian sect, she or he would likely spend many hours in Bible study learning a new approach to the Scriptures.

During the indoctrination period, which could last from a few months to a few years, the new recruits may spend all of their leisure time (or in the case of communal groups, all of their waking hours) in the practice of and education in their new faith. This indoctrination completes the process of religious striving which each convert began prior to any contact with the group. The early stages of religious concern in a young adult begin in a period of dissatisfaction and investigation. The events of this period may be totally internal and completely hidden from family and close friends. The internal process often becomes visible only when potential new cult members discover a group that seems to meet their religious concerns. They then begin to investigate the group, sometimes on their own or frequently through structured recruitment activities and visits to worship services. More or less gradually, the decision to join is made. That decision is often influenced by far more than the teachings and practices of the group; the friendliness of the members, the spirituality and quality of the leader(s), and the rigorousness of the demands are all elements to be considered. During the period of investigation, potential new members will adopt some outward signs of the religion, which might include uniform dress, specific religious practices (chanting, Bible reading, meditation, vegetarian diet, etc.) and changing relationships as group members take their place in the circle of the new member's closest associates (replacing former ones).

Spiritual Disciplines. Life in many nonconventional religions includes the practice of a "spiritual discipline," a specific set of exercises designed to produce various "altered" or mystical states of consciousness. While quite common to the East, such practices have not been as common to Western Christianity apart from the monastic orders. However, the normal role of a guru or swami in India is to teach a set of spiritual practices which will lead the practitioner into a state of religious enlightenment. The systems and practices vary widely from kundalini yoga to zazen to the twirling dances of the dervishes. In the West, meditation and chanting have been the most common spiritual disciplines. Loyola's *Spiritual Exercises* are possibly the most famous system of spiritual practice. Also in the West, the guru, i.e., the teacher of spiritual wisdom, has usually been given the more mundane title, "spiritual director."

Some critics of new religions charge that the spiritual practices that regularly produce altered states of consciousness lead to disassociative disorders. Psychiatric studies on cult members, however, find little or no evidence to substantiate such charges. Several researchers have reported a lower-than-normal incidence of psychological well-being among converts to several well-known cults, while noting a measurable improvement over the period of initial conversion and a retention of that improved state over a period of years as members. Also reported are a reduction of alcohol and drug abuse.

Psychiatrist Marc Galanter, in summarizing all of the research on cult life and psychiatric issues, notes that psychiatry has a significant problem in assessing individual cult members because the discipline has yet to develop satisfactory methodologies for understanding social adaptation to a religious group which may deviate from conventional behavior. Behavior which might signal a disorder in a person in a more conventional social setting can be perfectly normal within a cult. Psychotherapist Robert L. Moore has also reported that most of the negative symptoms reported as typical of cult members—blank stares, disassociative states, submission to a guru, etc.—are, when viewed in the context of the developmental process, perfectly normal. Individuals going through such a significant life transition as changing a religion may exhibit patterns that become pathological only if retained for an abnormal period of time—four to five years.

Social scientists have confirmed what psychiatrists and psychologists report. The nonconventional behavior reported as typical of members of new religions is a direct result of members adapting to the norms of group life and derives its meaning from the group context. Within the group, behavior that ordinarily would be strange, even weird, becomes logical and meaningful within the context of the group goals and beliefs.

Behavioral Patterns. Some sects and most cults make great demands upon their members. Sectarian groups are distinguished by their strictness in either doctrinal or behavioral standards and/or their adoption of a nonconventional pattern of worship or piety. Sect groups generally demand a greater commitment of time than the larger, more inclusive, denominations. As a corollary, sect members make a larger number of their social contacts within the group than among the general public. Church and sect groups can be placed along a continuum of strictness with the large liberal Protestant denominations (such as the United Methodist Church or the United Church of Christ) at one extreme and the small separatist sects (such as the Amish or Old Order Brethren) at the other.

Cults do not easily fit along that continuum. All demand allegiance to some belief(s) and behavior pattern(s) which strongly differ from more conventional religion. Some nonconventional religions are very loose in their structure and demands upon members. Some are so loose, for example, that their status as a religion has been questioned. Others are as demanding as any sect body. The Hare Krishnas are a semi-monastic group which adheres to a special dress, haircut, diet, and worship schedule. Other groups, less removed from secular work patterns, will ask for all the leisure time of members. A few groups will schedule meetings every evening and plan lengthy sessions for worship, teaching, and fellowship on the weekends.

Such high-demand, unconventional religions and the newer sectarian groups have been the major targets of the anti-cult movements. Their demands on members' time and almost exclusive hold on members' social contacts have provided a focus of parental concerns when sons and daughters joined. Critics have accused the high-demand religions of being "antifamily" as the groups life takes up time previously spent with the natural family. In the long run, such demands upon members can lead them to become dependent upon the group. Such dependency experienced over a period of years may create difficulty for members in adjusting to society if either the group dissolves or they decide to leave it.

The Aftermath of Cult Life

The great majority of people who join groups which deviate strongly from societal norms or have a high disapproval level in society leave after only a short period of time, typically within two years. For these people the time in the cult was what Robert Ellwood has termed an *excursus*, a spiritual journey away from the mundane structures of established religion. For most the excursion is brief, though it might assume an importance in shaping the more mature long-term religious existence. Having made the journey, former cult members return to a more conventional religion or, increasingly, to no formal religious affiliation at all. They may return to a life so integrated into dominant societal patterns that little evidence of the excursion is visible to the persons' acquaintances.

A minority of persons who join a cult leave under a situation of great stress. Some leave because of a bad experience within the group. Ex-members tell of psychological and even occasional physical abuse, the bitter disappointment of discovering corruption in the leader or leaders of a group, and the inability of a cult to deliver what it had promised in spiritual values. Members who have had a bad experience leave angry and hurt and often turn with vengeance upon their former faith.

Among those who leave cults under stressful conditions are those who have been deprogrammed. Under the pain of physical confinement and strong psychological pressure, cult members have been forced to renounce their allegiance to the group and join the chorus of cult critics.

Those who leave a cult under the stress of either a bad experience or deprogramming frequently have difficulty picking up the pieces of their life again. Psychiatrists such as Margaret Singer, who has worked with many excultists who left various groups under stress, have blamed the cults for the delayed stress syndrome found in their clients. They see the recruitment and indoctrination process as essential agents in the trauma but offer no discussion of how such practices induce pathology. More recent comparative studies have shown, however, that any delayed stress syndrome is almost exclusively limited to those former members who have left under stress (i.e., as a result of deprogramming). The great majority of people who leave simply because the group no longer meets their needs show no pattern of psychological disturbance.

A small percentage of those who join a new religion will remain in it for many years, even a lifetime. For these few, the group provides a satisfactory structure within which to discover a meaningful existence. It may motivate individuals to make significant contributions to life and culture. While some new religions and their members may appear to be withdrawing from society, especially during the first generation of the group and its newest converts, in the long run, alternative religions that survive their formative period generally integrate themselves into American culture, and their members have added greatly to its richness.

A Perspective on the "Cults"

Much of the contemporary debate about alternative religions revolves around the basic doubts concerning the legitimacy of nonconventional religions. They appear strange and foreign. They challenge the status quo, particularly the religious hegemony enjoyed by the more established religions. In their zeal and organization, cults often seem, to outside observers, to be accomplishing far more than they would claim for themselves. The proliferation of alternative religions and the obvious impossibility for any individuals to become acquainted with more than a few of them calls for some kind of overall perspective.

Critics of the cults have proposed programs for the elimination of cults. Secular critics have tried to mobilize public opinion against those cults they consider to be intrusive, harmful elements in the social order. Cults destroy families, harm individuals who join them, and threaten society. Christian critics, for somewhat different reasons, also view cults negatively. They see them as illegitimate parodies of God's true religion and a Satanic plot to lure people away from the pure faith. Both secular and Christian critics agree that efforts should be made both to discourage people from joining and to reclaim people who have joined.

This criticism, while stifling a few individual groups, has done nothing to slow the growth of alternative religions, which have steadily increased in both numbers and percentage throughout Western society during the twentieth century. On the other hand, the massive criticism of the new religions has widened the rifts in the social fabric which have divided families and even communities along religious lines. The cults, especially those nonconventional religions now entering their second generation, have developed deep roots in the American soil and are well on their way to becoming established elements in the social order. Older groups such as the Church of Jesus Christ of Latter-day Saints have already created a secure niche for themselves in both the religious and secular realms. The emergence of the radically pluralistic society suggests that not a continuation of hostilities but an attitude of acceptance and understanding of a new religious social order is needful. The United States, as is true for all of the West, is becoming home to Hindus,

Buddhists, Sikhs, Muslims, and a variety of psychic-occult and metaphysical religions just as it has been home to Christians and Jews.

Viewed parochially, cults can appear to be the strange activity of cultural outcasts, those small groups always on the edge of culture, always dissenting, always strange, sometimes sinister. If, on the contrary, one assumes a broader more historical approach, cults take on a quite different appearance. During the nineteenth century, riding the tide of colonial conquests, Christianity spread from Europe around the world. It swept across North America, Africa, and Latin America and made a significant penetration of Asia. On the heels of the Christian expansion, non-Christian religion began to come into the West. Its first significant appearance was in New England where Hinduism greatly influenced the Transcendentalist Movement. By the end of the century, groups of Asians began to bring their faiths, primarily Buddhism, to Hawaii and the West Coast. Then in the twentieth century, returning upon the ships and planes that brought Western culture to the East, Asian and Middle Easterners came to America to establish now thriving communities. They brought their religion and their often exotic culture. All the while, occult religions which had all but disappeared in the eighteenth century made their comeback.

The progress of Christianity in the East and the spread of Eastern religion in the West accelerated after World War II. What has been viewed as the rise of cults in America is actually but a single phase of a total global shift in world religion. The basic component of this shift in recent decades has been the very visible penetration of Asian religion in unprecedented proportions in the West. This massive migration of people and ideas is far larger than the momentary success of one single religion and far more significant than the human frailties of an individual guru. A microcosm of world religion is being created in the West. Instead of the twenty to thirty Christian denominations from which eighteenth-century Americans could choose, those living in the next century will be able to pick from over a thousand Christian denominations and literally hundreds of non-Christian alternatives. Given the change that is occurring in the West, approaches to nonconventional religions which attempt to comprehend their dynamics and build structures for people of diverse religious backgrounds to coexist in a high degree of social harmony offer a far more healthy and rewarding approach than those which perpetuate hostilities built upon an incorrect perception of the larger impact of the so-called cults.

Thus, this volume intends to provide an introduction to the world of unfamiliar religion. It will introduce the more important of these faiths that are challenging the hegemony of the established religions of America and offer information about others which are also making their impact. While this volume is not a substitute for the detailed studies of individual groups, it should provide a point from which in-depth investigation can begin. Most importantly it will furnish an overview and set the context for the understanding of any particular group.

Sources

This chapter has tried to summarize briefly the best current data on the major questions about contemporary nonconventional religions in America. Space has not allowed extensive footnoting, hence, a list of the most essential literature has been selected and listed at his point. These volumes (1) represent the range of scholarly opinion on the cult controversies and (2) draw from the most articulate critics of the nonconventional religions.

Not included in this list are a number of important articles from scholarly journals, the one exception being the article by Galanter which remains the best comprehensive survey of the psychological literature. To list all the important articles would have increased the size of this volume excessively, and in most cases the journal articles provide the substance from which the books are constructed. A companion book-length bibliographical volume of cult/new religion literature is being published simultaneously for the use of those who wish to continue their research on this fascinating new world.

Also, through the 1980s, the Institute for the Study of American Religion oversaw the production of a set of book-length bibliographies on the individual new religions and the associated issues. The volumes which have appeared to date are cited in this volume, either in this list, or, in the case of those related to a single group, in the relevant chapter. Additionally, Shupe, Bromley, and Oliver, one of the bibliographies, list a number of the scholarly articles.

Also not included in this list are those items specifically related to the secular anti-cult movement and the Christian-counter ministries, which may be found at the end of Section V.

Finally, some of the finest work on the broader cult issues has been included in books primarily about a single group, such as Eileen Barker's *The Making of a Moonie*, which has become a model for research on new religions. These items have been cited in the particular chapter to which they are related.

New material on the cults is constantly appearing, and books which should have been listed below have undoubtedly been omitted. However, the items cited will provide a broad introduction to the literature. The reader should note, as might be obvious from the range of opinion expressed in the many books on cult-related issues that (1) omission from the list below should not be taken as a condemnation of any book and in like measure (2) inclusion on the list by no means implies endorsement of the particular opinions and conclusions of any particular writer by this author.

Barker, Eileen, ed. *New Religious Movements: A Perspective for Understanding Society.* New York: Edwin Mellen Press, 1982. 398 pp.

—————. *New Religious Movements: A Practical Introduction.* London: Her Majesty's Stationary Office, 1989. 234 pp.

Beckford, James A. *Cult Controversies: The Social Response to the New Religious Movements.* London: Tavistock Publications, 1985. 327 pp.

Bromley, David G. *Falling from the Faith: Causes and Consequences of Religious Apostasy.* Newbury Park, CA: Sage Publications, 1988. 266 pp.

—————, and Anson D. Shupe, Jr. *Strange Gods.* Boston: Beacon Press, 1982. 244 pp.

—————, and James T. Richardson, eds. *The Brainwashing/Deprogramming Controversy.* New York: Edwin Mellen Press, 1983. 367 pp.

—————, and Phillip E. Hammond, eds. *The Future of New Religious Movements.* Macon, GA: Mercer University Press, 1987. 278 pp.

Coleman, John, and Gregory Baum, eds. *New Religious Movements.* New York: Seabury Press, 1983. 83 pp.

Creswell, Mike. *Your God, My God.* Atlanta: Home Mission Board of the Southern Baptist Convention, 1980. 172 pp.

Ellwood, Robert S., Jr. *Alternative Altars.* Chicago: University of Chicago Press, 1978. 192 pp.

—————, and Harry B. Parrin. *Religious and Spiritual Groups in Modern America.* 2nd ed. Englewood Cliffs, NJ: Prentice-Hall, 1983. 328 pp.

Fichter, Joseph H. *Alternatives to American Mainline Churches.* New York: Rose of Sharon Press, 1983. 199 pp.

Galanter, Marc, "Charismatic Religious Sects and Psychiatry: An Overview." *American Journal of Psychiatry* 139, 12 (December 1982): 1539-49.

Garvey, John, ed. *All Our Sons and Daughters.* Springfield, IL: Templegate Publishers, 1977. 131 pp.

Glock, Charles Y., and Robert N. Bellah. *The New Religious Consciousness.* Berkeley: University of California Press, 1976. 391 pp.

Kaslow, Florence, and Marvin B. Sussman. *Cults and the Family.* New York: Haworth Press, 1982. 192 pp.

Levi, Ken. *Violence and Religious Commitment.* University Park: Pennsylvania State University Press, 1982. 207 pp.

Levine, Saul. *Radical Departures: Desperate Detours to Growing Up.* San Diego, CA: Harcourt Brace Jovanovich, 1984. 196 pp.

Melton, J. Gordon. *The Directory of Religious Bodies in the United States.* New York: Garland Publishing, 1977. 305 pp.

—————. *The Encyclopedia of American Religions.* 3rd ed. Detroit: Gale Research Company, 1989. 1100 pp.

—————, and Robert L. Moore. *The Cult Experience.* New York: Pilgrim Press, 1982. 180 pp.

Needleman, Jacob. *The New Religions.* Garden City, NY: Doubleday, 1970. 245 pp.

—————, and George Baker, ed. *Understanding the New Religions.* New York: Seabury Press, 1978. 314 pp.

Richardson, Herbert, ed. *The New Religions and Mental Health.* New York: Edwin Mellen Press, 1980. 177 pp.

Robbins, Thomas, and Dick Anthony, eds. *In Gods We Trust.* New Brunswick, NJ: Transaction Books, 1990. 544 pp.

Robbins, Thomas, William C. Shepherd, and James McBride. *Cults, Culture and the Law: Perspectives on the New Religious Movements.* AAR Studies in Religion 36. Chico, CA: Scholars Press, 1985. 238 pp.

Rubenstein, I. H. *Law on Cults.* Chicago: Ordain Press, 1981. 120 pp.

Rudin, A. James, and Marcia Rudin. *Prison or Paradise?* Philadelphia: Fortress Press, 1980. 164 pp.

Saliba, John A. *Psychiatry and the Cults: An Annotated Bibliography.* New York: Garland Publishing, 1987. 601 pp.

————. *Religious Cults Today.* Liguori, MO: Liguori Publications, 1983. 48 pp.

————. *Social Science and the Cults: An Annotated Bibliography.* New York: Garland Publishing, 1990. 694 pp.

Shupe, Anson D., Jr. *Six Perspectives on New Religions: A Case Study Approach.* New York: Edwin Mellen Press, 1981. 235 pp.

————, David G. Bromley, and Donna L. Oliver. *The Anti-Cult Movement in America.* New York: Garland Publishing, 1983. 267 pp.

Tipton, Steven M. *Getting Saved from the Sixties.* Berkeley: University of California Press, 1982. 364 pp.

Wallis, Roy, ed., *Sectarianism.* London: Peter Owen, 1975. 212 pp.

Whalen, William J. *Strange Gods.* Huntington, IN: Our Sunday Visitor, 1981. 130 pp.

Wilson, Bryan, ed. *The Social Impact of New Religious Movements.* New York: Rose of Sharon Press, 1981. 234 pp.

Wuthnow, Robert. *The Consciousness Reformation.* Berkeley: University of California Press, 1976. 309 pp.

————. *Experimentation in American Religion.* Berkeley: University of California Press, 1978. 221 pp.

Zaretsky, Irving I., and Mark P. Leone. *Religious Movements in Contemporary America.* Princeton: Princeton University Press, 1974. 837 pp.

II.

The Established Cults

A. CHURCH OF CHRIST, SCIENTIST (CHRISTIAN SCIENCE)

The Church of Christ, Scientist, more popularly known as the Christian Science Movement, was founded in Lynn, Massachusetts, in 1875 by Mary Baker Eddy. Because of its espousal of spiritual healing and its affirmation that Christian Science is incompatible with reliance upon materia medica, the Church of Christ, Scientist has been one of the most important of the nonconventional religions in America as well as a matter of intense controversy from the day of its founding.

The Founder

The Church of Christ, Scientist was founded by Mary Baker Eddy (1821-1919) who as a young woman had been continually hobbled with poor health. Her condition worsened during the 1860s and she tried several alternative treatments, including the water cure, before learning in 1862 of Dr. Phineas Parkhurst Quimby, a mental healer in Portland, Maine. In October of that year she traveled to Portland and placed herself under his care. She soon experienced some relief of her symptoms which she ascribed to his efforts. She became his student and took the opportunity, when offered, to pass them on to others. While grateful for his help and generous with words of praise at the time of his death in 1866, she was disturbed by the periodic return of her illness and the conflicts of Quimby's ideas and those she found in the Bible.

Two weeks after Quimby's death, on February 1, 1866, she slipped on an icy pavement. Three days later while slowly and painfully recuperating, the "Biblical Truth" was imparted to her. Immediately her health was restored. That event marked the beginning of Christian Science. She quickly saw the conflict between the newly discovered Truth and some of Quimby's ideas and further study led her to abandon Quimby's mental and magnetic teachings altogether. She had realized that God was the only Life, and that Life was the only reality of being. There was no healing agent, as Quimby taught, either magnetic force or mind, only the unity with God in which there was no room for disease.

Within a few years she was ready to take students and began writing her first book, *The Science of Man*, and her major presentation of her teachings, *Science and Health with Key to the Scriptures*. Shortly before the first edition of *Science and Health* appeared, she was granted a letter of dismissal from the Congregational Church, in which she had been a member all of her adult life, and began the process of organizing those who were just beginning to follow her teachings.

In 1876 she formed the Christian Science Association, a fellowship of her personal students. Three years later she organized the Church of Christ, Scientist. In 1881 The Massachusetts Metaphysical College was chartered. That same year she was ordained as pastor for the Church. In 1883 the first issue of the *Journal of Christian Science* appeared, and in 1886 the National Christian Scientists Association was formed for the Christian Science practitioners who had not been trained personally by her.

No sooner had the movement been organized than Eddy began to doubt the soundness of the structures she had created. In 1889 she dissolved the church, the college and the Christian Science Association. The *Journal* was turned over to the National Christian Scientists Association. Only in 1892 was the church reorganized and the publication of the *Journal* resumed by the church.

In 1882, two other former students of Quimby, Julius and Annetta Dresser, settled in Boston. They aligned themselves with former Eddy student Edward Arens and began to teach mental healing following a combination of Quimby's and Eddy's teachings. Arens was in trouble for plagiarizing some of Eddy's writings and publishing them under his own name. In defense of Arens, Julius Dresser began to attack Eddy as a plagiarist of Quimby's ideas, an approach that Arens would use unsuccessfully in his subsequent trial. To account for the obvious differences between Eddy and Quimby, they accused her of distorting the

Quimby teachings. The plagiarism case began a lengthy and often bitter controversy between Christian Science and New Thought, the movement which developed in the late 1880s from the work of one of Eddy's former students, Emma Curtis Hopkins.

Eddy spent the majority of her life in perfecting the organization of the church and in clarifying and deepening her understanding of Christian Science. Her work manifested in large part through two books, *Science and Health with Key to the Scriptures* and the *Church Manual.* Each volume went through numerous editions, including several major revisions, during her lifetime. The texts were frozen at her death and remain as the authoritative documents for the Church. Also, after Eddy died, leadership in the Church passed to the five-person Board of Directors of the Mother Church in Boston, Massachusetts. They oversaw the production of standard editions of Eddy's writings, to this day the only ones used throughout the church.

Beliefs

A summary of the beliefs of Christian Science is found on page 497 of the Authorized Edition of *Science and Health with Key to the Scriptures.*

1. As adherents of Truth, we take the inspired Word of the Bible as our sufficient guide to eternal life.

2. We acknowledge and adore one supreme and infinite God. We acknowledge His Son, one Christ; the Holy Ghost or divine Comforter; and man in God's image and likeness.

3. We acknowledge God's forgiveness of sin in the destruction of sin and the spiritual understanding that casts out evil as unreal. But the belief in sin is punished so long as the belief lasts.

4. We acknowledge Jesus' atonement as evidence of divine, efficacious love, unfolding man's unity with God through Christ Jesus the Wayshower; and we acknowledge that man is saved through Christ, through Truth, Life, and Love as demonstrated by the Galilean Prophet in healing the sick and overcoming sin and death.

5. We acknowledge that the crucifixion of Jesus and his resurrection served to uplift faith to understand eternal Life, even the allness of Soul, Spirit, and the nothingness of matter.

6. And we solemnly promise to watch, and pray for that Mind to be in us which was also in Christ Jesus; to do unto others as we would have them do unto us; and to be merciful, just and pure.

While Christian Science affirms its oneness with other Christians in that it worships the One God revealed in Jesus Christ, it departs from orthodox Christianity at several significant points. Christian Scientists believe in what they term the "allness of God" and hence the "unreality of disease, sin and death." Thus Christ does not defeat evil but demonstrates its lack of any reality beyond our belief in it.

Christian Science emphasizes the impersonal aspect of God as Principle, Mind, Life, Truth and Love, though the personal aspect of God as Father is acknowledged. It also distinguishes between the man Jesus and the eternal spiritual selfhood, Christ, Son of God, which has been expressed by men and women throughout the centuries. Humans are saved through the Christ, which was demonstrated in Jesus and has been seen in others.

Organization

Authority in the Church of Christ, Scientist is derived from the Bible ; *Science and Health with Key to the Scriptures*, which sets forth its teachings and is the continuing voice of its founder; and the *Church Manual*, which includes the basic outline of the church's organization pattern and the laws governing its actions. Authority is vested in the Mother Church and its Board of Directors. They have direct oversight of the Mother Church congregation, the various church agencies (especially the large publishing concern), and all teachers and practitioners.

Individual congregations are democratically organized and elect their own officers. There is no separate ministry in the Church and the congregation is led by the First Reader. All officers of the congregation must be members of the Mother Church and, thus, fall under the direct authority of the Board of Directors, who are responsible for the correctness and purity of teachings. Each congregation is also in charge of at least one reading room where Christian Science literature is made available to the public.

Healing Activity

Belief and practice in Christian Science come together most concretely in the Church's healing activity. The promise of physical healing has been the most attractive aspect of Christian Science, and the Church boasts of many cures of illnesses of all kinds. Healing is one of the natural by-products of growing closer to God.

The Church undergirds its healing program through its Department of Care of the Mother Church which accredits sanatoriums where Christian Science treatment is given. One of the sanatoriums offers a three-year nurses' training school where sanatorium staff are trained. The Church also trains and accredits practitioners, to whom members can turn for help with specific problems. A list of recognized practitioners is printed in the monthly *Christian Science Journal.*

Current Status

Headquarters of the Church of Christ, Scientist is located at the Christian Science Church Center, a complex in downtown Boston. This complex contains the Publishing Society which publishes and sells the authorized literature including the several periodicals: *The Christian Science Journal*, a monthly magazine; the *Christian Science Sentinel*, a weekly magazine; *The Christian Science Quarterly*, and *The Herald of Christian Science*, which appears in a number of foreign languages. The Church's prominent newspaper, *The Christian Science Monitor*, issued daily with a weekly international edition, was joined during the 1980s by Monitor radio, shortwave, and television in-depth news programming, and *World Monitor*, a monthly magazine.

The Board of Education teaches a class of thirty pupils every three years for the purpose of providing authorized teachers of Christian Science. A Board of Lectureship, made up of approximately forty members, provides free lectures on Christian Science worldwide. The Board of Publication deals with the public in correcting errors about Christian Science and the Church of Christ, Scientist and looks into charges of injustices done to Christian Scientists.

The Church does not give out membership statistics. In 1972 there were 3,237 branches or congregations, of which approximately 2,400 were in the United States. At that time, the membership and constituency was estimated at 475,000. During the two decades prior to 1972, there was an approximate 50% decrease in the number of practitioners. Between 1972 and 1982 the Church experienced an annual decline of from 1 to 2% and closed almost 200 congregations. Circulation of *The Christian Science Monitor* went from 218,886 in 1970 to 157,942 in 1981. That decline has continued through the 1980s.

Controversy

The Church of Christ, Scientist, its founder, and her teachings were attacked from the moment they began to draw any attention and support. The controversy which grew out of the Arens case has lasted to the present day, in large part because of the work of Horatio Dresser, the son of Annetta and Julius Dresser, who brought the controversy into his several books on the history of New Thought. Critics of Christian Science have frequently adopted the Dresser perspective on the Church and see it as merely an extreme and somewhat distorted form of a Movement begun in the middle of the nineteenth century by Quimby. That perspective has spurred charges of plagiarism against Eddy and in one case the production of fraudulent documents by her enemies.

The major challenges to Christian Science have, however, not come from New Thought. At the time of the founding of the Church, spiritual healing was just beginning its revival. Its practice in Christian Science, as well as the other forms in Spiritualism and evangelical Christianity, received sharp criticism from a medical profession that was just consolidating its position as the normative authority in the treatment of illness in the United States. During the twentieth century, numerous court cases were fought over the rights of Christian Scientists to refrain from the use of doctors and the rights of Christian Science practitioners to care for the sick. An impressive body of legal decisions have given Christian Scientists a unique position in American life, including the right to deduct care received from a practitioner on their income tax as a legitimate medical expense.

The medical attack upon Christian Science has had inconclusive results. Critics cite many cases in which individuals, in some cases infants, have died in situations where proper medical care could have saved their lives. On the other hand, Church periodicals are filled with accounts of people, many unhelped by visits to doctors, who found health through Christian Science. Such testimonies remain the major appeal of the Church.

Periodically throughout the twentieth century, most notably in the case of Dorothy Sheridan in the 1950s, the practice of Christian Science has brought the Church and its members into court. These cases, bolstered by legislation in the states, also define the limits of Christian Science within the larger context of the freedom granted to individuals to accept or reject medical treatment. Christian Science practitioners may operate but must limit their activity to prayer. The one area which has remained a matter of intense controversy involves the children of Christian Science parents.

During the 1980s in the context of the larger public concern for child abuse and neglect, the issue of medical care for children, largely neglected since the Dorothy Sheridan case, was revived in a series of court cases across the United States, as Christian Science parents were charged with homicide, child abuse, and negligence. Ex-members such as Rita Swan, whose son had died in 1977 after receiving no medical treatment, swelled the attackers upon the Church. While each case had distinct aspects, and some were decided upon what might seem a minor technicality, each forced both judge and jury to consider as possibly criminal the actions of loving parents who deeply held religious beliefs against medical treatment and to respond to a church who argued for the effectiveness of Christian Science treatment over medicine, a position summarized in their 1989 booklet, *Freedom and Responsibility.*

The cases in the 1980s had mixed results. For example, a case from California led to the Supreme Court turning back a challenge to the prosecution of parents on the grounds of religious freedom, thus allowing the various court cases to proceed. In Florida, a couple was convicted of third-degree murder but given suspended sentences, a lengthy probation, and ordered to give their other children regular medical check-ups. In

Massachusetts, where the Church is headquartered, David and Ginger Twitchell were convicted of manslaughter. One couple in California was convicted of child endangerment, but meanwhile, another California couple was acquitted in a similar case. In Michigan and Minnesota cases filed against Christian Scientists were dismissed. These cases, which left inconclusive the status of parents who rely on Christian Science, were fought out at the same time cases involving children of several conservative Christian groups were proceeding, and various bills on both sides of the issue were being considered by state legislatures.

Almost as much as the medical controversy, charges of heresy from orthodox Christian churches have hounded the Church. Leaders of Christian Science insist that they are within the mainstream of Christian teachings, a concern which leads to their strong resentment of any identification with the New Thought movement, which they see as having drifted far from their central Christian affirmations. At the same time, strong differences with traditional Christian teachings concerning the Trinity, the unique divinity of Jesus Christ, atonement for sin, and the creation are undeniable. While using Christian language, *Science and Health with Key to the Scriptures* and Eddy's other writings radically redefine basic theological terms, usually by the process commonly called allegorization. Such redefinitions are most clearly evident in the glossary to *Science and Health* (pages 579-599). For example, the "Holy Ghost" is defined as "Divine Science; the development of eternal Life, Truth and Love."

While not as strongly organized or as large as the various groups which have come out of the Jehovah's Witnesses, several groups of former Christian Scientists do exist and continue an active polemic against the Church. There has always been a network of independent Christian Science practitioners, the first generation of which created the New Thought movement. However, in recent years the independents have become more aggressive and outspoken. Some, such as the United Christian Scientists headquartered in San Jose, California, attacked the Church for its undemocratic principles, and the independent Christian Science Church in Plainfield, New Jersey, successfully challenged the Mother Church both on its continued use of the name "Christian Science" and in having *Science and Health* declared in the public domain. One ex-practitioner, Joel Goldsmith, developed a large following before his death in 1964, and his very loosely organized students continue to circulate his popular books and tapes.

Other ex-Scientists have become Evangelical Christians and have organized to oppose the Church from that position. Typical are New Beginnings (Ex-Christian Scientists for Jesus) of El Toro, California, and Christian Way of Lancaster, California.

Sources-Primary

Beasley, Norman. *The Cross and the Crown.* New York: Duell, Sloan and Pearce, 1952. 664 pp.

—————. *The Continuing Spirit.* New York: Duell, Sloan and Pearce, 1956. 403 pp.

Eddy, Mary Baker. *Manual of the Mother Church, First Church of Christ Scientist in Boston, Massachusetts.* 89th ed.: Boston: Trustees Under the Will of Mary Baker Eddy, 1908. 138 pp.

—————. *Prose Works Other Than Science and Health.* Boston: Trustees Under the Will of Mary Baker Eddy, 1925. Various paging.

—————. *Science and Health with Key to the Scriptures.* Boston: Trustees Under the Will of Mary Baker Eddy, 1906. 700 pp.

Freedom and Responsibility: Christian Science Healing for Children. Boston: The First Church of Christ, Scientists, 1989. 127 pp.

Sources-Secondary

Braden, Charles S. *Christian Science Today.* Dallas: Southern Methodist University Press, 1958. 432 pp.

Corey, Arthur. *Behind the Scenes with the Metaphysicians.* Los Angeles: DeVorss & Co., 1968. 258 pp.

Gottschalk, Stephen. *The Emergence of Christian Science in American Religious Life.* Berkeley: University of California Press, 1973. 305 pp.

Peel, Robert. *Christian Science, Its Encounter with American Culture.* Garden City, NY: Doubleday & Company, 1965. 224 pp.

—————. *Mary Baker Eddy.* 3 vols. New York: Holt, Rinehart and Winston, 1966, 1971, 1977.

B. THE CHURCH OF JESUS CHRIST OF LATTER-DAY SAINTS (MORMON)

The most successful of the many groups which have over the years been labeled "cult," the Church of Jesus Christ of Latter-day Saints has over two million members and dominates the religious life of the Rocky Mountain area from Boise, Idaho, to Phoenix, Arizona. Started in the early nineteenth century, it has grown steadily into a multimillion member worldwide ecclesiastical body.

Founder and Early History

The Church of Jesus Christ of Latter-day Saints, popularly called the Mormons, was founded by Joseph Smith, Jr. (b. December 23, 1805, Sharon, Vermont). As a youth, Smith had moved from Vermont to western New York, near the town of Palmyra. Western New York was, during the early nineteenth century, one of the places in which the various Protestant churches fought vigorously over the allegiance of a largely unchurched population. Some of Smith's family joined the Presbyterians, but young Joseph was partial to Methodism.

Undecided as to which group to join, Smith's problem was solved by a vision he had in 1820. Two personages, whom he later identified as God the Father and Jesus, appeared to him and told him to join no church as they were all wrong. This vision was the first of a series that would lead to the founding of a new Church. In 1823 he was visited by the Angel Moroni who told him of some plates buried nearby upon which was written an account of the ancient inhabitants of North America.

Buried with the plates were two stones with which Smith could translate the plates. Smith was informed of the exact location of the plates in 1827 and began the task of translating them. The translation was published in 1830 as the *Book of Mormon* (hence the popular designation of Smith's followers).

Meanwhile Smith, and an acquaintance, Oliver Cowdery, had a vision of John the Baptist who conferred upon them a restored Aaronic Priesthood which carried the authority to re-establish the true Church of Christ which had been lost and replaced by the numerous "sects." In a second vision Peter, James, and John gave them the higher priesthood of the Apostles.

On April 6, 1830, Smith led a small group in the formation of the Church of Christ (a name soon changed to the Church of Jesus Christ of Latter-day Saints). Smith and Cowdery ordained each other as elders and, in turn, ordained others.

The new Church attracted a following almost immediately. In 1831 Smith moved the headquarters to Kirkland, Ohio, and the Church began construction of a Temple. Smith took control of the group as a prophet-revelator and guided the young group by his regular revelations that were gathered and published in a book—*The Doctrines and Covenants.* Unfortunately, soon after the Temple was completed, conditions necessitated a further move, and in 1838 Smith moved to Missouri. The stay was short as the governor ordered the Mormons from the state before the year was out.

In 1839 the Mormons established the community at Nauvoo, Illinois, which soon grew into the largest city in the state. A new Temple was begun, and the Church entered a growth phase. During this period the first of the European mission efforts (later a major source of members) was launched.

At Nauvoo Smith introduced the practice of polygamy and began by setting an example for the other Church leaders. The exact number of Smith's plural wives is still a matter of conjecture (estimates range from 27 to 84), but there is little doubt that polygamy caused immense problems for the Church and led to Smith's death and the destruction of the community. He lost the support of Sydney Rigdon, his prime counselor, who accused Smith of trying to seduce his daughter.

Polygamy also led a group of disgruntled members to challenge Smith through an independent newspaper, *The Nauvoo Expositor.* Smith ordered the paper destroyed. The resulting controversy led to Smith's arrest and confinement in the jail at Carthage, the county seat of Hancock county. There, on June 27, 1844, a mob broke into the jail and murdered Smith and his brother, Hiram.

The death of the Prophet threw the Church into confusion. Sydney Rigdon asserted his right to succession from his position in the First Presidency. However, the Council of the Twelve Apostles gave their support to Brigham Young, their senior member. He proved an outstanding leader and organizer and dominated the Church's life for the next thirty years.

Brigham Young (b. June 1, 1801) had joined the Church in Ohio and had become an original member of the Council of Twelve Apostles in 1835. He headed the first British Mission in 1840 and took his first plural wife shortly after his return in 1842. Within four years he had married seventeen more women.

Under Brigham Young's leadership the Mormons organized their forced exodus from Nauvoo and the migration to Utah in 1848. He was named governor of the proposed state of Deseret, a position that manifested h' ; role as both spiritual leader of the Church and temporal leader of the community established at Salt Lake City.

In 1852 Young announced the practice of plural marriage as public doctrine and began a battle with the United States government that was to last for the rest of the century. Young himself married nine more times. As the polygamy spread and became more openly practiced, public outrage increased. In 1862 the first federal anti-polygamy bill was passed, and efforts were increased to prevent its practice. These efforts were strengthened in 1882 with the passage of the Edmunds Bill, which disenfranchised all people living in polygamy, and the 5-member Utah Commission established to enforce the provisions.

The pressure on the Church and the disruption of secular life led Church President Wilford Woodruff to announce a reversal of Church policy toward plural marriage. Tension levels decreased greatly until 1900 when a polygamist was elected as a Congressman from Utah. He was denied his seat. In the face of renewed public hostility, the Church announced in 1904 that anyone who entered into plural marriage in the future would be excommunicated. During the twentieth century polygamy was eradicated from the Church of Jesus Christ of Latter-day Saints, but it continued to flourish in Mormon territory, especially in Mexico where it was not illegal. A large Fundamentalist (polygamy-practicing community) still exists in the Western United States and Northern Mexico.

Doctrine

The faith and life of the Church are based upon the revelations given to Joseph Smith and the restored priesthood. Smith is claimed to have been given a set of gold plates written in "Reformed Egyptian" which he translated as the *Book of Mormon*, which has authority equivalent to that of the Bible for Mormons. They also accept the set of revelations received directly by Smith (and later Church Presidents) contained in the *Doctrines and Covenants*. Finally, they accept a third volume which Smith claimed to be a translation from the inscriptions on a mummy he once owned called the *Pearl of Great Price*.

Smith's authority to establish the Church came in the restored priesthood given to him and Oliver Cowdery. On two separate occasions, the two were elevated first to the Aaronic (lower) priesthood and then the Melchizedek (higher) priesthood, both believed to have been lost centuries before.

What the Church understands Smith to have revealed is summarized in their Articles of Faith:

1. We believe in God, the Eternal Father, and His Son, Jesus Christ, and in the Holy Spirit.
2. We believe that men will be punished for their own sins, and not for Adam's transgression.
3. We believe that through the Atonement of Christ, all mankind may be saved, by obedience to the laws and ordinances of the Gospel.
4. We believe that the first principles and ordinances of the Gospel are: first, Faith in the Lord Jesus Christ; second, Repentance; third, Baptism by immersion for the remission of sins; fourth, Laying on of hands for the gift of the Holy Ghost.

5. We believe that a man must be called of God, by prophecy, and by the laying on of hands, by those who are in authority to preach the Gospel and administer the ordinances thereof.

6. We believe in the same organization that existed in the Primitive Church, viz. apostles, prophets, pastors, teachers, evangelists, etc.

7. We believe in the gifts of tongues, prophecy, revelation, visions, healing, interpretation of tongues, etc.

8. We believe the Bible (King James Version) to be the Word of God in so far as it is translated correctly; we also believe the *Book of Mormon* to be the word of God.

9. We believe all that God has revealed, all that he does now reveal, and we believe that He will yet reveal many great and important things pertaining to the Kingdom of God.

10. We believe in the literal gathering of Israel and in the restoration of the Ten Tribes; that Zion will be built upon this (the American) continent; that Christ will reign personally upon the earth; and that the earth will be renewed and receive its paradisiacal glory.

11. We claim the privilege of worshipping Almighty God according to the dictates of our own conscience, and allow all men the same privilege, let them worship how, where or what they may.

12. We believe in being subject to kings, presidents, rulers and magistrates, in obeying, honoring and sustaining the law.

13. We believe in being honest, true, chaste, benevolent, virtuous and in doing good to all men; indeed we may say that we follow the admonition of Paul—We believe all things, we hope all things, we have endured many things and have to be able to endure all things. If there is anything virtuous, lovely, or of good report or praiseworthy, we seek after those things.

Smith began work on a new translation of the Bible, the *Inspired Version.* However, the Utah church does not use it, preferring the King James Version. The *Inspired Version* is used by the Reorganized Church of Jesus Christ of Latter Day Saints.

Organization

The Church of Jesus Christ of Latter-day Saints is headed by the General Authorities, which consists of the First Presidency, the Council of Twelve Apostles, the First Quorum of Seventy, a Patriarch and the Presiding Bishopric. The First Presidency consists of three men, one of which is designated the President of the Church. It along with the Twelve Apostles and the Seventy (which is headed by the seven-member Presidency of the Seventy) administers the ecclesiastical affairs of the Church. The gift of prophecy is believed to reside in the President who may propound revelations binding upon the whole Church. The Presiding Bishopric administers the temporal affairs of the Church under the Patriarch of the First Presidency.

The membership of the Church is organized into wards (congregations) of 300 to 800 members, and the wards are grouped into stakes which consist of 6 to 10 wards. The stake is headed by a President, two counselors and a High Council of twelve members. A Bishop and two counselors head a local ward.

Members of the Church are expected to refrain from the use of tea, coffee, tobacco, and alcohol and to tithe their income.

Of particular concern to the organization of the Church is temple worship. A Mormon temple is not a public house of worship but a space set aside for special services for members of the Church only. The main ceremony is sealing of a married couple for time and eternity, it being a Mormon belief that marriage and family life continue into life beyond death. Each place the Church settled in the nineteenth century they immediately began to construct a temple. In the twentieth century they have constructed a number of them around the world wherever they have strength.

Present Status

In 1977 the Church reported 3,969,220 members worldwide. A decade later it reported 6,400,000 members in 1,666 stakes and 13,719 wards (congregations). In the United States in 1989 it reported 4,175,400 members in 10,049 congregations. The line between laity and clergy is not as sharp as in some churches. All male members are expected to receive the Aaronic priesthood and most do. Most men who function in ministerial leadership positions do so on a part-time basis while earning their living at a full-time job in the secular world.

In 1984 the First Presidency of the Church announced a partial decentralization in the Church's organization. Administration for the Church worldwide was placed in the hands of 13 General Authorities who would supervise the 13 areas of the world into which the expanding work had been divided. In 1987 four new areas were created and an additional one named the following year, bringing the total to 18.

Temples are located in Utah (7); Hawaii; Mesa, Arizona; Idaho Falls and Boise, Idaho; Los Angeles; Oakland; Seattle; Washington, D.C.; Atlanta; Dallas; Chicago; and Denver. Outside the United States temples can be found in Alberta, Canada; Switzerland; New Zealand; London; Sao Paulo, Brazil; Tokyo; Samoa; Tonga; Chile; Tahiti; Mexico City; Sydney, Australia; Manila; Taiwan; Guatemala City; Germany (2); Sweden; South Africa; Korea; Peru; and Argentina.

Controversy

During the first generation of the Church it experienced much the same hostility which the new alternative religions were subjected to during and since the 1970s although the Mormons experienced much more violence. Joseph Smith was tarred and feathered by an angry mob in Ohio, jailed for no reason in Missouri, and murdered in Illinois. The communities in which the Mormons settled were offended by their curious beliefs, threatened by the political power they represented, and upset by the loss of family members to a new religion.

Once the Church moved to Utah, polygamy was openly practiced and became the major focus of tension with the larger society. The Church eventually prospered in large part because of its distance from the major centers of population and power in the United States.

During the twentieth century, with the growth of Evangelical Christians who were specialists in counter-cult polemics, Mormonism became one of several major "cults" to receive extensive attention. The visible success of the Church in the last generation has but spurred Evangelical Christian missionary work among Mormons. Numerous books, booklets, and tracts have been written to refute Mormon teachings and the authenticity of Mormon revelation.

As it is given particular attention in Mormon/anti-Mormon polemics, the integrity of the *Book of Mormon* has been questioned from the moment it appeared. Critics have noted its anachronisms, its verbatim quotations from the King James Bible, and the coincidence that a document purporting to be thousands of years old dealt directly with many of the issues hotly debated in western New York in the 1820s. There have been a variety of attempts to track down possible mundane sources for the *Book of Mormon*, none of them conclusive. The Church has just as stoutly defended the *Book* and supported archeological research throughout the Americas to find evidence of its truth.

During the 1970s controversy flared over the small volume called the *Pearl of Great Price*. The mummy from which Smith supposedly translated the text was thought to have been lost many years ago; however, it was rediscovered and claims were made that it was nothing but a common funerary mummy and that the inscriptions on it contained nothing related to the text Smith produced. The *Pearl of Great Price* controversy turned out to be but the first round in a series of controversies involving Church authorities, Mormon intellectuals, and non-Mormon (but friendly) scholars of Mormon history. Through the 1970s and 1980s, Mormon scholarship, especially historical research, flourished. Numerous conferences were held and journal articles written. Debate centered upon three journals (*Dialogue*, the *Journal of Mormon History*, and *Sunstone*) which published a regular series of items debating sensitive points of the Mormon past, and several books which questioned standard interpretations of Latter-day Saint church history.

In recent decades there has also emerged a group of people who wanted to stay Mormons, but who accepted many conclusions about the historical accuracy of the *Book of Mormon*, the life of Joseph Smith, and the founding of the Church which conflict with the Church's official position. The publishing of such opinions have long irritated the Church's leadership and in recent years it took steps to curb further publication of what it saw as destructive critical works. Among its activities have been the limiting of access to Church archives, forcing the resignation of Brigham Young University professor D. Michael Quinn (author of a book on Joseph Smith's magical beliefs), and demanding that scholars submit their writings for approval before issuing them. This controversy will continue into the 1990s and its outcome far from certain.

Throughout this century, critics have questioned the Church's attitude toward blacks who have traditionally been denied the priesthood, the status and role of women, and the wealth amassed by the Church. In 1989 the issue of its treatment of Native Americans was added to the list when George P. Lee, the only Native American General Authority in the Church, resigned his post and accused the Church of racism. The Church then moved to excommunicate him.

Its very success and its strong influence in the several states in the Rocky Mountain region have given it the strength to deal with most of its critics with little effort. Occasionally, one of the general authorities answer a critic, and occasionally the Church has moved against dissident members. Also, as the Evangelical Christian attack on Latter-day Saints has increased, individual Mormons have provided a steady stream of polemic literature to answer the charges.

Sources-Primary

Arrington, Leonard J., and Davis Britton. *The Mormon Experience.* New York: Alfred A. Knopf, 1979. 404 pp.

Church History in the Fullness of Times: The History of the Church of Jesus Christ of Latter-day Saints. Salt Lake City, UT: Church Educational System, Church of Jesus Christ of Latter-day Saints, 1989. 643 pp.

Hinckley, Gordon B. *Truth Restored.* Salt Lake City: Church of Jesus Christ of Latter-day Saints, 1947. 156 pp.

Richards, Le Grand. *A Marvelous Work and a Wonder.* Salt Lake City: Deseret Book Company, 1968. 452 pp.

Smith, Joseph, Jr., trans. *The Book of Mormon.* (numerous editions).

————. *The Doctrines and Covenants.* Salt Lake City: Church of Jesus Christ of Latter-day Saints, numerous editions.

Sources-Secondary

Arbaugh, George Bartholemew. *Revelation in Mormonism*. Chicago: University of Chicago Press, 1932. 252 pp.

Brodie, Fawn M. *No Man Knows My History*. New York: Alfred A. Knopf, 1945. 495 pp.

O'Dea, Thomas. *The Mormons*. Chicago: University of Chicago Press, 1957. 289 pp.

Shipps, Jan. *Mormonism: The Story of a New Religious Tradition*. Urbana: University of Illinois Press, 1985. 211 pp.

Tanner, Jerald, and Sandra Tanner. *Mormonism—Shadow or Reality?* Salt Lake City: Modern Microfilm Company, 1972. 597 pp.

C. FUNDAMENTALIST OR POLYGAMY-PRACTICING MORMON GROUPS

With the Civil War and the slavery issue largely behind it, Congress turned its attention to eradicating polygamy in the Utah Territory. In response to the several anti-polygamy laws which were passed in 1874, Mormon leader Brigham Young's secretary, George Reynolds was chosen as the subject for a test case. The case reached the Supreme Court in 1879, and in its famous ruling in *Reynolds vs. U.S.*, the court sustained the government's ability to move against the practice.

In 1882 Congress passed the Edmunds Law which gave added teeth to the efforts to enforce its anti-polygamy stance. Eight years later, beleaguered by the jailing of its leaders and the threat of political disenfranchisement, President Wilford Woodruff of the Church of Jesus Christ of Latter-day Saints issued the manifesto withdrawing the Church's support from polygamy and threatening excommunication to any who practiced it. In spite of the public Church's stance, some, with the secret approval of the Church, continued quietly to perpetuate the practice, especially outside of the United States. Many of these polygamists relocated to Mexico because of that country's neglect in enforcing its anti-polygamy laws.

The polygamy issue continued to simmer and periodically burst into flame especially during the drawn-out hearings (1904-07) on the seating of Reed Smoot as a senator from Utah. In 1904 a second Manifesto was issued by President Joseph F. Smith which excommunicated those who defied the 1890 Manifesto. However, in 1910, a list of 200 men, including a number of Church leaders, who had entered into plural marriages since the 1890 Manifesto, was published, further spurring Church action against the so-called "new" polygamists. Over the next decades, as the Church moved to distance itself from its polygamist past, the practice was effectively driven out of the Church of Jesus Christ of Latter-day Saints.

The Emergence of Fundamentalism

The primary reaction against the actions of the Church in the first decades of this century came in the development of Fundamentalism, a movement which looked beyond the Church's hierarchy for its authority. The basis case for Fundamentalism was articulated by Lorin C. Woolley. As early as 1912 Woolley began to tell of a gathering on September 27, 1886. During that evening, John Taylor, president of the Church of Jesus Christ of Latter-day Saints, while staying at the Woolley home in Centerville, Utah, received a spirit visitation from Joseph Smith, Jr., the Church's founder. Smith's revelation concerned the continuance of plural marriage, and Taylor extracted a promise from all present that they would defend, sustain, and uphold the principle. The group covenanted together that no year would pass without children being born according to "the principle."

Later, according to Woolley, Taylor conferred the priesthood on five men, including Woolley and his father. At the time of the publication of the claim, all the men involved in the story except Lorin Woolley were dead. Only when he was the only one left, did Woolley assert any prerogatives based on Taylor's actions. In 1929, Joseph W. Musser gathered the accounts of the events of 1886 and published them. That same year, Woolley gathered followers and appointed a seven-member council to which he passed authority to govern the new movement. Woolley died in 1934 and was succeeded by J. Leslie Broadbent. Broadbent lived only a short time before he was succeeded by John Y. Barlow.

After the creation of an organization by Woolley, polygamists began to drift into Short Creek, a small town in the isolated northwest corner of Arizona. Short Creek was cut off from the rest of the state by the Grand Canyon and hence could be reached only from Utah or by air. The defiance of the new polygamists led in 1933 to a stronger statement by the Church of Jesus Christ of Latter-day Saints against the practice and offered the Church's active cooperation in stamping it out. In 1935 the Utah legislature declared polygamy a felony in the state, while the governor of Arizona launched a raid on the colony at Short Creek which not only failed to stamp out the colony but backfired politically. By the 1940s the colonists had reestablished communal living (the United Order) and reached a population of 36 men, 86 women, and 263 children. Musser, serving as one of its council members, emerged as the major public apologist of the polygamous tradition; he wrote several books and edited the group's periodical *Truth*.

Barlow's death in 1951 led to the first major split in the group. Musser succeeded Barlow; however, a paralytic stroke partially disabled him, causing many people to oppose his assuming an active leadership role. Opposition increased following his appointment of Rulon C. Allred, his physician, and Mexican leader Margarito Bautista to vacant positions on the council. Musser then totally disbanded the council and appointed a new one. He designated Allred as his successor. His defiant actions precipitated the schism. Subsequent to the schism in 1951, the Fundamentalist movement has fragmented into a number of factions.

United Order Effort

In 1936 the leaders of the Short Creek community formed the United Trust, generally referred to as the United Order Effort, a corporate expression of the communal life which they intended to live. In 1951 those who rejected the continued leadership of Joseph Musser, a Salt Lake City resident, lived in Short Creek and remained in control of the United Trust. They selected LeRoy Johnson to lead them. He accepted only after a vision of Christ confirmed his new role. His visions have guided the community through the years, and in the over thirty years of his leadership the community has grown and prospered. The United Trust now owns most of Colorado City, Arizona (the recently renamed Short Creek), and nearby Hilldale, Utah. It also owns businesses in St. George, Utah, and other towns in southern Utah.

The United Order Effort is the most conservative wing of the Fundamentalist Movement. It allows sexual relations only for the purpose of procreation and prohibits sexual contact altogether with a wife during her pregnancy, lactation (nursing), and menses. As of 1985 there are an estimated 3,000 members of the group residing in the Colorado

City-Hilldale area, with several thousand other adherents who accept the
Colorado City leadership. Johnson, who lived into his nineties, recently
died, but no successor had been named.

Apostolic United Brethren

Approximately 1,000 Fundamentalists remained loyal to Musser
and the new Council he appointed. He began a new periodical, the *Star
of Truth*, which he edited until his death in 1954. After his death, Rulon
Allred (1906-1977) reorganized his scattered following into the Apostolic
United Brethren. Allred, the son of a former Speaker of the House in the
state of Idaho, had joined the Fundamentalists in the 1930s. After his
father's death in 1937, he moved to Salt Lake City and opened his
practice of naturopathic medicine. His large suburban home became a
regular gathering place of polygamists in the urban area.

Allred's real prominence in the Movement came after his arrest
on March 7, 1944, during the last massive anti-polygamy raid attempted
in Utah. He went to prison but was paroled on his word to refrain from
either the practice or advocacy of plural marriage. In 1947 he violated his
parole and fled to Mexico. He returned to Salt Lake City in 1948 but
served only a few weeks for his parole violation.

After he took control of Musser's following, the Apostolic
United Brethren prospered. It grew as did Allred's own family. His major
losses came in Mexico, where Joel LeBaron left to form the Church of the
First Born of the Fullness of Times in 1955.

The Apostolic United Brethren is the more liberal branch of the
Fundamentalist Movement. It allows sexual relations apart from the strict
purpose of procreation.

During the 1970s Allred became the target of his former follower
Ervil LeBaron. Ervil, Joel's brother, had left the Church of the First Born
of the Fullness of Times and formed the Church of the Lamb of God. He
claimed authority over all of the polygamous groups and the right to
execute any who defied him. In 1972 he had Joel killed. On April 7, 1975,
he sent a pamphlet, *A Response to an Act of War*, and a handwritten
note to Allred. Allred ignored him. Then on May 10, 1977, two female
members of the Church of the Lamb of God murdered Allred in his office

in Murray, Utah. The women and LeBaron were eventually tried and convicted. LeBaron died in prison.

Allred was succeeded by his brother Owen Allred. The Apostolic United Brethren has approximately 5,000 members, many of whom live in the community at Pineville, Montana, and the several colonies still operated along the Mexican border.

The Church of Jesus Christ in Solemn Assembly

Possibly the single most well-known polygamist in the United States is Alexander Joseph, the mayor of Big Water, Utah. As a young man, Joseph had been a prominent leader in the Apostolic United Brethren but left in 1974 to form the Church of Jesus Christ in Solemn Assembly. In the years since, Joseph has actively pressed the rights of polygamists in general and his Church in particular. Shortly after founding the Church, he attempted to homestead federal land but was denied access by court order. He then moved to Glen Canyon, Kane County, Utah, and established a new town incorporated as Big Water, the current location of the Church's headquarters. Joseph became the first mayor of the town in 1983. He also founded the *Big Water Times*, the county's main newspaper.

Since the mid-1970s, Joseph has been in the news continually, beginning with his fight over the land in southern Utah he wanted to homestead. His various lawsuits attempted to establish his church and his polygamous practices in law. He has initiated a long-standing battle with the government, which owns much of the land in Kane County, to force it to surrender its claim to the land.

Joseph has nine wives (as of 1992). He has argued that polygamy, practiced as he does with a simple marriage contract not backed by a state granted license, is legal, but its legality has yet to be tested in court. He is the author of one book, *Dry Bones, A Resurrection of Ancient Understandings*, a commentary on *The Pearl of Great Price*, one of the Latter-day Saint scriptures.

During the 1990s, Joseph can expect a continued fight for control of the community he founded. As the population of Big Water increased during the 1980s, opposition to his strong if benevolent dictatorship of the town, which includes an opposition newspaper, has emerged around a vocal leadership.

The Church of the First Born of the Fullness of Times

The Church of the First Born of the Fullness of Times has a somewhat distinct origin from those polygamist groups tracing their origins to Lorin Woolley, though it derived from the same milieu of opposition to the 1890 Manifesto decrying the practice. It is the most successful of several churches founded by the sons of Alma Dayer LeBaron, a polygamy-practicing Mormon who lived at Colonia Juarez, a Mexican Mormon settlement where many went to escape anti-polygamy laws in the United States. His children, Benjamin, Ross Wesley, Joel, Ervil, and Alma, each became founders of a new Church.

First, in 1944 Benjamin declared himself a prophet. Several of the brothers supported his claim, most notably Ervil, but most of the family quickly recognized that his claims were mixed with some mental pathology. Few followed him and he spent much of his life in and out of mental institutions.

Next Ross Wesley proclaimed himself a prophet, specifically the "One Mighty and Strong" who would put the House of God in order as prophesied by Joseph Smith in the *Doctrine and Covenants* 85:7, and the heir to his father's patriarchal authority which the LeBarons believed had been passed through the family from Benjamin F. Johnson, A. D. LeBaron's grandfather. Reportedly, Ross Wesley still has a small following in Utah.

It was in the context of membership in a family within which two brothers had already claimed prophethood that Joel became the third. According to his account, in 1955 he was visited by two heavenly messengers and told that he was the "One Mighty and Strong." He incorporated the Church of the First Born of the Fullness of Times in September of that year in Salt Lake City and the next spring formally organized the new body. He appointed his brother Ervil secretary and head of the Mexican Mission.

Prior to the formation of the new Church, Joel was associated with the Apostolic United Brethren headed by Rulon C. Allred. He invited Allred to join his group, but Allred refused, while remaining friendly.

Joel propounded two unorthodox teachings. First, like his brother Ross Wesley, he claimed a lineage of priesthood (and the office of First Grand Head) through his family from Benjamin F. Johnson to himself rather than through Lorin Woolley and Joseph Musser. He also believed that a hereditary patriarchal office existed and was held by Margarito Bautista, a Mexican leader also with Allred's group. When Bautista died, Joel appointed his brother Ervil to that post. Second, Joel taught that the law, i.e., the Ten Commandments, were the basis of political life and only when the Commandments were kept would Christ return to earth.

During the 1960s trouble developed between Joel and Ervil. Joel was attempting to develop a group that practiced the Ten Commandments. Ervil came to believe that this new order should be established by force. This disagreement and other problems led Joel to excommunicate Ervil in 1971. Ervil asserted his right to lead because of his patriarchal office and founded the Church of the Lamb of God. The next few years became ones of bitter strife as Ervil attempted to force his will upon the polygamy-practicing groups in both Mexico and the United States.

On August 20, 1972, on orders from Ervil, some members of his Church shot and killed Joel. Joel's brother Verlan succeeded him as head of the Church of the First Born. Since Verlan's death in 1981, the church had been led by Siegfried Widmar. In the midst of the troubles, Alma LeBaron, the presiding bishop of the Church of the First Born, asserted his authority to control the economic affairs of the Church in ways that were disapproved by the majority of members. Alma left and founded his own Church which he now heads.

The Church of the Lamb of God

After he left the Church of the First Born, Ervil LeBaron founded the Church of the Lamb of God. Through the 1970s, beginning with the murder of Joel LeBaron, Church members carried out a variety of criminal acts in an attempt to survive and establish the Church as the dominant force in the polygamous community. Ervil LeBaron was soon arrested and tried in Mexico for his involvement in the killing of his brother, but then served only twelve months of a twelve-year sentence. A few days after he was released, on December 14, 1973, his followers attacked and burned Los Molinos, a town in Baja California where many members of the Church of the First Born resided. Two were killed. Again Ervil was tried and convicted but served only eight months. Then on May 10, 1977, several members of Ervil's Church murdered Rulon C. Allred in his office in Salt Lake City. After a lengthy and extensive manhunt, Ervil was arrested in 1979. The following year he was sentenced to life imprisonment. Finally, on August 16, 1981, he was found dead in his prison cell, apparently of natural causes. Incidently, on that same day, Verlan LeBaron, who had succeeded Joel as head of the Church of the First Born, was killed in an automobile accident in Mexico City.

Following Ervil's death it appeared that the Church was disintegrating, but while it lost many of its members, a small group quietly perpetuated its teachings. Members of the continuing church have been accused of a string of illegal actions including a number of murders. Among the deaths are those of two leaders of rival groups, Daniel Ben Jordan, shot in 1987, and Leo P. Evonik, who had claimed to be Ervil's successor and who has not been seen since his disappearance that same year. In 1988 the Church jumped back into the headlines when four former members of the group were killed on June 27 in Texas.

The Church of the Lamb of God is one of the few new religious groups both to develop a theology which sanctions violence and to carry out a number of killings based upon that theology. The use of violence in the attempt to coerce individuals into religious conformity has in past centuries been the norm, especially for those religions aligned with the power of the state. It has been the source of religious wars throughout human history, and, given the seriousness of religious claims upon people, it is possibly most surprising that so few groups such as the Church of the Lamb of God have emerged in the West in the past century.

Other Polygamy-Practicing Groups

Besides the several larger and more well-known groups discussed above, numerous small independent polygamy-practicing churches exist throughout the Rocky Mountain area from Montana and Idaho to Mexico. Most are confined to a single community (frequently communal in structure). Some have a lineage that can be traced to Lorin Woolley, but others have established their authority on quite divergent bases.

Controversy

Polygamy has produced numerous defenders and critics on both the theoretical and practical level since its widespread practice was advocated by Brigham Young in the mid-nineteenth century. Critics charge practitioners with degrading and even enslaving women. Mormons, however, claim polygamy is the answer to prostitution and lascivious behavior while providing a family context for every person. They have attempted to place their practice in the context of the advocacy of polygamy in the West (whose defenders include such Christian leaders as Martin Luther and John Milton) and its practice around the world.

The tacit acceptance of polygamy reached a new level in March 1991 when the Utah Supreme Court ruled that polygamy was not grounds for denying a couple the right to adopt a child. Then in August of that year, a circuit court judge in St. George signed a statement permitting the first such adoption under the new ruling.

Since the rise of Fundamentalism, the Church of Jesus Christ of Latter-day Saints has been at pains to refute the claims of Lorin C. Woolley. Most recently, J. Max Anderson has examined the Fundamentalist story and found it impossible, as the journals and other records of the movement of President Taylor and those who claimed to have been present in Centerville in 1886 show conclusively that they could not have assembled at the same place on the day in question. Anderson's research adds substance to the long-standing criticism of Woolley, namely, that no account of the Taylor revelation appears until twenty-four years after the event and no published account for almost a half century.

Sources-Primary

Allred, Rulon C. *The Most Holy Principle.* 4 vols. Murray, UT: Gems Publishing Company, 1970-75.

—————. *Treasures of Knowledge.* 2 vols. Hamilton, MT: Bitteroot Publishing Company, 1981.

Chynoweth, Rena (Mrs. Ervil LeBaron), with Dean M. Shipiro. *The Blood Covenant*. Austin, TX: Diamond Books, 1990. 370 pp.

LeBaron, Verlan M. *The LeBaron Story*. Lubbock, TX: Keels & Co., 1981. 316 pp.

Musser, Joseph W. *Celestial or Plural Marriage*. Salt Lake City: Truth Publishing Company, 1944. 154 pp.

Openshaw, Robert R. *The Notes*. Pinesdale, MT: Bitteroot Publishing Company, 1980. 616 pp.

Reminiscences of John W. Woolley and Lorin C. Woolley. 4 vols. Ed. by Mark J. and Rhea A. Baird. N.p.: [1972].

Silver, Stephen M. "Priesthood or Presidency." *Ensign* 2, 11 (January 1963): 1-127.

Sources-Secondary

Anderson, J. Max. *The Polygamy Story: Fact or Fiction*. Salt Lake City: Publishers Press, 1979. 166 pp.

Bradlee, Ben, Jr., and Dale Van Atta. *Prophet of Blood*. New York: G. P. Putnam's Sons, 1981. 350 pp.

Foster, Lawrence. *Religion and Sexuality*. Urbana: University of Illinois Press, 1984. 363 pp.

Richards, Henry W. *A Reply to "The Church of the Firstborn of the Fullness of Times."* Salt Lake City: The Author, 1965. 159 pp.

Shields, Stephen. *The Latter-day Saint Churches: An Annotated Bibliography*. New York: Garland Publishing, 1987. 281 pp.

Van Wagoner, Richard S. *Mormon Polygamy: A History*. Salt Lake City: Signature Books, 1986. 307 pp.

Young, Kimball. *Isn't One Wife Enough*. New York: Henry Holt and Company, 1954. 476 pp.

D. THE "I AM" RELIGIOUS ACTIVITY

The Great White Brotherhood is the name given in metaphysical/occult circles to those adepts of wisdom who have finished their earthly pilgrimages (the cycles of reincarnation and karma) and, while ascending to a higher state of existence as masters of space, time and material existence, have assumed responsibility for the cosmic destiny of the human race, both individually and collectively. Most occult groups assign a high level of importance to the Brotherhood, but some make ongoing interaction with the Ascended Masters of the Brotherhood a major focus of their existence. Of these several, two stand out as most prominent: the "I AM" Religious Activity, the original Ascended Masters group founded in the 1930s, treated below, and the Church Universal and Triumphant, founded in the 1960s, a discussion of which can be found elsewhere in this volume. The two organizations, though frequently confused in the public media, were never connected and vary widely in their teachings.

Founders

Guy W. Ballard (1878-1939), leader of the "I AM" Ascended Master Religious Activity and co-founder with his wife Edna of the Saint Germain Foundation (its corporate expression), was born in Kansas. He married Edna Wheeler (1886-1971) in 1916 and three years later their son Donald was born. After a period in the Army during World War I, he superintended his uncle's lead mine in Tucson, Arizona. Edna was an accomplished concert harpist, and like her husband, had a deep interest in metaphysics and the occult.

1930 became the turning point in the Ballards' lives. Guy Ballard, widely read in theosophical/occult literature, had heard the reports of strange occult events that had been said to occur at Mt. Shasta, a giant volcanic cone in northern California. He developed a desire to visit the mountain to investigate the rumor that a group of Divine Men called the Brotherhood of Mt. Shasta were to be found there.

One day in 1930, while hiking around the mountain he encountered another hiker, "Directly behind me stood a young man, who, at first glance, seemed to be someone on a hike like myself." The man turned out to be the Ascended Master Saint Germain. The Comte de Saint Germain was one of the most famous occultists of modern time. He had lived in eighteenth-century France, had claimed to be several centuries old, and possessed a great reputation as a mystic, alchemist and generally mysterious figure. At the time of their meeting, Ballard, thirsty from his hike, had been looking for a spring. Saint Germain offered a more refreshing drink, a creamy liquid, which had an astonishing vivifying effect upon him. Saint Germain identified the liquid as a substance coming from the Universal Supply. Over a period of time, he introduced Ballard to the astonishing powers of the Ascended Masters and led him into a number of experiences which prepared him to assume his new role as the Messenger of the Masters.

According to Ballard, Saint Germain had ascended to become a member of the Divine Spiritual Hierarchy which rules the life of the universe, and had been assigned the task of initiating the Seventh Golden Age, the permanent "I AM" Age of eternal perfection on this earth. He had searched Europe for several centuries to find someone in human embodiment through whom he could release the instructions of the Great Law of Life. Not finding anyone, he began a search in America, where he encountered Ballard. He subsequently designated Ballard, his wife Edna, and their son Donald as the only Accredited Messengers of the Ascended Masters.

As the initial experiences with Saint Germain and the other ascended beings were occurring, Ballard wrote lengthy letters to his wife in Chicago introducing her to the events. He returned to Chicago in 1931 to initiate Saint Germain's instructions. In 1932 Ballard began to release the message of Saint Germain and to bring forth the visible manifestation of the "I AM" Religious Activity. Together with his wife, he founded the Saint Germain Press and Saint Germain Foundation. Two years later, under the pen name Godfre Ray King, he published his first book, *Unveiled Mysteries* (1934), an account of the encounter with Saint Germain, quickly followed by its sequel, *The Magic Presence* (1935). He also held the first ten-day class in Philadelphia. The class was repeated in Chicago, New York, Washington, D.C., Florida, and Los Angeles. To assist in the work, the Ballards designated a group of "appointed messengers" from among their most capable students. These messengers gave classes and toured the country speaking at various sanctuaries.

Through the 1930s, the other publications which were to become the major literary expressions of the Activity were released: *"I AM"* *Adorations and Affirmations* (1935), which gave the texts for the decrees, the affirmations and invocations regularly repeated by students of the "I AM"; and *"I AM" Discourses* (1936), a series of lectures by Saint Germain which contain the tenets of the Activity (1935). The Saint Germain Press also issued *"I AM" Songs* (1938), a hymnal, while Mrs. Ballard had already launched the Foundation's magazine, *The Voice of the "I AM"* (1936).

The success in Los Angeles led the Ballards to move there and establish a second headquarters. They also encouraged students to establish "I AM" sanctuaries and reading rooms to help strengthen the movement around the country. They promoted the idea of "I AM" schools, and the first one was established in Tenafly, New Jersey. Another was opened in Los Angeles. The movement grew in the face of public recognition of its unorthodox beliefs and practices and at one point claimed over a million students.

In 1939, because of attacks by the media and the appearance of hecklers in the midst of the classes and in order to keep a serene atmosphere in the classes (which had been attended by some 7,000 people in Los Angeles), Ballard discontinued the open classes. It became necessary for sincere followers to obtain a special card of admission. He continued regularly to instruct those who had become students of the teachings until his death in December 1939.

Shortly before Ballard's death, several former members of the movement became vocal critics of the Ballards. One former student, Gerald B. Bryan, wrote a series of booklets and one book, *Psychic Dictatorship in America*, attacking Guy Ballard's integrity and accusing him of plagiarizing much of the religion from old occult books. Other students initiated lawsuits against the Foundation. These suits in turn led to a criminal indictment of Edna and Donald Ballard, along with several staff members. They were charged with mail fraud, i.e., "for using the mails to operate a religion they knew to be false in order to obtain the money of their students." Overwhelmingly the student body supported the Ballards and the Foundation.

When the case finally came to trial in 1942, the Ballards were convicted. Subsequently, the U. S. Postal Service denied the Foundation and Press use of the mail. The convictions were reviewed for the first time by the Supreme Court in 1944, and the Court ruled, in one of its most quoted opinions, that members of a new religion could not be held accountable before a judge and/or jury for the sufficiency of their faith as a grounds for continuing to propagate it. However, a lower court again upheld the conviction which was reviewed and reversed a second time by the Supreme Court in 1946.

The criminal charges behind it, the "I AM" turned to the correlative actions against the Foundation. Another eight years of legal action was required before the Post Office removed its ban on the Foundation's use of the mail in 1954. Up to that time, it had been forced to distribute literature by American Express. Finally, in 1957, the Foundation's tax-exempt status was granted.

In 1941, as legal actions proceeded, Edna Ballard moved from the hostile atmosphere in Los Angeles and established her headquarters in Santa Fe, New Mexico (though the official headquarters always remained in Chicago). A branch of the Saint Germain Press, which had just been established in Denver that same year, also moved to Santa Fe, as did the school previously opened in Los Angeles. It offered classes for elementary and high school grades. She further expanded the youth program by initiating the youth conclaves in 1943.

The rebuilding of the movement could begin in earnest, after the final dismissal of the various charges. It was done with little public fanfare. In 1948 national conclaves of the membership were resumed, and that same year a twelve-story building was purchased in Chicago's Loop to serve both the large concentration of followers there and to be a national teaching center. In 1951, a resort center, the famous Shasta Springs Water Co., was purchased, and Mt. Shasta became the scene of two annual national conclaves for both youth and senior students. The

Youth Conclave featured a pageant of the life of Christ, "I AM Come!," one of the few Activity events open to the public.

Throughout the 1950s Edna Ballard expanded the Teachings contained in The Saint Germain Series (the basic textbooks of the Activity which currently numbers eleven volumes). She also recorded over two thousand dictations from the Ascended Masters. Her son Donald had resigned in 1957 as vice-president of the Foundation and withdrew from the "I AM" Activity. He managed his own manufacturing business but continued to handle most of the recording activity for the Foundation and Press. By the mid-1960s she was heard on twenty-five radio stations. After her death in 1971, the movement's leadership passed to the Board of Directors, which had been established in 1932 and had previously served under the Ballards' guidance.

Beliefs and Practices

Though the spiritual hierarchy, that group of beings who constitute the spiritual cosmos and are popularly called the Great White Brotherhood, have been referred to in occult texts for generations, the contact begun with the Ascended Masters through Guy Ballard led to the releasing of what the "I AM" Religious Activity believed to be a three-fold Truth not previously known outside of the Masters secret retreat centers: This Truth includes (1) the knowledge of the Individualized Presence of God which is known as the "Mighty I AM Presence," God in Action; (2) the use of the Violet Consuming Flame of Divine Love; and (3) the Ascended Masters' use of God's Creative Name, "I AM."

The Activity affirms the reality of One God who is omnipresent, omniscient, and omnipotent and who rules all creation. As the Life of the Universe, God permeates all things and is individualized for dynamic action. From the "I AM" perspective, light is the dominant form taken by divine realities. At the heart of our universe the Great Central Sun, the source of God's power and authority, emanates forth as the "Mighty I AM Presence." As that Presence goes forth and is individualized, creation is brought into existence. Each individual begins as a spark from the divine flame. The "I AM Presence" is the light in the electron and the cells of the body; it is the light in the mind and heart. However, the misuse of the divine energy over the centuries has resulted in the present condition of humanity, manifest in discord, hate, impurities and death which hide the perfection, harmony, love, purity, and life which is God and His "I AM Presence."

As the individualized "I AM Presence," God is the Master within each person, the Christ Self. God is also individualized within each of the members of the hierarchy who govern the cosmos, this planet, and solar system. Members of the hierarchy are known as the Ascended Masters of Love, Light and Perfection. They are the guardians of humanity and have worked through the centuries from the invisible, as well as the physical, to awaken, bless, enlighten, and lift humankind out of the self-created situation in which it now finds itself. Once like other humans, they have, through a series of reembodiments, overcome the present condition and by attuning themselves to the "I AM Presence," ascended into the light. To follow their path is the goal of each person. One of the Ascended Masters is the Master Jesus. Through His ministry and ascension, He released the Christ Light, the "Mighty I AM Presence," to give the earth the forward movement out of darkness and hate into the Light of Divine Love. A picture of the Master Jesus adorns the platform of every "I AM" sanctuary, next to that of Saint Germain. The emphasis placed upon his work and teaching by the Activity leads the members to affirm themselves as members of a Christian religion.

The Activity also teaches that each Ascended Master radiates a certain color, an aspect of the divine light representative of a specific divine quality. "Clean, clear, bright colors," said Mrs. Ballard, "are rivers of blessing from the realms of light, the source of all perfection." However, members generally refrain from wearing red or black or having objects of these colors in their immediate environment. Black is indicative of hate, death and destruction. Red is associated with anger, irritation, and impurity. When impurity is removed from red, for example, it will be transformed instantly into gold.

Within the "I AM" Activity, contact with the Ascended Masters and cooperation with their work is a central goal of each individual's life. Through their Authorized Messengers, the Ballards, the Ascended Masters regularly communicated with the "I AM" membership. Those communications were delivered before gatherings of members, published in the monthly periodical, and the more prominent ones collected and reprinted in the textbooks. (In all, over 3,000 dictations from the Masters were received during the Ballards' lifetime.) These dictations present a total program of guidance for both individuals and society.

Each person in his fullness is pictured in the chart of the "Mighty I AM Presence" which also is to be found on the platform of "I AM" sanctuaries. The individual is shown possessing a "Mighty I AM Presence," a higher self, which is the focus of the Light and Power of God within the self. The "I AM" is the designation of God's creative Word or power in action in everyone. It is pictured as a being of light surrounded by a rainbow of lights, above each person and connected to each conscious self by a thread of luminosity. The purpose of the "I AM" Activity is to release the "I AM" power within and to make it available for the student to use, in cooperation with the Ascended Masters, in the elimination of evil and the advent of freedom and justice in the world.

Each person is also shown surrounded by a violet flame, a cylinder of light created by the "I AM Presence." It is released to function whenever the individual calls forth his/her "I AM Presence" to consume discord and impurity in the world.

The most definitive activities for "I AM" members, by which they seek to attune themselves to their "I AM Presence," and thus align themselves to the path of the Ascended Masters, are (1) quiet contemplation and (2) the repetition of affirmations and decrees. Affirmations are sentences that affirm the individual's attunement to God and the blessing due to the person as a result of that attunement. A decree is a fiat spoken from the standpoint of the higher self, the "Mighty I AM Presence," and may be, depending upon the occasion, peaceful, calming or powerful in content and/or enunciation. The repetition of decrees is devotional activity, and all decrees are given in the Name of God, the "Beloved Mighty I AM Presence" and in the Name of the Ascended Master Jesus the Christ. Decrees are repeated daily for the release of the Violet Consuming Flame and the dissipation of discord in the individual's environment. One typical decree, repeated in a strong commanding voice, might be:

> In the Name of God, the "Beloved Mighty I AM Presence," and in the Name of the Beloved Ascended Jesus Christ, "I AM" the Strength, the Courage, the Power to move forward steadily through all experiences, whatever they may be, by the glorious Presence with "I AM" "I AM" the Commanding Presence, the Exhaustless Energy, the Divine Wisdom, causing every desire to be fulfilled. The "Presence which I AM!" remains untouched by disturbing outer conditions. Serene, I

fold my wings and abide in the Perfect Action of the Divine
Law and Justice of my Being, commanding all things within
my radiance to appear in Perfect Divine Order!

Students are taught basic decrees from the beginning of their
work in the movement, and booklets of decrees for every occasion have
been published.

Freedom was a persistent theme in the teaching of the Ascended
Masters, who assigned America a special role in the unfolding Plan for
the coming Golden Age. As a result, the Activity and its members have
become known for their patriotism and love of country. American flags
are prominently displayed at all "I AM" centers, and patriotic literature
is integral to all their teaching activity.

Current Status

After the death of Edna Ballard, the governance of the Saint
Germain Foundation and the Saint Germain Press and the supervision
of the "I AM" Activity passed to a five-member Board of Directors. That
board was expanded to eighteen members in 1982. The Foundation
charters the local sanctuaries, which are otherwise autonomous centers
of the Activity. It oversees the work of Appointed Messengers of Saint
Germain who teach the introductory classes, which are open to the
public, and other classes for "I AM" Activity students, as well as the
several regional counselors, field workers, and local councils. The radio
programs begun by Edna Ballard have been continued and may be heard
weekly across the United States.

In 1978 the headquarters of the Foundation was moved into a
new Worldwide Headquarters in Schaumburg, Illinois. The Saint
Germain Press moved into the new facilities in 1982, and the property in
Santa Fe was sold. The Press publishes the Saint Germain Series, the
eleven textbooks of the Activity, and the monthly periodical, *The Voice
of the "I AM."* In 1990 there were over 300 "I AM" centers in over
twenty-five countries. One school owned and operated by the students of
the Activity is located in Denver, Colorado.

New students in the Activity begin by reading the first three
books of the Saint Germain Series and studying two series of

Fundamental Lessons. After completion of these materials, the student may receive an admittance card to an Introductory Class, which is offered periodically in Chicago. The Saint Germain Foundation emphasizes that it does not charge for the teaching or the classes. Students frequently make gifts to assist and support the work of the Foundation or a local sanctuary, but no charge is ever made for instruction.

Controversy

Soon after its establishment as a national movement, the "I AM" Activity came under attack. The first significant critic was Gerald Bryan, author of *Psychic Dictatorship in America* (1940). However, as soon as the Movement began to show signs of success, newspapers took a critical approach to what many saw as its very unusual teachings and frequently ridiculed the movement and its leaders. During the string of legal actions and especially the several trials during the 1940s, the sensational and hostile reporting drove many from the movement and drove the movement itself away from the public eye. Over the years, the leaders refrained from discussions with reporters and others who attempted to gather information about them. As a result little was written about the Activity after the lengthy chapter in *These Also Believe*, the 1949 survey of America's alternative religions by Northwestern University professor Charles Braden.

Thus while the movement has slowly rebuilt itself into a significantly large religious organization, it has been almost totally unnoticed and frequently reported as nonexistent. (The Foundation has a policy against advertising and promotion of itself and the Activity.)

During the decade, some recognition of the "I AM" Activity has come because other organizations that have derived some of its teachings and symbolism from the "I AM" Activity have received widespread media attention. One such group, the Church Universal and Triumphant, has emerged as a prominent and controversial organization. In the face of this variety of groups whose teachings resemble those of the "I AM" Activity, the Saint Germain Foundation has attempted to hold to the teachings of the Ascended Masters exactly as originally delivered by those whom they believe to be their only Accredited Messengers, the Ballards, unmixed with the teachings of other religious traditions or the words spoken through other Messengers.

Sources-Primary

Ascended Master Saint Germain. *The "I AM" Discourses.* Chicago: Saint Germain Press, 1936. 361 pp.

King, Godfre Ray (pen name of Guy W. Ballard). *The Magic Presence.* Chicago: Saint Germain Press, 1935. 399 pp.

————. *Unveiled Mysteries.* Chicago: Saint Germain Press, 1934. 263 pp.

The Great Cosmic Beings. *Ascended Master Light.* Chicago: Saint Germain Press, 1938. 536 pp.

Sources-Secondary

Braden, Charles S. *These Also Believe.* New York: Macmillan Company, 1949. 491 pp.

Bryan, Gerald B. *Psychic Dictatorship in America.* Los Angeles: Truth Research Foundation, 1940. 255 pp.

Stupple, David W. *A Functional Approach to Social Movements with an Analysis of the I AM Religious Sect and the Congress of Racial Equality.* Kansas City: University of Missouri, MA thesis, 1965. 170 pp.

E. THE IDENTITY MOVEMENT

What came to be known in the 1970s as the Identity Movement was previously termed Anglo-Israelism or British-Israelism. It is composed of those individuals and groups who identify the present day Anglo-Saxon people as the direct biological descendants of the ancient Israelites and, as such, God's chosen people, the heirs of all God's promises to Abraham and his progeny. Following the death of Solomon, Israel split into two nations, the northern kingdom (Israel) and the southern kingdom (Judah). The ten lost tribes of Israel, the former northern kingdom, are sharply distinguished from Judah, the ancient southern kingdom centered upon Jerusalem, which consisted of the tribes of Judah and Benjamin and some Levites. In like measure, modern Anglo-Saxons (Israelites) are to be sharply distinguished from the Jews (Judah).

Origin and History

The Anglo-Israelite hypothesis originated with Richard Brothers (1757-1824), a Canadian born visionary. His self-proclaimed right, as a descendant of King David, to the throne of England led to his commitment to an asylum. Dismissed as mentally deranged, Brothers found no support for his ideas before his death. They did not receive serious attention until 1840 when John Wilson published his restatement of them in *Our Israelitish Origin*. Throughout the rest of the nineteenth century, supporters of Wilson's presentation emerged in Bible student circles. In England, Piazzi Smith, famous for his study of the Great Pyramid, became a believer. In America, M. M. Eshelman, author of *Two Sticks or the Lost Tribes of Israel Discovered* (1887) and a prominent minister in the Church of the Brethren, became an early exponent. He was soon joined by Canadian minister W. H. Poole, author of *Anglo-Israel or the Saxon Race Proved to be the Lost Tribes of the Bible* (1889). Both of these early authors were eclipsed by J. J. Allen, whose *Judah's Sceptre and Joseph's Birthright* (1902) became the single most important instrument in spreading Anglo-Israel thought into Adventist and independent Bible student circles. Through the efforts of Merritt Dickinson, who had read and accepted the arguments in Allen, Anglo-Israel thought entered the Church of God (Seventh Day). Herbert W. Armstrong, a minister in the group, and later founder of the Worldwide Church of God, subsequently became the most successful exponent of Anglo-Israelism.

In spite of the efforts of the early teachers, and the founding of both British and Canadian Anglo-Israelite organizations, the message did not find a large audience until the 1920s when Howard B. Rand began a small Bible study group in Haverhill, Massachusetts. He began a periodical, and in 1930 organized a national convention of Identity people to be held in Detroit. At the convention, he met W. J. Cameron, formerly the editor of the *Dearborn* (MI) *Independent* in which Henry Ford had published his infamous series of articles on "The International Jew." Cameron became president of Rand's Anglo-Saxon Federation of America. Assisted by public relations executive Clarence S. Warner, the Federation promoted the formation of Anglo-Israelite groups across the United States. Some of these groups matured into large independent congregations, which in turn became publishing centers for the movement.

In identifying the Anglo-Saxon people as the modern descendants of ancient Israel (as distinguished from ancient Judah) and in concentrating attention upon the promises of God to Israel, His chosen people, the movement was inherently racist. However, while supporting Britain's colonial empire and America's manifest destiny during their first decades, American believers did not crusade against those God had not chosen, particularly blacks and Jews. Inevitably, as the movement gained national support, some supporters of the Ku Klux Klan and neo-Nazi movements found Anglo-Israelism an acceptable ideology. By World War II, most Anglo-Israelite leaders openly supported racial propaganda.

Rand's Anglo-Saxon Federation of America, which had dominated the movement, was joined after World War II by a score of new centers of activity. A new generation of leaders also emerged. Most prominent of the Anglo-Israelite leaders who placed great emphasis on racial themes was Gerald L. K. Smith. In 1947 he launched the Christian Nationalist Crusade, and its periodical, *The Cross and the Flag*, became one of the most vitriolic anti-black and anti-Jewish publications in the United States. Smith campaigned for the deportation of all Zionists, abolition of all "Jewish Gestapo organizations," shipping of all black people to Africa, and liquidation of the United Nations.

A survey of the movement made in the early 1950s appeared in Ralph Lord Roy's *Apostles of Discord*. Roy discovered centers in every part of the United States. Among the most important were the Beacon Light Ministry headed by William Kullgren of Atascadero, California; the Prophetic Herald Ministry headquartered at Bethel Temple in Spokane, Washington, pastored by William Schiffner; Destiny of America Foundation headed by Conrad Gaard of Tacoma, Washington; the United Israel World Fellowship headed by James A. Lovell of Fort Worth, Texas; and the Anglo-Saxon Christian Association headed by H. M. Greene and Hugh C. Krum of Portland, Oregon. For a few years in the 1940s, the movement sponsored the Dayton Theological Seminary in Ohio.

Beliefs

Members of the Identity Movement do not consider themselves a new sect or denomination, rather they believe themselves to be a group of orthodox Christians who accept the Bible as the inspired and hence literally true Word of God. While affirming their belief in God, Jesus Christ, and the Holy Spirit, they generally stop short of belief in the Trinity. Their belief in the literal truth of the Bible is manifested by a firm belief in the biblical account of creation as described in Genesis, the virgin birth of Jesus, the personal return of Jesus to earth, and the final battle to be fought between the Israel of God and the enemies of Jesus. Following the tradition of free church Protestantism, two ordinances, baptism (by immersion) and communion, are practiced.

Some Identity groups have also adopted both sabbatarianism and sacred name emphases from Adventism. Joe Jeffers, head of the Kingdom of Yahweh, was possibly the first person to combine a belief in the British-Israel hypothesis with the keeping of the sabbath on Saturday and the use of transliterations of the Hebrew names of the Creator and His Son ("Yahweh" and "Yahshua") in place of "God" and "Jesus."

The movement is most at variance with the larger body of Christians by its belief that, as Identity pastor Sheldon Emry asserts, ". . . the Anglo-Saxon, Celtic, Scandinavian, Germanic, and related peoples, often called the 'Christian nations' are the racial descendants of the tribes of Israel." The modern Anglo-Saxon nations continue those ten tribes of ancient Israel to whom the law and the promises of God were given. Israel is first of all a literal nation and then a Church. Britain and the United States possess what Israel was to possess and are doing what Israel was to do.

The New Covenant first mentioned by the prophet Jeremiah was made with Israel, and Jesus Christ came to confirm that covenant and hence to redeem Israel. Jesus' death re-established the relationship between Israel and God broken at the time just prior to Israel's being cast out of the Holy Land (II Kings 17).

The perspective on Scripture and history adopted by the Identity movement has led to distinctly pro-white racial bias and an anti-black and anti-Jewish stance that varies in militancy within various segments of the movement. Modern-day Jews, the surviving remnant of the House of Judah, are sharply distinguished from Israel, with which they have no part.

Organization of the Movement

The Identity Movement is composed of numerous independent congregations and ministries, each of which is built around one prominent minister who frequently combines the roles of congregational leader, writer and radio-TV spokesperson. Only one person, Herbert W. Armstrong, has been able to build a large denominational structure. (His Worldwide Church of God is considered in a separate chapter elsewhere in this volume.) Though independent, various congregations form networks and distribute the literature of the movement as a whole. Among the most important centers of the movement are the following:

The Anglo-Saxon Federation of America

Founded in 1928 by Howard B. Rand, the Federation is the oldest identity group currently operating, though its work has been considerably reduced as its leader has aged. It is headquartered in Haverhill, Massachusetts, and continues to distribute Rand's books and a newsletter to its several thousand members scattered across the country.

Christian Conservative Churches of America

The Christian Conservative Churches of America grew out of the spiritual experience of John R. Harrell while recuperating from cancer at the Mayo Clinic. He founded the Church and donated his 55-acre estate to it in 1959. The Church suffered a major setback five years later, however, when Harrell disappeared on the eve of a scheduled IRS hearing. Arrested the following year, he was sentenced to 10 years in jail. Although paroled in 1969, he was not allowed to participate in the work of the Church until his probation was ended in 1975. He immediately began to rebuild the Church whose purpose was to blend Christianity and Patriotism to effectively oppose Zionism (i.e., Jews) and communism.

Harrell teaches that the present governmental systems of North America are in imminent danger of collapse, and he encourages members of the Identity Movement to band together for survival and the preservation of the heritage of the white race. He has designated an area in the middle of the United States (roughly the land between Pittsburgh, Atlanta, Lubbock (Texas), and Scottsbluff (Nebraska), which he terms the "golden triangle," as prime territory within which Christian Survivalists can defend themselves when the collapse occurs.

Associated with the Church are three auxiliary organizations. The Christian-Patriots Defense League, founded in 1977, is a dues-free organization which educates and organizes Christian patriots for the coming collapse. It is dedicated to preserving Anglo-Saxon culture against any form of miscegenation. The Citizens Emergency Defense System is a private militia standing ready to be activated should the situation deteriorate sufficiently. The Paul Revere Club receives funds to support the other organizations. The Church and its auxiliary organizations are headquartered at Harrell's estate in Louisville, Illinois, in a full-scale replica of Mt. Vernon, George Washington's home.

Church of Jesus Christ Christian, Aryan Nations

The Church of Jesus Christ Christian was founded after World War II by Wesley A. Swift, a Ku Klux Klan organizer on the West Coast and close associate of Gerald L. K. Smith. Swift died in 1970 and was succeeded by his widow. Richard Butler, a pastor at the Church moved to Idaho and began an independent branch at Hayden Lake. Due to Butler's open identification with both Klan and Nazi groups, this branch has become one of the most notorious centers of the Identity Movement. In 1982 he organized the International Congress of Aryan Nations, which attracted numerous white supremacy groups. The single congregation in Idaho has around 300 members, but claims some 6,000 additional members across the country.

The Aryan Nations describes itself as a white racial theo-political movement whose aim is the re-establishment of white Aryan sovereignty over the lands of Aryan settlement and occupation. It teaches that the preservation of the white race is demanded and directed by Yahweh and that a battle is presently being fought between the present-day children of darkness (i.e., the Jews) and the children of light (Aryan race).

The Church of Israel

The Church of Israel was formed in 1972 as a result of a disagreement in a small Mormon splinter group, the Church of Christ at Haley's Bluff, Missouri. That Church was, in turn, a splinter from the Church of Christ (Temple Lot) which claims to be the original church founded by Joseph Smith, Jr., the Mormon prophet. During the 1960s, Daniel Gayman, one of the Church's pastors, was appointed editor of the Church's periodical. He soon began to print articles reflective of his extreme racial views and then began to use the church's youth camp as a seminary for fellow white supremacists and as a military training ground to teach weapons use and military tactics.

Tension over Gayman's activities resulted in schism in 1972 after an election in which Gayman won control of the congregation and dismissed all the members of the congregation's priesthood. Those relieved of their office sued Gayman, and the court returned almost all of the Church's property to the Church of Christ at Haley's Bluff. In 1974, following the court ruling, Gayman's supporters reincorporated and at that time assumed the name Church of Christian Heritage. It took its present name in 1981.

In the place of the teachings of Joseph Smith, Jr., the Church of Israel has substituted the Identity Movement's theology and its belief in white supremacy. Gayman teaches that the British people have transmitted the apostolic succession of the early church through Joseph of Arimathea who brought it to the British Isles in the first century. Gayman has developed a theologically unique variation on the two-seed-in-the-spirit theory first popularized in the last century by Baptist minister Daniel Parker. Basing his interpretation upon *Genesis* 3:15, Parker argued that Cain and Abel represented two seeds carried within the human race, the former of Satan, the latter of God and Adam. Every person was born of one of the two seeds and was thus predestined from the beginning to be a part of either God's family or Satan's. Gayman turned Parker's theories into a racial polemic against blacks and Jews. White gentiles have descended from Seth (the murdered Abel's substitute), while blacks and Jews have descended from Cain, the child of Satan's impregnation of Eve.

At the time the church adopted its present name, it also reorganized. The Church was divided into twelve dioceses, each named for one of the twelve tribes of Israel. There is no diocese for either Levi or Joseph, but there is one for each of Joseph's two sons, Ephraim and Manasseh. Each diocese is headed by a bishop. The Diocese of Manasseh, covering the United States, is headed by Bishop Gayman. The Diocese of Ephraim covers the British Commonwealth and other dioceses have been designated for the various European countries. Only the Diocese of Manasseh has been activated as of the mid-1980s. There are five congregations with a combined membership of several hundred. Gayman edits *The Watchman*, the church's periodical.

The New Christian Crusade Church

The New Christian Crusade Church was founded in 1971 by James K. Warner, a former member of Lincoln Rockwell's American Nazi Party. Headquartered in a New Orleans suburb, it is closely associated with The Knights of the New Ku Klux Klan which used the Church's postal box for distributing its periodical, *The Crusader*. Warner has also founded two associated structures, The Christian Defense

League, an open membership organization for people who support the Church's racial policies (anti-black and anti-Jewish), and the Sons of Liberty, a publishing and literature distribution company. The church has a single congregation serving members in the New Orleans area, but has a significant outreach through its affiliated organizations.

The Covenant, the Sword, the Arm of the Lord

One of the most militant groups within the Identity Movement, The Covenant, the Sword, the Arm of the Lord was founded in 1976 by Rev. Jim Ellison, an independent minister from San Antonio, Texas. Following a vision of the coming collapse of American society, he established a survivalist commune, Zarephath-Horeb, near the Arkansas-Missouri border on land purchased from the Campus Crusade for Christ. The former campground was intended as a haven when the battle of Armageddon begins. The community was partially self-supporting. A farm produced its food, and education and medical services were provided by the members. Residents lived without either electricity or plumbing. A substantial part of the community's income derived from classes in military skills and survivalism at the communal site.

C.S.A. believed that the two-edged sword of God's Spirit is coming in judgment to the earth, and that God's arm, which will administer that judgment, will soon be manifest. C.S.A. was to have a significant part in the execution of God's judgment. In preparation for the difficult times ahead, the community stored food, stockpiled weapons, and learned to live an austere life. It fully expects a major internal war in which white Christians will be set against Jews, blacks, homosexuals, witches, and Satanists, as well as foreign enemies.

C.S.A. disbanded after the 1985 raid and the subsequent trial and convictions of Ellison and several other leaders.

Ministry of Christ Church

The Ministry of Christ Church, founded by William Potter Gale (1917-1988), was incorporated in 1964. The Church teaches that Jesus preached the Gospel of the Kingdom and the Kingdom is a government.

Further, Jesus accomplished the salvation from sin of his kinsmen, Israel, or modern-day Christians. Jesus' kinsmen are the white race, which began with Adam who suddenly appeared on the earth in approximately 5,500 B.C.E. The black and yellow races preceded Adam by thousands of years. The Bible is the book of the "generations" (i.e., race) of Adam, the white race, who are to bring God's government to this earth. That government is present in the United States, the New Jerusalem.

Founder Gale had been an aide to General Douglas MacArthur in the Philippines during World War II. His activities with his church and the Posse Comitatus earned him an arrest and conviction in January 1988 for sending threatening letters to agents of the Internal Revenue Service. He died a few months later. He had built a national following but only a single congregation located in Mariposa, California. His widow continues as head of the Ministry of Christ Church.

Other Centers

Besides the more prominent organizations in the Identity Movement, a number of others publish and distribute literature and/or regularly broadcast over radio. Such organizations include The Lord's Covenant Church, headed by Sheldon Emry of Phoenix, Arizona; The Church of Jesus Christ founded by Thomas Arthur Robb of Bass, Arkansas; New Beginnings headed by Eldon D. Purvis of Waynesville, North Carolina; the Mountain Kirk of Cohoctah, Michigan, headed by Robert E. Miles; the Gospel Temple in Hopkins, Minnesota, pastored by C. O. Stadsklev; and Your Heritage headed by Bertrand L. Comparet of San Diego, California.

Internationally, the Movement is represented by the British-Israel World Federation, headquartered in London. A similar organization, the Association of Covenant People, distributes literature throughout Canada from its headquarters in Vancouver.

Current Status

The informal *Identity Directory for All Anglo-Saxon, Celtic & Kindred Peoples* (periodically updated), reveals a network of individuals scattered across the United States but provides no basis upon which to estimate the number of supporters of the Identity philosophy in its several variants. No recent survey to determine the size of the Movement has been undertaken, and there is no way to tell how much overlap there is between the reported size of mailing lists from the several centers. Churches and publishing centers can be found throughout the United States, and a substantial amount of literature is circulated. The Sons of Liberty catalog lists hundreds of books and tapes for sale. Among the several Identity ministers on radio, none approaches Sheldon Emry, whose radio broadcast is currently heard on approximately 40 radio stations across the United States each weekend. However, most groups have only a single congregation with memberships averaging in the low hundreds. A few, such as the Church of Israel and the Christian Conservative Churches of America, have several congregations.

While based in a single congregation, Identity groups have frequently sought a national following through the circulation of a periodical or the building of a national auxiliary organization, the members of which may gather for a convention annually. Among the prominent periodicals of the Movement are: *America's Promise Newsletter* (Lord's Covenant Church); the *Christian Vanguard* (New Christian Crusade Church); *The C.D.L. Report* (Christian Defense League); *From the Mountain* (the Mountain Kirk); *Identity* (Ministry of Christ Church); *New Beginnings, Our Nation* (Church of Jesus Christ Christian, Aryan Nations); *The Torch* (edited by Thomas Arthur Robb); and *The Watchman* (Church of Israel).

Apart from the Worldwide Church of God, adherents to the Identity Movement seem to number approximately 10,000 to 20,000. Of these only a minority seem to be involved in the more violent Ku Klux Klan and Nazi-oriented wing of the Movement.

Controversy

From the beginning of its appearance in the nineteenth century, scholars have attacked the basic ideas of British-Israelism. They have noted that the ten lost tribes of Israel did not migrate to Europe, they were assimilated within the cultures of the Middle East. No evidence for Anglo-Saxon roots in the ancient Middle East has been found. Scholars have also refuted the particular claims of British-Israelites, such as their philology (most British-Israelites, for example, derive the word British from the Hebrew "b'rith," i.e., covenant) and their archaeology. (Movement writers, for example, generally assert that the Stone of Scone came from the Holy Land. In fact, it came from Scotland.)

However, most of the recent criticism of the Movement has focused upon the racial teachings inherent within the Movement's basic assumptions. While less than half of those associated with the Identity Movement seem to support the overt and frequently violent racist rhetoric, the racial (anti-black and anti-Semitic) teachings of white supremacy pervade the Movement. Within the Movement, bitter anti-Semitic documents circulate freely (including the fraudulent *Protocols of the Learned Elders of Zion*), and leaders openly advocate racist and anti-Semitic beliefs. Several of the Identity churches keep strong ties to the Klan and the several Nazi groups. Jewish organizations, such as the Anti-Defamation League, have taken the lead in attacking the Identity Movement in this regard.

To the longstanding criticism of the racial teaching of the Identity Movement has been added concern about its potential for violence. Through the mid-1980s much of that concern centered upon two groups, C.S.A. and the Posse Comitatus, a populist organization which has become well known for its protest of the income tax system. Posse Comitatus' national membership includes members from Identity Churches, and many Posse members have formed congregations of the Life Science Church or the Basic Bible Churches of America, two churches which offer ordination by mail, merely upon application. They brought Identity beliefs into these two churches. For many years, C.S.A. used its rural location as a school for members of other Identity groups to teach a variety of courses in weapons use, military tactics survival, and related subjects. They also dealt in weapons as a means of supporting their commune.

Through the 1980s the government, urged on by various civil rights groups and organizations such as the Anti-Defamation League, took steps against the movement in so far as it had stepped across the line from rhetoric to illegal actions. On February 17, 1983, Posse Comitatus leader Gordon Kahl was involved in a shootout in Medina, South Dakota, that left two U.S. Marshals dead and three other law officers wounded. Kahl fled but was discovered and killed June 3, 1983, in Arkansas not too far from C.S.A. headquarters. The following year, in

July, an Arkansas state trooper, Louis Bryant, was killed. Richard N. Snell, formally a resident at C.S.A., was arrested and later convicted of the murder. In 1985 James Ellison, C.S.A.'s founder, and other members of the group were arrested and convicted on racketeering charges. Ellison was sentenced to twenty years in prison, and he would subsequently appear as a government witness against other Identity leaders.

During the mid 1980s authorities also moved against a militant semi-secret Identity group which had split off from the Church of Jesus Christ Christian, Aryan Nations, called the Order. Members were accused of a variety of crimes in the Northwest, including the murder of Denver talk-show host, Alan Berg. Investigating Order member Gary Lee Yarbrough, F.B.I. agents found the gun used to kill Berg. In December 1984 Order founder Robert Matthews died in a siege on a house on Whidbey Island, Washington. In February 1985 Yarbrough was convicted of assault for shooting at the FBI agents. Later that year, ten Order members were arrested and convicted of racketeering charges.

In 1988 in what was perceived to be a major action against the Identity Movement, a number of its leaders, including Richard Butler and Robert Miles, were put on trial for seditious conspiracy. The lengthy trial, however, resulted in not guilty verdicts. Meanwhile, attention turned to the emergence of a new phenomenon, the Skinheads, young adult groups whose members shaved their head as a sign of their membership. The skinheads adopted a Nazi-like perspective and made common cause with both secular Klan and racialist groups and the Identity Movement. However, many Skinheads used burglary and robbery as a means of support and their open hostility frequently resulted in actions of felonious assault. Easily identified by their shaved heads and black uniform-like dress, their numbers were decimated within a few years as a significant portion of the group found themselves in prison.

The Identity groups seem destined to continue as long as they limit their advocacy of racial ideas to rhetoric. Because of their potential threat, their activities are continually monitored.

Sources-Primary

Allen, J. H. *Judah's Sceptre and Joseph's Birthright.* Boston: A.A. Beauchamp, 1930. 277 pp.

Anti-Christ vs. Christians. Hayden Lake, ID: Church of Jesus Christ Christian, Aryan Nations, n.d.

Gale, William P. *Identity.* Glendale, CA: Ministry of Christ Church, n.d..

Identity Directory for All Anglo-Saxon, Celtic & Kindred Peoples. N.p.: n.d. Periodically revised.

The Pattern of History. Merrimac, MA: Destiny Publishers, 1961. 26 pp.

Stadsklev, C. O. *Tracing the Isaac-Sons—Anglo-Saxons.* Hopkins, MN: America's Hope Broadcasts, n.d..

Sources-Secondary

Coates, James. *Armed and Dangerous: The Rise of the Survivalist Right.* New York: Hill and Wang, 1987. 294 pp.

Corcoran, James. *Bitter Harvest: Gordon Kahl and the Posse Comitatus: Murder in the Heartland.* New York: Viking Press, 1990. 274 pp.

Darms, Anton. *The Delusion of British-Israelism.* New York: Loizeaux Brothers, n.d. 224 pp.

Hate Groups in America. New York: Anti-Defamation League of B'nai B'rith, 1982. 107 pp

Martinez, Thomas I., with John Gunther. *Brotherhood of Murder.* New York: McGraw-Hill Book Company, 1988. 246 pp.

Roy, Ralph Lord. *Apostles of Discord.* Boston: Beacon Press, 1953. 437 pp.

Schwartz, Alan M., et al. "The Identity Churches: A Theology of Hate." *ADL Facts* 28, I (Spring, 1983): 1-16.

Singular, Stephen. *Talked to Death: The Murder of Allen Berg and the Rise of Neo-Nazis.* New York: Berkley Books, 1987. 309 pp.

F. JEHOVAH'S WITNESSES

Since its founding in 1881, the organization known as Jehovah's Witnesses has been one of the most controversial religious groups to spring up on the fertile American soil. Its roots lie in the nineteenth-century Adventist movement begun by William Miller. Originally, Miller projected the imminent return of Christ in 1843. After the failure of that prediction and its revision to 1844, Adventists splintered into a number of factions, one group of which attempted to set other dates for the Second Advent. The Jehovah's Witnesses and their founder Charles Taze Russell emerged from among these people.

Charles Taze Russell (1852-1916)

Much of the history of the Jehovah's Witnesses can be told through the careers of its leaders. The first, Charles Taze Russell, was raised a Presbyterian but, as a young man, left that church. While still in his teens, he met Jonas Wendall, an Adventist minister who believed that the Second Advent would occur in 1874. Russell associated with Wendall and in 1868 formed his own Bible Study group to explore the Bible in the light of Wendall's ideas. Working with the small group, Russell developed the views with which he was to become identified. Over the next decade he began to teach that hell meant annihilation (death) not eternal torment; that humanity had been ransomed from that death, not from hellfire; and that there was no biblical basis for the doctrine of the Triune God.

Most importantly, Russell faced the fact that Christ had not visibly returned in 1874 by announcing that Christ did, in fact, return in 1874 but as an invisible presence. He adopted the view that the Greek word "parousia," commonly translated "coming," in fact should be translated "presence."

In 1879 Russell began to publish a magazine, *The Watch Tower and Herald of Christ's Presence*, to expound his ideas. Tracts and a booklet, *Food for Thinking Christians*, soon followed. By the end of 1880, approximately 30 groups of worshippers had formed. In 1881, Russell sent two people to England to distribute literature. From the incorporation of the Watch Tower Bible and Tract Society (originally Zion's Watch Tower Tract Society) in 1884 the work progressed steadily. Congregations of believers led by local elders sprang up across the United States and in Canada, Australia, and Europe.

Russell's popularity rested, in part, on his prediction that the end of gentile sovereignty over the nations would occur in 1914. The beginning of World War I seemed to confirm Russell's prophecy, but the War continued and the lack of supernatural intervention became obvious to all. In the midst of the confusion, Russell died.

Joseph Franklin Rutherford (1869-1942)

J. F. Rutherford, the Society's lawyer, had joined Russell's group after reading *The Studies in the Scriptures*, Russell's six-volume exposition of the Bible. He became the Society's attorney in 1907 and oversaw the movement of the headquarters to Brooklyn, New York.

Following Russell's death, Rutherford was elected President of the Society but not without a struggle and the loss of a number of congregations who opposed his leadership. No sooner had his position been consolidated, than he had to deal with the government. He and other members of the board were arrested and sentenced to prison for advising men to refrain from military service. Rutherford emerged from prison in 1918 embittered by his imprisonment to lead a group discouraged by the failure of the 1914 prediction.

And over the next decade, Rutherford made monumental changes in the Society. He began to weld the loosely organized congregations into a close-knit body, described as "theocratic," whose job was to inform the world of Jehovah's reign. He attacked the established structures of Satan's world—the Church, particularly the Roman Catholic Church, and government. Members of the Society were mobilized to distribute the ever-growing number of Watch Tower books and pamphlets.

Rutherford became the first popular religious leader to raise the issue of God having a name in Hebrew. That name, asserted Rutherford, was Jehovah, and Jehovah's people should be called by his name. Thus he led the members of the congregations affiliated with the Society to adopt the new name, Jehovah's Witnesses, in 1931. [This concern with the "name" of God in the 1930s would give rise to separate denominations within Adventism generally referred to as the Sacred Name Movement.]

Rutherford had created the strong organization he had envisioned in the 1920s. He died in 1942 as government persecution of the pacifist Witnesses began to disrupt the international work.

Nathan Knorr (1905-1977)

Rutherford was succeeded by Nathan Knorr, the former manager of the Society's printing plant. Knorr put his managerial skill to work in perfecting the organization built by Rutherford, but he approached his task in a much lower key. Increasingly, the board had been seen as directing the organization's activities, rather than any one person. As in the days of Rutherford, books and materials flowed from the Watch Tower publishing plant, but beginning in 1943, no author's name appeared on them.

Knorr placed great emphasis upon training members and instituted the Service Meetings and the Kingdom Ministry School as a lay education effort to assist Witnesses in communicating their beliefs effectively. He also enlarged the international conventions, which were held in multiple locations around the United States and the world in stadiums or other large structures where large crowds could gather. The same program would be held in each site.

The last decade of Knorr's tenure was filled with the expectation that the Second Advent would occur in 1975. He only lived a short time after that prediction failed, a fact which has shaken the organization in recent years.

Fred Franz (1893-)

Possibly the most lasting accomplishment of the Knorr years was the publication of the *New World Translation of the Holy Scripture*, which embodied all the Witnesses' ideas about translation of the Bible, especially in its use of Jehovah as God's name. However, the man generally given most credit for the Bible was Fred Franz who succeeded Knorr as President of the Society. A scholarly man, he, even more than Knorr, was a retiring man. He has, nonetheless, provided strong leadership and done nothing to allow the strong central authority in the board to slip, in spite of the defections of many Witnesses due to the failure of the 1975 prophecy.

Beliefs

Jehovah's Witnesses consider themselves Bible-believing followers of Christ; however, they have come to different conclusions about what the Bible teaches from those of orthodox Christianity. Their position resembles that of Arius (ca. 256-336 A.D.), a teacher whose opinions were condemned by the Council of Nicea (325 A.D.). Arius, like other Witnesses, held that Christ was not the second person of the Triune Godhead but rather the first of God's creations. Christ's death, which occurred on a stake, not a cross, was a ransom for obedient humanity.

Humans are saved by their faith and obedience to God (Jehovah). At death their soul (i.e., their life) ceases. They go to the grave (hell) and their hope is in a future resurrection. Humankind looks for the imminent end of Satan's reign upon earth. After his reign is destroyed in the Battle of Armageddon, Jehovah's rule will be established on earth. A select 144,000 will go to heaven and reign with Christ, while the remaining Christians will live forever on earth. Most present-day Witnesses do not expect to go to heaven. After Armageddon, the dead in Christ will be raised to enjoy eternal life.

Witnesses also believe in creation as opposed to evolution. They consider saluting the flag to be idol worship. They do not use blood transfusions because of the biblical admonition to refrain from drinking blood.

Organization

The Jehovah's Witnesses are organized as a theocracy, that is, the Witnesses see their organization under the direct rule of Jehovah through Christ. Their first allegiance is to that rule, even if it conflicts with various national governments, and most especially if such governments demand what Witnesses consider idolatrous or otherwise against Jehovah's moral precepts. Jehovah's authority on earth is manifest in a remnant of spirit-anointed leaders, the president, and Governing Board of 17 members. In carrying out their global task, they have formed corporations recognized by various secular governments. The most important of these are the Watch Tower Bible and Tract Society of Pennsylvania (1884), the Watch Tower Bible and Tract Society of New York (1909), and the International Bible Students Association (1914).

The Society is divided into various zones or branches which consist of one or more countries. Each branch is led by a committee of three or more elders. Local congregations are led by local elders, from among whom are appointed a presiding overseer, a secretary, a service overseer, a Watch Tower study conductor, and a Theocratic Ministry School overseer. Congregations in any branch territory are grouped into circuits under a circuit overseer. Circuits are grouped into districts, under a district overseer. Literature, the distribution of which is a major item on the Witnesses' agenda, is written at the headquarters in Brooklyn. Copies are than distributed to the branch offices. Those with their own printing presses will print the material (and translate where appropriate). Other branches will obtain their material directly from the presses in Brooklyn.

Members of the Witnesses are expected to attend Sunday Worship and the several meetings each week. They are also expected to spend some time distributing copies of the Society's two magazines, *Awake* and *Watch Tower*, as well as current books. Such activity is the main source of new members. The immediate area around the Kingdom Hall is canvassed regularly by members, each of whom is designated a minister by the organization. The Witnesses have not designated a special "ministerial" class, though certain elders are assigned traditional ministerial tasks.

Witnesses have generally disapproved of higher education, though in 1943 they founded a training school for missionaries, the Watch Tower Bible School of Gilead, at Brooklyn, New York.

Current Status

The 1990 *Yearbook* of the Jehovah's Witnesses reported 3,430,926 active "publishers" in 47,670 congregations in 212 countries. Of these, 762,960 publishers in 8,754 congregations could be found in the United States. Brazil, Germany, Mexico, and Nigeria each reported slightly over 100,000 publishers. The 1980s were a decade of significant growth for the Witnesses, with over 200,000 new adherents in the United States, and over a million worldwide. Spectacular growth was reported in Brazil and Mexico which became the first countries other than the United States with over 200,000 Witnesses. However, Great Britain, France, Germany, Italy, Japan, Nigeria, and the Philippines all report over 100,000 active publishers.

Europe has been particularly receptive to the Witnesses, and in most countries they are the second largest religious body next to the national church. Since World War II they have also been quietly active in Eastern Europe, though little was reported because of possible retaliation. With the recent changes in Eastern Europe, it is to be expected that Witnesses will come out into the open and experience rapid growth.

While most of the printing for the Witnesses is done in the massive plant in Brooklyn, a number of printing shops around the world provide local material, especially in other languages. The number of pieces of literature distributed annually has taken on astronomical proportions, reaching well into the hundreds of millions. The two magazines, *Awake* and *The Watch Tower*, both published biweekly, are the primary items used in witnessing activity along with tracts, pamphlets and a selection of current books in print.

Controversy

The Witnesses have never been far from controversy. From the moment Russell began to teach, other Adventists warned followers of his dangerous ideas. However, his major opposition came from mainline churches after it became known that he did not believe in either the

Trinity or the divinity of Christ, bedrock beliefs of orthodox Christianity. A number of Evangelical Christian groups, many made up of ex-members of the Witnesses, have arisen to counteract what they see as group heresy. Together, these groups have produced as much material as the Witnesses themselves.

Ever since World War I, the Witnesses have encountered attacks from both the community and the government. In the patriotic atmosphere of the War, their pacifist stance made the Witnesses (then known simply as Bible Students) objects of government suppression, and their refusal to salute the flag made them objects of community scorn and popular prejudice. That popular prejudice carried over into the post-war years and led many communities to attempt various measures to prevent the Witnesses from distributing their literature. Such attempts led to a series of court battles and a number of Supreme Court landmark decisions. The rights won by the Witnesses in the 1940s set the context in which the new religions of the 1970s and 1980s operated and from which more decisions on religious freedom have been built.

Among the most unacceptable of the Witnesses' beliefs is their refusal to allow blood transfusions, a conclusion reached from consideration of Leviticus 17: 11-14 and Acts 15: 28-29. This belief also led to numerous court cases and, especially in the case of children, was often overruled. During the 1980s, the growing public concern over neglect and abuse of children led to a new round of confrontations between the Witnesses and legal authorities. The issue was joined when a woman giving birth by cesarian section refused transfusions. In a decision handed down by the New York Supreme Court, her right to direct her medical treatment, even in potentially fatal situations, was upheld. In general, courts have for many years assumed parental prerogatives in cases involving minors.

The Witnesses faced their most severe persecution outside the United States. The Nazis were possibly the first government to attempt to destroy the organization entirely and many Witnesses died in concentration camps. The story of their perseverance in the face of such persecution is impressive even to those who do not agree with their religious beliefs. In more recent years other governments have attempted to limit their activities and suppress them, the most bloody persecution arising in the tiny nation of Malawi.

During the years immediately following the failure of the predicted events of 1975, the Witnesses experienced an intense period of inner turmoil. Not only did many members, citing their dislike of the arbitrary authority exercised by the leadership and the failure of the prophecy, leave, but a number of leaders resigned or were disfellowshipped. Among the most important to depart was Raymond Franz, nephew of Frederick Franz, and member of the governing body. Others included Canadian professors James Penton, and Heather and Gary Botting. The Bottings, Franz, and Penton all wrote books attacking the organization.

Evangelical Christians have attacked the Witnesses as one of the major (most successful) cults in North America, and during the twentieth century have written a large body of anti-Witness literature. In the 1980s such groups as Bethel Ministries in Manhattan Beach, California, and Witness, Inc. in Clayton, California, have been formed exclusively to oppose the Witnesses, while numerous other counter cult ministries have singled out the Witnesses for special activities. Concern over the growth of the Witnesses in traditionally Roman Catholic territory (including Italy) has aroused that church into activity as well.

Sources-Primary

Jehovah's Witnesses in the Divine Purpose. Brooklyn, NY: Watch Tower Bible and Tract Society, 1959. 315 pp.

Life—How Did It Get Here? By Evolution or by Creation? Brooklyn, NY: Watch Tower Bible and Tract Society, 1985. 255 pp.

Make Sure of All Things, Hold Fast to What Is Fine. Brooklyn, NY: Watch Tower Bible and Tract Society, 1965. 512 pp.

Organization for Kingdom-Preaching and Disciple-Making. Brooklyn, NY: Watch Tower Bible and Tract Society, 1972. 192 pp.

Organized to Accomplish Our Ministry. Brooklyn, NY: Watch Tower Bible and Tract Society, 1983. 224 pp.

The Truth That Leads to Eternal Life. Brooklyn, NY: Watch Tower Bible and Tract Society, 1968. 190 pp.

Sources-Secondary

Beckford, James A. *The Trumpet of Prophecy.* Oxford: Basil Blackwell, 1975. 244 pp.

Botting, Heather, and Gary Botting. *The Orwellian World of the Jehovah's Witnesses.* Toronto: University of Toronto Press, 1984. 213 pp.

Franz, Raymond. *Crisis of Conscience.* Atlanta: Commentary Press, 1983. 375 pp.

Gruss, Edmond Charles. *Apostles of Denial.* [Nutley, NJ]: Presbyterian and Reformed Publishing Co., 1970. 324 pp.

Penton, James M. *Apocalypse Delayed.* Toronto: University of Toronto Press, 1985. 400 pp.

Rogerson, Alan. *Millions Now Living Will Never Die.* London: Constable, 1969. 215 pp.

Sterling, Chandler W. *The Witnesses.* Chicago: Henry Regnery Company, 1975. 198 pp.

White, Timothy. *A People for His Name.* New York: Vantage Press, 1967. 418 pp.

G. THE REORGANIZED CHURCH OF JESUS CHRIST OF LATTER DAY SAINTS

After the death of Joseph Smith in 1844, the Church he founded splintered into several groups each of which claimed to be the legitimate successor to Joseph Smith's Restorations. Of the several groups, over twenty-five of which currently exist, only one has attained a large membership. Unlike the other branches, the Reorganized Church of Jesus Christ of Latter Day Saints was formed by the coming together of a number of individuals and remnants of the Church who did not follow Brigham Young to Utah, rather than a group which formed around one leader who claimed to be Smith's successor though the story of the Reorganized Church begins with such a claimant.

The Formation of the Reorganized Church

The events leading up to the formation of the Reorganized Church began with Joseph Smith's brother, William. In May 1845, William was named Patriarch of the Church in place of Hyrum Smith, who had been killed along with Joseph. William, who had had a stormy relationship with the Church, almost immediately began to claim the office of President by right of his relationship to Joseph. Eventually he was excommunicated and joined the Church of Jesus Christ (Strangite). James J. Strang welcomed William as his Patriarch, but the two argued when Strang invited Joseph Smith's son to share the post of Patriarch with William. William left Strang and in 1848 called the Church members to gather under his leadership at Palestine Grove, Illinois. In 1850 he called a conference at Covington, Kentucky, to organize a Church, but by that time had significantly changed his stance. He named himself "President pro tem," an act by which he for the first time asserted that the real President should be Joseph Smith III. This was the first assertion that the right of succession to the Presidency was by lineal descent. Among William Smith's twelve apostles was Jason Briggs.

Jason Briggs had supported Brigham Young and the twelve apostles against the claims of Sidney Rigdon but in 1848 left Young and became a missionary for Strang in Wisconsin. He soon left Strang and joined William Smith. On November 18, 1851, he had a revelation that in due time God would call Joseph Smith, Jr.'s son to lead His Church.

A similar experience was claimed by Zenos Gurney. A senior president of one of the ruling quorums of seventy at Nauvoo, he advocated Young's cause but then left to work for Strang. Gurney had a revelation which said, "The successor to Joseph Smith is Joseph Smith, the son of Joseph Smith the Prophet. "

Briggs heard of Gurney and, upon meeting him, shared his revelation. The two decided to reorganize the work under their control and in 1853 formed the "New Organization." The New Organization offered the presidency to Joseph Smith III but he refused the offer. However by 1859 he changed his mind and accepted it. At this same time William Marks, a onetime supporter of claimant Sidney Rigdon who had joined several of the different Mormon splinters, joined the New Organization. At a meeting held April 6, 1860, the New Organization became the Reorganized Church of Jesus Christ of Latter Day Saints. There were about 300 members.

From the small beginning, the Reorganized Church grew as it gathered Mormons across the Midwest into membership. Much of Strang's Church was absorbed after Strang was murdered. Headquarters were established in Plano, Illinois. During the 1870s Decatur County, Iowa, on the Missouri border, became a site for gathering, and the town of Lamoni was founded. Headquarters were moved there in 1881.

The Reorganized Church also moved to obtain the property formerly owned by the Church as temple sites. In 1880 the courts awarded the Reorganized Church the temple lot in Kirkland. In 1891 the Church went to court to obtain the Temple Lot in Independence,

Missouri, the site designated by Joseph Smith as the city of Zion. Though initially given the land, the Supreme Court returned it to the Church of Christ (Temple Lot), a small faction that had bought the property earlier.

Eventually, the Reorganized Church moved their headquarters to Independence and erected a large building, the Auditorium, across the street from the Temple Lot.

Doctrine

While following the teachings of Joseph Smith and basing its authority upon the revelations received by Joseph Smith and the priesthood he reinstituted, the Reorganized Church has taken pains to distinguish its beliefs from what it considers the innovations of the Utah branch of the Church. Its statement of faith affirms that the Church believes:

> In God the Eternal Father, Creator of the heavens and the earth. In the divine Sonship of Jesus Christ the Savior of all men who obey the gospel.
> In the Holy Ghost, whose function it is to guide all men unto salvation.
> In the gospel of Jesus Christ, which is the power of God unto salvation.
> In the six fundamental doctrinal principles of the gospel, named in the sixth chapter of Hebrews: (1) faith; (2) repentance; (3) baptism by immersion in water, and the baptism of the Holy Ghost; (4) the laying on of hands (for the healing of the sick, conferring of the Holy Ghost, ordination, and blessing of children); (5) the resurrection of the dead; (6) the eternal judgment.
> In the justice of God, who will reward or punish every man according to his works, and not solely according to his profession.
> In the kind of organization that existed in the primitive church: apostles, prophets, evangelists, pastors, teachers, elders, bishops, seventies, etc.
> In the word of God contained in the Bible, so far as it is correctly translated.
> In the willingness and ability of God to continue the revelation of his will to men until the end of time.

> In the powers and gifts of the gospel: faith, discernment of spirits, prophecy, revelation, healing, visions, tongues and their interpretation, wisdom, charity, temperance, brotherly love, etc.
>
> In marriage as instituted and ordained of God, whose law provides for but one companion in wedlock, for either man or woman, excepting in cases of death or when the marriage contract is broken by transgression.
>
> In the Book of Mormon declaration: "There shall not any man among you have save it be one wife; and concubines he shall have none. "

The most obvious difference between the Reorganized Church and its larger cousin is in the former's denial of polygamy. The Reorganized Church opposed polygamy from its beginning, and, in fact, the immediate occasion of its formation was due in no small part to Strang having introduced polygamy into his Church. The Reorganized Church holds the increasingly untenable historical position of denying that Joseph Smith ever taught polygamy.

The Reorganized Church has also opposed the "polytheistic" interpretation of Smith's teaching introduced into the Utah Church by Brigham Young. It holds strongly to a strict monotheism that approaches a traditional doctrine of the Trinity.

In practice, the Reorganized Church believes in a tithe, not of one's income but of one's increase, that is, a tenth of what you earn above and beyond that needed to feed, clothe, and house yourself.

Finally, the Reorganized Church recognizes the most obscure of Joseph Smith's writings, the *Inspired Version* of the Bible, a Bible with revisions given to Joseph Smith. (The Utah Church uses the King James Version of the Bible.)

Organization

The organization of the Reorganized Church follows the pattern laid down by Joseph Smith and followed by the Utah Church—First Presidency, Council of Twelve Apostles, Patriarchy, Presidency, Bishopric, stakes, and wards. It differs only in the perpetuation of the descendants of Joseph Smith, Jr., in the position of President. Joseph Smith III headed the Church until 1915 and was succeeded by Frederick M. Smith, his son. Having no sons, Frederick designated Israel Smith, his brother to the post. Upon Israel's death, since his oldest son had died and the other was disinterested in the post, Israel's half-brother W. Wallace Smith became President.

The power to receive revelation, of course, rests in the President of the Church and on occasion new revelations are received by the President and delivered to the Church. These revelations are printed in the *Doctrine and Covenants*. Thus, because of additional revelations since 1845, the editions of the book used by the Reorganized and Utah Churches differ in content. The Reorganized Church has, as have several other Latter Day schisms, produced their own edition of the *Book of Mormon* in which the verses are divided quite differently from the Utah edition. The Reorganized Church members also do not accept the designation "Mormon. "

Present Status

The Reorganized Church reported 190,083 members, 1,040 congregations and 16,912 clergy in 1989. The Church is headquartered in Independence, Missouri. Graceland College at Lamoni, Iowa, is sponsored by the Church. Branches of the Church are found in 35 countries around the world.

The current President (1991) of the Church is Wallace B. Smith, great-grandson of Joseph Smith, Jr.

In 1988, no longer waiting to obtain control of the Temple Lot property, the church announced plans to build a temple immediately east of the designated site. The large carefully designed spiral structure is in process and due to be completed early in 1993.

Controversy

Through the 1980s, controversy raged in the Reorganized Church between the leadership and conservative members opposed to new paths the church was following. The controversy began with the publication of a series of position papers in the late 1960s which many felt perceptively revised some of the church's distinctive teachings. However, the issue became focused in the decade long trends that resulted in the first female being ordained to the priesthood in 1985. As it became obvious what would happen, dissenting members began to organize and a number of splinter groups began to form. The most substantive of these has become known as the Restoration Branches Movement whose principle spokesperson is Richard Price. Price advocates the formation of independent congregations (branches) which would serve as holding tanks until the church leadership repented of its apostasy. Price and his colleagues adhere to the authority of the *Book of Mormon* and the *Inspired Version* of the Bible, and reject the historical-critical approach to the Bible and the *Book of Mormon* which has become evident in the writings of some of the seminary-trained leadership.

Sources-Primary

Church Members' Manual. Independence, MO: Herald Publishing House, 1964. 128 pp.

History of the Reorganized Church of Jesus Christ of Latter Day Saints. Independence, MO: Herald Publishing House, 1951.

Koury, Aleah G. *The Truth and the Evidence.* Independence, MO: Herald Publishing House, 1965. 112 pp.

Reorganized Church of Jesus Christ of Latter Day Saints. *Rules and Resolutions.* Independence, MO: Herald Publishing House, 1980. 351 pp.

H. ROSICRUCIANS

The Rose Cross (the juxtapositioning of a cross and one or more roses) has, since the early seventeenth century, become one of the most popular occult symbols. From its origin in Germany, it spread throughout the Western world and gathered to it fanciful legends and colorful stories of mystery and adventure. It entered into Freemasonry where various ritual degrees derived their name and meaning from the Rosicrucian legend. At least eight occult orders currently functioning in the United States accept the name Rosicrucian and a version of the Rosicrucian legend as their history.

History

According to the Rosicrucian legend, the Order began with one Christian Rosenkreuz, born in 1378 in Germany. Beginning in 1393, he visited Damascus, Egypt, and Morocco where he sat under the masters of the occult arts. Upon his return to Germany, he began in 1407 the Rosicrucian Order with three monks from the cloister in which he had been raised. He also erected the House of the Holy Spirit (the Spiritus Sanctum) which was completed in 1409. The original group was enlarged to eight. Christian Rosenkreuz died in 1484 (at the age of 106) and was entombed in the Spiritus Sanctum. Knowledge of his tomb was lost, but it was rediscovered in 1604. Its opening led to the spread of the Order.

Modern Rosicrucian groups have different opinions about Christian Rosenkreuz. Some believe he actually existed as the early documents assert; others see the name as a pseudonym for one or more historic personages (Francis Bacon?); still others view the story as a parable, an occult legend that points to more profound truth.

Knowledge of Christian Rosenkreuz and the Order he supposedly founded was given to the world in three documents in the second decade of the seventeenth century: *The Fama Fraternitas of the Meritorious Order of the Rosy Cross* (1614); *The Confession of the Rosicrucian Fraternity* (1615); and *The Chymical Marriage of Christian Rosenkreuz* (1616, but purportedly written by Christian Rosenkreuz in 1459). While the full facts of the case may never be known, research indicates that these three documents and the idea of the Order originated with a German Lutheran pastor Johann Valentin Andreae (1586-1654). Andreae had envisioned a society for the reformation of social life—and he, with or without assistance from others, created the legend and published the documents describing it. A few have seen Rosicrucianism as a complete hoax. Most believe, however, that either Andreae formed an order combining his interest in esotericism and the reformation of society, which the documents promoted, or, more likely, Andreae wanted the documents to catalyze others to initiate the Rosicrucian work.

The response to the documents was immediate and intense. Rosicrucian societies emerged, and the rose and cross symbol (which seems to have derived from Andreae's coat of arms) became popular. The Rosicrucian groups combined a vision of social transformation, the study of alchemy, Cabalism, and mysticism with an otherwise "orthodox" Christian theology. The Rosicrucian groups blended into the larger community of Christian pietism which could be found throughout Germany at this time.

During the seventeenth century Rosicrucianism spread throughout Europe. It found its first exponents in England almost immediately in the persons of Robert Fludd (1574-1637) and Michael Maier (1568-1622). In 1616, the same year *The Chymical Marriage* appeared, Fludd published his *A Compendius Apology for the Fraternity of the Rosy Cross.* Maier, an alchemical physician, both during his years in England and after his 1619 retirement to Germany, did much to bring Rosicrucianism and alchemy together.

The mystical piety of German Rosicrucianism produced the first Rosicrucian group in America. The Chapter of Perfection, as it was called, was formed by scientist-theologian Johann Jacob Zimmerman. Zimmerman joined other pietist groups in accepting the invitation of William Penn to migrate to Pennsylvania. However, just before the group sailed, Zimmerman died. Their beliefs included a strong millennialism, and the group brought a hope for the imminent return of Christ to earth with them when they came to America in 1694. Zimmerman's role was assumed by Johannes Kelpius (1673-1708) who led the small band to Germantown where they established headquarters on the bank of the Wissahickon Creek. On top of their building they erected an observatory so as to discern the moment of Christ's second advent.

The Chapter lasted only a few years. After Kelpius' death, his successor Conrad Matthai allowed the breakup of the communal structure, and the small group became a community of mystical hermits. Several of the members worked in the community as healers and practitioners of the occult arts. They passed along their knowledge of magic and occultism to later generations and became the source of the modern hexmeister tradition.

Rosicrucianism almost completely disappeared in the eighteenth century, but in the nineteenth century reemerged as one component of the occult revival in the West. It was largely rooted in a revived Freemasonry. In Great Britain, in 1866 Robert Wentworth Little (1840-1878) formed the Societas Rosicruciana in Anglia, open only to Masons. A Scottish branch was formed a few years later. Rosicrucianism had never completely died in France, but in the mid-nineteenth century it also received a new impulse from occultist Eliphas Levi (1810-1875) who wrote three monumental works on magic: *The Doctrine of Transcendental Magic* (1855); *The Ritual of Transcendental Magic* (1856); and *History of Magic* (1860). American Rosicrucian P. B. Randolph mentions meeting Levi on his trip to Rosicrucian gatherings in France. The renewed interest begun in Levi's time led to the formation of the Qabalistic Order of the Rosy Cross in 1888.

Rosicrucian groups are occult orders and as such make their central and most important teachings available only to members. In like measure no examination of documents and archives is allowed, and little independent corroboration of the claims of the various groups, especially their claims to ancient origins and European alliances, is possible.

Fraternitas Rosae Crucis

The oldest Rosicrucian body in the United States, the Fraternitas Rosae Crucis was founded in 1858 by Pascal Beverly Randolph (1825-1875), one of the most important figures in occult history. Randolph's role in reviving magic and occultism in North America was the equivalent of Levi's role in Europe. A self-educated orphan of mixed blood, Randolph developed an early interest in the occult and in 1850 traveled to Europe and was initiated into a Rosicrucian Fraternity in Germany. On his third trip to Europe in 1858, he was made the Supreme Master for the Western World, at a Conclave headed by Supreme Grand Master Eliphas Levi. He returned to the United States and founded the Fraternitas Rosae Crucis. Two years later he returned to Europe and was initiated in 1861 in the Order of the Rose, a group headed by Rosicrucian historian Hargrave Jennings, and traveling on to Syria, he was initiated by the Ansaireh.

During the 1860s Randolph wrote a series of pioneering occult texts: *Dealing with the Dead* (1861), *Ravalette, the Rosicrucian's Story* (1863); and *Seership* (1868). As a physician Randolph became interested in the problems of sexuality and in his last book, *Eulis: The History of Love* (1874), he described his occult theories on sexuality which became the basis of the first modern system of sex magic.

Randolph was succeeded by ex-Spiritualist Freeman B. Dowd (b. 1812) who had been drawn to the Fraternity by reading Randolph's writings. He established temples in Philadelphia, San Francisco, and Denver. He also formed the Rosy Cross Publishing Company in San Francisco. He retired in 1907 and was succeeded by Edward H. Brown (1868-1922). Upon Brown's death, Reuben Swinburne Clymer (b. 1878) became head of the Fraternity.

Under Clymer, the Order, whose growth had been slow, blossomed. Clymer had joined the Fraternity in 1897 and coupled his training in the occult with a career in non-conventional medicine. His career kept him in continual conflict with the American Medical Association and the government. In 1904 Clymer founded the Philosophical Publishing Company, which reissued many of Randolph's books.

Upon his assumption of the leadership of the Fraternity, Clymer established the headquarters at Beverly Hall in Quakertown,

Pennsylvania. He wrote voluminously, and his numerous books remain standard reading material for Rosicrucians. He brought his healing concerns into the Fraternity, and the headquarters complex still includes a chiropractic office and a clinic specializing in natural healing methods. Upon his death, Clymer was succeeded by his son Emerson M. Clymer.

Associated with the Fraternity is the Church of Illumination, a religious body and outer court for the Fraternity. The Church defines its task as teaching the Divine Law, the exoteric teachings of the esoteric group. The Church is the tool for bringing about the Masisis Aeon, in which the two natures in humanity (male and female) will reach a state of equilibrium.

Members of the Fraternity receive private instruction through lessons mailed from the headquarters. Teachings focus upon the transmutation of the base and inglorious aspects of humanity into the self pure and refined. Progress in the course can lead to ordination into the Council of Initiated Priests.

Societas Rosicruciana in Civitatibus Foederatis (S.R.I.C.F.)

The Societas Rosicruciana in Civitatibus Foederatis was founded in 1880 as the Societas Rosicruciana Republicae Americae. Charles E. Meyer was named the first Supreme Magus. The S.R.I.C.F. originated with a group of Masons who traveled to England in 1878 and were initiated into the Societas Rosicruciana in Anglia at the college at York. They applied to the S.R.I.A. for permission to begin an American branch. Rebuffed, they turned to the Scottish branch which chartered American colleges at Philadelphia in 1879 and New York the following year. These two colleges established a High Council in April 1880 for what became an autonomous American branch. During 1880 three additional colleges were authorized for Boston, Baltimore, and Burlington, Vermont.

The S.R.I.C.F. is one of the smallest Rosicrucian groups. One must be a Mason to join. The last issue of their magazine, *The Rosicrucian Fama*, published in 1973, set the membership at less than 600. In 1912 it adopted the rituals of both the British and Scottish branches.

Societas Rosicruciana in America (S.R.I.A.)

The Societas Rosicruciana in America originated with members of the Societas Rosicruciana in Civitatibus Foederatis who wished to open the Rosicrucian teaching to the general public (i.e., non-Masons). In 1907 Sylvester C. Gould, a member of the Boston college of the S.R.I.C.F., in collaboration with other Rosicrucians, began the S.R.I.A. and a periodical, *The Rosicrucian Brotherhood.* Unfortunately Gould died in 1909 and the periodical died with him. The leadership of the infant Society, however, was picked up by George Winslow Plummer (1876-1944), who had assisted Gould in its formation, and under his leadership the Society began to grow.

Plummer incorporated the Society in 1912. In 1916 he founded the Mercury Publishing Company and began issuing *Mercury,* the official quarterly for the Society. By 1920 seven colleges (including one in Sierra Leone) had been established. Two more were added in 1921. By 1930 eighteen colleges had been chartered (though not all remained active) and there were seven study groups in other cities. After his death, Plummer was succeeded by his widow, known as Mother Serena (1894-1989), who published much of his work in a series of booklets.

Plummer had a strong interest in Christian mysticism and liturgical religion. Intimately connected to his Rosicrucian work, the Seminary of Biblical Studies operated out of the Society's headquarters and offered lessons in mysticism. Then in 1934 Plummer was consecrated as a bishop by Archbishop William Albert Nichols of the American Orthodox Church. He formed the Holy Orthodox Church in America, also headquartered at the Society's office. Two years later the Church reported four congregations, all located in cities which had S.R.I.A. colleges or study groups.

Plummer's widow married Stanislaus Witowski (a.k.a. De Witow), whom Plummer had consecrated and who succeeded Plummer as head of the Church. After Witowski's death, Mother Serena became head of the Church and in 1982 was consecrated as bishop by Archbishop Adrian Spruit of the Church of Antioch. In 1983 Mother Serena was succeeded by Lucia Grosch, the present Supreme magus and imperiatrix of the Society.

The Ancient and Mystical Order Rosae Crucis (A.M.O.R.C.)

The largest and best known of the several Rosicrucian groups in America, the Ancient and Mystical Order Rosae Crucis, was formed by Harvey Spencer Lewis (1883-1939), a writer, artist, and occultist living in New York City. In 1904 he had formed The New York Institute for Psychical Research, an occult interest group. Four years later, he met Mrs. May Banks-Stacey, a Rosicrucian who put him in touch with members of the Order in Europe. In 1909 he went to France, where he was initiated and given authority to begin an organization in America. He pulled together a group of interested occultists and in 1915 the A.M.O.R.C. was formally organized and a magazine, *The American Rosae Crucis*, began.

In 1917 the first national convention was held. The convention approved a plan for offering its teaching to individuals through correspondence lessons. These lessons, which have been widely advertised over the years, became the major tool for the rapid spread of the Order.

In 1918 headquarters of the Order were moved to San Francisco. During these years Lewis formed ties with several occult groups and in 1921 received a charter from the Ordo Templi Orientis. In 1925 Lewis moved to Florida for two years but moved back to California in 1927 and established headquarters at San Jose on land the Order had acquired. He reincorporated the Order in California and incorporated the Pristine Church of the Rose Cross, an affiliated religious group over which he served as bishop. The Church lasted only a few years as the Order began to stress its non-religious fraternal aspect and hence dropped its "religious" structure.

During the 1930s Lewis developed the headquarters complex which came to include the Rose-Croix University (1934), a Planetarium (1936), and the Rosicrucian Research Library (1939). Possibly the most famous structure at the headquarters, the Egyptian Museum, has received wide acclaim and become a popular tourist attraction for San Jose.

In 1990 the Order claimed 250,000 members worldwide and has lodges and groups spread throughout the world including almost all of the non-Communist countries. It publishes two magazines, *The Rosicrucian Digest*, a monthly, and the *Rosicrucian Forum*, the latter for members only. Lewis was a voluminous writer and the Order circulates his many books, as well as those of his son Ralph M. Lewis (1904-1987), who succeeded him as Imperator of the Order.

Ralph Lewis was succeeded by Gary L. Stewart, a rather young man to lead such a large organization. Soon afterward, a power struggle began within the organization. In April 1990 the board of directors of the Order fired Stewart and accused him of embezelling $3.5 million which he had transferred into a European bank account. Christian Bernard, formerly head of the Order in France, was appointed to succeed him. He was formally installed August 7, 1990.

The Rosicrucian Fellowship

Several Rosicrucian groups have a direct lineage from the Theosophical Society, the largest one being the Rosicrucian Fellowship founded by Max Heindel (1865-1919) in 1907. Heindel, born Carl Louis Von Grasshoff, was an engineer whose occult interests led him to the Theosophical Society shortly after the beginning of the century. By 1905 he was a theosophical lecturer. Then in 1907 he traveled to Germany where there appeared to him several times one whom he described as an "Elder Brother of the Rosicrucian Order." He was sent to work with a knowledgeable teacher, believed by most to have been Rudolf Steiner, founder of the Anthroposophical Society.

Returning to the United States, he wrote down what he had been taught and published it as his first book, *The Rosicrucian Cosmo-Conception*, still the major introductory text of the Fellowship he founded. The first center was founded in Columbus, Ohio, but within a few years centers could be found along the West Coast from Seattle to Los Angeles. In 1910, while recuperating in a hospital from his recurrent heart condition, he had a vision of the future center on Mt. Ecclesia in Oceanside, California. That center remains the headquarters of the group.

The Rosicrucian teachings of Heindel advocate the occult worldview of Theosophy. Heindel also picked up the astrological emphases of Theosophy and two of his books, *Simplified Scientific Astrology* and *The Message of the Stars*, were major factors in the twentieth-century revival of astrology in America. The Fellowship also publishes the popular *Ephemeris*, the annual table of the position of the planets in the astrological signs, a necessary tool for constructing astrological charts. A monthly astrology column continues to be an important feature in the Fellowship's monthly *Rays from the Rosy Cross*.

Heindel was succeeded by his wife, Augusta Foss Heindel, an accomplished occultist in her own right. In 1920 Mt. Ecclesia was dedicated. The Society has established some small groups, but the majority of its efforts are through various mail order courses it offers in astrology and the occult.

Rosicrucian Anthroposophic League

Hearkening back to the influence of Rudolf Steiner on Max Heindel, S. R. Parchment, a former member of the Rosicrucian Fellowship, formed the Rosicrucian Anthroposophic League in San Francisco in the 1930s. Parchment wrote a series of books to expound his version of the Rosicrucian teachings: *The Middle Path, Steps to Self Mastery, Operative Masonry*, and *The Just Law of Compensation*. Parchment offered a variety of correspondence courses using the texts. The League also published a magazine, *Rosicrucian Quarterly*.

The occult basis of the League is spelled out in its six objectives:

1) To investigate the occult laws of nature and the superphysical powers of man;
2) To promote the principles which will eventually lead to recognition of the truth of the universal brotherhood of man, without distinction as to sex, creed, race or color;
3) To acquire, disseminate, and exemplify a knowledge of spiritual truth as given to the world by the Elder Brothers of the White Lodge;
4) To study and teach ancient religion, philosophy and astrology in the light of modern needs;
5) To encourage the study of science and art in the hope that religion, art and science—which are a veritable trinity, the equilateral triangle which has always been used as a symbol of the Divine—may again be recognized as portals through which egos must pass in attaining to the mastery of self;
6) And finally, to attain to self-conscious immortality which is the crowning feat of evolution.

Like Heindel, Parchment had a prime interest in astrology and wrote an astrological classic, *Astrology, Mundane and Spiritual.* Since his death, the book has been kept in print by the American Federation of Astrologers. Recent information about the status of the League had been unavailable.

Lectorium Rosicrucianum

The Lectorium Rosicrucianum was formed in 1971 by former members of the Rosicrucian Fellowship in Holland under the leadership of J. Van Rijckenborgh. The Lectorium sees itself as a new instrument for the Universal Brotherhood, the spiritual hierarchy popularly known as the Great White Brotherhood. Its basic teaching is termed "transfigurism," based upon the idea of two natural orders. The first is of God, the second that in which we normally live, the result of a catastrophe due to man's disobedience to Divine Law. The way to escape this order in which we are bound by the endless cycles of reincarnation is through transfiguration, i.e., giving up our lives in order to participate in God's original order. The transition is exemplified in Jesus Christ's resurrection.

There are two American headquarters for the Lectorium, the Western North American headquarters in Bakersfield, California, and the Eastern in Chatham, New York. English editions of Rijckenborgh's books, including his main work, *Dei Gloria Intacta*, and lesson material, are disseminated from there by mail to students across the United States.

Ausar Auset Society

The Ausar Auset Society was formed by R. A. Straughn, known by his religious name as Ra Un Nefer Amen, a member during the 1970s of the Rosicrucian Anthroposophic League. A black man, Straughn became an occult teacher to the black community and in 1980 established an independent organization which applied the universal occult truths of Rosicrucianism to the Afro-American situation. Straughn has written several occult texts: *The Realization of Neter Nu, Health Teachings of the Ageless Wisdom* (2 volumes), and *Meditation Techniques of the Kabalist, Vedantins and Taoists.* Other books manifest the particular interest in the needs of black Americans: *Black Woman's, Black Man's Guide to Spiritual Union, Black Woman, Black Man in Quandary,* and *How Marijuana Affects You.*

In 1980 he started a magazine, *The Oracle of Thoth* (now *Metu Neter*), and by 1982 offered classes in the Society's occult teachings in New York, Washington, D.C., Chicago, Philadelphia, New Haven, and Norfolk, Virginia. By 1988 he had trained and initiated 60 men and women to the priesthood.

Sources-Primary

Clymer, R. Swinburne. *The Rosy Cross, Its Teachings.* Quakertown, PA: Beverly Hall Corporation, 1965. 287 pp.

Heindel, Max. *The Rosicrucian Cosmo-Conception.* Oceanside, CA: Rosicrucian Fellowship, 1909. 536 pp.

Lewis, H. Spencer. *Rosicrucian Questions and Answers with Complete Answers.* San Jose, CA: Supreme Grand Lodge of AMORC, 1969. 343 pp.

Parchment, S. R. *Astrology, Mundane and Spiritual.* San Francisco: Rosicrucian Anthroposophic League, 1937. 500 pp.

Plummer, George Winslow. *Principles and Practice for Rosicrucians.* New York: Society of Rosicrucians, 1947. 43 pp.

Straughn, R. A. *The Realization of Neter Nu.* Brooklyn, NY: Maat Publishing Co., 1975. 98 pp.

Voorhis, Harold V. B. *Masonic Rosicrucian Societies.* New York: Press of Henry Emerson, 1958. 146 pp.

The Way of the Rosycross in Our Times. Haarlem, Netherlands: Rozekruis-Pers, 1978. 43 pp.

Sources-Secondary

Allen, Paul M., ed. *A Christian Rosenkreutz Anthology.* Blauvelt, NY: Rudolf Steiner Publications, 1968. 704 pp.

McIntosh, Christopher. *The Rosy Cross Unveiled.* Wellingborough, UK: Aquarian Press, 1980. 160 pp.

Waite, Arthur Edward. *The Brotherhood of the Rosy Cross.* London: Rider, 1924. 249 pp.

Yates, Frances A. *The Rosicrucian Enlightenment.* London: Routledge and Kegan Paul, 1972. 269 pp.

I. SATANISM

Concern over the widespread presence of Satanism, the worship of the Christian devil, reached a new peak in North America during the 1980s. Beginning with the publication of the account of a woman who claimed to have been forcefully abused by parents who were Satanists, a new myth about the nature of Satanism, its beliefs, and practices began to develop. The new myth was fed by the adoption of Satanic imagery by rebellious adolescents who picked up the symbolism from some popular musical acts.

Traditionally Satanism has been associated with a variety of practices which parody Roman Catholic Christianity. The major ritual is the black mass, the essence of which is the profaning of the central acts of worship, and might include the repeating of the Lord's Prayer backwards, the use of a host which has been dyed black, the slaughter of an animal (usually a cat or dog) to parody the crucifixion, or the rape of a woman upon the altar. The climax of the worship is the invocation of Satan for the working of malevolent magic.

This form of Satanism, as a parody of Catholicism, appeared in the fifteenth century as the construct of the Inquisition in preparation for its move against "witchcraft," which was redefined as Satanism. Previously, church documents had equated witchcraft with Paganism, a non-Christian religion and hence outside of the agenda of the Inquisition whose assignment was limited to Christians who had fallen into either heresy (false belief) or apostasy (denial of the faith). By redefining witchcraft as the worship of the devil (rather than Pagan gods), its practitioners became subject to the Inquisition's action. No well-documented case of a devil-worshipping group appears until the famous incident of the group which developed among the courtiers around Louis XIV who used black magic in the attempt to remain in favor with the king. When discovered, the scandal almost brought down the government.

Prior to the 1960s actual Satanist groups are quite rare; however, Satanism has provided a steady stream of imaginative material for novels and, more recently, horror movies. Such books and movies have done far more to create the popular understanding of Satanism than reference to any actual Satanic groups and practitioners. For example, British novelist Dennis Wheatley wrote a series of best-selling novels which developed the theme of an ancient worldwide secret and powerful Satanic society which regularly gathered its conspiratorial forces to attack the structures of order and goodness. While novels such as these make entertaining stories, there is no evidence that such novels even remotely reflect an existing social phenomenon. An examination of all the evidence shows no large organized Satanic movement or group.

Satanism emerges as a most unusual cult. Prior to the 1970s, it produced almost no literature. Its several groups have organized and disbanded without connecting with any previously existing group or leaving any progeny. The maintenance of the tradition fell to non-Satanists, primarily conservative Christians, who authored many books thoroughly denouncing Satanism. Though none had ever seen a Satanist ritual or met a real Satanist, these Christian writers described their practices in great detail. That is to say, the Satanist tradition was created and sustained by generation after generation of anti-Satanist writers. Over the last two centuries, groups and individuals have tried to reproduce groups which conform to the Satanism portrayed in the Christian literature.

Such Satanic activity showed a rise in the early 1970s with police reports showing an increase in the number of ritual remains found in graveyards, church break-ins and vandalism, and mutilated bodies of animals. A steady stream of similar reports continued through the 1980s, but during the decade the emphasis shifted radically to the New Satanism and the emergence of the claims by several hundred women of being survivors of Satanic ritual abuse.

As the 1990s begin, several distinct forms of Satanism can be said to exist: a traditional Satanism primarily consisting of ephemeral groups of teenagers and young adults; a new form of Satanism initiated by Anton LaVey and developed in various directions by the several groups which split off from his Church of Satan; and the New Satanism as defined by those who claim to be its survivors.

Traditional Satanism

Through the 1970s and 1980s a handful of cases of small groups which practiced a form of traditional Satanism were reported in the press. Overwhelmingly, these were teenage groups and most were also into heavy drug use. In 1984 a particularly dramatic incident of such a group became the focus of national media coverage when members of a group on Long Island killed (sacrificed?) one of their own. Then one of the youths arrested for the crime hung himself in his jail cell. As details of the incident were uncovered, the case, apart from the deaths, proved to be fairly typical. The group was small, consisting of several classmates, and had no associations or connections with any other Satanist groups. Members had a history of drug use prior to the emergence of any Satanism. The Satanism thus emerges as an expression of (rather than the cause of) the youth's social alienation.

A somewhat similar case emerged a few years later in Sacramento, California, in which a small Satanic group (less than ten members) murdered one of their members who was the loser in a love triangle involving two other members. This group was unusual in that it had existed for several years, had a designated ritual sight, and was beginning to develop its own mythology above and beyond the several books the members had read. Like other such groups, they had no connection with any other Satanist group.

The kinds of social and psychological forces which lead to these ephemeral traditionalist Satanist groups also underlie the widespread use of Satanist symbolism by many teenagers, most devotees of hard rock music. Several rock artists such as Ozzy Osborne and the group Judas Priest have used Satanic symbolism and content in their music and stage performances. One rock group, Slayer, seems to move beyond the imagery of social alienation and rebellion of Osborne into advocating Satanism as a viable way of life. As a whole, however, the use of Satanic imagery by teenagers has rarely grown into the practice of full-scale devil worship.

Most tragic of all the phenomena surrounding Satanism has been the emergence of the serial killers who have adopted Satanic trappings. In these cases, individuals who have no connections to a Satanist group pick up information on Satanic symbolism from the culture and utilize it as an additional expression of the rage which also leads them to become murderers. Again, it is not the cause of their actions but a result of the same forces operating on their life. These cases are most tragic in that they alone account for the majority of all deaths associated with Satanism.

The Church of Satan

Although drawing upon the reputation and images of more traditional Satanism, the Church of Satan has attempted to take modern occult and magical teachings and reorganize them around a Satanic motif. Within the Church, a philosophy of individual pragmatism and hedonism seems to be more important than the worship of Satan. Having devised a new form of Satanism, founder Anton LaVey institutionalized his ideas and gave the resultant movement all of the formal trappings of an organized religion.

Anton LaVey (b.1930) began to read occult books as a teenager and developed a deep fascination for real magic, i.e., the practice of creating change in the world through the use of cosmic powers controlled by the individual's will. During his adult years he worked in the circus. In the 1960s he began to hold informal meetings built around his interest in magic. Then on April 30, 1966, he shaved his head, donned a black garb, and announced the formation of the Church of Satan, with some members of the magic groups among his first members.

The Church was an object of significant media attention in 1967 following LaVey's performance of the first Satanic wedding in January and a funeral for a sailor (with accompanying full Navy color guard) in December. Membership grew rapidly though, contrary to many media reports, the active membership was rarely over 1,000. [The Church had an initial membership fee which included a formal lifetime membership, and it had generally stated the cumulative lifetime memberships when questioned about the number of adherents, even though the great majority of those who at one time joined have nothing to do with the Church presently.]

In 1969 LaVey authored the first of three books, *The Satanic Bible*, which became an occult best-seller and has remained in print through the last two decades. It was followed by *The Compleat Witch* (1970) and *The Satanic Rituals* (1972). LaVey also extended his consulting work (which he had done for many years for the police department) to the movie industry and became the occult advisor on several films, most notably *Rosemary's Baby*, in which he appears briefly as the Devil.

The perspective of the Church of Satan is summarized in the 9 Satanic Statements found at the beginning of *The Satanic Bible*:

1. Satan represents indulgence, instead of abstinence!
2. Satan represents vital existence, instead of spiritual pipe dreams!
3. Satan represents undefiled wisdom, instead of hypocritical self-defense!
4. Satan represents kindness to those who deserve it, instead of love wasted on ingrates!
5. Satan represents vengeance, instead of turning the other cheek!
6. Satan represents responsibility to the responsible, instead of concern for psychic vampires!
7. Satan represents man as just another animal, sometimes better, more often worse than those that walk on all fours, who because of his divine spiritual and intellectual development has become the most vicious animal of all!
8. Satan represents all of the so-called sins, as they lead to physical or mental gratification!
9. Satan has been the best friend the church has ever had, as he has kept it in business all these years.

The Church of Satan promotes the development of strong individuals who seek gratification out of life and practice the selfish virtues as long as they do not harm others undeservedly. An individual's birthday is considered the most important date on the Church calendar.

Current Status

By the 1970s the Church of Satan had a national membership and groups in many cities around the United States. It had been dubbed the largest occult organization in America, but always counted its active membership in the hundreds. LaVey edited a newsletter, *The Cloven Hoof.* There were several schisms in the early 1970s. Group leaders in Michigan, Ohio, and Florida left to form the Church of Satanic Brotherhood in 1973. The Church lasted only a few years, its death kneel being sounded in 1974 when one of the founders announced his conversion to Christianity in a dramatic incident staged for the press in St. Petersburg. Church of Satan members in Kentucky and Indiana left to form the Ordo Templi Satanis, also short lived.

In the wake of the several schisms, LaVey disbanded the remaining grottos (the name given local units of the Church of Satan) and reorganized the Church as a fellowship of individuals related through the Church headquarters. Though the Church refuses to diverge current membership statistics, there is no reason to believe that its active membership has grown beyond the level reached in the 1970s. Besides the organizations mentioned above, there are several presently existing groups which ultimately derive from the Church of Satan. The most important one is the Temple of Set, treated below, but also includes the Church of Satanic Liberation founded in 1986 by Paul Douglas Valentine and the Temple of Nepthys founded in the late 1980s. Over the years other small Satanic groups have emerged only to soon disappear, and it is assumed that such will continue to be the case.

Note: Important in distinguishing the Church of Satan and the several churches which ultimately derive from it, from the more informal traditional Satanic groups, are the prohibitions issued by LaVey against participation in any illegal activity, the consequences being expulsion from the Church. Specifically singled out for consideration was the practice of animal sacrifices, a practice antithetical to the Church of Satan philosophy of life affirmation. To date no serious allegations linking the Church to any crimes, especially those related to traditional Satanist groups, have been put forth.

The Temple of Set

One of the major events in the development of the Church of Satan was the departure of Michael A. Aquino, a Magister Templi with the Church, and Lilith Sinclair, head of the largest of the grottos, in Spottswood, New Jersey. The pair established the Temple of Set as a group dedicated to Set, the ancient Egyptian deity believed to have become the model for the Christian Satan. At issue in the split was the status of Satan as a real being, a fact Aquino affirmed and LaVey denied.

Aquino (b. 1946), with a Ph.D. from the University of California at Santa Barbara and a lieutenant Colonel in the U. S. Army, was the leading intellectual in the Church of Satan. In 1975 he invoked Satan to receive a new mandate for continuing the Church of Satan apart from LaVey. Satan appeared as Set and gave to Aquino the content of a book, *The Book of Coming Forth by Night*, and authorization to found the Temple of Set to carry forward the thrust initiated by the Church of Satan.

The goal of the Temple is to awaken the divine power of the individual through the deliberate exercise of will and intelligence. It is believed that over the centuries Set has manipulated human evolution in order to create a new species possessing an enhanced nonnatural intelligence. The program of the Temple is geared to work with an intellectual elite and includes a lengthy list of required readings.

Over the years the Temple grew to include approximately 500 members in North America and some additional members in Europe. It is headed by a Council of Nine which appoints a High Priest of Set and the Executive Director. There are six degrees of magical attainment recognized, and members have several internal specialized orders through which they can work.

By the end of the 1970s, in part because of his holding a responsible position in the Army, Aquino became well known as a Satanist and the subject of a variety of media coverage. In 1987-88, Aquino was briefly charged with sexually molesting a young girl at the Presidio, the army base in San Francisco, but was later exonerated of all charges.

The New Satanism

In the late 1980s, Michael Aquino, as the high profile leader of a Satanist organization, found himself caught up in a new wave of public concern about the possible presence of Satanism in the United States. That new concern, some would label it hysteria, which has been centered upon the sexual abuse of children in Satanic rituals, was largely disseminated from California through the 1980s and by the end of the decade was reaching into Europe. It began with a book, *Michelle Remembers* (1980), the account of a woman, Michelle Smith, who under hypnosis claimed to have been the victim of Satanism in her childhood. She told of her family involving her for a period of time in a Satanic group in Vancouver, British Columbia, in which she was systematically tortured and raped. In later years she forgot the traumatic events but remembered them while under psychiatric care.

Smith in effect created a new story of Satanism in which Satanic groups reveled in child abuse. Most importantly, they forced young girls into the group, systematically tortured, raped, and impregnated them, often while to all outward appearances the girls were leading normal lives attending school and participating in a social life outside their home. Then at some point the group simply let them go and risked that none of the victims would ever talk.

Smith's story led in two directions. By the mid-1980s there were several reports of contemporary Satanic groups operating at locations around the United States doing to children exactly what had been done to Michelle Smith. Many of these cases began with reports of divorced parents reporting their estranged spouses who had gained custody of the children. Others centered upon nurseries and day-care facilities. In both instances accusations were built totally upon the reports of the children, usually following lengthy sessions with child psychologists, and without any independent verifying data. Many of the cases fell apart as contradictions to the account mounted.

Also, by the mid-1980s other women began to come forward to tell a story similar to that of Michelle Smith, i.e., of being forced into a Satanic cult and of forgetting the events until they were later brought up during hypnosis or as part of psychotherapy and as fragmentary memories were gradually assembled into a narrative. Many of the survivors have been termed breeders as they have told stories of being impregnated and the resultant babies being used in human sacrifices. Like the stories of the children, however, these accounts have failed to produce any corroborating evidence.

The accounts of the children led to several court cases, the most important one being the McMartin Day School case in which the members of the school's staff were accused of terrorizing and abusing the children over a number of years. The case led to verdicts of innocence as accounts of how the children were coached by psychologists were revealed and as possibly verifiable claims by the children proved false. For example, many of the children reported events occurring in a room below ground level at the center which has never had such a room.

As the number of accounts of survivors of childhood Satanic involvement increased, the story they have told has become increasingly unbelievable. Taken together, they tell of hundreds of Satanic groups operating twenty to thirty years ago and still active in cities and towns across the United States. They did so without a hint of their existence both in the past and until the 1980s. They killed thousands of people, and in spite of the difficulty, never slipped up in disposing of a body. They own(ed) elaborate paraphernalia none of which has ever been discovered. They carried on a trade in kidnapped children used in sacrifices without ever being foiled or records of their transactions being uncovered.

Psychologists have yet fully to account for the survivor stories. The basic argument for their being taken seriously is the obvious belief in the truth of the story by the teller and the fact that so many have come forward with the same story independently of each other. However, it should also be noted that the stories bear a strong formal resemblance to the now hundreds of UFO abduction stories (in which a person reports their abduction aboard a space ship followed by a period of amnesia).

As the 1990s begin, the level of hysteria concerning reports of Satanic activity has greatly diminished. However, a variety of anti-cult groups, parent groups, and professional psychological counseling associations have remained supportive of the claims of Satanic activity. Critics of the stories have pointed out the role of the psychological counselors, beginning with Michelle Smith's psychiatrist, in generating stories and the increasing number of incidents of the diagnosis of Satanic abuse being offered before any evidence has been produced in the patient's narrative.

The continuing controversy on the existence of widespread Satanism will likely continue through the 1990s. However, under the impact of critical voices, it will gradually die, unless someone is able to produce some corroborative evidence to back up the many unsubstantiated stories. Until such a time, as will be the case for those who have reported UFO abductions, some other cause of the distress being suffered by the ritual survivors will have to be sought.

Meanwhile, the issue of the role of Satan and Satanism has been renewed within Christianity, at least the Evangelical Protestant branch, and a number of popular works decrying the present growth of Satanism have appeared. These have not so much contributed to the ongoing debate as they are products of it.

Sources-Primary

LaVey, Anton S. *The Compleat Witch.* New York: Lancer Books, 1971. 274 pp.

―――――. *The Satanic Bible.* New York: Avon Books, 1969. 272 pp.

―――――. *The Satanic Rituals.* Secaucus, NJ: University Books, 1972. 220 pp.

Smith, Michelle, and Lawrence Pazder. *Michelle Remembers.* New York: Congdon & Lattes, 1980. 310 pp.

Sources-Secondary

Carlson, Shawn, and Gerry O'Sullivan. *Satanism in America: How the Devil Got Much More Than His Due.* El Cerrito, CA: Gaia Press, 1990. 283 pp.

Hicks, Robert D. *In Pursuit of Satan: The Police and the Occult.* Buffalo, NY: Prometheus Books, 1991. 420 pp.

Lyons, Arthur. *Satan Wants You: The Cult of Devil Worship in America.* New York: The Mysterious Press, 1988. 192 pp.

Richardson, James T., Joel Best, and David G. Bromley, ed. *The Satanism Scare.* Hawthorne, NY: Aldine de Gruyter, 1991. 320 pp.

Wolfe, Burton H. *The Devil's Avenger.* New York: Avon Books, 1974. 222 pp. A biography of LaVey.

J. SPIRITUALISM

Spiritualism is a religion based upon the belief that mediumship, the ability demonstrated by a few select persons to contact the world of spirits, proves that the individual survives bodily death. It arose in mid-nineteenth-century America and has spread around the world.

Origins

During the centuries prior to Spiritualism's emergence, Western society received a massive attack upon its belief in the supernatural world, first from Protestants, who did away with some of the more basic elements in Roman Catholicism's supernaturalism (transubstantiation, relics, indulgences), and then from eighteenth-century Deism and Freethought, which decried the very notion of the supernatural itself. The United States also provided a fertile context for the emergence of a new religion, as less than 30 percent of the populous were formally attached to a church. Thus, when reports of an outburst of extraordinary paranormal experiences spread from upstate New York in the 1840s, it was little surprise that a host of individuals began to examine them for any verification that the supernatural world actually did exist.

As early as 1684, Puritan patriarch Increase Mather produced the first of several volumes of accounts of supernatural occurrences out of his observations and reading and that of his son, Cotton Mather. While the Mathers and, in the next century, such Christians as Methodist founder John Wesley, appealed to paranormal experiences to substantiate a traditional Christian faith, others observing similar phenomena developed new movements that had psychic paranormal experiences at the core of their belief. Among the most prominent were Swedish seer Emanuel Swedenborg and Austrian physician Franz Anton Mesmer, who believed that he had discovered a Universal Fluid, "animal magnetism," the manipulation of which led to hypnotism, spiritual healing, and a trance-like state. The popularity of both Swedenborgian thought and Mesmerism set the stage for Spiritualism.

Spiritualism dates to 1848 and the so-called Hydesville rappings. In that year, two female children in the Fox family of Hydesville, New York, in response to some mysterious noises in their home, discovered that the rapping sounds would intelligently react to their questions and commands. After a system of communication had been established, the girls learned that the rappings were produced by the spirit of a man who had been murdered in the house some years before. The phenomena continued when the girls moved to the home of their sister in Rochester. A public investigation the following year discovered neither a mundane explanation of the occurrences nor evidence of fraud.

The publicity given the Fox sisters struck a resonant chord in people across the secularized country and within a short time circles in which similar phenomena were exhibited appeared. The popular movement also attracted a young magnetist, Andrew Jackson Davis (1826-1920), who had been receiving material from the spirit world for several years while in trance. As early as 1844, Davis had been hypnotized and communicated with two spirit entities who called themselves Galen and Emanuel Swedenborg. He began to do magnetic healing and to receive metaphysical teachings. He published his first book, *The Principles of Nature*, in 1847. He followed with his most important book, *The Great Harmonia*, which appeared in five volumes from 1850 to 1855 and went through numerous editions.

Davis gave Spiritualism a coherent system of thought to substantiate the central experience of mediumship. He offered an alternative to orthodox Christianity with a belief in an immanent God, who was the active moving principle in nature. Davis also developed the image of "Summerland," the land of perpetual summer to which the dead go, the primary idea of heaven within Spiritualist circles.

The movement spread as numerous autonomous groups of people gathered to experiment in spirit contact. As mediums were discovered and their ability to contact what were believed to be spirit entities perfected, they traveled the country lecturing and giving demonstrations. Newspapers such as the *Spiritual Messenger*, *Shikinah*, and *The Spiritual Telegraph* appeared. The movement became the subject of great interest and controversy for a decade but suffered in the late 1850s as a result of reports of fraudulent mediums and the general disruption of the Civil War. After the War, state and local associations, such as the Society of Spiritualists and Progressive Lyceum founded in St. Louis by Davis, were formed, and as early as 1864 an attempt to form a national organization was made at the convention in Chicago.

That initial attempt at organization failed and Spiritualism settled into a three-decade period of slow but steady growth and the establishment of several strong state associations, such as the one in New York. Finally in 1893 the National Spiritualist Association (later changed to the National Spiritualist Association of Churches) was formed and, as Spiritualism expanded, other national associations formed in its wake.

Beliefs

The beliefs of Spiritualism center upon the phenomena produced by mediums. Mediums are special people who have, for whatever reason, the ability to communicate with and to be used for communication with the spirit world. Mediumship has proven, Spiritualists believe, personal survival after death. Most of the activity of Spiritualists is concerned with developing and demonstrating mediumship.

Most Spiritualists would also agree with the basic statements concerning God, ethics, and the afterlife included in the N.S.A.C. Declaration of Principles:

1.   We believe in Infinite Intelligence.
2.   We believe that the phenomena of nature, both physical and spiritual, are the expression of Infinite Intelligence.
3.   We affirm that a correct understanding of such expression and living in accordance therewith, constitute true religion.
4.   We affirm that the existence and personal identity of the individual continue after the change called death.
5.   We affirm that communication with the so-called dead

is a fact, scientifically proven by the phenomena of Spiritualism.

6. We believe that the highest morality is contained in the Golden Rule: Whatsoever ye would have that others should do unto you, do ye also unto them.

7. We affirm the moral responsibility of the individual, and that he makes his own happiness or unhappiness as he obeys or disobeys Nature's physical and moral laws.

8. We affirm that the doorway to reformation is never closed against any human soul here or hereafter.

Spiritualism grew up in a context in which Christianity was the primary option for those people who chose to be religious, but it departed from orthodox Christianity at many points. It affirmed the essential goodness of humanity (as opposed to the idea of original sin and human depravity), denied any need for salvation, and opposed any idea of hell as a place where God punished evildoers.

Organization

Spiritualists are organized into numerous autonomous congregations. Individual churches may or may not be affiliated with one of the several Spiritualist associations, but most are. Church property is either owned by the congregation and administered by a board or owned by the medium-minister and totally controlled by her/him.

Mediums are licensed by the several associations, some of which require a modest amount of study and examination. Several organizations, however, have been organized merely to issue and hold ministerial credentials by otherwise independent mediums and require no more for a license than the payment of a small annual fee.

Associations exist primarily for fellowship, the training of mediums, publication of books and other printed matter, and some low-key coordination of the movement. Possibly more important than the associations are the many camps which provide summer employment for many mediums and have established schools for the training of new ones. Many Spiritualists vacation at these camps, which offer a full round of lectures, public demonstrations, and seances.

Current Status

No recent survey of Spiritualism has been made, and any estimate of its size would be highly speculative. The emergence of other psychic groups has often obscured its continued and vital presence within American religion. A cursory survey of several Spiritualist publications and the phone directories of the larger urban areas indicate that they are concentrated in urban centers and those states with the highest percentage of senior citizens—Florida, California, Arizona, etc.

Spiritualism has been somewhat neglected as the field of new religious studies emerged. In spite of Geoffrey Nelson's important study of British Spiritualism which did much to revise the understanding of nonconventional religion, the movement had become somewhat invisible on the religious landscape. Few were aware of its continued vitality and growth over the twentieth century. Most recently it has been rediscovered by a few feminist scholars fascinated with the role played by women in the leadership of the movement in the nineteenth century.

Among the larger associations are those discussed below.

National Spiritualist Association of Churches (N.S.A.C.)

Oldest of the several Spiritualist bodies, the National Spiritualist Association of Churches was formed in 1893, and most of the other Spiritualist associations derive from it. In 1982 it had 136 congregations and associated congregations in Canada, which are affiliated with the National Spiritualist Churches of Canada. It sponsors the Morris Pratt Institute as its educational bureau and several camps, the most prominent of which are Lily Dale in New York and Cassadaga in Florida. *The National Spiritualist Summit* is a monthly magazine.

The N.S.A.C. represents the mainstream of Spiritualist thought, and its conservative stance led to the first schisms in the movement. During the early years of the twentieth century it was split by several controversies. First, one group wished to replace the Declaration of Principles with a Confession of Faith based upon the authority of the Bible. Unable to prevail, the group left to found the Progressive Spiritualist Church, which reported 21 churches in 1930 but seems to have disappeared.

Reincarnation, which has steadily gained adherents throughout this century, is an issue that has continually divided the N.S.A.C. The first group to leave because of a belief in reincarnation was the National Spiritual Alliance in 1913. Then in 1930 the N.S.A.C. adopted a strongly worded statement condemning reincarnation as being subversive of Spiritualism. This resolution led to the loss of the New York State Association, which formed the General Assembly of Spiritualists.

Finally, Spiritualism was split by the same issue that affected other American churches, race. As Spiritualism spread among black people, the N.S.A.C. moved to segregate them and curtail their participation in the national conventions. An initial schism of black members occurred in 1925, and those who left formed the National Colored Spiritualist Association of Churches. An anti-black resolution passed at the N.S.A.C. convention in 1930 became a second factor in the loss of New York members to the General Assembly of Spiritualists.

Universal Church of the Master

The Universal Church of the Master was formed in Los Angeles, California, in 1908 by West Coast Spiritualists and for many years was a small regional body. However, during the 1960s it began to grow and became national in scope. In 1980 it reported approximately 300 congregations, 1,300 ministers (mediums), and 10,000 members. Headquarters are in Santa Clara, California.

Universal Harmony Foundation

The Universal Harmony Foundation was founded in 1942 as the Universal Psychic Science Association by Revs. J. Bertrand and Helene Gerling. It combines Spiritualism with both Eastern and New Thought teachings.

Headquarters of the Association are in Seminole, Florida, where a seminary for training ministers is located. A periodical, *The Spiritual Science Digest*, serves Association members.

Controversy

Controversy has been integral to Spiritualism's life. Its emergence called forth scientists and other researchers to examine the claims of spirit contact (which had immense implication for human life if substantiated). The results of the studies of mediumship repeatedly reached a dead end without convincing results and by World War II had, as a whole, been abandoned in the more modest search for the verification of more basic psychic phenomena—telepathy, clairvoyance, precognition, and psychokinesis. Thus Spiritualism failed to convince the majority of experts who examined it, and the power of its "demonstration" of life after death was considerably weakened.

However, Spiritualism was harmed even more by the continued accusations of fraudulent activity against its mediums. Charges of deception date to the very beginning of Spiritualism, as Margaret, one of the Fox sisters, in 1888 confessed that she and her sister Kate had faked the original rappings. By the time she made the confession, which she later recanted, numerous incidents of fake phenomena had been uncovered. Many of the frauds revolved around attempts to materialize spirits, frequently accomplished by the mediums having accomplices covered in luminous cheesecloth. Mediums kept files on regular and potential clients so they could produce convincing information supposedly derived from the spirit world during seances. Mediums also attempted to produce objects (called "apports") from the spirit realm, which would mysteriously materialize during a seance.

The constant repeated exposure of fraudulent mediumship slowed but by no means stopped Spiritualism's growth or the practice of fake seances. For example, a rather detailed 1960 exposure of fake materialization seances at Camp Chesterfield in Indiana did not noticeably effect the status of the offending mediums but *The Psychic Observer*, the paper which printed the story, was destroyed as a Spiritualist newspaper by the loss of advertising and subscriptions. The failure of the movement as a whole to rid itself of the openly operating pockets of fraudulent leaders has prevented its acceptance as a legitimate religion in many quarters. More recently, the confessions of fake medium Lamar Keene had little effect upon either the movement he served or the individual congregations with which he was directly associated.

Sources-Primary

Centennial Book of Modern Spiritualism in America. Chicago: National Spiritualist Association of United States of America, 1948. 253 pp.

Grand Souvenir Book, World Centennial Celebration of Modern Spiritualism. San Antonio, TX: Federation of Spiritualist Churches and Associations, 1948. 200 pp.

A New Text of Spiritual Philosophy and Religion. San Jose, CA: Universal Church of the Master, 1972. 192 pp.

Toph, Ollah Eloise, ed. *The Centennial Memorial of Modern Spiritualism, 1848-1948.* St. Louis: Thomas E. Tororovich (for the National Spiritualist Association of U.S.A.), 1948. 157 pp.

Wallis, E. W., and M.H. Wallis. *Mediumship Explained.* Summit, NJ: Stow Memorial Foundation, n.d. 88 pp.

Sources-Secondary

Braude, Anne. *Radical Spirits: Spiritualism and Women's Rights in 19th Century America.* Boston: Beacon Press, 1991. 268 pp.

Brown, Slater. *The Heyday of Spiritualism.* New York: Hawthorn Books, 1970. 264 pp.

Lawton, George. *The Drama of Life After Death.* London: Constable, 1933. 668 pp.

Nelson, G. L. *Spiritualism and Society.* New York: Schocken Books, 1969. 307 pp.

Pond, Mariam Buckner. *Time Is Kind.* New York: Centennial Press, 1947. 334 pp.

Skultans, Vieda. *Intimacy and Ritual.* London: Routledge and Kegan Paul, 1974. 106 pp.

K. THEOSOPHY

The Theosophical Society was one of the first and has certainly been the most successful of the occult/metaphysical organizations in the modern West. Much of that success has come through people trained as Theosophists who have left to found their own organizations. At least 100 groups currently functioning in North America have a lineage which can be traced directly to Theosophy.

Founders and History

The Theosophical Society was founded in 1875 by Helen Petrovna Blavatsky (1831-1891), Henry Steel Olcott (1832-1907), and William Q. Judge (1851-1896). The previous year Blavatsky and Olcott had met in Chrittenden, Vermont, where each had gone to observe the phenomena generated by the Eddy brothers, two famous materialization mediums. Blavatsky joined in and demonstrated her skills as a medium. Olcott, a reporter, attended the seances and wrote several enthusiastic accounts.

Back in New York City, Olcott became the leader of an informal circle of people interested in the psychic and occult which had grown around Blavatsky. Judge, an Irish-born lawyer, was a member of this circle and joined with Blavatsky and Olcott in forming the new organization. Olcott was elected president; Madame Blavatsky, corresponding secretary; and Judge, counsel to the Society.

Of the three founders, Blavatsky was by far the most important. Born in Russia, she was first introduced to the occult by her family. She left home at the age of 17 and for the next quarter of the century traveled the world and became active in the Spiritualist movement. She moved to the United States in 1873 where the continuation of her Spiritualist interests led her to her meeting with Olcott. Increasingly, however, she was developing a perspective quite opposed to Spiritualism.

In 1877 Blavatsky finished her first important book, *Isis Unveiled*, in which she summarized her own views on Western occult philosophy, including her disagreements with Spiritualism, the dominant psychic movement in America at that time. The next year she and Olcott moved to India, leaving the American work to Judge. Abner Doubleday, of baseball fame, was designated the new president in Olcott's stead.

Blavatsky and Olcott settled in Bombay and in 1879 began a magazine, *The Theosophist*. In 1882 they moved to Madras. Once in India, both began to pay increasing attention to Hinduism and Buddhism. Olcott became an enthusiastic supporter of Buddhism and spent much of the rest of his life in helping Buddhists in Ceylon resist British missionaries; attempting to promote international Buddhist unity; and spreading Buddhism to the West. Blavatsky increasingly absorbed Eastern esoteric ideas into a more comprehensive and unique Theosophical system, which she described in her second major work, *The Secret Doctrine* (1888). Instead of the spirits of the Spiritualists, Blavatsky drew her authority from a number of masters or mahatmas, highly evolved beings who taught her and demonstrated their powers by various paranormal events, primarily the mysterious materialization of objects and messages. At Adyar, near Madras, where permanent headquarters were established, Blavatsky had a cabinet built into which messages and other gifts from the masters frequently were found.

Blavatsky died in 1891. Her death was followed by a decade of internal dissension within the larger Theosophical movement. In 1888 Annie Besant (1847-1933), an atheist and leader in the British Freethought movement, converted to Theosophy. An outstanding orator, Besant had become a leading public spokesperson for atheism, and Blavatsky, recognizing her capabilities, quickly moved her into a leadership position. She succeeded Blavatsky as head of the Esoteric Section, an inner group of Society members which experimented with magic and occultism. When Olcott died in 1907 she became the president.

Meanwhile, in America, Judge had built the American Section of the Society into a large group. He had authored several books and launched two periodicals, *The Path* (1886) and the *Theosophical Forum* (1889). After Blavatsky died, a power struggle developed between Besant and Judge. Unable to resolve the conflict, in 1895 the American Section under Judge became independent of the British and Indian branches. Only a few lodges remained affiliated to Besant and Olcott.

In 1896 Judge died. Like Blavatsky, he had a few years before his death met a talented young woman who became his successor—Katherine A. Tingley. She took complete control in 1898 and the Theosophical Society in America experienced further schisms. Members in Syracuse, New York, left to form the Temple of the People, and others in New York City broke away to found the Theosophical Society of New York.

Twentieth Century

Tingley brought to Theosophy not only a background in Spiritualism but in social work. Upon taking control of the Theosophical Society in America, she reorganized it as the Universal Brotherhood Organization and Theosophical Society. She purchased land on Point Loma at San Diego, California, and introduced American Theosophy to a community she built there. She invited members to move to Point Loma and created a communal society that included a school, the Isis Temple of Art, Music and Drama, a Greek theatre, and a hotel-sanatorium.

Tingley moved the Society into social work beginning with the establishment of the War Relief Corps and a hospital on Long Island for soldiers wounded in the Cuban campaign of the Spanish-American War. She brought Cuban children to Point Loma to be educated and set up schools on the island after the war ended.

Tingley died in 1929. Gottfried de Purucker succeeded her. He immediately began to refocus the organization. He sold the property on Point Loma and began to build the chapters, many of which had been lost through Tingley's neglect. Membership, which had declined nationally, rose again. Shortly before his death in 1942, he moved the headquarters to Covina, California.

The early years of the twentieth century were a time of rebuilding for the Theosophical Society under Annie Besant. Soon after the Judge schism and the reorganization of the Society, a major setback occurred when it was revealed that the new head of the American section, Alexander Fullerton, was a homosexual who had seduced a minor. He was arrested and eventually sent to a mental institution, but the society rebounded and by 1925 could claim 7,333 members in 268 lodges in the United States.

In 1912 A. P. Warrington established the Krotona Institute of Theosophy, a Theosophical community in Hollywood, California, and a rival to Point Loma. It was primarily designed to be the headquarters of the Esoteric Section (officially an independent corporation though its members had to be Theosophists). For a decade, Krotona functioned as both the headquarters of the Society and the Esoteric Section. However, after World War I, the Society voted to separate the two organizations and moved the headquarters to Illinois. The land was soon sold, and in 1924 Krotona moved to a 118-acre site in Ojai, California, where it remains. In 1926 land was purchased in Wheaton, Illinois (a Chicago suburb), and a national headquarters built.

Membership in the Society peaked in the late 1920s. This was the era in which Krishnamurti was most active. Besant had come to believe that the young man was the vehicle for the manifestation of Maitreya, the Avatar of the New Age which many Theosophists felt was soon to dawn. However, in 1929 Krishnamurti publicly denounced the idea and withdrew from participation in the Society. Coupled with the worldwide depression in the fall, Society membership plummeted from a peak of almost 8,000 to around 3,000. Only in recent years has it made visible strides in regaining that level of membership.

Theosophic Perspectives

The Theosophical Society set three objectives for itself:

1.   To form a nucleus of the Universal Brotherhood of Humanity without distinction of race, creed, sex, caste, or color.

2.   To encourage the study of comparative religion, philosophy and science.

3. To investigate the unexplained laws of nature and the powers latent in man.

Within the context of these objectives, Theosophy sees itself as a body of the truths that form the basis of all true religions; hence, Theosophy sees itself not so much as a new religion as a restatement of the essence of religion. This Theosophical perspective was preeminently stated by Blavatsky in *The Secret Wisdom*, a most difficult book to read without one of the many study guides and summaries published by the several Theosophical organizations.

Theosophy posits one eternal, infinite Reality, the Divine, which underlies everything. From this infinite unknowable Reality, the creative principle is emanated, and from the creative principle, God, many and various spiritual beings—angels, etc.—have emanated. Thus the universe is a manifestation of the life of God.

Each human being is a monad, a spark of the Divine, a microcosm of the macrocosm, which enters into physical embodiment to evolve from a latent divinity into full perfection. To enter physical manifestation, the monad passes through the various planes of existence from the Divine through the Monadic, Atomic, and Buddhic down to the Upper and Lower Mental, Astral (Emotional), and Physical. As the monad descends into the lower realms, it acquires a set of sheaths or bodies termed the causal body (Upper Mental), mental body (Lower Mental), astral body, and physical body. These allow the monad to function in various appropriate manners.

The monad develops through a series of embodiments, i.e., reincarnations. Gradually it gains enough knowledge and experience to be free from the need to reincarnate.

The spiritual hierarchy bridges the gap between humans and the Divine. Individuals who have completed their cycle of development through successful incarnations now work for the evolution of the race. At the bottom of the hierarchy are the Masters or Mahatmas who periodically select a few members of the human race to become their messengers for a generation. Blavatsky was such a select messenger. The majority of the disagreements within the Theosophical Movement concern the acceptance and rejection of the claims of people to be messengers of the masters. Claimants have been many and include: Alice

Bailey, William Q. Judge, Guy Ballard, and Francia LaDue, to mention only a few.

The Theosophical perspective has been accepted by many occult organizations, some of which do not realize that the source of these ideas is the Theosophical Society. A number of individuals have claimed contact with one of the Masters first described by Blavatsky and have begun new organizations based upon the individual revelation imparted. Alice Bailey was contacted by the Master Djwhul Khul; Ballard regularly spoke with St. Germain; and LaDue received her messages from Hilarion. Each assumed a basic agreement with Theosophy but found new emphases according to their special revelations. The Theosophical Society in America and the Theosophical Society have been the least open to the claims of new messengers, while those growing out of the work of Guy Ballard ("I AM" Movement, the Church Universal and Triumphant, etc.) have relied upon the leadership of a messenger.

Present Status

During his years of leadership, Gottfried de Purucker changed the name of Tingley's Universal Brotherhood Organization and Theosophical Society to, simply, the Theosophical Society. Headquarters moved from San Diego to Covina and eventually to Altadena, California, where they are located today. Associated with the Theosophical Society is the Theosophical University Press, which issues *Sunrise*, a periodical, and operates a large library for the members. There are only a few centers remaining of this branch in North America, but it has a significant following in Holland.

The Theosophical Society in America, the branch of the Society chartered by the international Society in India, is headquartered in Wheaton, Illinois. The large headquarters building houses the Olcott Library for members. The American branch of the Theosophical Publishing House and Quest Books are also located at Wheaton. They publish several periodicals, including *American Theosophist* and *Discovery*. *The Theosophist*, founded in 1979, is still published in India. During the 1980s the Society's membership edged over the 5,000 mark.

A smaller branch of Theosophy is the United Lodge of Theosophy, formed in 1909 by Robert Crosbie, a former member of the

Point Loma community. Headquarters are in Los Angeles, as is the associated Theosophy Company, the publishing arm. *Theosophy* is their monthly periodical. There are 11 lodges in the United States.

Quite apart from the several groups which retain the word "Theosophical" in their name, Theosophy has spawned numerous occult bodies in the United States. The main groups, each of which has splintered into several factions, include the Arcane School, the "I AM" Religious Activity, the Liberal Catholic Church, and the Rosicrucian Fellowship (founded by Max Heindel). All are discussed elsewhere in this volume.

Controversy

One cannot understand the development apart from an encounter with the several major scandals and controversies which hindered its growth, contributed to its splintering, and could have proved fatal to a weaker organization. First, in 1885, in the face of numerous claims of extraordinary occurrences attributed to Blavatsky, Richard Hodgson and the British Society for Psychical Research issued their report of Hodgson's extensive investigations of the claims of paranormal phenomena produced by her. Hodgson concluded that most of the phenomena had been fraudulently produced by Blavatsky and several associates. The previous year, a disgruntled former employee, claiming to be one of her confederates, Emma Coulomb, had turned over incriminating documents to the *Christian College Magazine* in Madras, which had published the extracts in several exposé articles. Coulomb also demonstrated to Hodgson how some of the phenomena were produced by simple trickery.

The Hodgson Report accused Blavatsky of writing the messages which she claimed came from the master and placing or dropping them so that they would appear mysteriously. She was also accused of planting objects that would "materialize" to the amazement of the naive and gullible.

Efforts to investigate further and defend Blavatsky only increased the accounts of fraud, which have been kept alive over the years by writers hostile to Theosophy. The several branches of the Society assumed a low profile in discussing the charges, but because of the marked influence of her books and the Society, and the key roles claimed for the Masters in the development of both, the cloud that remains over her life is still a matter of intense interest. Only in recent years has there been some active attempt to reopen the case and seek some reappraisal of Blavatsky. In 1963, the Society published an attack on the Hodgson Report by Walter A. Carrithers, Jr., citing inaccuracies and inadequacies throughout. Through Carrithers's efforts, the Society for Psychical Research published an article in the April 1986 issue of their *Journal* in which some distance was set between the Report and the S.P.R.

A more studied account of the issues surrounding Blavatsky has been made by Michael Gomes, a talented young historian, who has already published one volume of his revisionist approach to the society's history, *The Dawning of the Theosophical Movement* (1987) and who has further works in progress.

Following Madame Blavatsky's death, when leaders were striving for control of the Society, Judge claimed to have received messages from the Masters. His opponents in the Society accused him of forgery. When Besant turned against him, Judge gathered his supporters and led them to assert their autonomy of Europe and India.

After Judge left, the small minority of supporters of the Besant-Olcott position reorganized and elected Alexander Fullerton as its leader. The fighting between the two groups became intense, especially after Katherine Tingley succeeded Judge. Thus when Tingley received word of Fullerton's attempted seduction of a male minor, she released the information to the authorities, who arrested him.

Finally in 1906 Besant's major associate, the Rev. Charles W. Leadbeater, became the center of a sex scandal on the very eve of Besant's becoming president of the Society. He was accused of teaching masturbation to some youths placed in his charge, as a means of controlling their emerging sexual drives. Besant and Leadbeater had been closely identified, were good friends, and had authored a number of books together. The scandal forced Besant to ask for his resignation. He was allowed to return to membership, a few years later, but spent most of the rest of his life in Sydney, Australia, where he authored a number of books, including the basic texts of the theosophically inclined Liberal Catholic Church.

About that same time, Besant inaugurated the Order of the Star of the East, an organization to proclaim the coming of a new World Teacher Savior. In 1909 Besant announced that the Lord Maitreya, the master most closely associated with the person who walked the earth as Jesus of Nazareth, was returning and would be embodied in a young Indian named Jiddu Krishnamurti. Krishnamurti became head of the Order, traveled on its behalf, and accepted the promotion given him until 1929. That year he dissolved the Order, denied any role as the World Teacher, and became an independent guru. Besant lived the last few years of her life in the aftermath of the Krishnamurti affair. Membership worldwide dropped by half, and the society did not really begin to recover until after World War II.

While the Besant branch of the Society suffered through its travails with Fullerton, Leadbeater and Krishnamurti, the branch under Katherine Tingley also had to survive several attacks on its credibility. In 1902 Tingley won a major lawsuit against the *Los Angeles Times*, which had accused her of permitting gross immoralities among her disciples. She also won a battle with the New York Society for the Prevention of Cruelty to Children which had tried to block the arrival of a group of Cuban children she had brought to the United States for education at Point Loma.

After these early tumultuous years, both Societies have been relatively free of major controversies for half a century, though their critics have not been allowed them to forget their past.

Sources-Primary

Gomes, Michael. *The Dawning of the Theosophical Movement.* Wheaton, IL: Theosophical Publishing House, 1987. 248 pp.

Johnson, Paul. *In Search of the Masters Behind the Occult Myth.* N.p.: The Author, 1990. 305 pp.

Mills, Joy. *100 Years of Theosophy: A History of the Theosophical Society in America.* Wheaton, IL: Theosophical Publishing House, 1987. 215 pp.

Murphet, Howard. *When Daylight Comes.* Wheaton, IL: Theosophical Publishing House, 1975. 277 pp.

Ransom, Josephine. *A Short History of the Theosophical Society.* Adyar, India: Theosophical Publishing House, 1938. 589 pp.

Rogers, L. W. *Elementary Theosophy.* Wheaton, IL: Theosophical Press, 1956. 269 pp.

Ryan, Charles J. *H. P. Blavatsky and the Theosophical Movement.* Pasadena: Theosophical University Press, 1975. 358 pp.

The Theosophical Movement, 1875-1950. Los Angeles: Cunningham Press, 1951. 351 pp.

Waterman, Adlai E. (pseudonym of Walter A. Carrithers, Jr.). *Obituary: The "Hodgson Report on Madame Blavatsky.* Adyar, India: Theosophical Publishing House, 1963. 92 pp.

Sources-Secondary

Campbell, Bruce F. *Ancient Wisdom Revisited.* Berkeley: University of California Press, 1980. 249 pp.

Greenwalt, Emmett A. *California Utopia: Point Loma: 1897-1942.* San Diego: Point Loma Publications, 1978. 244 pp.

Meade, Marion. *Madame Blavatsky, the Woman Behind the Myth.* New York: G. P. Putnam's Sons, 1980. 528 pp.

Nethercot, Arthur H. *The First Five Lives of Annie Besant.* Chicago: University of Chicago Press, 1960. 419 pp.

―――――. *The Last Four Lives of Annie Besant.* Chicago: University of Chicago Press, 1963. 483 pp.

L. UNITY SCHOOL OF CHRISTIANITY

The Unity movement, which has visible form through two organizations, the Unity School of Christianity and the Association of Unity Churches, is the largest of the several metaphysical churches usually grouped together under the name New Thought. From its founding in the 1880s, it has grown steadily and now has congregations across North America and is expanding overseas.

Founders and Early History

The Unity School of Christianity was founded in 1887 by Charles and Myrtle Fillmore. They were among the first organizations to develop from the new metaphysical movement begun by Emma Curtis Hopkins, the founder of New Thought. Hopkins (1849-1925) had been a prominent student of Mary Baker Eddy and in 1884 succeeded Eddy as editor of the *Christian Science Journal*. In 1885, however, she had a falling out with her teacher, and, resigning her position in Boston, she moved to Chicago. In the summer of 1886 she opened her own office and school and began to teach her modified version of Christian Science. Over the next year and a half she taught hundreds of students who opened centers across the United States. She brought her teachings to Kansas City, Missouri, and to the Fillmores in 1889.

Charles S. Fillmore (1854-1948) had grown up in Minnesota and moved to Texas as a young man. There he met Mary Caroline "Myrtle" Page. Before they were married in 1881, he had moved to Colorado and entered the real estate business. When the real estate market turned sour, they moved to Kansas City. Meanwhile, Myrtle had developed tuberculosis, at the time incurable.

In 1886, Myrtle attended a lecture by Eugene Weeks, a student of the Illinois Metaphysical College, headed by independent Christian Scientist George B. Charles. She was greatly affected by his words, especially the phrase, "I am a child of God and therefore do not inherit sickness." By putting what she had learned into practice, she improved considerably over the next year. Her cure was remarkable and Charles finally began to take an interest in it. He began to attend the lectures given by various teachers who came through town and read widely in metaphysical and occult subjects. In 1989 he began to publish *Modern Thought*, a magazine for the discussion of all of the new religious impulses which were emerging in America at the time, and to teach some classes for supporters of his magazine who lived in the Kansas City area. They also heard of Emma Curtis Hopkins and helped to arrange her visit to Kansas City.

Hopkins came to Kansas City at the beginning of 1890. Both Charles and Myrtle enthusiastically received her message and became her students. Over the next two years they made significant transitions in their expanding ministry. Myrtle suggested the formation of what became known as the Society of Silent Help for magazine subscribers across the country. They also traveled to Chicago on several occasions to take classes at Hopkins' school. While in Chicago in 1891, they decided upon the name "Unity" and the symbol of the winged sphere for their work. Gradually all the names of their various efforts were altered to include the new designation. In June of 1891 they were ordained by Hopkins. About the same time, the first issue of a new magazine, *Unity*, appeared. It eventually absorbed the older magazine.

Over the remainder of the decade, a movement began to take shape. Silent Unity (as the Society of Silent Help had been renamed) had membership in the thousands. H. Emilie Cady, a student of Hopkins' in New York City, began to write for *Unity* and in the middle of the decade authored a series of lessons later reprinted as *Lessons in Truth*, the standard Unity textbook over the next century. A children's magazine, *Wee Wisdom*, was first issued in 1893. Until its discontinuance at the end of 1991, it was the oldest children's magazine in America. As Unity developed, similar movements were appearing around the country. A general meeting of other New Thought groups, who met under the name

"Divine Scientists," as they then termed themselves, was held in Kansas City in 1896.

The work of Unity steadily expanded as an impressive prayer (Silent Unity) and literature ministry. It published numerous tracts, booklets, and books, which were widely read and studied by gatherings around the country. In 1903 he incorporated the Unity School of Practical Christianity (the word "practical" was dropped in 1914) as an umbrella organization for the various activities. Three years later he devised a plan to begin ordination through Unity, and he and Myrtle were reordained with the first class of new Unity ministers. In 1909, Charles' first book, *Christian Healing*, was published. It reprinted a series of lessons he had written for the magazine.

Unity developed very informally as people utilized the publications from Kansas City and established "Unity" centers. However, as will happen, some of the teachers were offering students ideas not in agreement with what Charles and Myrtle saw as Unity teachings. Thus in 1925 the Unity Annual Conference was formed as a means of providing some organization and accountability for people who used the Unity name. The conference would later mature into the Association of Unity Churches.

Myrtle died in 1931. Two years later Charles married Cora G. Dedrick. He died in 1948.

Beliefs and Practices

Unity considers itself a noncreedal church organized primarily to help people acquire what it considers to be the practical benefits of Christianity. The movement is more about prayer and healing than belief. It also considers whatever teachings it offers to be open to change should greater insight so dictate. That being said, however, Unity does have distinctive teachings which find their standard presentation in such volumes as *Lessons in Truth* and the various books written by Charles Fillmore, and several recent textbooks, *Foundations of Unity* and *Metaphysics.* At one point an attempt was made to summarize these teachings in what was termed "Unity's Statement of Faith." This statement is not in use today, but it remains one of the better succinct presentations of Unity's perspective.

1. We Believe in God, the one and only omnipotent, omniscient, and omnipresent Spirit-mind.
2. We believe in Christ, the Son of God, in whom is imaged the ideal creation, with perfect man on the throne of dominion.
3. We believe in Christ-Jesus, the Son of God made manifest in Jesus of Nazareth, who overcame death, and who is now with us in His perfect body as the Way-Shower in regeneration for all men.
4. We believe in the Holy Spirit, which baptizes the universe and man with the thoughts of God and perpetually establishes the divine law in all manifestation.
5. We believe in the supremacy and eternity of the good, as the one and only objective of man and of all things visible and invisible.
6. We believe in the twelve disciples, the twelve powers of man, going forth into mind and body with power and authority to teach, preach, heal, and wholly save man and the world from sin, sickness, and death.
7. We believe that "God is spirit," as Jesus taught, and that all of his Spirit is with us at all times, supplying every need.
8. We believe that Divine intelligence is present in every atom of man and matter, and that the more abundant life, which Jesus promised, is flooding the world and quickening the minds and bodies of men everywhere.
9. We believe that the original authority and dominion given to man was over his own thoughts, emotions, feelings, and passions, and that, in the lawful exercise of this authority, he will harmonize all discords within and without and restore the Kingdom of God on the earth.
10. We believe in the creative power of thoughts and words.
11. We believe that the "kingdom of God" can be attained here and now by overcoming the world, the flesh and the Adversary through Jesus Christ.
12. We believe in the at-one-ment that Jesus established between God and Man, and that through Jesus we can regain our original estate as sons of God.
13. We believe that the prayer of faith will save the sick, resurrect the body from "trespasses and sins," and finally overcome the last enemy, death.
14. We believe that the more abundant life, which Jesus promised, is poured into the race stream as a vitalizing

energy, and that, when accepted in faith, it purifies the life-flow in our bodies and makes us immune to all diseased thoughts and germs.

15. We believe that sense consciousness may be lifted up . . . and that all men may be again restored to paradise through faith, understanding, and practice of the divine law, as Jesus Christ taught and demonstrated.

16. We believe that creative Mind, God, is masculine and feminine, and that these attributes of Being are fundamental in both natural and spiritual man.

17. We Believe that we live, move, and have our being in God-Mind; also that God-Mind lives, moves, and has being in us, to the extent of our consciousness.

18. We believe that the body of man is the highest-formed manifestation of creative Mind and that it is capable of unlimited expression of that Mind.

19. We believe that . . . man can transform his body and make it perpetually healthy, therefore immortal, and that he can attain eternal life in this way and in no other way.

20. We believe that the blood of Jesus represents eternal life; that the body of Jesus represents incorruptible substance.

21. We believe that spirit, soul, and body are a unity, and that any separation of these three is transgression of the divine law.

22. We believe that the dissolution of spirit, soul, and body, caused by death, is annulled by rebirth of the same spirit and soul of man to be a merciful provision of our loving Father.

23. We Believe that the kingdom of heaven of harmony is within man and that through man the law and order existing in Divine Mind are to be established on the earth.

24. We believe that the "second coming" of Jesus Christ is now being fulfilled, that His Spirit is quickening the whole world.

25. We believe that the golden rule . . . should be the standard of action among men.

26. We believe that Jehovah God is incarnate in Jesus Christ and that all men may attain the Christ perfection by living the righteous life.

27. We believe that the Word of God is the thought of God expressed in creative ideas and that these ideas are the

primal attributes of all enduring entities in the universe, visible and invisible.

28. We believe in the final resurrection of the body, through Christ. We believe that we do free our minds and resurrect our bodies by true thoughts and words and that the resurrection is being carried forward daily and will ultimate in a final purification of the Body from all earthly errors.

29. We believe in all of the doctrines of Christianity spiritually interpreted.

30. Almighty Father-Mother God, we thank Thee for this vision of Thine omnipotence, omniscience, and omnipresence in us and in all that we think and do, in the name of Jesus Christ, Amen!

The statement ties Unity to the larger New Thought worldview in the positing of God as the basis of reality and God as best understood as Mind. Humanity is the expression of God. Since God is the only reality, atunement between God and humanity overcomes all of the problems of life—sin, sickness, and poverty. Unity differs with some New Thought in being distinctly Christian and seeing that the realization of Unity between God and humanity is accomplished by a relationship with Jesus the Christ.

Unity teaches all of the ideas of traditional Christianity but interprets them "spiritually," i.e., somewhat allegorically. The literal and material notions are thus seen as veils of spiritual truth. Spiritual or metaphysical interpretation guides Unity's approach to the Bible, and in this light, Unity has dropped traditional rituals and sacraments, though some rituals have been created to meet the needs of marking special occasions (Christmas, birth of a baby, etc.).

Reincarnation, an idea which came into North America in the late nineteenth century, was embraced wholeheartedly by Fillmore. It is accepted by most in New Thought today. Fillmore also taught some unique ideas not necessarily shared by the present leadership of the movement. Integral to his belief in reincarnation is the idea of the eventual immortality of the body. He saw a process of purification and spiritualization in various incarnations leading to a form of perfection that would allow for the transformation of the body. Once in possession of a transformed body the individual would gain eternal life. Fillmore also favored vegetarianism as an aid to the body's transformation.

In concert with most of New Thought, Unity also teaches what is called prosperity consciousness. It is the belief that just as a relationship with God handles the problems of sin and sickness, so it can handle the problem of poverty. Poverty is a matter of consciousness and success (measured in financial or other terms as the individual wishes) can be had as one realizes God is all abundance.

Organization

Unity has a rather unique organizational structure. The Unity School of Christianity is an umbrella organization for the various activities centered upon Unity Village. The Fillmores had originally purchased what is now Unity Village as a farm/retreat center near Lee's Summit, Missouri, in 1920. Some activities were held there during the years in which the headquarters remained in Kansas City, but the headquarters were finally moved there in 1949. Unity School is today headed by Connie Fillmore, president, and Charles R. Fillmore, chairman of the board of trustees.

Located at Unity Village are Silent Unity, the Unity School for Religious Studies (where Unity teachers and ministers are trained), the Village Chapel, Unity Inn, and a publishing concern which produces millions of pieces of literature annually. Wee Wisdom School (a preschool) was discontinued in 1982. Two magazines, *Unity* and *Daily Word*, are mailed out worldwide.

Also located at Unity Village is the headquarters of the Association of Unity Churches. The Association grew out of the old field department of Unity School and now has charge of the churches and ministers across the country and in foreign lands. It provides for ordination, the establishment of new Unity churches, and sets standards for congregations and ministers.

Unity is part of the larger New Thought movement but has tended to remain somewhat aloof from association with the International New Thought Alliance. Unity has kept a staunchly Christian perspective, while the Alliance has been open to a wide variety of perspectives. As such, neither the Unity School nor the Association of Unity Churches are members of the Alliance, although many local Unity congregations and ministers are members and active participants.

Present Status

The Unity movement has emerged as a strong church with congregations in every section of the United States. In 1987 the Association of Unity Churches had oversight of 437 congregations and 147 study groups in North America and an additional 42 congregations and 71 study groups overseas in 15 different countries, most being in Europe.

Controversy

Unity has escaped the major thrust of the anti-cult controversies of the 1970s and 1980s. It has, however, been consistently attacked as a cult by Evangelical Christians who are offended by what they perceive as Unity's use of Christian words and symbols while interpreting them in an unorthodox manner. Among the most often quoted passage is a version of the 23rd Psalm interpreted metaphysically:

> The Lord is my banker; my credit is good.
> He maketh me to lie down in the consciousness of omnipresent abundance;
> He giveth me the key to His strongbox.
> He restoreth my faith in His riches;
> He guideth me in the paths of prosperity for His name's sake.
> Yea, though I walk through the very shadow of debt,
> I shall fear no evil, for thou art with me,
> Thy silver and thy gold secure me.
> Thou preparest a way for me in the presence of the collector;
> Thou fillest my wallet with plenty, my measure runneth over.
> Surely goodness and plenty will follow me all the days of my life;
> And I shall do business in the name of the Lord forever.

From Unity's perspective, their understanding of God as the Supplier of all abundance, this rendition of the Psalm is a perfectly logical rendering of the meaning of the text. To orthodox Christians, it borders on blasphemy.

Critics of Unity have charged it, in essence, with denying basic Christian affirmations of the distinction between the Omnipotent God and His creatures, the reality of sin, and the nature of salvation. While any number of groups are equally guilty, Unity comes under special consideration because of its extensive literature ministry. The majority of the readers of *Unity* and *Daily Word* are not directly associated with a Unity congregation but are members of mainline churches who have added Unity literature to their reading. Evangelical Christians have charged that the infiltration of Unity literature constitutes an act of deception in that it parades as normal Christian devotional and inspirational material while denying essential teachings.

Unity has seen itself as adhering to the essential truths of Christianity as taught by Jesus from which the churches have largely departed. Only rarely has it replied to its critics, though in the mid-1980s an article in *Unity* magazine, later reprinted separately, answered charges that Unity was a cult. Such charges were dismissed as religious bigotry.

Sources-Primary

Cady, H. Emilie. *Lessons in Truth.* Kansas City, MO: Unity School of Christianity, 1919. 172 pp. Frequently reprinted.

D'Andrade, Hugh. *Charles Fillmore: Herald of the New Age.* New York: Harper & Row, 1974. 145 pp.

Freeman, James Dillet. *The Story of Unity.* Unity Village, MO: Unity Books, 1978. 269 pp.

Metaphysics. 2 vols. Unity Village, MO: Unity School for Religious Studies, n.d.

Sources-Secondary

Lytton, Kam. *Unity for the Millions.* Los Angeles: Sherbourne Press, 1969. 158 pp.

Tenner, John W. *Unity School of Christianity.* Chicago: Ph.D. dissertation, University of Chicago, 1942. 204 pp.

M. THE UNIVERSAL PEACE MISSION MOVEMENT OF FATHER DIVINE

No "cult" group aroused more attention in the period between World Wars I and II than the Peace Mission Movement of Father Divine. During this time, when the word "cult" was first adopted by social scientists, the Peace Mission was frequently cited as a typical example of the cult phenomena.

Founder

The Peace Mission was founded by the man known to his followers as Father Major Jealous Divine (1880?-1965). The "facts" of his life prior to 1914 remain a matter of disagreement. According to the most popular story (among those outside the Movement), he was born George Baker around 1880 on a rice plantation in Georgia. In 1899 he became the assistant of an itinerant preacher, Samuel Morris, who called himself Father Jehovia. The two split in 1912, and Father Divine began to gather his own following. Members of the Movement project a much earlier date of birth as they cite June 6, 1882, as the date of his first marriage.

In either case, he emerged in Brooklyn in 1914. Five years later, with his followers, he moved to Sayville, New York, where his wife, Sister Penny, bought them a home. He lived quietly. His followers were organized to work in the community. By the mid-1920s there were from 30 to 40 members, all of whom were black. Sometime during this period, however, the first white members joined. Approximately one-fourth of the membership has remained non-black.

The most famous events in the life of Father Divine, the ones that catapulted him into the public spotlight, began on November 13, 1931. On that day, responding to neighborhood complaints about traffic congestion around his home, police arrested Father Divine for disturbing the peace. Viewing the incident as racially inspired, he refused bail, pleaded not guilty, and was tried and convicted. The jury asked for leniency. The judge ignored them and handed down a sentence of a year in jail and ordered him to pay a $500 fine. Father Divine went to jail. Two days later the judge, apparently a healthy man, died, and Father Divine freely offered his opinion that the death was not the result of natural causes. One follower is said to have remarked on the day of sentencing, "The judge can't live long now. He's offended Almighty God." From his cell, Father Divine remarked simply, "I hated to do it!" (Since that date, the Peace Mission commemorates June 7, the day of the judge's death, by publishing accounts of disasters that befell people whose activities conflicted with Father Divine's program.)

Father Divine, spurred by the events in Sayville, moved his followers to Harlem in 1932. He had become a hero to the black community, and once in Harlem, he was able to expand the Mission in response to the Depression. He purchased hotels which he turned into Peace Mission "heavens." Members were able, through the Mission's assistance, to have cheap food, shelter, a job, and a reformed life. New members were instructed to pay off their debts, cancel insurance, return any funds they might have stolen, and in the future to pay their own way in cash.

His first wife having died, Father Divine married Edna Rose Ritchings, a white Canadian, in 1946. Their wedding day is a holiday for the Movement. About this time he also moved his headquarters to Philadelphia. In 1954 he was given Woodmont, an estate in suburban Philadelphia. It served as his country home until his death in 1965. His body is enshrined there. After his death, Mother Divine succeeded to leadership of the Movement and continues to administer its worldwide affairs.

Beliefs and Practices

The structure and practices of the Movement derived from Father Divine's perception of the situation of the downtrodden of society, particularly black Americans. He proposed a total economic and religious program to reform the individual and restructure society.

The Peace Mission affirms that Father Divine fulfilled all the Biblical prophecies for the Second Coming of Christ and the Coming of the Jewish Messiah. God as Father and Mother are personified in Father and Mother Divine and constitute humanity as one brotherhood. Woodmont is the Mount of the House of the Lord (Micah 4:1-2; Isaiah 2:2-3) from which the Law shall go to all nations. The Mission views itself as the fulfillment of specific Biblical prophecies and the essence of all religion: faith in the one God. It accepts both the Ten Commandments and the Sermon on the Mount.

From this religious perspective a social, economic, and political program has developed. Members look for a day when America, as the birthplace of the Kingdom of God, will become the Kingdom, in fact. The Kingdom is equated with the principles of true Americanism, Brotherhood, Democracy, Christianity, Judaism, and all other true religions.

The Mission teaches that each person is equal in the sight of God and, thus, entitled to basic rights (life, liberty, and happiness) and every convenience and comfort of modern society. Each individual also has the responsibility of protecting every other person's rights and privileges. One step in that protection would be the conviction of all members of a mob that commits murder as first-degree murderers.

Members of the Mission live communally. All possessions are owned cooperatively, and all properties are maintained by the members without compensation for their work on this endeavor. The Mission advocates full employment as a right and opposes life insurance, social security, and credit and installment buying. The Mission admonishes members to pay cash for all purchases.

On a personal level, all members adopt Father Divine's International Modesty Code: No Smoking. No Drinking. No Obscenity. No Vulgarity. No Profanity. No Undue Mixing of the Sexes. No Receiving of Gifts, Presents, Tips, or Bribes. Within the group men and women live apart. Within their businesses, the principles are enforced. For example, guests at the hotels run by the Movement must adopt the code while staying at the hotel. Men and women stay on separate floors (even married couples). Women cannot wear slacks or short skirts. Men cannot wear short-sleeved shirts. Visitors are not allowed in the guest's room.

On a social level the Mission teaches the equality of the individual and the right to freedom of worship and voting. Education should be free and in English, the universal language. All racial references should be deleted from books.

The Mission believes in the Declaration of Independence and the Constitution, particularly in the Bill of Rights. All people have a right to live safely and securely under the Constitution. Restitution is a basic step toward the ideal life as spelled out in the Constitution. The Mission advocates nations returning territory taken by force, governments restoring losses due to mob violence, and individuals returning all stolen possessions. It advocates mass production as the means of eliminating poverty and social inequality.

In putting his principles into action, Father Divine created a far-flung organization.

Organization

The Universal Peace Mission Movement began as a small group around Father Divine in his home in Sayville, New York. The group functioned as an extended family with Father Divine as patriarch. He took personal responsibility for the members by placing ads for employment opportunities and providing inexpensive food and shelter. During the Depression in Harlem, he became known for the lavish banquets he gave for his followers and guests at little or no cost.

As the organization grew, so did his personal staff. He hired secretaries for correspondence, filing, and typing. As the organization grew, the large secretarial staff became a personal entourage that included a cook and chauffeur.

The growth of the Movement soon required the acquisition of houses of worship, housing for followers, and restaurants. However, once the Sayville property was sold, no property or other assets were placed in Father Divine's name. Rather, groups of believers incorporated independently as a church and affiliated with Father Divine and his principles. Five separate corporations were formed that now hold all the property. They are held together within the Movement only by their allegiance to Father (and now Mother) Divine. During Father Divine's life, he approved all nominations to the Churches' boards, and the Churches conformed to Father Divine's rules.

Individual members of the Mission also formed businesses that they associated with the Movement. They named the businesses so as to identify them with Father Divine. They were allowed to make that identity if they followed Father Divine's rules: sell only for cash, sell below the price of their competitors, accept no tips or gratuities, refrain from dealing in tobacco or liquor.

Within the Movement, members may also participate in one of three religious orders, which together are estimated to include approximately fifty percent of the group. The younger women (up to middle age) can become Rosebuds. They wear dark red jackets with a white "V" (for virtue) over their hearts. Shirts are navy blue. They assist in conducting worship services, perform in dramatic productions, and participate in the Movement's holiday celebrations. Rosebuds ascribe to an extensive set of special rules aimed at inculcating the virtues of submissiveness, meekness, and sweetness.

Older women may join the Lily-buds. They wear green jackets trimmed in white and lead in music and reading at services. Men may join the Crusaders. Members of the orders must devote all of their free time to the Mission.

The Universal Peace Mission Movement now exists as a number of independent church corporations, businesses and religious orders interrelated by the participants' belief in Father Divine and his teachings.

Current Status

The Peace Mission had its greatest growth during Father Divine's life. At present it has churches meeting in Philadelphia (4), the Bronx, Newark (3), Los Angeles, and Sacramento. One congregation each can be found in Australia and Switzerland. The New Day Publishing Company publishes the biweekly newspaper, *The New Day*, which is, for the most part, filled with quotations from and pictures of Father and Mother Divine. Hotels (formerly known as "heavens") conducted by the Movement include the Divine Lorraine and Divine Tracy in Philadelphia, the Divine Riviera in Los Angeles, and the Divine Hotel in Ulster County, New York.

The home in which Father Divine lived from 1919 to 1932 in Sayville, New York, is owned by the Movement and has become a shrine.

Sources-Primary

Mother Divine. *The Peace Mission Movement.* Philadelphia: The Imperial Press, 1982. 191 pp.

Sources-Secondary

Burnham, Kenneth E. *God Comes to America.* Boston: Lambeth Press, 1979. 167 pp.

Harris, Sara. *Father Divine.* New York: Collier Books, 1971. 377 pp.

Weisbrot, Robert. *Father Divine and the Struggle for Racial Equality.* Urbana: University of Illinois Press, 1983. 241 pp.

N. WORLDWIDE CHURCH OF GOD

The Worldwide Church of God is the most successful of the several church bodies to grow out of the nineteenth-century Seventh Day Church of God Movement. In like measure, it is the most successful group to incorporate within its theology the teaching known as British-Israelism, and thus it shares some affinity with the Identity Movement.

Founder and Early History

The Worldwide Church of God was founded by Herbert W. Armstrong, born in 1892 to a Quaker family in Iowa. He began a career in advertising in Chicago where he met and in 1917 married Loma Dillon. In 1924 they moved to Oregon. In Salem, Loma met Ira Runcorn, a sabbatarian Bible student, who convinced her that the proper day of worship and rest was Saturday, not Sunday. Angered at his wife's new belief, Armstrong agreed to try to prove her wrong. He also began to study the Bible concerning evolution, the truth of which was being advocated by a neighbor. Six months of study convinced him of seven basic truths: God exists; evolution is a false theory; the Bible is God's inspired, infallible instruction book; the Saturday Sabbath is still binding today; the Jewish holy days and festivals are also binding; death, not eternal punishment, awaits the unsaved; and eternal life is God's Gift to believers.

Being convinced of these truths, in 1927 he sought baptism at the hands of a Baptist minister but joined no church. Rather, he began to seek for the true church and, through Ira Runcorn, was led to the Church of God headquartered in Stanberry, Missouri. This oldest branch of the Seventh Day Church of God, since splintered into numerous independent church bodies, was the Adventist group which accepted Saturday as the Sabbath but rejected the unique teachings and revelations of Ellen G. White, founder of the Seventh-day Adventist Church. It had only about 50 members in Oregon, but Armstrong joined, frequently preached for its congregations, and wrote for the denominational periodical.

Armstrong's entrance into the Church coincided with its period of turmoil. The members in Oregon, suffering during the Depression, did not wish to send money to Missouri. In 1930 Armstrong led the formation of the Oregon Conference of the Church of God, by which he was later ordained. In 1933, the Church of God (Stanberry, MO) split. A group in Salem, West Virginia, headed by A. N. Dugger, wanted a reorganization of the Church along what they felt were Biblical standards. The group rejected congregational church government and chose its leadership, 12 apostles, seventy evangelists, and 7 elders by lot. In the first drawing, Armstrong was selected as one of the seventy. He remained loosely connected with the Salem faction for several years, even after he began his own independent ministry.

Armstrong began that independent ministry in 1933. In April of that year he edited and issued the first copy of the *Bulletin of the Churches of God in Oregon.* That summer he began an evangelistic service in Eugene, Oregon, at the close of which the members decided to start a congregation independent of the Churches of God of Oregon. Then in September, he began a radio broadcast, "The Radio Church of God," over station KORE in Eugene. A second congregation was organized in October. These events are now seen as the beginning of the Worldwide Church of God.

On February 1, 1934, Armstrong issued the first copy of the magazine with which he has subsequently been identified, *The Plain Truth,* to 106 listeners to his radio broadcast. Growth proceeded slowly through the 1930s, but by 1940 *The Plain Truth,* now printed instead of mimeographed, reached a circulation of 3,000, and four radio stations (Eugene, Salem, Portland, and Seattle) carried the broadcast. Slowly, as the response to the broadcast increased, Armstrong became committed to using the mass media as the major means of reaching people with his teachings.

On a trip to California in 1941, Armstrong arranged to have his program broadcast over KMTR in Hollywood. He had decided to drop any remnants of a worship service and concentrate entirely on Biblical teaching and interpretation. He changed the name of the broadcast to "The World Tomorrow," the name by which it is still heard. The high response from his California audience and the opportunity for daily broadcasts led him to shift his attention to Southern California. The work expanded quickly, and in August 1942, he added the 50,000-watt WHO in Des Moines.

After World War II, the Radio Church of God, the corporate name of Armstrong's organization, bought its first printing facilities. He also went on his first baptizing tour to interview, baptize, and receive new members of the Church from among the listeners to the broadcast. Seeing the expansion of his efforts, he envisioned a college which would offer both a Christian liberal education and training for ministers. He moved to Pasadena, California, and opened Ambassador College in the fall of 1947. In December 1952 he ordained the first five ministers of the Church and added two more in January. In 1953 the work took on international proportions with the addition of Radio Luxembourg.

For the next two decades after the initiation of work in Europe, the Church grew impressively and Garner Ted, Armstrong's son, who in 1957 began to speak on most of the broadcasts, became one of the most recognizable figures on both radio and television. "The World Tomorrow" was heard in Spanish, French, and German. *The Plain Truth* became a full-color magazine. Two additional Ambassador College campuses opened (in England and Texas). In 1968 the Radio Church of God changed its name to the Worldwide Church of God.

The 1970s, A Period of Change

The two decades of spectacular growth were followed by a decade of intense turmoil, beginning in 1972. There was widespread expectation in the Church that 1972 would signal the beginning of God's kingdom in a time of disaster and turmoil and the necessity of God's true church to flee into hiding. That expectation was unfulfilled. Then Garner Ted Armstrong left the air in unexplained circumstances, only to reappear four months later. In 1973 the Church reorganized at the regional level. It announced a new policy of openness and, for the first time, offered *The*

Good News, a second periodical formerly issued only to members, to nonmembers.

Then in 1974 the Church was shaken by a massive scandal. Garner Ted Armstrong was charged with multiple counts of sexual improprieties. Added to the scandal was an intense internal theological conflict over the dating of Pentecost and the marriage of divorced members. A number of ministers resigned and began several independent churches, including the Associated Churches of God, the Twentieth Century Church of God, the Church of God, the Eternal, and the Foundation for Biblical Research. The exodus of the ministers and their supporters did little to decrease the controversy. A group of former members in Pasadena attacked the Church through a new periodical, *The Ambassador Report*, originally *The Ambassador Review*, claiming continued unresolved leadership problems.

Much of the continued controversy within the Church centered upon the person of lawyer Stanley Rader, a nonmember who was nevertheless managing much of the Church's business. Eventually, he and Garner Ted, at the time Armstrong's designated successor, openly clashed, their arguments being resolved only when Garner Ted left the Church in 1978 to begin the Church of God International. In the midst of this conflict, his father announced his marriage to a young divorcée (who he would, in turn, divorce in 1984).

Relative quiet did not return to the Church until 1980. In 1978, a group of former members filed suit against Rader and a number of the Church leaders on behalf of the Church, claiming fiscal mismanagement. The Church, defined by the state's attorney and the court as a "public trust," was placed under a temporary court-ordered receivership, which was only lifted when the California legislature passed a law against the state's movement on an ecclesiastical body in such a manner.

Beliefs and Practices

The Worldwide Church of God grew out of the Seventh Day Church of God and accepts many of its basic teachings. It considers the Bible to be the infallible Word of God. Following commonly accepted Adventist teaching, the Church affirms God the Creator and Father and the divinity of Christ but denies the Trinity. The Holy Spirit is God's power, shared by Christ and the Father, i.e., the family of God. Salvation is through faith in God and His son, Jesus Christ, who atoned for humankind's sins upon the cross. Baptism (by immersion), the annual memorial of the Lord's Supper, and foot washing (practiced in connection with the Lord's Supper) are ordinances.

The Worldwide Church of God also accepted the perspective on sabbatarianism held by the Seventh Day Church of God. It teaches that the Ten Commandments are God's eternal law and, as such, the keeping of the sabbath has never been abrogated. At the time of the Church's founding, Armstrong was among several Church of God ministers who felt that the Old Testament festivals should also be observed. It extended that belief into a keeping of all seven feasts (Cf. Leviticus 23)—Passover and the Days of Unleavened Bread, Pentecost, Trumpets, Atonement, Tabernacles, the Last Great Day and the First Day of the Sacred Year. In every country where the Church has a significant membership, feast grounds are designated where Church members gather to celebrate the Holy Days. Popular holidays such as Christmas, Easter, Valentine's Day, and Halloween are denounced as pagan. Evolution is also denounced as opposing Biblical teachings on creation.

Integral to Church beliefs is an understanding of the position and role of the Worldwide Church of God in history. That understanding originated in the second key doctrinal point that led to Armstrong's leaving the fellowship of the Church of God (Salem,WV)—his acceptance of British-Israelism. British-Israelism is the belief that the Anglo-Saxon people of Western Europe (and by extension the United States and the peoples of the British Commonwealth nations) are the literal descendants of the ten Northern (the so-called lost) tribes of ancient Israel. Great Britain and the United States, as the present tribes of Ephraim and Manasseh, respectively, have a special role in the inheritance of God's blessings and promises. Among the first books sent to people who receive *The Plain Truth* has been *The United States and British Commonwealth in Prophecy*, a detailed statement of the British-Israel perspective.

The Church has also adopted the dispensational view of the history of the Church of God from the Book of Revelation in which the seven churches of chapters two and three are identified as the seven church ages. The Worldwide Church is identified as the church at Philadelphia, which was to appear just before the "endtime" events described in the remainder of the Book of Revelation. The work of the

Philadelphian Church was supposed to occur in two nineteen-year cycles. The first was dated from the beginning of Armstrong's independent ministry in 1934; the second began in 1953 with the internationalizing of the work through the European radio program. It was widely held that in 1972 the Church would begin the tribulation and would have to flee the country to a place of safety. No significant event or move to refuge occurred in 1972, and the Church has since deemphasized the nineteen-year cycles.

Organization

During the split between the Stanberry and Salem factions of the Church of God, Armstrong sided with the Salem group, which denied any basis for democratic elections of Church leaders, believing instead that the correct method to choose leaders was by casting lots (Acts 1: 26). Armstrong moved toward an even more autocratic system. He saw himself as the chosen prophet and apostle of the Church in the last days, who had absolute authority in all matters, including the appointment and dismissal of ministers, the disfellowshipping of members, and the purchase and disposal of property.

The Church is administered through the national offices in Pasadena, California. Local churches are under a regional minister in the United States or a national director in foreign countries. Pastors are appointed from the national office. The national office also has control of the colleges, the several periodicals, the secular cultural programs, and the feast sites.

Current Status

Armstrong died in 1986. He was succeeded by Joseph William Tkach. Tkach had been ordained in the Church in 1963 and had emerged as a strong supporter of Armstrong during the era of turmoil through which the Church passed. He assumed the title of Pastor General. He is the Church's administrative head and editor-in-chief of *The Plain Truth*.

The Worldwide Church of God is headquartered in Pasadena, California, adjacent to the Ambassador College complex. By 1985, it had approximately 100,000 members worldwide. Most of the congregations meet in rented facilities and, as a rule, do not advertise locally, hence their presence is almost unknown within the communities in which they operate. Two Ambassador College campuses, one in Pasadena and one in Big Sandy, Texas, serve the membership. A third campus in England was recently sold. Feast sites, such as the ones in the Pocono Mountains of Pennsylvania and the Dells in Wisconsin, are located around the United States.

The Church publishes three international periodicals. *The Plain Truth* circulates in the millions and has several foreign-language editions (German, French, and Spanish). It is offered free to listeners of "The World Tomorrow" radio and television shows through ads in national periodicals and through displays at many public and business locations. *Youth*, as its name implies a magazine for teenagers, circulates beyond the Church's membership but to a lesser extent. Readers of these periodicals are asked to renew their free subscriptions annually. *The Worldwide News* is available to members only. Through the College, the Church also offers a free Bible Correspondence Course, which teaches basic church doctrine. Finally, the Church publishes numerous pamphlets which are offered free to readers of *The Plain Truth* and which spell out the Church's teachings and its approach to a variety of social concerns.

In the mid-1970s, Armstrong announced the formation of the Ambassador International Cultural Foundation, which had as its purpose the promotion of international understanding between peoples, and extended the work of the Church into secular areas. A magazine, *Quest*, was launched in 1978, but lasted only a few years. At the auditorium on the campus in Pasadena, the Foundation offers concerts and other nonchurch-related cultural programs to the general public. Though born in considerable controversy, the Foundation has built an impressive record of accomplishments through its many projects.

Controversy

The Worldwide Church of God became a matter of intense controversy as the Church programs appeared increasingly on radio and then television and as more and more people began to receive *The Plain Truth*. Other Church leaders opposed Armstrong's teaching which denied basic orthodox Christian doctrine (the Trinity), emphasized racial themes

(British-Israelism), and in general denounced mainline Christianity. By the late 1960s, substantial analyses with an accompanying denouncement of the Worldwide Church's teachings by Evangelical Christians began to appear.

Since 1972, the Church has moved from one intense controversy to another. The major upheavals of 1974 and 1978 caused many members and ministers to leave the Church, and they, in turn, released many confidential documents to the public. They revealed widespread opposition to the emphasis within the Church upon Armstrong's many foreign trips to meet with political leaders, the secular programs of the Foundation, the articles in *Quest* (many of which opposed Church teachings), and the leadership of Stanley Rader. Confusion erupted within the Church when doctrines on the keeping of Pentecost and the remarriage of divorced persons were revised. The large personal following of Garner Ted Armstrong left and joined his new organization.

Several ex-members such as former staff member Marion McNair, prominent minister John Robinson, and layman John Tuit, an active force behind the 1978 lawsuit, wrote books (all privately published) about their experiences with the Church denouncing its hypocrisy. Their charges centered upon the misuse of Church funds for secular programs and the enrichment of Armstrong, Rader, and other Church leaders. Both Tuit and Robinson also accused Armstrong of gross sexual improprieties.

The Worldwide Church of God has, as of the mid-1980s, outwardly recovered from the controversies of the past decades (including Armstrong's divorce from his second wife) and the loss of many key personnel. Membership lost during the height of the controversies (estimated at between 5,000 and 10,000) has been replaced by new converts, and the circulation of *The Plain Truth*, which had fallen drastically during the 1970s has resumed its earlier rate of growth. A number of new pamphlets have been published, and new editions of older ones released. The Church seems to have entered a period of relative tranquility, though those opposed to it, such as the staff of *The Ambassador Report*, continue to press their concerns.

Sources-Primary

Armstrong, Herbert W. *The Autobiography of Herbert W. Armstrong*. 2 vols. Pasadena, CA: Ambassador College, 1973.

——. *The United States and Britain in Prophecy*. Pasadena, CA: Worldwide Church of God, 1954, 1987. 53 pp.

Kelly, Ronald, and Peter Ditzel. *The Millennium and Beyond*. Pasadena, CA: Worldwide Church of God, 1990. 28 pp.

Recapturing True Values: The Story of the Worldwide Church of God. Pasadena, CA: Worldwide Church of God, 1989. 22 pp.

Stump, Keith W. *The History of Europe and the Church*. Pasadena, CA: Worldwide Church of God, 1984. 52 pp.

——. *The Middle East in Prophecy: Focus of End-Time Events*. Pasadena, CA: Worldwide Church of God, 1988. 36 pp.

Sources-Secondary

Bjorling, Joel. *The Churches of God Seventh Day: A Bibliography*. New York: Garland Publishing, 1987. 296 pp.

Hopkins, Joseph. *The Armstrong Empire*. Grand Rapids, MI: William B. Eerdmans Publishing Company, 1974. 304 pp.

McNair, Marion J. *Armstrongism: Religion . . . or Rip-off?* Orlando, FL: Pacific Charters, 1977. 339 pp.

Robinson, David. *Herbert Armstrong's Tangled Web*. Tulsa, OK: John Hadden Publishers, 1980. 283 pp.

Tuit, John. *The Truth Shall Make You Free*. Freehold Township, NJ: Truth Foundation, 1981. 307 pp.

III.

The New Age Movement

THE NEW AGE MOVEMENT

[*Note:* The New Age Movement differs considerably from the other groups treated in this volume. These other groups are cohesive religious communities with fairly recognizable boundaries and a unified organization. The New Age Movement is a religious-social movement with somewhat vague boundaries. It consists of groups and individuals who, more or less, share its basic vision. Several of the new religions considered elsewhere in this volume, such as the Sikh Dharma and the Church Universal and Triumphant, have been active participants, while others such as Jehovah's Witnesses and the Christian Foundation have just as actively opposed it. The movement entered the mass consciousness during the 1980s and has become an important force in presenting alternative religious ideas to Westerners by providing a forum for a wide variety of metaphysical, occult, and Eastern mystical spirituality.]

Origins

During the 1970s, religious observers became aware of a diverse new social and religious movement whose most visible proponents were teachers of Eastern and mystical-occult philosophies. Ira Friedlander, an early sympathetic observer, described it thusly,

> A great spiritual energy has been moved to this country and holy men of the East are following it, and, of course, they bring the Light within them to become our mirrors. They establish centers or ashrams and reconfirm the spiritual centers within ourselves. They plant the seeds of inner peace with their divine grace, which remains and nourishes like a

good rain that falls on fertile soil; long after the rain has gone, the seed in the soil continues to grow.

The New Age Movement, as it came to be called, grew on what many had perceived to be a great spiritual hunger in the West. David Vaughn, whose *A Faith for the New Age* (1967) was one of the harbingers of the Movement, saw the unmet religious need and yet reflected, ". . . this widespread spiritual hunger is symptomatic not of a healthy, virile Church, but of conditions of famine accompanying volcanic eruptions and earthquakes in the ecclesiastical domain."

Western society has periodically experienced widespread religious hunger accompanied by denunciations of the Church as dead, formal, and spiritually bankrupt. However, for the first time in many centuries, that spiritual hunger coincided with the presence of a number of Eastern religious teachers and a new wave of sophisticated mystical-occult teachers, many with a strong Eastern flavor to their teaching, prepared to feed the general public. The New Age Movement was and is the attempt to find the social, religious, political, and cultural convergence between the new Eastern and mystical religions and the religious disenchantment of many Westerners. While some who explored the new spiritual systems which emerged in the 1960s became members of one particular group, others found in the ferment a transformative vision of a new world which transcended the limitations of any particular culture or religion or political system and surpassed the outmoded thought forms of old world theologies and beliefs. That transformative vision ties together the bewildering diversity which constitutes the New Age Movement and gives the Movement its name.

Historic Background and Origin

The original stirrings which became the New Age Movement can be traced to Great Britain. While the hope of a New Age can be traced within occult groups at least back to the era of the French Revolution, it had found a most welcome home and had been particularly nourished with the Theosophical movement. Theosophy founder H. P. Blavatsky had first articulated the idea of a New Age and began to prepare her students to facilitate its arrival. However, by the 1960s there had arisen in Great Britain a number of what were termed "Light" groups, independent Theosophical groups which began to "network" around a common vision of a coming New Age and their role of facilitating the coming of the New Age by acting as channels of spiritual light.

This fresh vision of the New Age was hammered out through the 1960s and first shared internationally by Anthony Brooke, head of the Universal Foundation who traveled the world during the late 1960s and early 1970s lecturing to like-minded organizations. Through his (and others) efforts, the New Age was planted in North America, Australia and New Zealand, South Africa, and continental Europe. Within a very short time an international network was established and the New Age settled in to begin a slow process of growth through the 1970s and early 1980s.

The New Age Movement in the United States can best be dated from 1971. By that year, British teachers had brought their new vision across the Atlantic, Eastern teachers had opened ashrams and centers, books had been published representing the various strains of New Age concern, and a self-conscious social movement began to emerge. *East-West Journal* (now *Natural Health*), possibly the first national periodical to focus the issues of the New Age Movement, was begun by a Boston macrobiotic community, and the first popular book representative of the Movement appeared: *Be Here Now* by Baba Ram Dass. The first networks, a typical New Age organizational form, were created, and in 1972, the first national New Age directories were published: Ira Friedlander's *Year One Catalog* and the first edition of the *Spiritual Community Guide*. Even prior to the Movement, in the 1960s, small groups in various communities began to call themselves "new age" and adopt some of the elements which would in the 1970s characterize the Movement. For example, as early as 1967 Leland Stewart of Northridge, California, had captured much of the essence of the Movement in his International Cooperation Council and its ideal of a new civilization built on "unity in diversity."

The New Age Movement did not develop *de novo*, however; it had many precursors. Its roots can be clearly seen in previous attempts to find points of convergence between East and West. In the United States, possibly the first movement to synthesize the newly discovered wisdom of the East with Western thought was Transcendentalism. Growing out of the religious dissent in New England, the early Transcendentalists took the recently translated holy books of Hinduism and created a uniquely American form of mysticism. Transcendentalism was the first substantial religious movement in North America with a prominent Asian component. Its emergence signaled the arrival of an alternative religious tradition in America which has grown up and existed beside the more prominent churchly and sectarian Christian bodies. This alternative tradition valued mysticism and Eastern religious wisdom, with which it integrated Western values, particularly individualism and success orientation.

Transcendentalism passed its emphases upon mystical experience and Eastern religion to several popular movements: Spiritualism, Theosophy, New Thought, and Christian Science. Within these popular movements, Transcendentalism became wedded to Western occult thought and the new mental healing movement which had been brought to America by the disciples of Franz Mesmer. By the end of the nineteenth century, the alternative religious tradition had grown and splintered into various factions, each of which possessed its own national organization. During the twentieth century, both Spiritualism and New Thought divided periodically, thus producing numerous new organizations, several of which became national in scope. The membership of these groups supplied the initial support for the New Age vision once it was presented to them.

While Westerners were discovering and appropriating Eastern religious thought, Eastern religion itself was reeling under the impact of an imposed Western government and the Christian missionary movement which came with it. The Hindu Renaissance represented a significant adaptation to the Western critique of Hindu polytheism and village religion. It put forth what might be thought of as a Protestant Hinduism stripped of the deities and the accretions of traditional Indian religion so offensive to Western monotheists. It transformed the ashram, traditionally the small isolated residence of a guru, into communal structure analogous to a Christian congregation. It sought to appropriate the knowledge of the West and valued the opinion of Western religious leaders. Members of the Brahmo Samaj aligned themselves with the Unitarians. Ramakrishna had visions of the Blessed Virgin Mary. Swamis Vivekananda and Yogananda, two outstanding products of the Renaissance, were the first to plant Hinduism in America.

Emerging as a prime example of the Western alternative religious tradition, Theosophy stepped into the midst of the Hindu Renaissance when its founders, Madame H. P. Blavatsky and Col. Henry S. Olcott, moved to India in 1878. Once settled, the Theosophical Society began a conscious attempt to inform its members and the general public about Eastern wisdom and to integrate Eastern thought into Western life. The first book on Hinduism written in English not merely to inform but to "convert" Westerners to Hinduism, *Nature's Finer Forces* by Rama Prasad, was published in 1890 by the Theosophical Publishing House. Blavatsky and the Society standardized the language concerning what we now call reincarnation and became the major conduit of passing the concept to the West.

The classic theosophical statement of what has come to be an essential component of the New Age perspective is Bhagaven Das' *The Essential Unity of All Religions* (1932). Das argued for the "Truth of essential Unity in superficial Diversity" of religions. He demanded the emphasis on the unity of religions as a means to further world peace. He spent over 500 pages defining the elements of Universal Religion and saw its teaching as an imperative.

Theosophy, as did Spiritualism and New Thought, splintered into a number of factions after the death of Blavatsky. Early in the twentieth century, Alice Bailey left the Society to found the Arcane School, and during the 1930s Guy Ballard founded the "I AM" Activity. Each of these groups has further subdivided, producing scores of new organizations.

While propounding the vision of the essential unity of religion, theosophists also proposed the vision of a coming new world religious teacher who would teach the nations the new truth which was being revealed to theosophical leaders by the spiritual masters. Under the leadership of Annie Besant, Jiddu Krishnamurti was nominated as the embodiment of the teacher. After assuming the role for several years, he disassociated himself from Besant and the Society and became a teacher on his own. Alice Bailey gave impetus to the vision in her book, the *Reappearance of the Christ* (1948), and like Besant, equated the coming of the world teacher with the several prophesied future religious events, the second coming of Christ, and the return of the Buddhist bodhisattva Maitreya.

Another component of a convergence of Eastern and Western thought was the growth of the study of world religion in Western scholarly circles. Beginning in the nineteenth century, scholars stripped away many of the derogatory stereotypes of Eastern religions. Among the visible results of the scholarly enterprise has been the creation of a number of interfaith organizations and conferences, possibly the first being the World Parliament of Religions sponsored by the League of Liberal Churchmen in Chicago in 1893. This conference introduced most Eastern religions to the United States and led to the establishment of the first Hindu, Buddhist, and Islamic organizations. The convergence of religions has been a continued concern of the interfaith cooperatives.

The Coming of the New Age

When the New Age began to be announced in the early 1970s, there was already in place a large audience for its message, the members and constituencies of the several hundred alternative religions which had grown and spread since the mid-1800s. However, in 1965 a significant new factor, crucial for the emergence of the New Age Movement, appeared. In that year, the Asian immigration exclusion acts which had been in effect since the early twentieth century were repealed, and Asian and Middle Eastern countries were put on the same immigration quotas which had always been given to Europe. Annually, tens of thousands of Asians have moved to the United States. Where for decades only a trickle of Asian religious teachers came to America, and those primarily to serve Asian ethnic congregations, since 1965 numerous teachers have either moved to America or taken advantage of generous visa regulations to build followings in the United States. Many of these teachers came not to work within the new Asian-American communities but to spread their teaching among Westerners. The last days of the 1960s saw the launching of a major missionary thrust by the Eastern religions toward the West. It has not been centrally coordinated but has grown out of a popular idea within all the religious communities in Asia from Japan to India: the West is ready for and in need of the wisdom which the East possesses.

Once the idea of the New Age was articulated, the early exponents began to build the networks which have become so definitive of New Age organizational priorities. The early directories listed those groups and organizations seen to be aligned at least partially. They included centers of the various occult, Eastern, and mystical religions, health food stores, metaphysical book stores, yoga teachers, parapsychology research organizations, psychic development interest groups, communes, and alternative health care facilities. The early directories showed little discrimination and tended to include names of groups which appeared to offer any alternative spirituality, even traditional Christian groups with unusual names.

Once the national networks were defined and a broad community who accepted the basic vision of the Movement evolved, numerous services facilitated the Movement's development. Most important in any decentralized movement, periodicals tied the diverse groups and individuals across the country together and kept the Movement informed. The most important included *The New Age Journal* (created by former staff members from *East-West Journal*); *New Realities* (formerly *Psychic*); *Yoga Journal*; and *Body, Mind, and Spirit* (formerly *Psychic Guide*). Many periodicals also served particular Eastern and occult groups, and newsletters arose whose circulation was limited to a single metropolitan area or one organization's membership. In the early 1970s in San Francisco, *Common Ground* appeared as a directory of local New Age activities and services. Its format was copied in other cities and today almost every urban area in America has one or more similar periodicals which go under names such as *Chicago's New Spirit, Free Spirit* (New York City), *New Frontier* (Philadelphia), and *New Texas* (Austin). *Whole Life Times*, which copied *Common Ground's* format but has been primarily concerned with alternative health networks, appears in several local editions and has spurred similar periodicals such as *Organica* (Tampa) and *Wholistic Living* (San Diego).

As the Movement progressed through the 1970s, leading spokespersons began to appear. Baba Ram Dass was the first recognized national exponent of New Age consciousness. A former professor of psychology at Harvard, the Jewish-born Richard Alpert accompanied his colleague Timothy Leary through a period of experimentation with psychedelic drugs before going to India and finding his guru. He reappeared as Baba Ram Dass, a guru in his own right, just as the New Age was being announced. His excellent Western academic background as transformed by his new found Eastern faith made him the perfect symbol of the New Age. The Movement consumed his popular books: *The Only Dance There Is* (1973); *Grist for the Mill* (1976); *Journey of Awakening* (1978), and *Miracle of Love* (1979). He was joined by other popular figures, some of whom were, like himself, leaders of their own alternative religious movements: Kirpal Singh, Yogi Bhajan, Pir Vilayat Khan, Reb Zalman Schachter-Shalomi, Swami Kriyananda, Sun Bear, Swami Muktananda, and Rabbi Joseph Gelberman, to mention a few.

The Movement also brought forth teachers who were not just aligned to New Age Ideals but who founded or led organizations with a primary commitment to the New Age. Most prominent among these is Marilyn Ferguson of Interface Press, editor of *Brain/Mind Bulletin* and *Leading Edge Bulletin*. Ferguson jumped into prominence with her visionary survey of the Movement, *The Aquarian Conspiracy* (1980), which is the most commonly accepted statement of Movement ideals and goals.

David Spangler is possibly the least known of the major spokespersons for the Movement. After three years as co-director of the Scottish community at Findhorn, he returned to the United States and founded the Lorian Association, a New Age community near Madison, Wisconsin. His early volume, *Revelation, the Birth of a New Age* (1976), is one of the earlier systematic statements of New Age goals and perspectives. His subsequent volumes, possibly more than any set of writings, reflect the broad concerns and course of the movement through the years. By the end of the 1970s, Ram Dass, Ferguson, and Spangler were joined by other popular New Age teachers including Patricia Sun, George Leonard, Jean Houston, Norman Shealy, Irving Oyle, and Sam Keen.

The 1975 publication of *A Course in Miracles* by the newly formed Foundation for Inner Peace thrust Judith Skutch, an early New Age advocate in New York City, into the spotlight. The multi-volume *Course*, a simple restatement of New Thought metaphysics using the metaphor of "miracles," became a very popular study book throughout New Age circles, and several hundred groups were founded across North America during its first decade in print. As much as anything, the *Course* launched a renewed interest in mediumship, recast as "channeling" by the New Age. In the wake of the interest created by the *Course*, several new mediums appeared claiming to "channel" wise masters. The *Course* had been channeled by Helen Schucman, psychiatrist at Presbyterian Hospital, who claimed the source of the text to be the biblical Christ. During the 1980s, several new channels would come to prominence. Frank Alper, a longtime Spiritualist medium emerged as a channel of several entities claiming to be from Atlantis. They laid out the basic ideas on the power and use of crystals. Alper's channeling became the ideological basis for New Age interest in crystals. Joining Alper in popularity was J. Z. Knight, who channels an entity named Ramtha; Jach Pursel, who channels Lazaris; Ruth Montgomery, who developed the idea of walk-ins (entities which took over bodies of people ready to end their earthly existence), and Penny Torres, who channels Mafu.

Preferring cooperation to competition, New Age exponents tried several social structures to embody their ideals. Communes were a natural option, and some older communes were among the first groups to identify with the New Age perspective. Prominent among these communes are the Lama Foundation (NM), the Renaissance Community (MA) and Stelle Community (IL). Many of the Eastern teachers promoted communal living, and some nurtured such communities. Prominent among these communes are Sirius, founded by some former residents of Findhorn; the Abode of the Message, founded by Pir Vilayat Khan of the Sufi Order; and the Ananda Cooperative Community of Swami Kriyananda.

The most important elements in the New Age Movement are the many individuals, organizations, and businesses which have arisen to facilitate the process of transformation which is at the heart of the New Age vision. Every metropolitan area has scores of individuals who teach transformational techniques from meditation to the martial arts or who practice the various forms of alternative medicine, body therapies, and psychological processes. Organizations, primarily of a local and frequently ephemeral nature, support the practitioners and provide a point of contact between those seeking and those providing services. Particularly in the field of health, national professional and referral associations have arisen to bring some order to the competition among numerous forms of therapy (some of dubious value) offered by individuals with varying qualifications. Among the most prominent are the American Holistic Medical Association (Washington, D.C.) and the Association for Holistic Health (San Diego). Numerous businesses have also arisen which serve the New Age community through their distribution of a wide range of New Age products from yoga mats and meditation cushions to macrobiotic cookwear, health foods, natural vitamins, Oriental art, and incense. Many of these businesses are also trying to be a model of the New Age for the business community and embody New Age principles in the organization of their business.

The New Age Vision

The New Age Movement is among the most difficult of the recently prominent religious groups to grasp, primarily because it is a movement built much more around a vision and an experience rather than doctrines or a belief system. A decentralized movement, it entertains contradictory ideas, and among its more important spokespersons are people who voice opinions completely unacceptable to the Movement as a whole. Thus, it is easier to understand in terms of its ideals and goals rather than the beliefs to which it adheres.

The central vision of the New Age is one of radical mystical transformation on an individual level. It involves an awakening to such new realities as a discovery of psychic abilities, the experience of a physical or psychological healing, the emergence of new potentials within oneself, an intimate experience within a community, or the acceptance of a new picture of the universe. The essence of the New Age is the imposition of that personal vision onto society and the world. Thus, the New Age is ultimately a vision of a world transformed, a heaven on earth, a society in which the problems of today are overcome and a new existence emerges. There is a wide range of opinion about the nature of the New Age and the means of bringing it about, but each individual's personal experience of transformation gives the Movement its vitality.

The power to bring about the necessary transformation of both individuals and society comes from universal energy. Members of the New Age Movement assume the existence of a basic energy that is different from the more recognized forms of energy (heat, light, etc.) and undergirds and permeates all existence. This energy goes by many names—prana, mana, odic force, orgone energy, holy spirit, the ch'i, the healing force. It is the force believed to cause psychic healing. It is the force released in various forms of meditation and body therapies which energize the individual mentally and physically. It is the force passed between individuals in the expressions of love.

The fact that the Movement is based on the experience of radical transformation and universal energy does not deny the presence of concepts and ideas which members of the Movement affirm. Rather, this fact emphasizes the secondary role such ideas have and the nondoctrinaire approach taken toward the ideological framework of the Movement. Affirmation of particular propositions or beliefs is not a criteria for participation in or acceptance by the Movement, and members in good standing may vocally disagree with popular concepts without fear of chastisement or alienation.

The variety of ideas and goals that exist in the Movement have great appeal for some people. In the New Age, it is believed, people will recognize one universal religion. While that one religion will assume many different forms and draw from all the present religious traditions, the same mystical faith will underlie each no matter what its label (Christian or Buddhist). This faith finds inspiration in nature and the changing seasons and the growth and development of individuals through the common cycles of life. It also places great emphasis upon self-knowledge, inner exploration, and the participation in a continual transformative process begun in that initial transformation that led the individual to first identify him or herself as a New Age person.

The emphasis upon continual transformation will lead New Age persons on a *sadhana*, a spiritual path. For some that will mean commitment for a period or a lifetime to the practices taught by a single spiritual teacher. Others will continually sample transformative practices, picking and choosing from them, and thus develop a very individualized and constantly changing sadhana.

Since few individuals complete their sadhana in one lifetime, the commonly accepted belief of reincarnation and karma provides a long-term framework in which to view individual spiritual progression. Individuals will over a period of successive lifetimes in a physical body (reincarnation) accomplish their moral and spiritual development as they live out the consequences of prior actions from this life and previous ones. The law of karma, the rule by which the universe returns rewards and punishment, provides the authority for moral action. Immoral action produces a more or less exacting set of unpleasant consequences on its perpetrator (i.e., bad karma).

The sadhana will have as its goal a mystical consciousness or awareness (frequently called high consciousness, self-realization, Christ consciousness, or New Age awareness). To have a higher consciousness is to be aware of the universal energy which undergirds existence and of the metaphysical unity which underlies the appearance of diversity. Most (but not all) New Agers identify God with that Ultimate Unifying Principle which binds the whole together and the Power which gives it a dynamic. Thus some New Agers are pantheists, identifying God and the world as one reality. Using metaphysical speculations derived from Einstein's theory of matter, they will occasionally reduce all reality to energy. Others tend toward a form of dualism which sees spiritual reality as ultimately good and real, and matter as the evil which must be left behind in the spiritual-mystical life.

People participate in God as individualized manifestations of that Ultimate Unifying Principle and as channels of the universal energy to the world. Jesus, and the other significant religious teachers such as Buddha or Krishna, were particularly transparent bearers of the Divine, or Christ Principle. Such teachers appear regularly throughout history to illustrate the aware (fully realized) life, to teach individuals the goal of awareness, and to train them in particular techniques (the elements of the sadhana) to reach the awareness of their own Divinity. Some New Age people see the need to find a living guru who is a fully realized teacher. When such is found, he or she will be judged upon his or her perceived awareness (enlightenment) rather than on more mundane questions of his or her particular religious tradition, personal behavior (until it becomes scandalous or outrageous), or teaching idiosyncrasies.

Worship within the New Age Movement finds its typical expression in meditation and various transformative practices taught by the different spiritual teachers or gurus (to whom followers and critics will ascribe various levels of self-awareness). On the social level the Movement is most clearly expressed in the Universal Worship of the Sufi Order, which honors all religions while seeking to find the consciousness and understanding of the cosmos which underlie each one, and in the celebrations of those times which all the major religions seem to commemorate. For example, in late December, Christmas, Hanukkah, and Yule converge. Many people within the New Age Movement, primarily those with a Theosophical background, see the necessity of a particular person, a world teacher, a new avatar of the status of Jesus or Gautama Buddha, who will be a catalyst to bring about the New Age. The students of Alice Bailey have been energetic advocates of this position and have circulated uncounted thousands of copies of a prayer, "The Great Invocation," which calls for this avatar's appearance.

> From the point of Light within the Mind of God
> Let light stream forth into the minds of men.
> Let light descend on Earth.

> From the point of Love within the Heart of God
> Let love stream forth into the hearts of men.
> May Christ return to Earth.

From the centre where the will of God is known
Let purpose guide the little wills of men—
The purpose which the Masters know and serve.

From the centre which we call the race of men
Let the Plan of Love and Light work out.
And may it seal the door where evil dwells.

Let Light and Love and Power restore the Plan to Earth.

Not only will there be one universal religion recognized in the New Age, but there will be an allegiance to the planet and the human race which will supersede loyalties to the more limited groupings of clan, nation, race, or religion. This commitment to One World finds a typical expression in communes. Just as personal transformation is the symbol of social transformation, communes are the models of the new planetary society. They demonstrate the values of cooperation and sharing and the possibility of individual acceptance within an artificially created community.

Allegiance to the planet undergirds many new concerns (concerns also shared by many people in no way connected with the Movement): ecology, peace, natural foods and healing processes, humanizing technology, cooperative models of living, overcoming hunger, and global politics. While some leaders within the New Age community hold well-known and definite opinions on these issues, the Movement as a whole can be said only to share a focus and concern for these issues, which they see as planetary problems to be overcome during the transformation into the New Age. The concern with the planet and the development of networks to engage in social change has become a significant factor separating New Age people from more traditional occultists who tended to avoid social activism as irrelevant to spiritual development.

New Age people separate themselves from what is termed "fortune-telling," the trivialization of various occult techniques to catch a glimpse of the mundane future. Some traditional occult practices are accepted and used by many New Age people as tools in the acquisition of greater awareness. Most New Agers do not hesitate to consult astrologers, tarot card readers, and professional psychics. They will tend to avoid Spiritualist mediums who consult the dead, though they have little difficulty with mediumistic persons who are in contact with higher spirit teachers (conceived as ascended masters, the great white brotherhood, or the medium's own higher self). Such spiritual teachers do not establish contact with deceased loved ones; they limit themselves to religious-metaphysical teachings.

Current Status

The New Age grew slowly through the 1970s and began to build up a head of steam through the first half of the 1980s. Still, prior to 1987, few people outside of the metaphysical-occult community had heard of it. However, in the fall of 1987, the film version of actress Shirley MacLaine's autobiographical *Out on a Limb* aired in prime time. It was followed a few months later by *Time* magazine doing a cover story on the New Age. All of a sudden it was on the public agenda. What had been a movement counting its adherents in the thousands became the home of several million people who discovered that they had some ideological agreements with the New Age or that they were in need of some of the services provided by the New Age (from psychic readings to assistance with health problems). New Age sections appeared in secular bookstores and specialized New Age bookstores opened in most North American cities. Through the rest of the decade interest peaked.

If interest peaked, so did criticism, especially from Evangelical Christians. In 1983, lawyer turned religious writer Constance Cumbey published an attack upon the New Age Movement through a little-known publishing house. The book became an unexpected best-seller within the Evangelical Christian community. *Hidden Dangers of the Rainbow* developed the idea of a gigantic conspiracy behind the New Age Movement and called Christians to organize to fight it. The book caught the older counter-cult movement unprepared, and by the time it could react, Cumbey had been established as the Christian spokesperson on the New Age.

The counter-cult movement quickly recovered, and within a few years the New Age Movement had become the priority item on its agenda. Cumbey had, however, not only gotten the jump on the counter-cultists, but her ideas brought dissension to their ranks. Many, while equally opposed to the New Age, disagreed with her conspiracy theories and openly said so. The disagreements deepened as Cumbey began to accuse various Christian organizations of being New Age fellow travelers.

As the numerous Christian titles on the New Age appeared, they tended to take one side or another in the controversy.

Then almost as quickly as the New Age Movement came, signs of fading have appeared. Publishers began to discontinue "New Age" imprints. Attendance at New Age events began to creep downward. The first voices arose to declare the New Age Movement dead, even though it still has much life left in it.

Two factors have contributed to the decline of the New Age. While there is little noticeable response by the New Age Movement to the Christian anti-New Age literature, the secular press has had a significant effect upon it. Most importantly, the secular media has tended to emphasize the more questionable aspects of the Movement and hold up to ridicule such phenomena as channeling, crystals, and the leadership provided by media stars, especially Shirley MacLaine, who started leading workshops and authoring New Age textbooks soon after *Out on a Limb* appeared.

Possibly of even greater significance in the decline of the Movement has been the relinquishing of the hope of bringing in a New Age in this generation. Older leaders in the Movement have failed to see any significant changes in society that might suggest that a cultural transformation is occurring. As David Spangler, one of the Movement's architects stated in 1988, "To expect a magical transformation that will end history as we know it and start a whole new chapter of human experience is to misunderstand what the new age is all about and how it works."

In the wake of the popularization of crystals and channeling, serious leaders in the Movement were openly beginning to question their participation. By the beginning of the 1990s the leadership were speaking the Movement's epitaphs, but rather than walking away from it they were regrouping and searching for a new name to call the revamped Movement shorn of its emphasis upon the more superficial and faddish aspects. Such a reorientation has called for a reconsideration of essential values. In a March/April 1991 editorial, Paul Zuromski, publisher of *Body, Mind, Spirit*, called for the abandonment of the label New Age. With that issue, he changed the name of the subtitle of his magazine from "Your New Age Information Resource," to "Tools for Creating a Richer More Fulfilling Life." He had no new name to replace "New Age," and suggested none is needed. A variety of names which suggest the variety of changes needed by individuals and promoted by the former New Age is sufficient.

At this point it is felt that several million people have been directly involved in the New Age Movement. However, many more share New Age ideas and have participated in New Age activities. Over 20 percent of the population have reported that they believe in reincarnation and astrology. About the same number have meditated. Even more report having seen a ghost and/or having a psychic experience. The New Age Movement has brought to visibility a large spectrum of the American community who adhered to what have been considered nonconventional practice. The question which arises, of course, when as many people meditate as go to mass, when more people identify with astrology than with the Baptist church, and when far more people believe in astrology than attend the Methodist, Episcopal, Presbyterian, and Congregational churches combined, can we still think of the New Age as a fringe phenomenon? Has not the occult joined the mainstream?

Thus as the New Age as a movement fades through the 1990s, attention should be directed to its many components: the metaphysical churches, the health food stores, the offices of alternative health practitioners and the variety of growth centers. Through the many older organizations which have identified with the New Age and the many new organizations and businesses created by it, the substance of the New Age will continue into the indefinite future. The Movement has brought hundreds of thousands of people to openly identify with its alternative perspective and millions more to profess adherence to at least parts of it. While by the end of the century few may call themselves New Agers, the metaphysical occult milieu in the West, with a new, more positive image, seems destined to force its way forward to take its place beside the more established communities.

Sources-Primary

Bailey, Alice. *The Reappearance of the Christ.* New York: Lucis Publishing Company, 1948. 191 pp.

Brooke, Anthony. *Towards Human Unity.* London: Mitre Press, 1976. 133 pp.

Ferguson, Marilyn. *The Aquarian Conspiracy*. Los Angeles: J. P. Tarcher, 1980. 448 pp.

Heussenstamm, Karl. *Towards a Maitreyan Revolution*. Northridge, CA: International Cooperation Council, 1974. 267 pp.

Perrone, Ed. *Astrology: A New Age Guide*. Wheaton, IL: Theosophical Publishing House, 1983. 228 pp.

Ram Dass, Baba. *Be Here Now*. San Christobal, NM: Lama Foundation, 1971.

Satin, Mark. *New Age Politics: Healing Self and Society*. New York: Dell, 1979. 349 pp.

Spangler, David. *Emergence: The Rebirth of the Sacred*. New York: Dell, 1984. 176 pp.

—————. *Festivals for the New Age*. Forres, Scotland: Findhorn Foundation, 1975. 92 pp.

—————. *Revelation, the Birth of a New Age*. San Francisco: The Rainbow Bridge, 1976. 256 pp.

—————. *Towards a Planetary Vision*. Forres, Scotland: Findhorn Foundation, 1977. 151 pp.

Trevelyan, George. *A Vision of the Aquarian Age*. Walpole, NH: Stillpoint Publishing, 1984. 171 pp.

Vaughn, David. *A Faith for the New Age*. London: Regency Press, 1967. 160 pp.

Sources-Secondary

Basil, Robert, ed. *Not Necessarily the New Age*. Buffalo, NY: Prometheus Books, 1988. 395 pp.

Judah, J. Stillson. *The History and Philosophy of the Metaphysical Movements in America*. Philadelphia: Westminster Press, 1967. 317 pp.

Kautz, William, and Melanie Branon. *Channeling: The Intuitive Connection*. San Francisco: Harper & Row, 1987. 179 pp.

Klimo, Jon. *Channeling.* Los Angeles: Jeremy P. Tarcher, 1987. 304 pp.

Melton, J. Gordon, Jerry Clark, and Aidan A. Kelly. *New Age Encyclopedia.* Detroit, MI: Gale Research, 1990. 568 pp. Paperback edition as: *New Age Almanac.* Detroit: Visible Ink, 1991. 479 pp.

Sources-Christian

Chandler, Russell. *Understanding the New Age.* Dallas, TX: Word Books, 1988. 360 pp.

Cumbey, Constance. *The Hidden Dangers of the Rainbow.* Shreveport, LA: Huntington House, 1983. 268 pp.

Grootius, Douglas. *Confronting the New Age.* Downers Grove, IL: InterVarsity Press, 1986. 194 pp.

Hoyt, Karen. *The New Age Rage.* Old Tappan, NJ: Fleming H. Revell Company, 1987. 263 pp.

IV.

The Newer Cults

A. CHRISTIAN FOUNDATION

Also known as the Music Square Church, Holiness Tabernacle Church, and the Holy Alamo Christian Church, the Christian Foundation dates to the beginning of what became known as the Jesus People Movement in the early 1970s. As one of the original groups working among the street people who emerged in California urban centers in the later 1960s, the Foundation moved on to become a large, successful Evangelical Christian body. However, beginning with attacks in the late 1980s, the Foundation has been all but destroyed, and its future (as of the beginning of 1992) is very much in doubt.

Founders

The Christian Foundation was incorporated in 1969 by Susan and Tony Alamo. Susan, born Edith Opal Horn in Arkansas, came to California to begin a singing career under the name Susan Fleetwood. Though her musical efforts did not succeed, she married, converted to Evangelical Christianity, and began informally to preach and teach. In 1964 she founded the short-lived Susan Lipowitz Foundation (Lipowitz being her married name).

Tony Alamo was born Bernie Lazar Hoffman in a Romanian Jewish family in Missouri. He journeyed to California as a young man, changed his name, and became involved in show business as a singer and promoter. In 1964, he had a most remarkable experience in the midst of a business meeting. He became deaf to his normal surroundings, and he heard a voice say to him, "I am the Lord thy God. Stand up on your feet and tell the people in this room that Jesus Christ is coming back to earth, or thou shalt surely die."

Shortly after the experience he sought out Susan who became his Bible teacher. Eventually they were married and in the late 1960s began to evangelize among the street people in Hollywood. They moved into a house six blocks from Sunset Strip and obtained a brightly painted bus. They and their early converts "witnessed" on the street, and the bus carried interested people to the services each evening at the house. Their ministry was formally incorporated in January 1969. In 1970 they purchased a ranch near Saugus, about forty miles from Los Angeles, and soon the bus was carrying people to the ranch, converted into a camp retreat, for evening meetings. Of the many who attended the services, several hundred decided to stay and become full-time members and workers in the Foundation's ministry.

Soon after the move to Saugus, the Foundation became the target of the growing militant anti-cult movement which accused the group of improper recruiting techniques and brainwashing. If that was not enough, Susan realized that she had cancer. In 1973 the Alamos moved to Dyer, Arkansas, Susan's childhood home. Several of the Foundation members joined them. In 1974 they opened a small clothing shop in Nashville, Tennessee. The favorable climate in Arkansas combined with the growing hostility of the anti-cultists in California precipitated the movement of the headquarters and most of the members of the Foundation to Arkansas. Several businesses were purchased, and the expanding shop in Nashville supplied an economic base for the operation.

It did not take long for the anti-cult movement to follow the Alamos to Arkansas. The various businesses operated to support the Foundation became the focus of criticism and eventually led the government to enter the case. In the midst of the controversy, in 1982 Susan died. She was interred in a mausoleum at Dyer.

Beliefs

The Christian Foundation is conservative evangelical Christian. It has followed traditional Protestant teaching and not engaged in any doctrinal innovation.

It teaches that

> Jesus Christ is the Son of the living God, that he died on the
> cross and shed his blood for our sins, that he rose from the
> dead, ascended into the heavens, and took his seat beside God
> the Father, becoming the high priest, and the appropriation
> (propitiation?) for our sins. We believe that Christ is alive.
> That he lives forevermore and is coming back to earth very
> soon. We believe, as the Bible says, that you must be born
> again. It is a commandment of God that we repent of our sins
> and ask Christ to come into our hearts and make us a new
> creature, that old things must pass away and all things, all
> lives, become new in him.

The King James Version of the Bible is preferred to both the
Revised Standard Version and the Today's English Version as the latter
attack the Virgin Birth, the redemptive blood, and the deity of Christ.

The Foundation is against abortion and has frequently made
offers to pay for the delivery of any unwanted babies and to feed, clothe,
and house them after birth.

Current Status

The Foundation is headed by a three-person board which
includes Tony Alamo as its president. Through the 1980s, headquarters
of the Christian Foundation were at the Holiness Tabernacle in Dyer, six
miles east of Alma, Arkansas. Many of the members lived in houses
owned by the Foundation in Dyer and Alma. They operated several
businesses including a restaurant, service station, and clothing store; the
store in Nashville had grown into a large Western clothing outlet. Tony
also promoted country music in both Nashville and western Arkansas.

Members of the Foundation were totally supported by its
activities, and money from the businesses was used to support the total
program.

Besides the center in Saugus, California, churches were operated
in Omaha, Chicago, and Brooklyn, with mission centers in Miami,
Phoenix, and Tulsa. Each church held daily services, one each evening

and two on Sunday. Today members may still be found throughout the country doing missionary work, but local centers are extremely unstable. Besides the witnessing directed primarily to young adults and street people, members had developed a program of visitation to nursing and retirement homes.

Controversy

The militant anti-cult movement, which originated in the early 1970s in Southern California, directed its earliest efforts against several of the new Jesus People groups, and the Christian Foundation was among its initial targets. The Foundation attracted attention after the movement of its operations to Saugus. Critics charged that the Alamos would take unsuspecting young people to the isolated ranch and subject them to high-power conversion pressure. The accusations of deceit and brainwashing from the heyday of the Saugus center followed the Foundation to Arkansas where several attempts to deprogram members occurred.

With little success from the deprogramming attempts, the Foundation's enemies filed lawsuits charging the Foundation with holding members in "virtual slavery," in that members worked for the Foundation but received no wages and were forced to live in very poor conditions. While the civil suits did not bear direct fruit, the controversy led to the U.S. Department of Labor filing suit in 1977 demanding that the Foundation pay $15,500,000 in back wages to members of the group. When the suit was finally settled in 1985, the Foundation was ordered to pay minimum wages to those who work and had worked in the various Foundation businesses. Alamo remarried in December 1985, but a year later his new wife turned against him and accused him of dictatorial practices in attempts to control everything around him and beating her.

In the midst of the controversy, the Foundation gained new enemies as a result of its religious polemics. The group preached a strong anti-Catholicism which alienated it from the Roman Catholic Church. Both Evangelical Protestants and Jews came to the defense of the Roman Catholic Church after the widespread circulation of several strongly worded anti-Catholic tracts in the early 1980s. Alamo accused the Church of arranging the assassinations of Presidents Lincoln and Kennedy. The Jewish community had an additional reason for offense at the

Foundation, Alamo being an outspoken convert from Judaism to Christianity.

The settlement of the labor suit did not end the Foundation's legal problems. The IRS moved against the Foundation and in 1985 revoked its tax-exempt status and then moved against it for back taxes. It looked as if the Foundation was headed for a lengthy tax court battle. Then Alamo was accused of beating an 11-year-old boy at the Foundation's center in Saugus. Threatened with arrest, in 1988 he dropped out of sight, though he frequently appeared to have his picture taken with a celebrity or to call a talk show. As a result of his flight, charges mounted against him, and he was unable to defend the Foundation against civil actions aimed at stripping its assets.

In early 1991, the situation changed dramatically. On February 13, law enforcement agents seized the property in Arkansas. The store in Nashville, Tennessee, had already been seized. Within a week all of the residents left and Susan Alamo's body was taken from the mausoleum. In June, six former members of the Foundation won a $1.4 million lawsuit from the group. Finally in July, Alamo was arrested in Tampa, Florida. As of the end of 1991, he remains in custody awaiting trial.

With the seizure of the property, the membership scattered, and Alamo in jail, the future of the Foundation is in question. It is too early to count it out. The many members of the Foundation testify to lives changed by its ministry, and there have been strong professions of loyalty. Given its growth among people used to living on the streets, it could easily survive what are destined to be lengthy future legal battles. It could just as easily dissolve.

Sources-Primary

The Foundation published no substantive books but issued millions of copies of several tracts.

Alamo, Tony. *Duped.* Alma, AK: Holy Alamo Christian Church, n.d. 8-page tract.

—————. *Fugitive Pope.* Van Buren, AK: Music Square Church, n.d. 6-page tract.

————. *Jesus Said That Satan Would Have a Church and Government.* Alma, AK: Holy Alamo Christian Churches, n.d. 8-page pamphlet.

————. *The Pope's Secrets.* Alma, AK: Holy Alamo Christian Church, n.d. 8-page tract.

————. *Tony Alamo—My Side of the Story.* New York: Holy Alamo Christian Church, 1989. 8-page tract.

Alamo, Tony, and Susan Alamo. *Tricked.* Alma, AK: Christian Foundation, n.d. 4-page tract.

Sources-Secondary

Impact of Cults on Today's Youth. Sacramento, CA: State of California, Senate Select Committee on Children and Youth, 1974.

Poett, James. "Do They Have the Right to Be Weird?" *The Village Voice* (October 24, 1977).

Tracy, Phil. "The Jesus Freaks." *Commonweal* (October 30, 1970).

B. THE CHURCH OF SCIENTOLOGY

One of the few genuinely "new" religions to originate in the United States during the twentieth century, the Church of Scientology has become known for the numerous controversies, particularly with the Internal Revenue Service, and with those whom it claims have libeled and tried to destroy it.

Founder and Early History

The Church of Scientology was founded by L. Ron Hubbard (1911-1986). A man of varied experience, Hubbard grew up in rural Montana but during his teen years traveled internationally before settling briefly in the east. He attended George Washington University for a year (1931-32) and soon afterward began a successful career as a writer. Though he wrote a variety of true adventure and juvenile fiction, he is best remembered as a science fiction writer. He was made a member of the Explorers Club as his service in the Navy. Wounded in the South Pacific, he spent almost a year in the hospital.

During the years after his recovery, he synthesized the ideas which later became Dianetics and finally developed into Scientology. In 1948 he informally published and circulated copies of *Dianetics: the Original Thesis*, the first statement of his system. The volume brought him the interest and allegiance of John W. Campbell, Jr., editor of the popular *Astounding Science Fiction*, and Dr. J. A. Winter, a general practitioner from Michigan. In 1949 Campbell began to mention Dianetics in his magazine, and in May 1950 he published Hubbard's first article describing the new way to understand and treat mental health.

This article, along with Hubbard's general association with the community of fellow science fiction writers, led many people to label Scientology a "science fiction religion."

Even before the article in *Astounding Science Fiction*, Hubbard had formed the Hubbard Dianetic Research Foundation, headquartered in Elizabeth, New Jersey. By the end of the year, authorized branches were opened in New York, Washington, Chicago, Los Angeles, and Honolulu. Informal and independent dianetics groups sprang up around the country, especially after the publication of *Dianetics, the Modern Science of Mental Health*, which became a national bestseller in 1951.

Following a brief period of growth, problems arose. The medical and psychiatric community rebuffed Winter's attempt to describe Dianetics in professional journals, and individual doctors attacked the practice. A multitude of independent dianetics groups began to mix Hubbard's thought with occult and Eastern ideas and techniques, and Hubbard discovered that he had lost much control of Dianetic practice.

Amid the chaos and confusion, Hubbard also began to pay attention to a phenomenon which emerged during "auditing," the dianetics counseling practice, namely the phenonenon of "exteriorization" and resulting material on past lives. Exteriorization, similar to astral travel, is the separation of the consciousness from the body. Past lives are previous incarnations of the continuing essence of a person (in Scientology terminology, a "Thetan"). In 1952, Hubbard took these additional insights and, moving to Phoenix, Arizona, founded the Hubbard Association of Scientologists International, by which it is known today. He also published his first books on Scientology.

The additional material on past lives and exteriorization led to speculation on metaphysical and spiritual matters, with the further result that in 1953, Hubbard incorporated the Church of Scientology. The first congregations of the new Church were opened in Los Angeles and Auckland, New Zealand, the following year. The Founding Church of Scientology of Washington, D.C., was established in 1955. Once established, the Church spread quickly throughout the English-speaking world and in the late 1960s began to spread through all of Europe. In 1959 the Church purchased the St. Hill Manor as a residence for Hubbard and a headquarters for the growing movement.

The year 1966 proved an important one for the prospering Church. First, in the face of a growing number of attacks upon Scientology, the office of the Guardian was established and assigned the double task of defending Scientology from attacks by outside critics and keeping the teachings and practice correct throughout the Church. Shortly after the office was created, Hubbard resigned all formal positions within the Church and began to devote his life to further development of the system. Finally a ship, renamed the *Apollo*, was purchased and the Sea Org(anization), a fraternal group made up of the most dedicated Church members, was formed. Hubbard, a former naval officer, moved on board the vessel and made it his research facility.

The Sea Org became the center for the development of the more advanced grades of Scientological work. In 1967, the Advanced Organization was created to run the new advanced courses. In 1970 the Flag Management Bureau was created to oversee the management of the advanced courses. In 1975, the operation aboard the *Apollo* was abandoned, and the Advanced Organization moved into the facilities of the Church at Los Angeles, which had previously had oversight of the Sea Org. Flag was moved into newly purchased facilities at Clearwater, Florida, and designated the Flag Land Base.

Beliefs and Practices

The beliefs and practices of the Church of Scientology are based upon the extensive research, writings, and taped lectures (most of which have now been transcribed) of L. Ron Hubbard. These writings consist of some 44 million words and are considered the scriptures of the faith.

Though the Church published a creedal statement in 1954, the Creed of the Church of Scientology says little about the Church's unique beliefs, emphasizing instead the conditions under which it hopes people can function. It reads much more like a Bill of Rights than a traditional creed. It does, however, affirm the essential goodness of humans and the basic drive for survival.

According to Scientology, human beings are naturally good, but their goodness has been disturbed by an aberrant state. The immortal Thetan moves from life to life, but looses its memory of past existence when the body dies. As the Thetan takes up a new body in a mother's womb, a new problem is added. The problem is caused by a part of the mind, the "reactive" mind, a stimulus-response mechanism created by the true self (the Thetan) that records impressions on an unconscious level. The reactive mind provides programmed responses to specific repeated stimuli. The reactive mind carries images of pain, destructive moments, and injuries. The action of the reactive mind, though on an unconscious level, blocks the Thetan from realizing its true potentials and functioning properly. The individual, through ignorance and the automatic acts of the reactive mind, is led to destructive counter-survival actions.

The Church offers members a series of techniques and disciplines that deal with the problems of the reactive mind and train the Thetan to remember its true nature and express itself. The primary discipline involves work with an auditor, a spiritual counselor and teacher, who leads the member through a series of exercises to erase the effects of the reactive mind. The auditing sessions confront individuals with counter-survival aspects of their lives and allow them to be more free and responsible. When the reactive mind is eliminated and no longer exerts involuntary control over life, people are said to be "clear." Further work in Scientology is devoted to exercising the abilities of the operating Thetan, particularly the ability to exteriorize.

The goal of the Thetan is survival. The individual seeks to express the urge to survive in eight sectors, "the eight dynamics." The urge to survive begins as a drive to exist as a self. It is further expressed in a drive to live through sexual activity, through identification with progressively select groups of human beings (tribe or nation), humankind, the larger animal kingdom, and the physical universe. The seventh dynamic finds the self in the purely spiritual realm and includes the urge toward immortality. The eighth dynamic is the urge to exist as infinity or to find expression in the light of the Supreme Being. While individuals can expand their abilities so as to increasingly function in all dynamics, only when the seventh dynamic is reached can the meaning of the eighth be encompassed. For the Scientologist, God is approached after a lengthy process as the end product of their development as an operating Thetan. The Church has been reluctant to speculate on the nature of God and has concentrated on the spiritual problems of humanity and the necessary metaphysical conclusions of its more practical emphases.

The goal of all Scientology is a clear planet on which the effects of the reactive mind are eliminated. The immediate sign of a clear planet would be freedom from war, pollution, insanity, drugs, and crime. Humans, fully aware of their true nature, could operate along all eight dynamics. The Church's social programs have begun to implement their social goals.

Worship in Scientology takes second place to the daily work of becoming clear and exercising one's life as an operating Thetan. However, weekly worship services are held at all churches and missions following the order prescribed in the book of *Ceremonies*. A number of holidays have been designated, the most prominent being March 13 (Founder's Birthday) and May 9 (May 9 Day), which commemorates the publication of *Dianetics: the Modern Science of Mental Health* in 1950.

Organization

During the 1980s Scientology went through a complete reorganization which involved, among other factors, the dissolution of the Guardian's Office, which had become deeply involved in some of the illegal actions which had gotten the Church in trouble with the government, and the setting apart in separate corporations the Church's social action programs.

World headquarters of the Church of Scientology is in Los Angeles, California. The major corporate expression of the Church is the Church of Scientology International. The international leadership of the Church is located in the International Board of Scientology Organization, which guides the propagation of the Church's beliefs and the development of its program internationally, and the Board of Directors of the Churches of Scientology, which appoints the directors of the local churches of Scientology. The International Board concerns itself at the highest levels with the viability of Scientology and issues both doctrinal directives and advice of a technical nature. The Religious Technology Center, created in 1982, owns and controls the trademarks and copyrights of the Church. The Watchdog Committee is the inspection and policing arm of the Church which checks the other parts of the organization to make sure that they are following the administrative technology developed by Hubbard.

The central structure of the Church is geared to provide Scientology training. As Church members avail themselves of the training offered by the Church and move to more advanced levels, they encounter a variety of organizations. The most basic training in Dianetics and Scientology is available from local churches. Counseling in Scientology is offered by "auditors" who also receive their basic training locally. However, as progress is made, members are encouraged to receive the levels available first from an Advanced Organization and/or a Saint Hill Organization. These offer the basic introduction to the OT (operating Thetan) courses. Advanced training for auditors is taken through the Saint Hill Organization. Advanced Organizations are currently located in Denmark, England, Australia, and Los Angeles, California.

The higher level Operating Thetan courses (OT 1-7) and the most advanced auditor training are offered at the Flag Land Base in Clearwater, Florida. Flag was originally established as the Church's research arm aboard the *Apollo* but has been on land for many years. Recently, however, a new OT 8 course was opened and is offered aboard the *Freewinds*, a new large oceangoing vessel.

The Sea Org, the elite fraternal organization in the Church, is headquartered at the Flag Land Base in Clearwater, Florida. It had been assigned the tasks of assisting Hubbard in his continuing research and development and now oversees the higher levels of the program and of generally promoting Scientology worldwide. Each local church of Scientology is incorporated separately, but its leadership is appointed by the Board of Directors and is bound to follow the beliefs and practices of the Church in a high degree of exactitude.

In addition to the organizations whose main function is the delivery of training, various departments carry out specific tasks in its overall program. Among these are: Scientology Missions International which assists in the development of new Scientology churches around the world; the Office of Special Affairs which concerns itself with the Church's interaction with the outside world; and the Publications Organization which oversees Bridge Publications in Los Angeles and New Era Publications in Denmark.

Other organizations are more loosely affiliated to the Church, at least on the formal level. The International Association of Scientologists was formed in 1984 to support Scientology and to oppose any attacks upon it. The occasion for its founding was the multimillion dollar judgment made against the Church in the case of an ex-member who sued the Church. Some advanced services of the Church are available only to active members of the Association.

Still other organizations, now incorporated separately from the Church, are largely staffed by Church members and seek to apply Hubbard's teachings to all of life. The World Institute of Scientology Enterprises (WISE) was organized in 1978 to apply Scientology technology to the world of business. It is a separate corporation though generally aligned to the Church and its teachings. The Way to Happiness Foundation circulates copies of *The Way to Happiness*, a philosophical moral treatise by Hubbard which outlines the basic behavior patterns which he believed produced a happy existence and most contributed to the survival of individuals.

The various social reform activities of the Church were set aside as separate corporations through the 1980s, and in the later 1980s the Association for Better Living and Education (ABLE) International was created with the purpose of ensuring that Hubbard's teachings were applied to society's betterment. ABLE grew out of the Association of Scientologists for Reform which had been founded in 1975. Among the organizations cooperating through ABLE are Narconon, Criminon, Applied Scholastics, and the Citizens Commission on Human Rights. Narconon was founded in 1966 by Willie Benitz, an inmate at the Arizona State Prison who had found freedom from his own drug problem through his studies of Hubbard's writings. The program began to expand to other facilities and through the Church following Benitz's release in 1970. Narconon became an increasingly important aspect of the Church's program through the 1980s. Criminon is the name given to the Narconon program now functioning in the prison system. Applied Scholastics applies Hubbard's ideas to the field of education. Among other programs it has developed are management training courses which are marketed to businesses. Applied Scholastics also manages the Apple and the Delphian school systems.

The Citizens Commission on Human Rights was founded in 1969 to combat abuse in the psychiatric profession. The Church is basically opposed to the practice of psychiatry but has special condemnation for psychosurgery(lobotomies),shock treatments,and consciousness-altering drugs. Most recently the Church has joined in the fight to have the drug "prozac" removed from the market. Similar to the Commission is American Citizens for Honesty in Government founded in 1978 as a watchdog organization which exposes and publicizes illegal government activities.

Current Status

Both the national and international headquarters of the Church of Scientology are at the Church of Scientology of California, in Los Angeles. Flag Operations Liaison Offices for the Eastern and Western United States are in New York City and Los Angeles, respectively.

The Church publishes a number of periodicals; many serve primarily to inform members of programs, classes, schedules, and new publications. Among the more substantive national periodicals are *Source*, published by the Flag Service Organization; *Advance*, published by the Church of Scientology of California, Advanced Organization of Los Angeles; *The Auditor*, published by the Church of Scientology of California, and *Freedom*, published by he Church of Scientology International, which details many of the more intense conflicts of the Church with practices and organizations which it believes restrict individual freedom especially in the psychiatric and religious area.

In 1988 the Church reported approximately 7,000,000 members worldwide in 600 churches, missions and groups. The Church is active in more than 50 countries. Scientology counts members in terms of those who have received training, and there is no way currently to measure how many of the reported members consider themselves Scientologists.

Controversy

The history of the Church of Scientology has to a large extent been a history of controversy. Since 1958 the Church has been in almost constant litigation with the Internal Revenue Service. It fought a ten-year battle with the Food and Drug Administration, and in Australia it ended over sixteen years of war with the government in 1983. In addition to its problems with various government agencies, the Church became enmeshed in the anti-cult controversies of the 1970s, which led to a number of civil lawsuits. Finally, the Church sent several members incognito to selected government agencies which were collecting data on the Church. The members involved with this operation were arrested, tried, and convicted of theft of government documents. In 1958 the Internal Revenue Service revoked the tax-exempt status of the Founding Church of Scientology in Washington, D.C., and the Church of Scientology of New York. The Church filed suit to have its tax-exempt status reinstated. Meanwhile, as the tax case was awaiting trial, in 1963 the Food and Drug Administration seized the E-meters used in auditing, claiming that they were unauthorized devices in the diagnosis and treatment of disease. After ten years of litigation, the E-meters were returned to the Church, although much of the literature seized along with the meters was destroyed over the decade. The continuing tax issue reached its most recent juncture in 1984, when a court, in a lengthy 200-page decision, once again denied tax-exempt status to the Church.

Trouble in Australia began in 1967 when the Chairman of the Victoria Mental Health Authority initiated an investigation of Scientology. In 1965, Victoria passed the Psychological Practices Act, popularly called the Scientology Prohibition Bill. Western Australia and Southern Australia did the same in 1968. The Church assumed the name of the Church of the New Faith. Litigation in Australia finally ended in 1983 when the nation's Supreme Court ruled in favor of the Church, thus legitimizing its status as a religious organization.

The controversy in the courts concerning the status of the Church gave way to public controversy, and a number of books attacking the Church were written. Among these, some were considered so libelous and harmful by the Church as to warrant a lawsuit. The most famous of these books, *The Scandal of Scientology*, was published in 1971. Tower Books settled out of court and withdrew the book in 1973. In 1976 Paulette Cooper signed a lengthy statement with a retraction of over 50 significant erroneous and unsubstantiated accusations. Cooper has remained an active critic of the Church and has since disclaimed her statement and retraction. In like measure, the Church has continued to monitor and attack Cooper. Periodically, other writers, some former members, have also written exposé-like volumes against the Church.

The suits against books that attacked the Church were joined by several against deprogrammers who had attempted unsuccessfully to persuade members to leave the Church. However, the most famous case of this type was brought by Julie Christofferson, a member in Oregon, who was successfully deprogrammed and sued the Church. She charged the Church with outrageous conduct leading to severe emotional distress. Awarded $2,000,000 by a jury, the case was reversed on appeal in 1978. Retried in 1985, the case led to a second multimillion dollar award by the jury. However, the judge declared a mistrial and the case was dropped.

Possibly the most notorious series of events in the Church's often intense interaction with its critics began in 1977. In July of that year, the FBI conducted a raid on the Washington, D.C., and Los Angeles churches and seized many files of documents. Though the raid was declared illegal, the documents remained in government possession and were open to public scrutiny. They yielded the information that the Church kept files on people it considered unfriendly and that there had been various attempts to infiltrate anti-cult organizations. Labeling the Alliance for the Preservation of Religious Liberty as a front group for the Church largely destroyed that organization's credibility.

Most importantly, after the raid, a number of top officials of the Church, including Guardian Jane Kember and Hubbard's wife Mary Sue, were indicted and convicted for theft of government documents. After their conviction, the Church withdrew support for any appeal. Those convicted were released from their Church offices, and the Church began a thorough reorganization and eventual closing of the Guardian's Office.

Through the 1980s and into the 1990s, legal problems with the Internal Revenue Service has continued. In the early 1980s, the IRS charged L. Ron Hubbard with criminal tax evasion, i.e., using the tax-exempt church to hide taxable income. That investigation ended in 1986, but the IRS has still tried to move against the Church in ways which question its tax-exempt status. In 1991, the Church filed a lawsuit against the IRS, which claimed that the IRS had engaged in a 33-year campaign that included many illegal actions in order to destroy the Church.

Through the 1980s the Church also experienced growth and controversy in Europe. One of the most significant battles took place in Italy. After a five-year investigation in Italy, in which a number of Church officials were charged with both tax evasion and various criminal acts, the court in Milan found the officials not guilty. In another ruling, the Church received full tax-exempt status.

In 1991, as this volume was being written, *Time* magazine published a front-page story attacking Scientology. A short time before the *Time* article, the *Los Angeles Times* had published a series on the Church. The Church responded to both with a massive public relations campaign. The Church reprinted favorable quotes from the *Times* articles on bulletin boards around the metropolitan area. It answered the *Time* attack with a lengthy series of full-page ads in *USA Today*. Much of the material in these two attacks upon the Church had come from material that surfaced in the lawsuit of Larry Wollersheim, who won a multimillion dollar judgment against the Church in 1989. Early in 1992 the Church announced the filing of a major lawsuit against *Time*.

The Church has complained throughout the period of its controversies with both public and private critics that it has been unjustly singled out and targeted. It has responded aggressively. Some of its social action has been directed toward correcting abuses in areas of medical practice, particularly in the mental health field. It has responded to government attacks by claiming an anti-Scientology conspiracy and pursuing (and, in part, documenting) the conspiracy with documents obtained through the Freedom of Information Act. A 1984 tax ruling against the Church was followed by a series of advertisements in *The New York Times* that attacked the IRS and called for present and former employees to supply information about any illegal IRS activities.

Throughout the controversies, the Church has continued to grow and to develop its program. As the 1990s begin, while the Church still has legal fights ahead of it, it seems to have put the major issues behind it, though it still has a massive image problem with the significant negative publicity it has received. There is every reason to believe that, barring further negative disclosures, the Church will be able to lower its confrontational stance through the 1990s.

[Note: The Church of Scientology notes that the terms "Scientology," "Dianetics," "Narconon," "Criminon," and "Applied Scholastics" are registered trademarks of the Church, and we are happy to call this fact to the attention of readers.]

Sources-Primary

Hubbard, L. Ron. *Ceremonies of the Founding Church of Scientology*. Los Angeles: The American St. Hill Organization, 1971.

―――――. *Dianetics, the Modern Science of Mental Health*. New York: Hermitage House, 1950. 452 pp. Frequently reprinted.

————. *Have You Lived Before This Life?* Los Angeles: Publications Organization, 1977.

————. *Scientology: The Fundamentals of Thought.* Los Angeles: Bridge Publications, 1956, 1984. 181 pp.

————. *The Way to Happiness.* Los Angeles: Bridge Publications, 1984. 263 pp.

Meldal-Johnson, Trevor, and Patrick Lusey. *The Truth About Scientology.* New York: Tempo Books, 1980.

What is Scientology? Los Angeles: Church of Scientology of California, 1978. 347 pp.

Sources-Secondary

Wallis, Roy. *The Road to Total Freedom.* New York: Columbia University Press, 1976.

Sources-Critical

Over the last two decades, a series of exposé books on Scientology have been written. As these have appeared, the Church has complained that each of these books is based upon false data and half-truths. And for each one the Church has put together a response listing what it feels are the errors each volume perpetuates. The Church's response offers an opportunity for researchers to evaluate claims in the controversy. The response for the more recent titles can be obtained from the Church of Scientology International in Los Angeles.

Atack, Jon. *A Piece of Blue Sky: Scientology, Dianetics and L. Ron Hubbard Exposed.* Secaucus, NJ: Lyle Stuart, 1990. 428 pp.

Cooper, Paulette. *The Scandal of Scientology.* New York: Tower Books, 1971. 220 pp.

Corydon, Bent, and L. Ron Hubbard, Jr. (Ronald De Wolf). *L. Ron Hubbard: Messiah or Madman?* Secaucus, NJ: Lyle Stuart, 1987. 402 pp.

Miller, Russell. *Bare-Faced Messiah: The True Story of L. Ron Hubbard.* New York: Henry Holt, 1987. 390 pp.

C. THE CHURCH UNIVERSAL AND TRIUMPHANT (SUMMIT LIGHTHOUSE)

Frequently confused with the "I AM" Religious Activity, and often presented as its modern embodiment, the Church Universal and Triumphant was founded quite apart from the "I AM" Activity. Though there is some historical linkage between the two organizations, the founders of the Summit Lighthouse (the name under which the Church Universal and Triumphant was organized) were never affiliated with the "I AM" Religious Activity or its corporate manifestation, the Saint Germain Foundation, and its teachings are at considerable variance with the older organization founded by Guy and Edna Ballard.

At the same time, the similarities of the two organizations, at least to the public and the media, has led to their constant confusion. Both organizations were founded by and during their first generation led by individuals designated as Messengers of the Ascended Masters. Both groups assign a special importance to the Ascended Master Saint Germain and Jesus and recognize Guy Ballard, the founder of the "I AM," as an Ascended Master. Finally, the art and iconography are similar. The Church Universal and Triumphant circulates portraits of Saint Germain and Jesus which not only closely resemble those circulated by the "I AM" but were in fact originally used by the Saint Germain Foundation. In like measure both groups use very similar pictorial representations of the "I AM" Presence, though not without important differences.

Founders and Early History

The lineage of the Church Universal and Triumphant can be traced to 1952 when leaders of the New York and Philadelphia sanctuaries of the "I AM" Religious Activity broke away to form The Bridge to Freedom (now the New Age Church of the Christ). Several years later, Francis K. Ekey, the leader in Philadelphia, separated her work which she named the Lighthouse of Freedom. Among those associated with Ekey was Mark L. Prophet (b. December 24, 1918, Chippewa Falls, Wisconsin), who headed the Washington, D.C., center for her organization. However, during the later 1950s he began to receive messages from the Ascended Masters and in 1958 the Ascended Master El Morya anointed him as a new Messenger of the Masters, the Great White Brotherhood, and appointed him to begin a new thrust of Ascended Master activity. He began to lecture and to publish dictations (teachings of cosmic law) he received from the Masters in a series of *Ashram Notes.*

Prophet founded the Church Universal and Triumphant (CUT) in Washington in 1958. Prior to this time he had served in the United States Air Force in World War II. In 1961, while delivering the Ascended Masters' teachings in Boston, Prophet met Elizabeth Clare Wulf (b. April 8, 1940, Red Bank, New Jersey), who was studying political science at Boston University. Several years later they were married. In the meantime, Elizabeth became a student of the Ascended Masters and was tutored both by Prophet and directly by El Morya. Eventually she was also anointed as a Messenger.

That same year El Morya announced the formation of the Keepers of the Flame Fraternity through which students could receive systematic and graded instruction in the teaching of the Masters. A religious teaching center was founded in the Prophets' home in Beacon's Head, Virginia. At the "Holy Tree House," as the center became known, Prophet conducted classes that centered upon the dictations of the Masters who spoke through him. These dictations were published and distributed to students around the country.

In 1966 headquarters of the Summit Lighthouse, as the work was called, moved to Colorado Springs, Colorado. Growth was slow but steady. The weekly *Pearls of Wisdom* succeeded the *Ashram Notes* and was sent free to all who requested it. During these years, Elizabeth, while continuing to assist the growth of the movement, became the mother of four children.

On February 26, 1973, Mark died suddenly of a stroke, and Elizabeth took on the full responsibility for and leadership of the Summit Lighthouse. According to Church teachings, Mark Prophet ascended immediately and is now known as Ascended Master Lanello, the Ever-Present Guru. From his Ascended Master state, through Elizabeth, he has given a series of dictations later compiled into a book, *Cosmic Consciousness, The Putting on the Garment of the Lord* (1976), later reissued as *Cosmic Consciousness as the Highest Expression of Heart.* In 1981, Elizabeth married Ed Francis, a longtime Church member.

From Summit Lighthouse to the Church Universal and Triumphant

The Summit Lighthouse expanded dramatically during the 1970s. In 1970, Montessori International was founded to offer both secular education and spiritual nurturance for children and youth, nursery through high school. Summit University was established in 1972 to provide a three-month retreat experience with accompanying studies in science, culture, and religion. In 1974 Mrs. Prophet and the Board of Directors incorporated the Church Universal and Triumphant and designated the Summit Lighthouse as the publishing arm of the new Church. It continued to publish *Pearls of Wisdom*, numerous books, and a growing collection of tapes. In 1975 she announced the formation of Summit International as an umbrella organization for the various parts of the Church and laid out the plans for the establishment of teaching centers around the country.

Even before Mark's death, efforts had begun to raise funds and build a headquarters complex, including a church and school, in Colorado. However, these plans were revised and Southern California selected as the new site for the complex. In 1976 the former Pasadena College was leased, and the administrative center of the Church moved on campus. Nine regional teaching centers had been chartered by this time, and growth continued at a steady pace. Also, during this same period, the White Lodge, an ascended master group headquartered at Del Mar, California, decided to affiliate with the Church.

The Church stayed in Pasadena only a short time. In 1978 it purchased the 218-acre former campus of Thomas Aquinas College near Malibu, California, and moved all its offices to the new site, renamed Camelot. The Malibu site soon proved too confining to the growing movement and in 1981 12,000 acres were purchased in southwestern Montana north of Yellowstone National Park. Subsequently other blocks of land were acquired, and in 1986 the headquarters were transferred to Montana.

Beliefs

The Summit Lighthouse and Church Universal and Triumphant sees itself as a distinctive activity of the Ascended Masters initiated by the Ascended Master El Morya through the Messengers Mark and Elizabeth Prophet. In carrying on the work of the Great White Brotherhood, the Messengers have brought forth new teachings both from those Masters who spoke initially through Madame Blavatsky or Guy Ballard and other Masters from both the East and the West. The Church sees itself as the true church of Jesus Christ and Gautama Buddha as well as the hosts of the Lord ascended, referred to in the Bible as "the saints robed in white." It also venerates the Virgin Mary and sees her as an outstanding representation of the Divine Mother. The nature of the Brotherhood and their basic teachings are clearly outlined in two books, *Climb the Highest Mountain* (1972) and *The Great White Brotherhood in the Culture, History and Religion of America* (1983), and summarized in the Church's twelve "Tenets."

The Church affirms belief in God, The Source of Life and Being. From the Great Central Sun, the metaphysical center of the Cosmos, light came forth and was individualized in numerous individual sparks, each a replica of God, a personalized fragment of the Deity. These seeds of light are the "I AM" Presence, the Lord, or godly part of each individual.

Each person was created as a soul, an infinite potential intended to return to the source of its creation, to fully unite with its individualized God-presence. Mediating the process of the soul's return and eventual union with the "I AM" Presence is the universal Christ consciousness, individualized as the Real Self of each child of God. Individuals, souls, may choose to walk the path of initiation that leads to self-mastery, at which time they are wed to their Christ self. Eventually, each soul ascends into the light, at which time they become one with the "I AM" presence. The historical Jesus walked the earth as one whose soul was one with his Christ consciousness. At the end of his earthly existence, he ascended immediately.

In this age, the particular challenge for each individual is to raise up the feminine principle, i.e., to master the energies appropriate to the life of the soul, the feminine aspect of each individual, often spoken of as the inner mastery of the planes of matter, and then to wed the soul to the Universal Christ consciousness in a balancing action of Alpha (Spirit) and Omega (Matter), representative of the fusion of the energies in God who is both Father and Mother.

As a means of assisting individuals in their goal of self-mastery, the Church stresses a practical path of discipleship which includes instruction in the lost arts of healing, an understanding of the laws of karma and reincarnation, and the use of the science of the spoken word (which includes prayers, affirmations, decrees, and mantras) to invoke light, to expose evil, and to give illumination to God's people. It expects members to tithe ten percent of their income. Strongly patriotic, the Church encourages members and students to assume an active role on various social issues. It has spoken against abortion, child pornography, nuclear warfare, terrorism, and world communism. It vigorously supports family life, the four sacred freedoms, and a strong defense for America.

Though somewhat unorthodox, the Church considers itself a Christian organization and through the 1980s has given particular insistence to that identification. Prophet has publicly aligned the Church with gnostic Christianity and in this regard has issued *The Lost Years of Jesus* (1984), reviving the tradition that Jesus traveled to India and Tibet during his early adulthood, and a four-volume set, *The Lost Teachings of Jesus* (1866-198?), which reconstructs the essential teachings of Jesus believed to have been left out of the New Testament.

Organization

The Church is headed by Elizabeth Clare Prophet, the Messenger of the Ascended Masters. The administration of the Church is in the hands of a Board of Directors, which has responsibility for directing the centers and appointing their leadership. The various departments of the

Church are located at Camelot and the Inner Retreat at the Church's 30,000-acre Royal Teton Ranch in Montana, where regular conclaves (conferences), all open to the general public, are held.

The Keepers of the Flame Fraternity remains the heart of the Church. It consists of men and women who have pledged to keep the flame of the inner self, in reality God within the self, nurtured, and who are dedicated to the freedom and enlightenment of humanity. Some weekly services at the various teaching centers are designed especially for and limited to Keepers of the Flame.

The most dedicated members of the Church are the communicants. To become a communicant (i.e., full member) one must be a Keeper of the Flame, subscribe to the "Tenets" of the Church, be formally baptized and tithe his/her income. Individuals must make application to become a communicant member, and periodically ceremonies are held for christening or accepting new members.

At the center in Montana and through various centers scattered around the world, the Church offers communicants the opportunity to live in a spiritual community. Though only a minority of communicants have chosen such a living arrangement, those who do form a core of highly dedicated people. They accept upon themselves additional duties of devotional service and activity to spread the Church's teachings. Each teaching center carries on a daily program of worship and classes, led by the resident members. Members at the center also hold weekly study groups at various locations in the community.

Summit University, also located in Montana, offers spiritual training for Keepers of the Flame and advanced classes especially for those who plan to become ministers. The publishing arm, Summit Lighthouse, greatly expanded during the years in Malibu and continues to serve the Church through its publication of books, booklets, devotional (decree) materials, and cassettes of the conferences at which the Ascended Masters have spoken through the Church's Messengers.

Current Status

As a policy, the Church Universal and Triumphant does not release figures on the number of students or members, and only estimates can be given. Church centers were located across the United States from New York and Washington, D.C., to Chicago, Minneapolis, and San Francisco. Each center housed approximately twenty communicant members. Additional centers and members are to be found in Europe and West Africa.

Since moving to Montana, Church activities have developed in four locations designated Royal Teton Ranch North and South and Glastonbury North and South. Most of the Church activity takes place on the Ranch sites, and Glastonbury is primarily being used to locate single-family dwellings for Church members. By the end of the 1980s, approximately 800 Church members had moved to Montana.

Controversy

Through the 1980s, the Church Universal and Triumphant had joined the more well-known newer religions such as the Unification Church or the Hare Krishnas as a major target of the anti-cult movement. The adoption of a communal life-style by members in-residence at the centers and the exacting requirements on those who lived at Camelot and now at Grand Teton Ranch brought the common charges of excessive indoctrination and brainwashing. Such charges have been aired on national television news shows and in newspaper and magazine articles featuring ex-members.

One initial set of attacks on the Church relates to its outward financial success. Critics have cited Prophet's wardrobe and jewelry, the acquisition of property, and the proliferation of publications and audio-visuals. The Church has countered with its observations that the wardrobe was donated, the jewels (the property of the Church, not of Prophet personally) are focuses of spiritual light and healing power, and that the expansion of the Church's program and membership has required a greater amount of property. The many books, tapes, and videos are like the education materials produced by other similar churches and religious groups.

Shortly before their move to Montana the Church became involved in a lengthy court battle with an ex-member, Gregory Mull. His lawsuit resulted in a $1.5 million judgment against the Church though Mull died while the judgment was under appeal.

Since moving to Montana, the Church has continually been in the headlines. One set of issues involved its purchase and use of the land. Some local residents were upset over the quiet manner in which the large tracts of land were purchased, and anger mounted as development proceeded. Much of the controversy was blunted by the Church's having conducted an extensive ecological survey prior to beginning its development. The Church won most of the court challenges to its work.

In the midst of the controversy about its development of the property, the Church began to build nuclear-proof shelters for members in case of a significant future disaster. It was widely and incorrectly reported that such a disaster had been predicted to occur in April 1990 at which time members would go underground. In fact Prophet had stated that a period of dangerous times was beginning, and the shelters were a precaution should war or other emergency occur. The controversy was dying out when Church members did not behave as the media predicted they would, but was extended when a fuel spill from one of the shelters threatened the water purity of the immediate area. However, the leak was quickly contained.

While the Church was countering the "end-of-the-world" reports, its head of security was arrested for illegally purchasing firearms. Subsequently, Prophet's husband was arrested and convicted on a firearms violation.

Having lived through the controversies of the late 1980s, the Church has turned attention to a long-term public relations program to communicate its concern for the natural environment and the low level of interference with the natural processes during their decade of development. They have continued an open-door policy with the residents of their area in order to squelch any rumors about activities at the several Church facilities. It remains to be seen how successful these efforts will be, though much appears to depend upon their passing through a period of time without any major ecological disasters.

Sources-Primary

Prophet, Elizabeth Clare. *Astrology of the Four Horsemen: How You Can Heal Yourself and the Planet Earth.* Livingston, MT: Summit University Press, 1991. 619 pp.

————. *The Great White Brotherhood.* Los Angeles: Summit University Press, 1983. 352 pp.

————. *The Lost Years of Jesus.* Livingston, MT: Summit University Press, 1984. 401 pp.

Prophet, Mark, and Elizabeth Clare Prophet. *Climb the Highest Mountain.* Colorado Springs, CO: Summit Lighthouse, 1972. 516 pp.

————. *The Lost Teachings of Jesus.* 4 vols. Livingston, MT: Summit University Press, 1986-1987.

————. *My Soul Doth Magnify the Lord!* Colorado Springs, CO: Summit Lighthouse, 1974. 350 pp.

D. ECKANKAR

Though often missing from the surveys of world religion, the Sant Mat tradition of India has had an important role both in broadening the religious options on the Indian subcontinent and increasing the number of religious groups in the United States. Several of the popular new religions of the 1970s sprang directly from the large Sant Mat groups of India. Some such as Ruhani Satsang and the Radhasoami Satsang were openly representative of the tradition, while others, such as the Divine Light Mission, were less evidently attached. A few, such as ECKANKAR and the Movement of Spiritual Inner Awareness (discussed elsewhere in this volume), while relying almost totally on Sant Mat teachings, have attempted to distance themselves from the Sant Mat tradition.

Founder and Early History

ECKANKAR was founded by John Paul Twitchell (d. 1971). After World War II, while working as a correspondent in Washington, D.C., Twitchell joined the Self-Revelation Church of Absolute Monism, an independent congregation begun by Swami Premananda who had left Swami Yogananda's Self-Realization Fellowship. For several years he edited *The Mystic Cross*, the group's periodical. Then in 1955 he met Kirpal Singh, founder of the Ruhani Satsang. He left the Self-Revelation Church and was initiated by Singh. At the same time he became a member of the newly founded Church of Scientology and was among the first to attain the level of "clear."

In the early 1960s he moved to Seattle where he met Gail Atkinson, a librarian whom he eventually married. He introduced her to Kirpal Singh and she was initiated in 1963. Before the year was out, however, he had broken relations with Kirpal Singh and the following year he moved to San Francisco and began to teach classes which emphasized techniques for bi-location, the ability of a person's consciousness (soul or spirit) to separate itself from the body. Then in 1965, he declared himself the Living ECK Master. He incorporated ECKANKAR and established headquarters in Las Vegas, Nevada. The organization grew quickly, especially after the publication of popular paperback editions of *The Tiger's Fang* (1967), Twitchell's account of his visits to the inner world, and *In My Soul I Am Free* (1968), a biography by popular occult author Brad Steiger. A number of other titles by Twitchell quickly appeared, some in paperback and some in hardcover from ECKANKAR's Illuminated Way Press.

In his writings Twitchell claimed that he was the 971st ECK Master, the descendant of an unbroken chain of masters in the Order of the Vaiargi. He received his rod of power from ECK Master Rebazar Tarzs, a Tibetan. Twitchell died on September 17, 1971, six years after ECKANKAR was founded. On October 22, 1971, Darwin Gross received the rod of power and was acknowledged as the 972nd ECK Master.

Gross' tenure as the leader of ECKANKAR began and ended in controversy. A former professional musician and engineer from Oregon, he had been given a copy of *In My Soul I Am Free* in 1969. He immediately recognized the picture of Twitchell on the cover as the person he had encountered in his own inner journeys. He sent for the ECK lessons, the *Discourses*, attended the Third World Wide Seminar held that year in Portland, Oregon, and before the year was over, helped organize the first satsang group in the state. Then, with less than two years as an ECKist, he suddenly became the new ECK Master and was so acknowledged in a ceremony by Twitchell's widow.

In disagreement over the choice of Gross, ECKANKAR Vice President Dr. Louis Bluth and several other organization notables left. Gross married Gail Twitchell, and for the next several years the organization prospered. A new headquarters was built in Menlo Park, California, and membership more than doubled. He expanded the artistic and cultural development, especially in music. However, all was not well. In 1978 he announced his divorce. The next year Twitchell and

ECKANKAR were attacked for plagiarizing from Sant Mat materials and creating the lineage of ECK masters. Gross married again, but after a few months, the marriage was annulled. Then on October 22, 1981, he passed the rod of power to a new ECK Master, though he still retained a leadership role and a lifetime salary, and the organization continued to circulate and publish his several books: *Your Right to Know* (1979), *Gems of Soul* (1980), *From Heaven to the Prairie* (1980), *Leadership in ECK* (1982) and *Music from Spirit?* (1982, with Paul Twitchell).

Several years later, however, Gross was officially cut off from the ECKANKAR organization. He is no longer officially recognized as a genuine ECK master, and his books were withdrawn from circulation. Gross has since moved back to Oregon where, with his supporters, he began a new organization, Sounds of Soul.

Gross was succeeded by Harold Klemp, the 973rd Living ECK Master. According to Klemp's autobiography, *The Wind of Change* (1980), Klemp had had spontaneous astral travel (bi-location) experiences. He had joined several open membership occult organizations looking for some explanation of the questions raised by these experiences. Then in 1967 he answered an ad placed by ECKANKAR in *FATE* magazine and began the *Discourses*. In 1968 he bought a copy of *In My Soul I Am Free*, and like Gross, recognized Twitchell as someone he had met on his out-of-body trips. The announcement of Klemp's new position occurred at the 1981 ECK World Wide Seminar in Los Angeles.

Under Klemp's leadership the organization has taken steps to put the controversy of the 1970s behind them. He moved the headquarters to Minnesota and has authored a new set of books which have taken their place beside those of Twitchell.

Belief and Practice

ECKANKAR, the Ancient Science of Soul Travel, is, according to official ECK teachings, the most ancient teaching known to humanity. It has been handed down through an unbroken lineage of masters, the present Living ECK Master being the 973rd.

ECKANKAR beliefs begin with the "Sugmad," defined as the formless, All-embracing, impersonal, and infinite, the Ocean of Love and

Mercy, from which flows all of life, the equivalent of God in theistic religions. All life comes from the Sugmad via the ECK current, the Audible Life Current, which can be heard as sound and seen as light.

Humans are an immortal Soul incarnated in a set of bodies. The Soul body resides within the astral, causal, mental-etheric, and physical bodies to protect it from the coarse lower worlds. The ECK Masters teach the precise techniques and spiritual exercises whereby the soul can be released from the limitations of physical life and travel in the higher spiritual realms to the Sugmad. Travel is along the ECK, the Audible Life Current.

The path back to the Sugmad is through a series of twelve invisible planes. They may, in part, be distinguished by the sound typical of each level. According to ECKANKAR, most occult teaching never get beyond the second or astral plane, the realm of ghosts, spirits and psychic phenomena. The fifth plane is the first in which the soul reaches the pure spiritual worlds. The twelve planes and the sound associated with them are:

12. Sugmad	music of God
11. Sugmad World	music of universe
10. Anami Lok	sound of a whirlpool
9. Agam Lok	music of woodwinds
8. Hukikat Lok	thousand violins
7. Alaya Lok	deep humming
6. Alakh Lok	heavy wind
5. Soul	single note of flute

___Dividing line between psychic and spiritual worlds____
Etheric (top of mental plane) buzzing of bees

4. Mental	running of water
3. Causal	tinkle of bells
2. Astral	roar of the sea
1. Physical	thunder

The *Discourses* and other material available to "chelas" (students) teach a variety of techniques to contact and travel the ECK Current. The exact techniques are confidential, although an examination of ECKANKAR texts reveals that they are identical with those taught by the various Sant Mat teachers. Chelas are also taught to expect to encounter the ECK Master on their inner journeys, especially while asleep, during the dream state. Once contacted, the Master will guide the student through the various planes.

Organization

ECKANKAR is headed by the corporation's Board of Trustees, which operates under the spiritual leadership of the Living ECK Master. Trustees are drawn from different geographical locales and are active leaders at a regional level. The Trustees appoint the Area Madhis who are responsible for the activities in a particular region, and the Universal Madhis who travel wherever they are needed. Some Madhis are appointed to conduct the lower-level initiations. Working directly with the Board are the North American and European Advisory Councils and the Creative Arts Council.

The basic unit of ECKANKAR is the ECK Satsang class which is conducted, usually monthly, for chelas by an accredited Area Representative. In many areas, an ECKANKAR center has been opened. Such centers distribute ECK literature, offer seminars and introductory classes, and assist in the spread of ECKANKAR.

The international headquarters of ECKANKAR, for many years in Menlo Park, California, were moved to Minneapolis, Minnesota, during the 1980s. For many years Illuminated Way Press has been responsible for the publication of ECKANKAR books. *Mystic World* and *New from ECK* are issued quarterly. In 1988 the organization reported 127 centers in the United States and 284 worldwide scattered in 99 countries. Recent estimates of active membership range between 20,000 and 30,000 worldwide. The organization is strong in Europe.

New members are introduced to ECK teaching through the *ECK Dream Discourses*, monthly lessons authored by Klemp. Most live near a center in which regular weekly and monthly meetings are scheduled. Annually four major international seminars at which Klemp speaks are sponsored by the headquarters office.

Controversy

ECKANKAR grew steadily and quietly, in spite of the internal controversies which surrounded Darwin Gross, until David Christopher Lane, then a student at California State University, Northridge, and an initiate of Sant Mat Master Charan Singh, began to look into Twitchell's writings for a term paper. That exercise led to a lengthy investigation of Twitchell's life and resulted in two books which questioned the legitimacy of Twitchell's experiences and the truth of many of the claims upon which ECKANKAR is based. While Lane's book circulated informally as a manuscript, the Spiritual Counterfeits Project, the Evangelical Christian counter-cult group in Berkeley, California, developed his material in a special issue of the *SCP Journal* devoted entirely to ECKANKAR, "A Hard Look at a New Religion." In 1983, Lane's complete work was published as *The Making of a Spiritual Movement*. He subsequently published articles continuing and broadening the attack on ECKANKAR through the 1980s in his magazine *Understanding Cults and Spiritual Movements*.

Lane charged Twitchell with covering up his relationship with his former teachers—Swami Premananda, Kirpal Singh, and L. Ron Hubbard. He produced the original copies of articles Twitchell had written for various periodicals which later became chapters in his ECKANKAR books. They showed that Twitchell had deleted the names of these three teachers and replaced them with the names of ECKANKAR Masters such as Rebazar Tarzs (who no one outside of ECKANKAR has ever met). Lane charges Twitchell with creating Rebazar Tarzs out of the biographies of several Sant Mat teachers, such as Kirpal Singh and Sawan Singh.

Further, Lane has charged Twitchell with largely plagiarizing several of his books from the writings of Sant Mat author Julian Johnson. He demonstrated, by a detailed comparison of texts, the many passages Twitchell lifted directly out of Johnson's *The Path of the Masters*. During the years of Gross' leadership, ECKANKAR made no attempt to answer the substantive case put forth by Lane, but Klemp has moved to blunt the criticism by acknowledging Twitchell's role as a compiler of scattered and forgotten fragments of Truth.

Sources-Primary

Gross, Darwin. *Your Right to Know.* Menlo Park, CA: Illuminated Way Press, 1979.

Klemp, Harold. *The Book of ECK Parables.* 2 vols. Minneapolis, MN: ECKANKAR, 1988.

—————. *The Living Word.* Crystal, MN: Illuminated Way Publishing, Inc., 1989. 269 pp.

—————. *The Wind of Change.* Menlo Park, CA: Illuminated Way Press, 1980. 194 pp.

Twitchell, Paul. *ECKANKAR.* New York: Lancer Books, 1969. 254 pp.

—————. *The Spiritual Notebook.* Menlo Park, CA: Illuminated Way Press, 1979. 219 pp.

—————. *The Tiger's Fang.* New York: Lancer Books, 1969. 174 pp.

Sources-Secondary

Lane, David Christopher. *The Making of a Spiritual Movement.* Del Mar, CA: Del Mar Press, 1983. 154 pp.

Steiger, Brad. *In My Soul I Am Free.* New York: Lancer Books, 1968. 190 pp.

E. ELAN VITAL
(DIVINE LIGHT MISSION)

The arrival in the United States in 1971 of a 13-year-old religious leader from India was met with some ridicule from a culture which assumed that the possession of religious wisdom could only follow some years of living as an adult. However, many young adults not only were free of such assumptions, but more importantly, demonstrated an extraordinary amount of interest in seriously examining the claims of this teenager of being able to impart direct knowledge of the Divine. From that initial support, Guru Maharaj Ji would go on to establish a flourishing American organization, the Divine Light Mission, only in the 1980s to disband it and replace it with a loosely organized, informal network of followers, which he labeled Elan Vital.

Background

The original Divine Light Mission grew out of the Sant Mat movement, a spiritual tradition which developed in Northern India in the nineteenth century. It draws heavily on Sikhism, but posits a central role for the living guru as teacher and guide in spiritual realities. Over the years, as new gurus have appeared, a number of different Sant Mat groups have arisen. The Divine Light Mission was founded by Shri Hans Maharaj Ji (d.1966), the father of Maharaj Ji. Early in life he encountered Sarupanand Ji, a guru of the Sant Mat tradition by whom he was initiated. Though Sarupanand Ji reportedly had told his disciples to follow Hans Maharaj Ji, after the guru's death another disciple, Varaganand, claimed the succession and took control of the guru's property. Hans Maharaj Ji began to spread the teaching independently in Sind and Lahore, and in 1930 he established an informal mission in Delhi. His following grew steadily. In 1950, shortly after Indian independence had been declared, he commissioned the first mahatmas, followers who had the ability to initiate and who devoted themselves full time to the work of propagating the teachings of Shri Hans Maharaj Ji. He also began a monthly magazine, *Hansadesh*. By 1960 followers could be found across northern India from Bombay to Calcutta, and the need to organize them more formally led to the founding of the Divine Light Mission (Divya Sandesh Parishad).

Just six years after the founding of the Mission, Shri Hans Maharaj Ji died and was succeeded by his youngest son, Prem Pal Singh Rawat (b. 1957), who was but eight when he was recognized as the new "Perfect Master" and assumed the title Maharaj Ji. Maharaj Ji had been recognized as spiritually adept, even within the circle of the Holy Family, as Shri Hans Maharaj Ji's family was called. He had been initiated (i.e., given knowledge) at the age of six and soon afterward gave his first *satsang* (spiritual discourse). After his father's death he heard a voice commissioning him as the one to take the knowledge to the world. He assumed the role of Perfect Master at his father's funeral by telling the disciples who had gathered, "Dear Children of God, why are you weeping? Haven't you learned the lesson that your Master taught you? The Perfect Master never dies. Maharaj Ji is here, amongst you now. Recognize Him, obey Him and worship Him." Though officially the autocratic leader of the Mission, because of Maharaj Ji's age, authority was shared by the whole family.

During the 1960s, Americans in India searching for spiritual guidance discovered the Mission and a few became initiates (i.e., "premies," or "lovers of God"). They invited Maharaj Ji to the United States. In 1970 Maharaj Ji announced his plans to carry the knowledge throughout the world and the following year, against his mother's wishes, made his first visit to the West. A large crowd came to Colorado the next year to hear him give his first set of discourses in America. Many were initiated and became the core of the Mission in the United States. Headquarters were established in Denver, and by the end of 1973, tens of thousands had been initiated, and several hundred centers as well as over twenty ashrams, which housed approximately 500 of the most dedicated premies, had emerged. The headquarters staff expanded to 125, and social service facilities, such as a medical clinic in New York City, were opened.

Two periodicals, *And It Is Divine*, a magazine, and *Divine Times*, a tabloid, were begun. Enthusiasm ran high.

After a spectacular beginning in North America, the Mission suffered a major setback in November 1973. It rented the Houston Astrodome for "Millennium 73," an event celebrating the birthday of Maharaj Ji's father and designed to announce the beginning of a thousand years of peace and prosperity. The event failed; attendance was minuscule. The Mission was left with a $600,000 debt which required it to cut its staff and programs.

Millennium 73 was but the first of a series of events which gradually led the Mission to withdraw from the public scene. It was staged just as the anti-cult movement reached national proportions and turned its attention upon the Mission. Several deprogrammed ex-members became vocal critics of the Mission. Through his executive secretary, Maharaj Ji announced that he was replacing the predominantly Indian image with a Western one. Among other changes, he began to wear business suits instead of his all-white Indian attire. Many of the ashrams were discontinued.

To the problems caused by the debt and the attack of anti-cultists were added internal problems within Maharaj Ji's family. In December 1973, when Maharaj Ji turned 16, he took administrative control of the Mission's separate American corporation. Then in May 1974, he married his 24-year-old secretary, Marolyn Johnson, and declared her to be the incarnation of the goddess Dulga, usually pictured with ten arms and astride a tiger. Premies purchased an estate in Malibu into which the couple moved. Mataji, Maharaj Ji's mother, disapproved of the marriage and the life-style of the now-successful guru. Relations within the Holy Family were strained considerably. Accusing her son of breaking his spiritual disciplines, Mataji took control of the Mission in India and replaced him with his eldest brother. In 1975, Maharaj Ji returned to India and took his family to court. In a court-decreed settlement, he received control of the movement everywhere except in India, where his brother was recognized as its head. Publicity about the marriage and the subsequent family quarrels caused many Western followers to leave the Mission, though a large membership remained.

Following the incident at Jonestown in 1979, the Mission, which had slowly assumed a lower and lower profile, all but disappeared from public view. Maharaj Ji refused to give interviews, and contacts with non-members were largely avoided. By the end of the decade, an estimated 80 percent of the membership had left the Mission, though this left a sizable following (50,000+ in the United States and 1,000,000+ worldwide).

Finally, without public announcement, in the early 1980s, Maharaj Ji ordered all of the ashrams disbanded, though local informal gatherings (primarily in members' homes) were not discouraged. Maharaj Ji was no longer to be venerated as God. The Divine Light Mission was disbanded and in its stead Elan Vital was created as an informal organization to relate Maharaj Ji to his students on a one-to-one basis. He established a plan by which he would regularly travel the world speaking in those cities where a large number of his followers lived. He developed the "North American Sponsorship Program" to raise the financial support needed to undergird his travels. Meetings are held annually in approximately 75 cities (the largest number in the United States) and in 34 countries worldwide, primarily in India and Europe.

Beliefs and Practices

Elan Vital is derived from Sant Mat (literally, the way of the saints), a variation of the Sikh religion which draws significant elements from Hinduism. It is based upon a succession of spiritual masters generally believed to begin with Tulsi Sahib, an early nineteenth-century guru who lived at Hathras, Uttar Pradesh, India. It is believed that the person mentioned as Sarupanand Ji in Mission literature is in fact Sawan Singh, a prominent Sant Mat guru. In any case Hans Maharaj Ji claimed a Sant Mat succession which he passed to Maharaj Ji. Maharaj Ji, as do many of the other Sant Mat leaders, claims to be a Perfect Master, an embodiment of God on earth and hence a fitting object of worship and veneration.

The Mission had as one of its stated goals the instruction of the world in "the technique of utilizing the universal primordial Force, that is, the Holy Name (Word) which is the same as the Divine Light and which pervades all human beings thus bringing to the fore the eternal principle of unity in diversity." In the Sant Mat tradition this practice is called *surat shabd yoga*, the practice of uniting the human spirit with the universal divine sound current. The particular methods of accomplishing that union vary from group to group and are one reason for their separation. Within the Divine Light Mission, initiation into the yoga is by a process known as giving knowledge. Though those who received knowledge were instructed not to talk about their initiation to outsiders, details of the process were soon revealed by ex-members.

At initiation, an instructor (formerly called a *mahatma*), the personal representative of Maharaj Ji, introduces new members to four yogic techniques, all of which are quite common within Sant Mat circles, although equally unknown to the average person, even to the average Indian. These four techniques reveal the means of experiencing the divine light, sound, word, and nectar. To experience the divine light, one places the knuckles on the eyeballs, a process which produces flashes of light inside the head (and also pinches the optic nerve). To discover the divine sound or music of the spheres, one plugs the ears with the fingers and concentrates only on internal sounds. The third technique involves concentration upon the sound of one's own breathing. Finally, to taste the nectar, the tongue is curled backward against the roof of the mouth and left there for a period of time. Once learned, these techniques are practiced daily. Frequently, meditation is done under a blanket, both to block outside disturbances and to conceal the techniques.

Unlike many Sant Mat groups, the Divine Light Mission developed a social program during the 1970s. It was based upon Shri Hans Maharaj Ji's call for a balance between temporal and spiritual concerns. The original Mission's stated goals included the promotion of human unity, world peace, improved education for all (especially the poor), and relief from the distress caused by ill health and natural calamities. The Mission made provision for the future establishment of hospitals, maternity homes, and residences. This emphasis has been lost in the transformation of the Mission into Elan Vital.

Current Status

Elan Vital is virtually invisible in the United States. In 1979 the Denver headquarters of the Divine Light Mission quietly closed, and both it and Maharaj Ji moved to Miami Beach, Florida. From there, two periodicals were published, *Divine Times* and *Elan Vital*. In 1980, the Mission reported 10,000 to 12,000 active members in the United States.

Since the disbanding of the ashrams and local meetings, there has been no way to estimate the number of followers who have remained attached to Elan Vital. However, enough followers remain in the more than 25 U.S. and Canadian cities which Maharaj Ji regularly visits to warrant a stop.

Controversy

During the first years of the Divine Light Mission in the United States, both it and Maharaj Ji were constantly involved in controversy. The teachings of the Mission, particularly the public discourses of Maharaj Ji, were condemned as lacking in substance. Maharaj Ji, who frequently acted like the teenager that he was in public, was seen as immature and hence unfit to be a religious leader. At one point, a pie was thrown in his face (which led angry followers to assault the perpetrator). Ex-members attacked the group with standard anti-cult charges of brainwashing and mind control.

However, as the group withdrew from the public eye, little controversy followed it except for the accusations of Robert Mishner, the former president of the Mission, who left in 1977. Mishner complained that the ideals of the group had become impossible to fulfill and that money was increasingly diverted to Maharaj Ji's personal use. Mishner's charges, made just after the deaths at Jonestown, Guyana, found little support and have not affected the course of the organization. Through the late 1980s, not only has there been no controversy, but even information has been rare since the organization has granted no interviews and publishes no general announcements of Maharaj Ji's visits.

Sources-Primary

Light Reading. Miami Beach, FL: Divine Light Mission, 1980. 77 pp.

Maharaj Ji, Guru. *The Living Master.* Denver: Divine Light Mission, 1978. 109 pp.

————. *Reflections on an Indian Sunrise.* Divine Light Mission, 1972.

Shri Hans Ji Maharaj. Delhi: Divine Light Mission, n.d.

Who Is Guru Maharaj Ji? New York: Bantam Books, 1973. 303 pp.

Sources-Secondary

Collier, Sophia. *Soul Rush: The Odyssey of a Young Woman in the '70s.* New York: William Morrow and Company, 1978. 240 pp.

Downton, James V., Jr. *Sacred Journeys.* New York: Columbia University Press, 1979. 241 pp.

Price, Maeve. "The Divine Light Mission as a Social Organization." *Sociological Review* 27, 2 (May 1979): 279-96.

F. FAMILY OF LOVE
(CHILDREN OF GOD)

The Family of Love is the current name of the group which became infamous in the 1970s as the Children of God. When the Jesus People Revival began in the late 1960s on the West Coast, David Berg had already begun to gather the Children of God at a center in Huntington Beach. With some justification, Berg claims to be the originating force of the revival, even though the Children of God were the first of several Jesus People groups to be ostracized by the growing movement because of their doctrinal divergences.

Founder and Early History

The Family of Love was founded by David Brandt Berg, formerly a minister in the Christian and Missionary Alliance Church, a conservative holiness denomination. His mother was an evangelist with that church and had on several occasions received prophecies of future events. In 1967 Berg went to work for Fred Jordan who ran an independent pentecostal ministry, the Soul Clinic, in Los Angeles. In December 1967, alerted by his mother to the growing number of street people (hippies) in Huntington Beach, California, he moved there and took over a work previously begun by Teen Challenge, the Youth ministry of pentecostal minister Dave Wilkerson. It centered upon the Light Club Mission, a coffeehouse near the Huntington Beach pier.

Berg had already developed a critical attitude toward many establishment structures, particularly the organized church, and his message of withdrawal from worldliness and total commitment to a Jesus revolution appealed to the street people. Many of them gave up drugs, and a small group began to live communally. They called themselves Teens for Christ.

In 1969 Berg received a revelation that California was threatened by an earthquake and that he and his followers should leave. They moved to Tucson, where over the summer their number grew from 50 to 75. In the fall they divided into four teams to take their message of the Jesus Revolution across America. After several months, some of the Teens for Christ reassembled at a campground near Montreal. Here they formally organized and Berg ordained about fifty of them as bishops, elders, deacons, and deaconesses, though the highest offices remained in his immediate family.

Berg then called the entire membership together at Vienna, Virginia, to inform them of some secret revelations he had received in Canada. One of these, called "Old Church, New Church," was directly related to an adulterous affair with his secretary. In a lengthy session before the group, rather than repenting and announcing an end to the liaison, he sought to justify it. His wife and his secretary were, he asserted, models of the church. God had abandoned the old denominational church and had taken a new church (the revolutionary Jesus people), just as Berg had abandoned his wife, who, like the old church, had become a hindrance to God's work, for his new love. This theological metaphor of his sexual life undergirded the development of sex as a major metaphor of the Children's life and thought. Berg began to speak of America as the Great Whore. He began to articulate, first to the inner leadership, an understanding of revolutionary Christian love that involved communal sex. The practice soon spread to the entire membership.

The group departed Vienna for Washington, D.C., whereas the capital mourned the death of prominent Senator Everett Dirksen of Illinois, Berg's followers dressed in red sackcloth and ashes and mourned the death of the nation which had forsaken God. Similar demonstrations occurred in other cities. A reporter called them the "Children of God," and the group adopted this name. Also, in a prophecy spoken during this period, one of the members referred to Berg as Moses. Thus by February 1970, when Jordan turned over his Soul Clinic ranch near Thurber, Texas, to the group, they had become "Moses and the Children of God."

During the period at Thurber, William Rambur, a parent whose daughter had joined the Children of God, organized other angry parents into the "Parents Committee to Free Our Sons and Daughters from the Children of God," later popularly called FREECOG. Claiming their children were under drug-induced and hypnotic control, they aligned themselves with Theodore Patrick, who initiated the practice of deprogramming (discussed more fully in the chapter on the Anti-cult Movement), physically kidnapping members of the group and forcing them to renounce their allegiance to it. A few hostile ex-members began to relate vivid accounts of life among the Children which further increased the public opinion against them. Before the year was out Berg left the country and began to live in seclusion, and Jordan evicted the Children from the Thurber property.

Berg had incorporated the Children of God but, partly as a result of the bad publicity, tax-exempt status was denied. Hence, a second corporation, Youth for Truth, Inc., was quietly established to receive any financial assets, and the original corporation was abandoned.

The Children of God dispersed around the nation in some forty colonies. Some followed Berg's example and left the country. By the middle of the decade, spurred in part by Berg's warning of the destructive potential of Comet Kohoutek, most had emigrated. Berg exercised his leadership of the movement through a series of "Mo Letters," which guided the evolving organization and doctrine of the group. Some letters became internal documents, while others were sold on the street and became the means of spreading the group's message. Berg's understanding of himself as a prophet became more central and his prophecies, increasingly seen as coming from discarnate spirits, assumed the dominant role in molding the group's ideas.

During this period, Berg extended his increasingly radical ideas about sexual freedom to include by far the most controversial practice of the group, "flirty fishing." In a Mo Letter at the beginning of 1974, Berg ordered the women of the group to use their natural sexual appeal and talents to gain new members, to become fish bait, hookers for Jesus. The practice declined in the late 1970s after venereal disease ravaged the group.

In the face of the increasingly negative image of the Children of God, given a measurable boost following the deaths of Peoples Temple members in Guyana, Berg decided to change the organization of the group using a family model. Integral to the new structure, he asked followers to call him "Dad" and gave the Children their present name, the Family of Love.

Through the 1980s the Family of Love has assumed a very low profile. They had no mailing address in North America, and only on rare occasions were members spotted. They did surface to pass out tracks refuting charges made by Linda Berg (Deborah Davis) who had defected from the Children and wrote an account of her experiences. The headquarters, located in a London suburb, has refused to answer inquiries, and little new literature has been written. Otherwise, scattered reports of the Family, which retains colonies around the world have been the only source of information.

Beliefs and Practices

Beginning as a conservative holiness Christian group, the Family of Love adopted David Berg's extreme, but by no means unacceptable, ideas about the imminent end of the world, God's abandonment of worldly structures (governments, churches, economic systems), the coming Jesus revolution, and communalism. As they evolved, however, they thoroughly left orthodox Christian belief and practice. That deviation began with Berg's assumption of the role of, and not just the image of, Moses, a prophet of the endtime. Like Moses, Berg declared war on the evil system of things. The present system was so corrupt that reformation was not possible, only a complete revolution could bring in God's world.

In like measure, the Children of God assumed the role of the harbingers of God's New World. They were to be the living example of a totally new loving society. One sign of the Children's role was their new sexual ethic. Spelled out in a number of Mo Letters, love and sex were equated, and the free expression of sexuality including fornication, adultery, lesbianism (though not male homosexuality), and incest, were not just allowed but encouraged.

As a prophet, Berg increasingly received revelations that were completely divorced from the Bible. He issued Mo Letters concerning various spirit entities with whom he had established contact—especially

Abrahim (a gypsy king). He claimed to fulfill specific biblical prophecies, and as the endtime prophet, he claimed authority to teach new truth regardless of its substantiation in the Bible. He discarded the concept of the Trinity and adopted a belief in universal salvation.

Organization

The Children of God were organized into a pyramid of authority with Berg at the top. Under him were apostles, elders, and deacons. By the time of the loss of the colony at Thurber, the Children could count several thousand members. Berg dispersed them into numerous colonies nationally and internationally and created the new position of shepherds. Apostles oversaw the work nationally and internationally; elders were regional leaders; and shepherds led the individual colonies. In 1975, the colonies were broken into even smaller units, and the leadership roles on the lower levels expanded. By this time, the membership, approaching 7,000-10,000, was scattered internationally throughout Europe and Latin America. Berg supplied direction through the Mo Letters. Members lived communally. New members went through an indoctrination period as babes, soon progressing to become a brother or sister.

In 1979 Berg proposed a radical change in structure. He dismissed the entire leadership and reorganized the Children as an extended family. He disbanded the existing colonies into small family groups and encouraged everyone to call him "Dad." Taking a new name, the Family of Love, the group has tried to leave the negative image of the Children of God behind it.

As of 1991 there are no known Family of Love centers in North America, though it is believed that the Family has several hundred members scattered around the country.

Current Status

After leaving the United States, Berg settled in London, where he directs the Family of Love from his suburban estate. The Family has largely abandoned the United States and has no official center, headquarters, or even postal box address. International headquarters is in London. Publishing centers have been established in Geneva, Switzerland, and Hong Kong, though their present status is uncertain.

Into the early 1980s publishing was done by Gold Lion Publishers in Hong Kong, which in the late 1970s issued collected editions of the Mo Letters. A one-volume edition, *The Basic Mo Letters*, included the primary doctrinal tracts and outlined the family's perspective on religion, politics, economics, and sex. *New Nation News*, published in several languages and editions, is the major periodical.

No current statistics on the Family are available. There are an estimated 7,000-10,000 members widely dispersed internationally. Occasional reports of encounters with legal authorities from different countries, especially from Spain where they are outlawed, appear in news reports. The Family has claimed membership in the millions, but no verification of these figures has been found. Only a few hundred Family members reside in the United States. They are on rare occasions seen on the street distributing literature.

Controversy

The Children of God was the first of the new "cults" around which organized opposition developed and toward which the first deprogrammings were directed. It has been a central focus of anti-cult activities. It was prominently mentioned in legislative hearings such as that conducted by the Senate of the State of California in August 1974. A month later, New York Attorney General Louis Lefkowitz released the final report (an interim report issued in January 1974 had received wide publicity) of a lengthy investigation he had conducted. The report gave early justification to the theory of cults assaulting the psyche of new members by brainwashing. The report concluded, "Brainwashing techniques are deliberately employed under the rationalization that it is in the service of a good cause." The report emphasized and condemned the nonconventional sexual practices spreading though the group, though Lefkowitz was not yet aware of the institution of the "flirty fishing" policy. The report accused the leaders of arbitrarily forcing sexual relations upon members and, in one case, of condoning the rape of a 14-year-old runaway. The Children of God issued a lengthy reply to the Lefkowitz Report, but it had little circulation. Also, by that time, most of the members had left the country. In addition, all of the criminal charges made in the report concerned cases outside of Lefkowitz's jurisdiction, thus, no action followed its issuance.

The abandonment of the United States lessened, but by no means killed, hostile attitudes toward the group. The parents of members and ex-members remained key figures of the anti-cult movement, and they used the continuing reports of evangelism by prostitution and Berg's own sexual excesses as appalling examples of the degeneration of life within cults in general.

In the investigation conducted by Lefkowitz, Sarah Berg, the wife abandoned in the "Old Church, New Church" revelation, offered her story as witness to the truth of Berg's immorality. In the late 1970s, Deborah Davis, one of Berg's daughters left the group and published a book about her experience. She goes far beyond the account of her mother in detailing her father's personal excesses, including incest, as well as an account of the flirty fishing at the resorts at Tenerife in the Canary Islands. Shortly after the book appeared, Berg wrote a short rebuttal, but did not answer any of the specific charges. He merely labeled her account a lie.

In 1988 the account of former member Ruth Gordon, who had left the group in 1980, provided further documentation of the group's activities in the 1970s. The sexual manipulation in the Children of God has now been so thoroughly documented that it is doubtful whether the organization can ever, in spite of whatever future reforms it might initiate, regain any respectable place in the larger religious community.

Sources-Primary

Berg, David (under pen name Moses David). *The Basic Mo Letters*. Hong Kong: Gold Lion Publishers, 1976. 1521 pp.

—————. *The Mo Letters*. 8 vols. Hong Kong: Gold Lion Publishers and Zurich: World Services, 1977-1981.

—————. *Thoughts from Mo*. Hong Kong: Gold Lion Publishers, 1976. 220 pp.

Warner, Samson. *We Are the Children of God*. Rome, Italy: Children of God, 1977. 32 pp.

Sources-Secondary

Brogan, Frankie Fonde. *The Snare of the Fowler.* Lincoln, VA: Chosen Books, 1982. 198 pp.

Davis, Deborah (Linda Berg). *The Children of God.* Grand Rapids: Zondervan Publishing House, 1984. 244 pp.

Final Report of the Activities of the Children of God to Hon. Louis J. Lefkowitz. New York: Charities Fraud Division, Attorney General's Office, 1974. 65 pp.

Gordon, Ruth. *Children of Darkness.* Wheaton, IL: Living Books, 1988. 312 pp.

McManus, Una. *Not for a Million Dollars.* Nashville, TN: Impact Books, 1980. 182 pp.

Pritchett, Douglas. *The Children of God/Family of Love, An Annotated Bibliography.* New York: Garland Publishing, 1985. 177 pp.

G. THE INTERNATIONAL SOCIETY FOR KRISHNA CONSCIOUSNESS (HARE KRISHNA)

The International Society for Krishna Consciousness became for many people the symbol of the invasion of Asian religion into American life in the 1970s. Of all the groups, they were the most visible, most frequently pictured in illustrations accompanying media coverage of the new religions, and most often the target of humor and satire.

Background

During the debates on cults in the 1970s, the International Society for Krishna Consciousness (ISKCON) was frequently referred to as the prime example of a "new" religion. But while ISKCON was founded in the United States in 1965, when Swami Prabhupada began his public ministry, its tradition goes back at the very least to the sixteenth century and the career of a Bengali saint, Chaitanya (or Caitanya) Mahaprabhu (1486-1534?). Chaitanya was a promising young scholar without any particular religious inclination. Then, at about the age of twenty-one he went on a pilgrimage that changed his life. He met the ascetic Isvara Puri who introduced him to chanting. Accepting his new acquaintance as his guru, he returned to his hometown only to spend all his time chanting the names of Krishna. Some considered him mad; others attracted by his fervency became disciples. He moved to Puri in Orissa near the Jagannatha Temple. With the support of the king, he was able to build a strong movement among the Vaishnava Hindus who worshiped Jagannatha as a form of Krishna.

Chaitanya combined the ascetic monastic ideal with a life of intense devotional activity focused upon dancing and chanting. A mystic life came easily to him and he frequently would go into a trance while chanting. Some historians believe that his sudden disappearance in 1534 is best accounted for by assuming that he drowned in the sea while in a trance.

After his disappearance the movement declined but experienced revivals in the seventeenth and mid-nineteenth centuries. One of those who led the revival in the nineteenth century, contemporaneously with the national Hindu revival, Swami Bhaktivinode Thakur founded the Gaudiya Vaishnava Mission in 1886. After his death, his son Sri Srimad Bhakti Siddhanta Goswami, a former professor of mathematics and astronomy, continued his work. He founded the Gaudiya Math Institute and some sixty-four missions. He was also the guru of Abhay Charan De, the founder of the International Society for Krishna Consciousness.

Founder

A.C. Bhaktivedanta Swami Prabhupada was born in Calcutta, September 1, 1896, as Abhay Charan De. He graduated from the University of Calcutta in 1920 with majors in English, philosophy, and economics and went to work as the manager of a chemical plant. In 1922 he met Bhakti Siddhanta of the Gaudiya Vaishnava Mission and accepted him as his guru. Noting his ability in English, the Swami asked the young devotee to write about Krishna Consciousness in English, and he authored a commentary on the *Bhagavad-Gita*. In 1933 he was formally initiated into the Gaudiya Mission, just three years before its leader died. During those years the Swami gave his new initiate a charge to carry Krishna Consciousness to the West.

Abhay Charan De did not at first take the charge seriously. He continued to produce English-language material for the Mission. During World War II he began a magazine, *Back to Godhead*, but it lasted only a few issues due to a paper shortage. (He revived it in 1952 and made a third try in 1956). As the war ended however, he found himself saddled with unwanted responsibilities that directly conflicted with his desire to spend his entire life in Krishna devotion.

Finally, in 1950 Bhaktivedanta retired and began to give some thought to the task his guru had set for him. In 1954 he adopted the *vanaprastha* (retired) order and moved to Vrndavana and the Vamsi-gopalaji Temple. During this period he began to translate the massive Hindu classic, the *Srimad-Bhagavatam*, three volumes of which appeared in the next decade. He also wrote a small work, *Easy Journey to Other Planets*. In 1956 he had a vision of his guru telling him to go to the West, and he reconciled himself to the journey. In 1959 he took a further step in realizing his goal by taking the vows of a *sannyasin*, the renounced life, and separating from his wife and family. Family obligations had been the primary barrier keeping him from moving to the United States.

Then at the age of 70, in 1965, A.C. Bhaktivedanta Swami Prabhupada took up his mission. A short time after he arrived, the Oriental Exclusion Act (which had prevented Asians from migrating to America) was rescinded, and he was able to exchange his tourist visa for a residency visa which allowed him to stay in the country for an extended period of time. He began his missionary work in New York City on the Lower East Side. He daily went to Tompkins Park to chant and talk with passersby. A few hippies discovered the Swami and adopted him as their guru. Within a year a center had been opened and his magazine, *Back to Godhead*, revived again with the aid of a Xerox machine. A San Francisco center was opened in 1967, and the movement experienced a steady growth from that point on.

Swami Prabhupada, while leading the movement, continued to write and translate. He pushed the publishing venture with vigor. In 1968 a copy of his translation of the *Bhagavad-Gita, As It Is*, appeared. He continued to work on the *Srimad-Bhagavatam* and began translation of the *Caitanya-Caritamrta*. In 1972 the Bhaktivedanta Book Trust was established and published over 60 400-page volumes of his work.

Prabhupada lived long enough to see his venture transform into an international movement and some of his disciples turn into accomplished leaders. He also lived to see the first attacks on the movement by deprogrammers and anti-cultists. He passed away on November 14, 1977. He left the movement in the hands of a 22-person Governing Board Commission which included eleven gurus designated as initiating gurus. The work was divided geographically and an initiating guru assigned to each zone.

Belief and Practice

The International Society for Krishna Consciousness is a transplanted conservative form of Hinduism centered upon the practice of *bhakti yoga,* a path of devotional service. For ISKCON devotees, the prime method of devotional service is the repetition of the Hare Krishna mantra but includes a number of practices which, taken out of their context in India and thrust in the midst of modern American society, seem very strange. The worldview that underlies the Krishnas' *bhakti* practices is summarized in a widely circulated statement:

1. By sincerely cultivating a bona fide spiritual science, we can be free from anxiety and come to a state of pure, unending, blissful consciousness in this lifetime.
2. We are not our bodies but eternal spirit souls, parts and parcels of God (Krsna). As such, we are all brothers, and Krsna is ultimately our common father.
3. Krsna is the eternal, all-knowing, omnipresent, all-powerful, and all-attractive Personality of Godhead. He is the seed-giving father of all living beings, and He is the sustaining energy of the entire cosmic creation.
4. The Absolute Truth is contained in all the great scriptures of the world. However, the oldest revealed scriptures in existence are the Vedic literatures, most notably the *Bhagavad-Gita,* which is the literal record of God's actual words.
5. We should learn the Vedic knowledge from a genuine spiritual master—one who has no selfish motives and whose mind is firmly fixed on Krsna.
6. Before we eat, we should offer to the Lord the food that sustains us. Then Krsna becomes the offering and purifies us.
7. We should perform all our actions as offerings to Krsna and do nothing for our own sense gratification.
8. The recommended means for achieving the mature stage of love of God in this age of Kali, or quarrel, is to chant the holy names of the Lord. The easiest method for most people is to chant the Hare Krsna Mantra:

       Hare Krsna, Hare Krsna
       Krsna Krsna, Hare Hare
       Hare Rama, Hare Rama
       Rama Rama, Hare Hare

In joining ISKCON a devotee not only accepts a belief structure but an ascetic, semi-monastic life and disciplines. Like Roman Catholic monks, the new devotee takes a new name. Most devotees also don the traditional clothing associated with the religious life in India. The head of a male devotee is shaved except for a tuft called the *sikha*, a sign of surrender to the spiritual master. A set of japa beads are carried to assist in chanting the mantra. Daily, a clay marking called the *tilaka* is applied to the forehead and nose as a sign that the body is a temple of the Supreme Lord.

Diet for a Krishna devotee is strictly vegetarian. Their food, *prasadum*, is prepared for and offered to Krishna before eating. On the eleventh day after the full and new moons, a partial fast in which grains, cereals, and beans are deleted from the diet is observed. Krishna cooking has become a popular part of New Age gatherings, though Krishnas rarely take part in other New Age activities, and several Krishna cookbooks are now on the market.

For most devotees the important activity of the day is *sankirtan*, the congregational chanting of the holy names of God. Frequently this occurs in the temple setting, but, following the example of Chaitanya, the public chanting is also a regular feature of devotee life. Public sankirtan has become that aspect of ISKCON's life to be most satirized by the media.

The devotees, in accepting a life of devotional service, give up a great deal, most notably the close company of nondevotees as is common with all monastics. This cutting off from people outside the community has caused the greatest tension, especially among family members of devotees.

Organization

During the lifetime of Swami Prabhupada, he headed up the organization. Before his death, he appointed a Governing Board Commission (GBC) consisting of 24 senior disciples to administer ISKCON internationally. Eleven of the commissioners were also named as *initiating acharyas*, and hence authorized to take disciples as he had done. The eleven were each responsible for a particular area of the world. They assumed full authority and appointed the temple presidents who administratively head individual temples. Collectively, the GBC has over the years assumed authority to both depose several of the initiating gurus, disfellowship another, and appoint new gurus as the organization has expanded internationally.

Individual members are initiated only after a trial period. They enter either the unmarried (*brachmacari*) or married (*grhasthas*) order. If they remain celibate, they may enter the renounced order as *sannyasins*. Two orders are defined by function. *Brahmins* serve as priests, teachers, and administrators. *Vaisyas* produce foodstuffs. Ultimately all devotees receive the second initiation as brahmins and take on responsibilities for worship, instruction, and the spreading of the message of Krishna devotion.

Each temple is organized on a strict schedule that begins before sunrise. Morning activities include bathing, application of the clay markings, worship and chanting, the eating of *prasadam*, food which has been offered to Krishna, and veneration of the temple deities. During the day, each devotee has an assigned task which may include work at the temple or sankirtan. Some spend the day at the local airport distributing Krishna literature and collecting donations from passengers, an activity that has earned them the antagonism of many.

Growth

Although he arrived in the United States with neither income nor following, Swami Prabhupada accumulated both swiftly. The second temple in San Francisco was opened in 1967. By 1970 21 centers in the United States had been created, and the work spread to Japan, Germany, Canada, England, and Australia. By 1982 they reported 50 centers in the United States including several farms, plus a string of vegetarian restaurants. Centers (more than 175) were found throughout Canada, the British Isles, Europe, and on other continents.

Through the 1980s, two trends in Krishna membership were evident. First, with the growing population of first-generation immigrants from India, the attendance at Krishna temples expanded. A large percentage of their current support now comes from Indian-Americans. Secondly, the number of full-time non-Indian Krishna devotees dropped, and subsequently a number of the centers were consolidated into the larger temples. There were 43 temples, 6 farm communities, and 13 restaurants in 1990. ISKCON claims 3,000 initiated members and 500,000 lay members who regularly visit a temple at least once a month.

International headquarters of the movement are Sridhama Mayapur, West Bengal, India. Since the movement has decentralized, there is no official United States headquarters, but a public information ministry is located in San Diego. The Bhaktivedanta Book Trust is located in Los Angeles. There are several other publishing concerns, the most important being Gita-Nigari Press of Pontiac, Maryland. *Back to Godhead*, the movement's primary magazine which ceased publication in the mid-1980s, was revived in 1991. It is published in Philadelphia.

Controversy

Through its public activities—annual Rathayatra Festival, soliciting money at airports, and the practice of sankirtan on city streets—the International Society for Krishna Consciousness has maintained a high profile in American life. While trying to project an image of a bona fide religion following the traditions of ancient India, it has been seen as a foreign and enigmatic group whose ascetic, communal, and separatist lifestyle opposes dominant American values (to which it offers a distinct alternative) and threatens common family patterns (which, in many cases, it does).

The tension between the Society and the culture increased as the anti-cult movement focused attention upon the group. Various anti-cult groups have made members the object of a series of deprogrammings, beginning with Ed Shapiro who was deprogrammed by Ted Patrick in the early 1970s. Deprogrammed Krishnas have received wide media coverage. Anti-cult groups have also attempted to arouse public opinion against the Society and block attempts by ISKCON to carry out its program. They have moved to stop their public soliciting at the airports and, after years of frustration, finally were able to have some restrictions imposed. They have also lobbied to require building permits (for the establishment of Krishna temples) and parade permits (for street-corner solicitation).

The efforts of the anti-cult groups have been aided by some events within the Society. Annually, beginning in the mid-1970s, Krishnas were arrested for soliciting without a permit while dressed in Santa Claus suits. Since the Krishnas as Hindus do not celebrate Christmas, such solicitation attempts were widely interpreted as efforts to deceive the public.

In the wake of Jonestown, the Krishnas were reported to be stockpiling weapons. They denied the reports but later confirmed that, in spite of their pacifist stance, they had weapons at several of their farms where local citizens had harassed the residents. Then a leader in the Bay Area in California was discovered to have a car trunk full of guns. Not widely reported was the fact that the individual had refused to follow the Society's orders to rid himself of the weapons and after the incident was severely disciplined by the Society.

The single most famous incident in the Krishnas' interaction with the public concerns David Yanoff. As a child, David had been given to his father by an Illinois court when his parents divorced. However, his mother took him to California and disappeared into the movement and eventually moved to a Krishna community in Europe. David's father and grandfather launched a public crusade to force the Society to locate and return the boy. They organized public opinion which led to the denial of a zoning change for the temple in Evanston, Illinois, disrupted soliciting at Chicago's O'Hare Airport, and initiated a suit. After over a year of effort David was returned to his father's custody.

While attacks in the media and from anti-cult groups continued, the Society received a more cordial welcome from the scholarly community. Religious scholars praised Swami Prabhupada's translations, and individual scholars who had studied the group—J. Stillson Judah, Harvey Cox, Larry Shinn, and Thomas Hopkins—have defended it against what they saw as distorted media images and misrepresentations by anti-cultists. Members of the society were welcomed into academic organizations such as the American Academy of Religion.

During the 1980s, the life of the Krishnas became focused on two issues, one internal and one external. Internally, the movement was shaken by a reform movement. While the movement raised a variety of concerns, the issue of the authority of the new initiating gurus was possibly the most important. Following Prabhupada's death, several of the gurus asserted their belief that the new gurus were essentially taking his place and hence were the heirs of all the power, prestige, and privilege he enjoyed. In 1979 the GBC confirmed the gurus' authority to receive *guru puja*, a worship in which the guru is venerated. However, some of the gurus had not lived up to their assigned role. The GBC assumed authority to discipline Hansadutta (guru in Berkeley, California) and to remove Jayatirtha in London. Then in 1983 it appointed three new gurus. In 1985 the GBC voted to have the seats of the new gurus lowered below that of Prabhupada's (which is retained in each temple) and to initiate a number of new gurus so that the majority of initiating gurus would be GBC appointees. The practice of guru puja was discouraged and began to be abandoned.

Kirtanananda Swami Bhaktipada emerged as one of the most conservative voices in ISKCON as the reform movement gained strength. In 1987 he was disfellowshipped. As head of ISKCON of West Virginia, he reorganized and has continued with his separate work independently. With his departure, the strongest voice against reform was removed.

The second issue diverting the movement in the 1980s was the case of Robin George. George had joined the movement while still a minor. When her parents tried to locate her for deprogramming, she was shielded by the movement and moved among several temples. Finally located, she was deprogrammed and in 1977 filed a suit against the movement. The suit directly involved the Los Angeles temple and those associated with it. In 1983 the jury awarded her a $32.5 million judgment. The judge cut it to $9.7 million and an appeals court to $3 million in 1987. The appeals court ruling was sustained by the California Supreme Court. Since that time it has gone to the Supreme Court and is still in process of adjudication. In the meantime, the most damaging testimony concerning brainwashing, admitted in the original trial, has been tossed out of several other cases as having no basis in science.

The future of the appeals in the case remains in doubt (as of the end of 1991), but however it is finally decided it will have a decisive effect on both the Krishnas (who will be largely relieved of their property on the West Coast should the current judgment stand) and the anti-cult movement (which will be further discouraged from similar civil suits should the judgment be overturned).

Sources-Primary

The KRSNA Consciousness Handbook. Los Angeles: ISKCON Press, 1970. 110 pp.

Prabhupada, A. C. Bhaktivedanta Swami. *Bhagavad-Gita: As It Is.* New York: Bhaktivedanta Book Trust, 1972.

————. *KRSNA Consciousness: The Top Most Yoga System.* Boston: ISKCON Press, 1970. 57 pp.

————. *Teachings of Lord Caitanya.* New York: Bhaktivedanta Book Trust, 1974. 292 pp.

Satsvarupa dasa Goswami. *Guru Reform Notebook.* Washington, DC: Gita-Nigari Press, 1986. 70 pp.

————. *Prabhupada.* Los Angeles: Bhaktivedanta Book Trust, 1983. 362 pp.

Sources-Secondary

Bromley, David G., and Larry D. Shinn, eds. *Krishna Consciousness in the West.* Lewisburg, PA: Bucknell University Press, 1989. 295 pp.

Gelberg, Steven J., ed. *Hare Krishna, Hare Krishna.* New York: Grove Press, 1983. 276 pp.

Judah, J. Stillson. *Hare Krishna and the Counterculture.* New York: John Wiley & Sons, 1974. 301 pp.

Knott, Kim. *My Sweet Lord: The Hare Krishna Movement.* Wellingborough, UK: Aquarian Press, 1986. 112 pp.

Levine, Faye. *The Strange World of the Hare Krishnas.* Greenwich, CT: Fawcett Publications, 1974. 189 pp.

Rochford, E. Burke, Jr. *Hare Krishna in America.* New Brunswick, NJ: Rutgers University Press, 1985. 324 pp.

Shinn, Larry D. *The Dark Lord: Cult Images and the Hare Krishnas in America.* Philadelphia, PA: Westminster Press, 1987. 204 pp.

H. THE INTERNATIONAL SOCIETY FOR KRISHNA CONSCIOUSNESS OF WEST VIRGINIA

The International Society for Krishna Consciousness (ISKCON) of West Virginia was for many years an integral, but separately incorporated, part of the International Society for Krishna Consciousness. However, in 1987, following years of growing tension within ISKCON's Governing Body Commission, the West Virginia corporation was separated from ISKCON and has since made its own way in the world. It had already become one of the most controversial centers in the world of new religions, and that controversy has continued to the present.

Founder

The story of ISKCON of West Virginia begins in 1966 when a young Columbia University graduate student, Keith Ham, dropped out of his program to become the disciple of A. C. Bhaktivedanta Swami Prabhupada (1896-1977). After several tumultuous years, which included his leaving his teacher for several short periods, he moved to West Virginia (where he had found some inexpensive land), and began to create a Krishna-oriented community. It came to be known as New Vrindaban, named out of the holy city associated with Krishna in India. Ham steadily grew in Prabhupada's eyes, took the vows of a *sanyassin*, the renounced life, and emerged as Kirtanananda Swami Bhaktipada. As a senior disciple, in the early 1970s, he was named as one of the members of the Governing Body Commission which Swami Prabhupada named to carry on the Society after his death. Over the years his various books showed him to be an accomplished spokesperson of the Vaishnava Hindu tradition.

New Vrindaban grew slowly at first and was thought of as a rural farm center. Then in 1973 Bhaktipada began the first of several projects which would lift New Vrindaban into the spotlight. He began construction of a palace as a home for his revered guru, Swami Prabhupada. The Palace would not be completed until 1979, by which time Prabhupada had died. It was an elaborate building built of the finest materials and emerged as one of West Virginia's most visited tourist stops. Meanwhile the community began to grow as ISKCON members who had been initiated by Prabhupada moved to New Vrindaban to live.

As the Palace was taking shape under the skillful hands of devotees, Bhaktipada began to develop a vision of an expanded facility on the mountaintop that New Vrindaban occupied. He first conceived of the development of what were termed the Gardens of Transcendental Knowledge with the Palace at one end and a Krishna temple at the other. The gardens, apart from being a beautiful park, would also depict incidents in the life of Krishna and thus serve as a means of introducing visitors to Krishna Consciousness.

As plans were being announced for the temple, the ideas for development of New Vrindaban continued to germinate, and Bhaktipada allowed them to grow into the idea of a new kind of community, the City of God, a sacralized urban community to facilitate the development of body, mind, and soul. New Vrindaban would be the first of 12 such cities to be located in different parts of the world. The City of God would be an interfaith enterprise and become a place of pilgrimage for believers of the different religions.

Initial plans for the City of God were announced in the mid-1980s, but work on actualizing them was delayed following the almost fatal assault upon Bhaktipada by a former community member in October 1985. Finally the first of the annual summer conferences inaugurated an active interfaith program. By 1990 the interfaith program had grown into an entire series of conferences and retreats.

The development of the interfaith work and the dominance of the City of God theme in the community coincided with the emergence to prominence of the reform movement within the larger Krishna movement. The major issue in reform was the role of the initiating gurus who collectively had become the spiritual leaders of ISKCON following Prabhupada's death. Most of the gurus had assumed the roles and prerogatives of Indian spiritual teachers which included the reception of veneration by the devotees in a *puja* (worship) service. However, several of the gurus had proved inadequate in adhering to their vows of chastity and nonuse of drugs and alcohol. The reform movement called for, among other things, the lowering of the status of the gurus, especially in refraining from continuing to receive *guru puja*.

Bhaktipada emerged as one of the most conservative voices in the Governing Board Commission. Tension between Bhaktipada and his colleagues increased as calls for reform gained strength and as controversy swelled around New Vrindaban. The concerns came to a head in March 1987 when Bhaktipada was excommunicated. He reorganized the community and the several associated centers under his guidance in Ohio and Pennsylvania and prepared to go on independently, though informal contacts have been retained with the larger community looking for possible signs of reconciliation.

Beliefs and Practices

ISKCON of West Virginia is almost identical in belief and practice with the larger International Society for Krishna Consciousness, differences being largely on administrative matters. The larger movement has discontinued the guru puja service which is still integral to the worship at New Vrindaban.

Since the break, some innovations have been introduced at New Vrindaban which further distinguish it from its parent body. In place of the saffron robes worn by most ISKCON devotees, New Vrindaban residents adopted a new dress modelled on a Franciscan habit. As part of their emphasis on interfaith concerns (and reflective of the inclusive spirit of Hinduism), a *murti* (statue) of Jesus was installed in the temple, as was an organ.

Present Status

Very soon after the founding of New Vrindaban, the center was incorporated and a 12-person board of trustees elected. The board has ultimate responsibility for the land, now approximately 5,000 acres.

Members of the board serve for life. The community is headed by a president who is elected by the resident members. Associated with the community is Palace Publishing, its book publishing arm. The Interreligious Affairs Council plans and administers the interfaith program. A periodical, *New Vrindaban World*, is issued biweekly.

As of 1990, over 500 devotees resided at New Vrindaban. There were also affiliated temples in Brooklyn, New York, and Columbus, Ohio.

During the 1980s the community also developed a membership plan for nonresidents. A number of residential lodges and an apartment complex have been constructed, and guaranteed shared time for individuals who would like to come to New Vrindaban are available. These have proved especially popular among Indian-Americans, a large number of whom support the community.

Controversy

Through 1985, New Vrindaban, as part of ISKCON, shared the controversy which involved the larger movement. Part of that controversy surrounded the use of drugs in ISKCON. During its early years, ISKCON recruited members from the drug culture and offered the practice of yoga as a substitute for the psychedelic experience. The overwhelming majority of ISKCON members were former drug users and many were former dealers. During the 1970s, the international spread of ISKCON provided what some saw as an opportunity to make money off of drugs. Some members began to smuggle drugs into the United States, on occasion placing them inside of deity statues destined for ISKCON. Critics charged that this was done with the consent and to the profit of the organization. Defenders have noted that the offenders were in fact members who had lost their faith, who had fallen away from practice of their devotional life, and who decided to use the organization to their advantage before they left. It is among such "marginal" members that the troubles at New Vrindaban began.

The events at New Vrindaban also have to be understood against a background of tension with the local community. These tensions seemed to be on the wane when beginning in 1985 a series of events rocked the community and created a situation that had the potential of destroying it completely. In October 1985, Swami Bhaktipada was almost killed when a member of the community (who had previously been asked to leave another Krishna temple) attacked him. Then, during Bhaktipada's lengthy recovery, Stephen Bryant, another former resident of New Vrindaban, was shot and killed in Los Angeles. Bryant had blamed Bhaktipada for the dissolution of his marriage and had previously come to West Virginia carrying a pistol and threatening Bhaktipada.

A week after the Bryant murder, Thomas Dresher, a member of the community, was arrested and charged with the murder of one Charles St. Denis. St. Denis, a marginal member of New Vrindaban and former drug dealer, had disappeared in 1983 and had not been seen since. His body had not been found. However, authorities had put together evidence that St. Denis had been killed by Daniel Reid. Reid had accused St. Denis of raping his wife and after the killing had sought Dresher's assistance in dealing with the body. Reid gave state's evidence and received a light sentence. Dresher was given a life sentence. He was also tied to the Bryant murder.

In September 1986 a grand jury investigation of a variety of charges which had been leveled at New Vrindaban opened. In January 1987 the FBI raided the community and confiscated most of its records. The raid signaled the launching of a long-term federal investigation. A month later, two teachers at the New Vrindaban school were accused of child molestation. The growing questions about the community prepared the was for Bhaktipada's excommunication by ISKCON's Governing Board Commission. In April 1987, Dresher took the vows of the renounced life, an event widely publicized in the media as his becoming a swami.

The first results of the federal investigation were announced late in the year. Dresher and Swami Bhaktipada were indicted on a series of charges growing out of the arson of a building owned by the community and the subsequent collection of insurance. Dresher was convicted, and Bhaktipada found not guilty. Through 1988 and 1989, the community felt some confidence that the worse was over, even though a widely publicized book-length attack upon the community, *Monkey on a Stick*, was released in 1988. Then in May 1990 Bhaktipada and other community members were indicted on a series of conspiracy and racketeering charges, some of which originated in some questionable fund-raising practices in the community's earlier days. The trial was held in 1991 with the result that Bhaktipada was convicted on most of the charges. He was shortly thereafter released on bail but confined under house arrest awaiting his appeal. Meanwhile Dresher was tried for the Bryant murder in Los Angeles. The first trial resulted in a hung jury, but he was convicted in a second trial. Further efforts on his case are being continued by defense attorneys.

Much hinges on the appeals in the racketeering case. With the conviction looms the possibility that the state will move to claim the community's property in the light of its having been purchased with illegal money. Thus while the community moves ahead with its devotional program and interfaith efforts, it will have constant diversions for legal problems claiming its energy during the next decade.

Sources-Primary

Bhaktipada, Kirtanananda Swami. *Christ and Krishna: The Path of Pure Devotion.* Moundsville, WV: Bhaktipada Books, 1985. 180 pp.

—————. *Eternal Love: Conversations with the Lord of the Heart.* Moundsville, WV: Bhaktipada Books, 1985. 248 pp.

—————. *On His Order.* Moundsville, WV: Bhakti Books (Palace Publishing), 1987. 108 pp.

—————. *The Song of God: A Summary Study of the Bhagavad-Gita: As It Is.* Moundsville, WV: Bhaktipada Books, 1984. 304 pp.

Murti Swami. *Protection for Culture: The Cities of God.* Moundsville, WV: Interreligious Affairs Council, New Vrindaban Community, n.d.[1987]. 16 pp.

Tirtha Swami [Thomas Dresher]. *From Saigon to San Quentin: A Spiritual Odyssey.* N.p.: The Author, n.d. [1991]. 181 pp.

Sources-Secondary

Bromley, David G., and Larry D. Shinn. *Krishna Consciousness in the West.* Lewisburg, PA: Bucknell University Press, 1989. 295 pp.

Houriet, Robert. *Getting It Back Together.* New York: Avon Books, 1971. 408 pp.

Hubner, John, and Lindsey Gruson. *Monkey on a Stick: Murder, Madness, and the Hare Krishnas.* San Diego, CA: Harcourt Brace Jovanovich, 1988. 414 pp.

I. THE LOCAL CHURCH
(WATCHMAN NEE AND WITNESS LEE)

For a period in the early 1980s the Local Church became the focus of the most intense battles in the cult/anti-cult controversy, as several Evangelical Christian counter-cult organizations accused it of being a cult. While it claims, and appearances back its assertion, to be an orthodox evangelical Christian body of believers, recognizable differences of theological language (if not beliefs) and particular practices unique to the Local Church led to heated polemics. The polemics largely dissolved following the resolution of a series of lawsuits. The saga of the Local Church remains a significant episode effecting the course of the cult controversy as a whole, especially that phase revolving around the Christian counter-cult ministries. Hence its inclusion in this volume.

Founders and Early History

The group that is variously called the Little Flock, the Assembly Hall Movement, or the Local Church was founded in the 1920s in China by Ni Shu-tsu, popularly known by the English translation of his name, Watchman Nee (1903-1972). Nee was born into a Chinese Christian family. His grandfather had been a Congregational minister. His parents were Methodists. He changed his original name Ni Shu-tsu (Henry Nee) to To-Sheng (Watchman), to remind himself that he was a bell-ringer who would raise up a people for God. Not particularly religious as a youth, he was converted by Dora Yu, a Methodist missionary. Soon after, working with an independent missionary, Margaret E. Barber, he discovered the writings of John Nelson Darby and the exclusive Plymouth Brethren. He adopted the nondenominational approach to church organization espoused by Darby and soon became the leader of a small group of evangelical Christians. By the end of the decade, he had made contact with a branch of the Brethren led by elder James Taylor. At their invitation, he visited England in 1933, but soon broke with the group because of his unauthorized fellowship with a non-Brethren group headed by T. Austin-Sparks.

From its rather modest beginnings in Foochow, Nee's movement spread through China. He traveled widely, founding congregations based upon his idea that there should be only one local church (i.e., congregation) in each city as the basic expression of the unity of Christianity (in the face of divisive denominationalism). He expressed this position in his most famous book, *The Normal Christian Church Life*. He also authored *The Spiritual Man*, in which he espoused his conception of the tripartite nature of human beings as body, soul, and spirit.

During World War II, to prevent his becoming a financial burden to the Church, Nee took a job at his brother's chemical factory in Shanghai. After the War, he returned to full-time evangelical work and turned the factory over to the Church in Shanghai to own, manage, and, most importantly, collect the profits. Other members soon followed his example. This action became Nee's downfall, as the People's Republic of China, which came to power in 1949, accused Nee and the churches affiliated with him of imperialism. Exiled from Shanghai, he was arrested in 1952 and spent the rest of his life in prison. To protect itself, the Church excommunicated him and, for the most part, went underground.

During the 1930s, Nee gained a convert, Witness Lee, a former Protestant minister, who became an elder of the church at Chefoo. By the end of the decade he was among Nee's most valuable assistants. After a three-year absence caused by tuberculosis, Lee joined Nee upon his return to full-time church work in 1946. In 1947 Nee sent Lee to Taiwan to work among the growing number of refugees from the post-war conflicts in mainland China. Nee made one visit to Taiwan in 1949. Lee inherited Nee's mantle of leadership and under his guidance, the Church flourished and soon became the fastest growing church in Taiwan. Having no financial backing in the West, the Church relied upon the efforts of unsalaried workers, but by 1960 had a membership of over 20,000. Growth was slowed for awhile as other churches siphoned off members, but by 1967 there were 35,000 adherents. Subsequently, the Local Church had emerged as one of the largest Christian groups in the country.

The Church spread among immigrant communities in the Philippines and Hong Kong and soon around the entire Pacific basin. Members migrating to the United States brought the movement to the West Coast. Lee moved to the United States in 1962 and founded the Living Stream Ministry. Recognized as the leading full-time worker among the local churches, he has provided overall direction for the spread of the Local Church.

Lee has also been a source of innovation within the movement. He has introduced several theological emphases not found in the writings of Watchman Nee and initiated several practices such as pray-reading and "calling upon the name of the Lord," which became the subject of controversy.

Organization

The local churches affirm the unity of the Church, the corporate nature of Church life, and the direct headship of Christ over the Church. Great emphasis is thus placed on Church life, meeting together (several times a week), and the function and responsibility of each member in keeping alive a relationship with God and sharing the duties of congregational life. In rejecting the clergy-laity distinction, a pattern for the practical expression of the Church's life has been established.

Beginning with the critique of the denominational fracturing of the unity of Christianity found in John Nelson Darby, through his study of Scripture, Watchman Nee developed his own ecclesiology. He saw a pattern in the New Testament of founding a local church in each city and came to believe that that was the proper pattern for church life. Roman Catholicism and Protestant denominations had departed from that pattern, to which they should return. He also saw the local churches under the control of elders rather than an ordained clergy or episcopal hierarchy.

The rejection of denominationalism created a problem of naming the group. As did other nondenominational groups, such as the Plymouth Brethren before them, they took no name. The brethren were simply the believers who were called the Plymouth Brethren by others because an early prominent congregation was located in Plymouth, England. The Local Church sees itself simply as the Church. The term "local church" is a convenient designation but not a name. Thus local congregations are called "The Church in (name of the city)."

Following Nee's idea, the Local Church is organized as a fellowship of autonomous congregations, one to a city. Each congregation is headed by a small group (usually from two to five) of elders who are in charge of its teaching, preaching, and administrative responsibilities. Elders are generally appointed from those among the congregation who seem to be most dedicated and capable.

Nee also saw that there was a need for a continuing apostolic function—for men who would travel among the local churches teaching and training the leadership and initiating new congregations in cities without a local church. Such men are set aside, as was the apostle Paul, as workers. Workers organize their efforts, more or less formally, as an independent ministry. In the case of Witness Lee, his work is incorporated at Living Stream Ministry and is at present the most prominent such ministry among Local Church congregations. Workers travel, speak, and publish as they are led and supported and as their work proves fruitful. While such ministries are formally associated with one congregation as a base of operations. For example, Living Stream shares a building with the Church in Anaheim (California).

Throughout its history the Local Church has spread through the evangelical efforts of the co-workers or the happenstance movements of members, whose migration to the United States led to the founding of the first Local Church congregations in New York and California. However, in recent years, with Lee's encouragement, the Local Church has adopted a process termed the "Jerusalem Principle," by which Church members form a group and migrate together to a new locale for the single purpose of seeding a new congregation.

Beliefs

The local churches follow the teachings found in the numerous books and writings of Watchman Nee and Witness Lee. A convenient summary of these teachings has been compiled by a group of co-workers into a booklet, *The Beliefs and Practices of the Local Churches*. The booklet professes a belief in fundamental Christianity, very similar to that of the Plymouth Brethren. The Trinity, the deity of Christ, the Virgin Birth, the substitutionary atonement, the Resurrection, the Second Coming, and the verbal inspiration of the Bible are all affirmed.

Particular attention is given to an emphasis upon the unity of the Church, the Body of Christ. Sectarianism, denominationalism, and interdenominationalism are rejected, and the oneness of all believers in each locality affirmed. Because of their unique ecclesiology, believing that there can be only one "church" to a city, the Local Church refrains as a corporate group from joining with Christians from other "churches" in cooperative activities. To do so would deny an essential statement of their faith by recognizing that more than one church does exist. However, they are happy to work with Christians not of the Local Church on an individual basis.

The local churches place themselves in a history of recovery (or restoration) of the Biblical church, whose full life and unity were lost over the centuries. That restoration process began with Martin Luther and the Protestant Reformation and continued through the pietist recovery of Count Zinzendorf and the Moravians, John Wesley and the Methodists, and the Plymouth Brethren. Through the local churches, the Christian's experience of the riches of Christ (i.e., the enjoyment of Christ as life), and the practice of church life according to Scripture are being recovered. The newly recovered practices, which have become the focus of criticism, include: pray-reading, calling upon the name of the Lord, burning, and burying.

"Pray-reading" is a devotional practice which uses the words of verses of Scripture as the words of prayer. Individuals or groups when praying will repeat words and phrases of Scripture over and over, frequently interjecting words of praise and thanksgiving, as a means of allowing the Scripture to impart an experience of the presence of God to the person praying. "Calling upon the name of the Lord," as the term implies, is an invoking of God by the repetition of such phrases as "O Lord Jesus." It is similar to the use of the Jesus prayer in Eastern Orthodoxy.

"Burning" implies a close contact with God. When a person impresses another with the Gospel, that person has been burned.

"Burning" is also an occasional practice by which objects representative of a person's pre-Christian life or a time of lesser commitment are destroyed in a fire. Like burning objects from one's past, "burying" is also a sign of a newer level of Christian commitment and is accomplished through a rebaptism. Thus, a member might be baptized several times.

Worship in the local churches is spirited, with much time given to singing, pray-reading, and testimonies. Speaking in tongues is allowed but not encouraged. Emphasis is also placed upon the elders' teaching of scripture. The Lord's supper is observed weekly during Sunday worship. Most women wear a head covering during worship, but it is not required.

Current Status

The local churches, being autonomous congregations in fellowship with each other, have no central headquarters. However, Living Stream Ministry, which publishes most of the literature used by the churches and is the headquarters for its most prominent ministry, has served as an informal center for information. Living Stream publishes all of Witness Lee's work which includes numerous books, pamphlets and study guides to the Bible. Living Stream regularly holds regional and national training sessions for elders and the more dedicated members in both the United States and Taiwan. Many of Lee's books are the transcribed talks of such sessions.

Increasingly, as the local churches expanded nationally, other ministries emerged and several local churches have begun publishing literature and issuing their own periodicals. The most prominent of these independent ministries was Northwest Christian Publications of Seattle, Washington, the ministry of William T. Freeman. During the late 1980s, however, the publishing arms of most of these ministries were closed and the Church now uses the material of Living Stream Ministry almost exclusively.

In 1983 congregations in fellowship could be found around the globe, although most members could be found in North America (129 churches and 11,889 members) and Taiwan (77 churches and 119 members). Other prominent congregations could be found in the Philippine Islands, Hong Kong, and England. According to the latest information, the movement has survived on mainland China in spite of persecution. There were reported to be approximately 130,000 members worldwide.

Controversy

The last fifteen years have been a time of continual conflict between the Local Church and those in the larger Evangelical Christian community who perceived the theological innovations of Witness Lee as departing from acceptable Evangelical thought and disagreed with the new expressions of piety with the congregations. Much of that controversy began in the early 1970s when the Church in Berkeley (California) was housed in a building across the street from the World Christian Liberation Front, one of the early Jesus People groups. The two groups had several emotionally charged encounters. Eventually, the WCLF split into two groups, one known today as the Evangelical Orthodox Church and the other as the Spiritual Counterfeits Project. Out of each group a harshly critical book about the Local Church emerged (*The Mind Benders* by Jack Sparks and *The God-Men* by Neil T. Duddy and the SCP).

Both books charged Lee with heresy. Using quotes from a number of Lee's books, they suggested that Lee denied the traditional doctrine of the Trinity. They suggested that he did not believe in the essential distinctions between the three Persons of the Trinity, a position known as "monarchianism." They also took strong exception to the use of the metaphor "mingling" to describe the nature of the relationship of God to redeemed humanity. Lee answered that he was both biblical and orthodox in his doctrine of the Trinity and his use of "mingling." He claimed that he had been misquoted and made to appear heretical. Both authors also associated the Local Church with a variety of cultic practices. Duddy's more extensive volume, devoted entirely to Witness Lee and the Local Church, went much further and accused Lee, among other charges, of mismanagement of Church funds and of being the source of psychological damage to members.

Claiming libel and being unable to obtain a retraction and apology from either author or their publishers, Lee and several of the congregations filed suits. In the suit against *The Mind Benders*, an out-of-court settlement brought an apology from the publisher, the withdrawal of the book, and a financial settlement. In the case against *The God-Men*, an $11,000,000 judgment against its author and Spiritual Counterfeits Project was rendered in an uncontested trial (neither Duddy nor SCP appeared in court). Among other results, the publisher of *Bob Larson's Book of Cults*, Tyndale House, announced it was withdrawing the chapter on the Local Church from future printings and apologized for any damage it might have caused.

Since the settlement of the libel issues, the Local Church has returned to a rather quiet, non-controversial existence. The lawsuit had immense implications for the future management of the Christian cult ministries and the level of research which they had come to accept in their work.

Sources-Primary

Freeman, Bill. *The Testimony of Church History Regarding the Mystery of the Triune God.* Anaheim, CA: Living Stream Publishers, 1976. 40 pp.

Lee, Witness. *Elder's Training.* 8 vols. Anaheim, CA: Living Stream Ministry, 1985-86.

—————. *The History of the Church and the Local Churches.* Anaheim, CA: Living Stream Ministry, 1991. 140 pp.

—————. *The Practical Expression of the Church.* Los Angeles: Living Stream Publishers, 1970. 188 pp.

Nee, Watchman. *The Normal Christian Church Life.* Washington, DC: International Students Press, 1969. 127 pp.

—————, and Witness Lee. *Outlines for Training.* 4 vols. Anaheim, CA: Living Stream Ministry, 1980.

Sources-Secondary

Chen, James. *Meet Brother Nee.* Kowloon, Hong Kong: Christian Publishers, 1976. 104 pp.

Cheung, James Mo-oi. *The Ecclesiology of Watchman Nee and Witness Lee.* Fort Washington, PA: Christian Literature Crusade, 1972. 176 pp.

Duddy, Neil T., and the Spiritual Counterfeits Project. *The God-Men.* Downers Grove, IL: Inter-Varsity Press, 1981. 79 pp.

Kinnear, Angus I. *Against the Time.* Fort Washington, PA: Christian Literature Crusade, 1973. 191 pp.

Melton, J. Gordon. *An Open Letter Concerning the Local Church, Witness Lee and The God-Men Controversy.* Santa Barbara, CA: Institute for the Study of American Religion, 1985. 28 pp.

Roberts, Dana. *Understanding Watchman Nee.* Plainfield, NJ: Haven Books, 1980. 192 pp.

J. THE MOVEMENT OF
SPIRITUAL INNER AWARENESS

Coming out of the same Sant Mat tradition as ECKANKAR is the Movement of Spiritual Inner Awareness (MSIA).

Founder and Early History

John-Roger Hinkins (b. 1934), a former Mormon and high school teacher, was one of the early students of ECKANKAR and by 1968 was a second initiate and convenor of an ECK meeting in Southern California. That year he left ECKANKAR and founded MSIA. Sri John-Roger, as he is generally called in MSIA publications, claims that in 1963 he had a meeting on the inner planes with Sawan Singh (1858-1948), prominent leader of the Radhasoami Satsang Beas, the largest of the Sant Mat groups. At the time of his association with ECKANKAR, he believed that he had encountered Rebazar Tarzs, the ECK Master. He discovered his mistake and left ECKANKAR. Hinkins claims that Sawan Singh passed to him the role of Mystical Traveler Consciousness.

In 1971, informal gatherings around Hinkins were formally organized as the Church of the Movement of Spiritual Inner Awareness (usually referred to simply as MSIA). The organization was expanded in stages through the 1970s with the founding of Prana (now Peace) Theological Seminary (1974), Baraka Holistic Center (1976), and Insight Training Seminars (1978). In 1982, the John-Roger Foundation was created both to coordinate the various programs initiated by MSIA and to celebrate what has come to be known as Integrity Day, a means to focus the Foundation's goal of promoting global transformation by the enrichment and uplift of individuals. Since 1983, the Foundation has held an annual Integrity Award banquet in which awards are given to individuals for their achievement along with checks which may be donated to their favorite charities. In 1988 the John-Roger Foundation was divided into the Foundation for the Study of the Individual and World Peace and the International Integrity Foundation.

Beliefs and Practices

Although it employs a different vocabulary, MSIA adheres to the basic teaching which ECKANKAR inherited from the Sant Mat tradition through Kirpal Singh. The Mystical Traveler Consciousness functions almost identically to its ECKANKAR counterpart, the Living ECK Master. The description of the inner planes follows their delineation in the writings of Paul Twitchell, including, as observers have noted, the retention of those peculiarities introduced into the tradition by Twitchell. MSIA has, however, gone beyond ECKANKAR by identifying itself with the larger New Age/Eastern/metaphysical community and adding many of its practices and emphases to their own program.

MSIA contends that every person is involved in a movement of spiritual inner awareness, and the Movement of Spiritual Inner Awareness is an outward reflection of that universal inner movement. The focal point of the Movement is the Consciousness of the Mystical Traveler. The Mystical Traveler (i.e., John-Roger) exists simultaneously on all levels of consciousness in total awareness and can teach individuals who request his assistance how to develop the same total awareness and, thus, free themselves from the necessity of reincarnation. The Mystical Traveler also can read the karmic records of individuals and assist them in understanding and releasing themselves from their karmic responsibilities.

MSIA has taken a primary interest in helping individuals adjust to the rapid changes and resultant stresses so they are not hindered or distracted in their spiritual quest. Very early in the Movement, several New Age healing techniques, each dealing with a different aspect of the self, were offered to students (and the public): "aura balancing" is a technique to clear the auric (magnetic) field that exists around each individual; "inner-phasings" reach into the subconscious to bring to consciousness and remove the dysfunctional patterns learned early in life; and "polarity balancing" releases blocks in the physical body. These initial services blossomed into a major emphasis upon holistic healing and the development of the Baraka Holistic Center for Therapy and Research in Santa Monica, California.

Soon after the success of *est* (Erhard Seminar Trainings) and Lifespring, intensive seminars aimed at personal transformation, MSIA developed its own training seminars, which provide a similar intense transformational experience. While frequently compared to *est*, and some inspiration for its formation came from *est* and Lifespring, Insight Training Seminars developed its own emphases and format as a catalyst of self-awareness and the ability to move beyond self-imposed limitations.

Organization

During its early years, MSIA developed in a pattern similar to ECKANKAR. John-Roger wrote a set of Soul Awareness Discourses to introduce new members to the basic perspective and practices of the Movement. As members increased in one area, students were urged to form seminar groups. These were organized first in Southern California from whence they spread along the West Coast, and, then, from an initial group in Miami, Florida, they spread along the East Coast. The first international groups were organized in England and Japan.

In 1972, *The Movement*, the organization newspaper, began publication and is now offered for sale on newsstands. It has featured interviews with different New Age teachers, news of other Eastern mystical groups, and articles on general New Age concerns while presenting the program and services of MSIA to its readers.

During the past decade the programming offered at the national level has expanded to keep pace with the Church of the Movement of Spiritual Inner Awareness (as the organization is officially known) as a growing national and international concern. The official headquarters of the Church is in Los Angeles, but a major complex of facilities can be found in nearby Santa Monica. It is served by two educational facilities: Kor-I-Nor University in Santa Monica, California, is a graduate school which offers a master's degree in Applied Human Relationships as well as a non-degree extension program and counseling training for clergy;

and Peace Theological Seminary and College of Philosophy, in Los Angeles, offers master's and doctoral programs in theology and ministerial education. Baraka Holistic Health Center for Therapy and Research, also in Santa Monica, is a fully staffed alternative health center with practitioners in chiropractic, acupuncture, nutrition, and a variety of other therapies.

Insight Transformational Seminars offers training programs throughout the United States to the general public. A variety of advanced and special interest programs have been developed to supplement the week-long introductory seminar.

MSIA offers many tapes by John-Roger for sale. His numerous books have been published by Baraka Books of New York.

While recent statistics have not been forthcoming, in 1984, the Church reported 250 seminar groups in the United States which met regularly, mostly in private homes. Additional groups could be found in 12 countries. Membership is estimated at between 5,000 and 10,000. Members who have studied the *Discourses* for two years are eligible to apply for ordination as ministers in the Church.

Controversy

MSIA has grown slowly and quietly and remained virtually unknown beyond those people involved in the New Age Movement or one of the other alternative religions similar to MSIA.

Then in 1988 the *Los Angeles Times* published a two-part expose-like article on MSIA and a similar article appeared in *People Magazine.* Both articles highlighted charges by ex-staff members Wesley and Wendall Whitemore, who attacked Hinkins personally for sexual involvement with his followers (in spite of a vow of chastity), luxurious living (in spite of a vow of poverty), and the improper use of the Church's money. These charges led to the defections of some of the Church's leaders, but controversy remained inside the Movement until 1984, when David Christopher Lane, himself a Radhasoami initiate, attacked John-Roger and MSIA, in part using information supplied by several of the defecting ex-members. Lane accused John-Roger of plagiarism and repeated the charges of sexual misconduct and of being a charlatan. In response, an organization called the Coalition for Civil and Spiritual Rights came forward to defend MSIA and attack Lane's credibility as a researcher. In the midst of the exchange of correspondence with lane, the material and the records of his magazine, *Understanding Cults and Spiritual Movements*, were stolen, thus leaving the issues unresolved, until 1988.

In the wake of the 1988 articles, the Integrity Awards were canceled, and MSIA assumed a much lower profile.

Sources-Primary

About MSIA. Los Angeles: Movement of Spiritual Inner Awareness, n.d. 13 pp.

Beck, Sanderson, and Mark T. Holmes. *Across the Golden Bridge*. Los Angeles: Golden Age Education Publications, 1974. 206 pp.

John-Roger [Hinkins]. *The Christ Within*. New York: Baraka Press, 1976. 45 pp.

————. *Possession, Projections and Entities*. New York: Baraka Press, 1976. 84 pp.

————. *The Spiritual Family*. New York: Baraka Press, 1976. 90 pp.

————. *The Spiritual Promise*. Rosemead, CA: Movement for Spiritual Inner Awareness, 1973. 40 pp.

McWilliams, Peter, and John-Roger. *You Can't Afford the Luxury of a Negative Thought*. Los Angeles: Prelude Press, 1988. 622 pp.

The Teachings of the Traveler: A Reference Manual. 2nd ed. Los Angeles: Movement of Spiritual Inner Awareness, 1988. 102 pp.

K. NICHIREN SHOSHU

Nichiren Shoshu Soka Gakkai of America and Nichiren Shoshu Temple are the names of the two organizations representing the Nichiren Shoshu, the most successful of the several groups which have grown out of the work of 13th-century Japanese Buddhist teacher Nichiren Daishonin. The movement is somewhat unique in that in the last generation its lay organization, Soka Gakkai, has become one of the most successful evangelistic organizations outside of Japan, and many people who have become actively involved with Soka Gakkai are only vaguely aware of the temple-oriented movement to which it is related. While there are over 40 Soka Gakkai centers across the United States, there are only six temples.

History

Nichiren Shoshu derives from the work of Nichiren Daishonin (1222-1282 C.E.), a Buddhist reformer whose early adulthood was lived in the tension of, on the one hand, disgust at the corruption he felt had overtaken all of the Buddhist groups of his time and, on the other hand, a strong desire to find the true Buddhism. Having found what he came to believe was the Truth, he became a staunch critic of the whole range of Buddhist groups in Japan and attempted to get the government to suppress them. These actions earned him the enmity of fellow Buddhists who often attacked him as he preached throughout the country.

From his exploration of Buddhist holy books, however, Nichiren believed that he discovered the path for this degenerate age. He promoted the Lotus Sutra as the most holy of Buddhist books and taught his followers a mantra, "Namu-myoho-renge-kyo," the repetition of which leads to enlightenment. Through his reform activity he sought to unify Buddhists and reform Buddhist practice.

Following Nichiren's death, disagreements among his major disciples led to splits in the movement, and over the ensuing centuries a number of distinct Nichiren sects appeared. The Nichiren Shoshu traces its lineage to Nikko who had for many years served at Nichiren's temple at Minobu. Because of disagreements with the other major disciples, he left Minobu in 1289, and several years later he built a temple at Kitayama where he lived out the rest of his long life. By the end of the century an irreconcilable break had developed between him and his former colleagues. In 1913 Nikko's branch of the Nichiren community took the name Nichiren Shoshu (Orthodox Nichiren Sect) and increasingly stressed its difference from both the other schools of Buddhism and the other branches of the Nichiren Shu (i.e., the Nichiren sects).

Until after World War II, Nichiren Shoshu was merely one relatively small Buddhist group among many. However, with the coming of religious freedom, through the efforts of its lay organization the Soka Gakkai, it experienced a phenomenal growth. Soka Gakkai, the lay organization of Nichiren Shoshu members, was founded in 1930 as the Soka-kyoiku-gakkai (literally, Value-Creating Education Society) by the two men who were to become its first presidents, Tsunesaburo Makiguchi (1871-1944) and Josei Toda (1900-1958).

Makiguchi, an elementary school principal, was converted to Nichiren Shoshu in 1928. An enthusiastic convert, he began writing a series of books on education and values. In 1937 at the ceremony establishing Soka Gakkai in Tokyo, Makiguchi was elected president. Unfortunately, the new society ran counter to the policies of the increasingly militaristic Japanese government. The Nichiren Shoshu refused to unite with other Nichiren sects, and Makiguchi defied government orders to place a Shinto shrine in every home. In 1943 he and Toda were among a group of Nichiren Shoshu leaders arrested. Makiguchi died in prison.

Josei Toda immediately moved to rebuild Soka Gakkai after the War. He shortened the name and broadened the program from the educational field and saw its purpose as bringing peace and happiness to all. In 1951 he assumed the presidency of the revived movement. In his inaugural address he urged an aggressive proselytizing campaign. His announced goal was 750,000 members in seven years. Shortly after that goal was attained, Toda died.

In 1960 Toda was succeeded in the presidency by Daisaku Ikeda (b. 1928), the executive director of the organization and student of Toda since 1947. Since his becoming president, the Soka Gakkai and Nichiren Shoshu has spread around the world. Among his first actions was a trip to the United States to rally and organize Nichiren Shoshu members.

The Nichiren Shoshu faith had been brought to the United States after World War II by Japanese immigrants and American servicemen who had been influenced toward the movement while stationed in Japan. Much of the preparation for Ikeda's visit had been made by Masayasu Sadanaga who had migrated to the United States in 1957, organized the Soka Gakkai in Washington, D.C., and began to contact members around the United States. Ikeda appointed him director and the work began to flourish. The Los Angeles *Kaikan* (headquarters), the first outside of Japan, was established in 1963. To assist in the growth among Caucasian Americans, Sadanaga changed his name to George M. Williams in 1972.

In 1967 the first Nichiren Shoshu priest arrived and completed the structure of the movement, within which the Soka Gakkai is officially but a lay organization. The movement was reorganized around the several temples which were established and the name Soka Gakkai fell into disuse. About this same time the movement was Americanized. Japanese was discontinued except for chanting and repeating the Lotus Sutra.

By the mid-1970s, through the efforts of Soka Gakkai, Nichiren Shoshu had spread around the world. In January of that year, delegates from 51 nations gathered in Guam to create Soka Gakkai International as an umbrella organization to coordinate the growth of the movement internationally. Daisaku Ikeda was named its first president.

Beliefs and Practices

Nichiren Shoshu considers itself the True Buddhism. Within Nichiren Shoshu the individual can find Enlightenment (Buddhahood), or the fulfillment of life within and involvement to the fullest in society and the world. Enlightenment and the happiness it brings can be achieved by being in harmony with universal law, *Namu-myoho-renge-kyo*, i.e., reverence to the wonderful law of the Lotus. Nichiren taught that the Lotus Sutra contained the one needful truth and should be given exclusive place as the essential Buddhist teaching. From his study he began to chant Namu-myoho-renge-kyo, which totally captures the essence of the Lotus Sutra.

From the teachings of Nichiren, three essential practices are extolled. First and foremost is the repetition of the chant. Both morning and evening Namu-myoho-renge-kyo is repeated many times accompanied by the recitation of portions of the Lotus Sutra (*Gongyo*). Members are encouraged to fill leisure moments with the chant and to use it when in distress, doubt, or need.

Gongyo and chanting are usually done before the *Gohonzon*, a scroll measuring approximately 10" x 20", upon which are inscribed the names of the principal enlightened beings mentioned in the Lotus Sutra. It represents the entity of life itself. Each successive high priest delegates the authority to inscribe the Gohonzon, and one is given to each member. It must be appropriately enshrined in the member's home in an altar that contains offerings of fruit, evergreen, candles, and incense.

During the daily worship before the Gohonzon the scroll is unrolled. The worship is done with prayer beads and a bell. After the worship the Gohonzon may be rolled up but should be kept in a "protected area."

Nichiren Shoshu also believes in the principle of *Kaidan* (literally ordination platform), pilgrimage to the headquarters, since 1972 the Shohondo located at the foot of Mt. Fuji. The first pilgrimage by American members of Nichiren Shoshu found 68 people traveling to Japan in 1961. In 1972, 1,800 attended the dedication of the Shohondo.

Organization

Nichiren Shoshu is headed by the High Priest who has followed in succession from Nikko Shonin since the thirteenth century. The High Priest appoints the priests and has administrative responsibility for the total organization, including its lay branch.

Officially, Soka Gakkai International also operates under the High Priest of Nichiren Shoshu, but because the tremendous growth of Nichiren Shoshu has in fact been due to the activity of Soka Gakkai, it exercises influence and power far beyond its assigned role as merely a lay organization within the larger sect. The work in America began as a missionary activity out of Soka Gakkai headquarters in Japan and was formally organized in 1960. With the creation of Soka Gakkai International, NSA became an independent organization. It remains tied to the movement in Japan, however, through Soka Gakkai International. In 1967 the first temple was established in the United States, an acknowledgment of the growth of the movement in America

In the United States two corporations control the separate Nichiren Shoshu functions. Lay believers are organized through the Nichiren Shoshu Soka Gakkai of America or the Nichiren Shoshu Academy. Most believers in America came to Nichiren Shoshu through the lay organization and affiliate through the numerous community centers it has sponsored. Once the priesthood arrived, it was incorporated as Nichiren Shoshu Temple. Though officially in charge of Nichiren Shoshu work in America, the size, power, and prior history of Soka Gakkai gave it a position it has retained.

Current Status

World headquarters for Nichiren Shoshu are at the Taisekiji compound near Mt. Fuji. That compound has been built up by the Soka Gakkai, and the Shohondo (main grand temple) completed in 1972 has become a new focus for the faith. Within its 55,660 square meters, the Dai-Gohonzon is now enshrined. The Soka Gakkai is headquartered in Tokyo. It publishes several periodicals including the monthly English-language *Soka Gakkai News*, which is mailed out internationally. There are over 3,500,000 members.

In the United States, the Nichiren Shoshu Soka Gakkai of America is headquartered in Santa Monica, California. From its presses come the monthly magazine *Seikyo Times*, an American edition of a periodical published in Japan, and the weekly *World Tribune*, a newspaper. The NSA World Cultural Center is located in California and is the focus for the Soka Gakkai's numerous cultural and musical events and programs. Over 40 NSA centers found across the United States serve the more than 300,000 members. A significant sign of growth in NSA is the opening of Soka Gakkai University in Calabasas, California.

Nichiren Shoshu Temple has six temples under its hegemony—Flushing, New York; Kaneohe, Hawaii; Chicago, Illinois; Silver Spring, Maryland; Rancho Cucamonga, California; and the headquarters temple in Los Angeles.

Soka Gakkai has published a large number of English-language books, including the writings of Ikeda. George Williams has begun to publish English translations of the *Gosho*, the collected writing of Nichiren Daishonin. The first volume appeared in 1976.

Controversy

In Japan, Soka Gakkai has been a controversial organization from the time of its founding, though most Americans would support its attempts to keep its organizational integrity in the face of government pressure prior to World War II.

During the 1970s, Soka Gakkai broke into the news following some noteworthy successes of its political arm, the *Komeito*, or Clean Government Party. Founded in 1964, the Komeito had, by the mid-1970s, become the third largest political party in Japan. As the Komeito grew, Ikeda moved into the political arena and launched a campaign for international world peace. Throughout the 1970s Ikeda traveled and met with such world leaders and intellectuals as Arnold Toynbee, Henry Kissinger, and John Kenneth Galbraith.

The success of the Komeito underscored the most controversial practice of the Soka Gakkai, *shakubuku*, literally "to break and subdue" the evil spirits and make straight the true teaching of Buddha. It is a principle of Nichiren Shoshu that it is the true religion and true form of Buddhism, and it is the duty of every believer aggressively to pressure family, friends, and acquaintances into converting. Shakubuku includes strong polemic against other faiths, the use of rational argument, and the application of psychological and even physical pressure. In Japan numerous accusations of violence by Nichiren Shoshu members arose during the 1970s, and opponents charged that much of their growth came through strong-arm tactics.

In the United States shakubuku has primarily appeared as high-pressure evangelism, without the physical coercion noted in the Japanese situation. Once the more objectionable aspects of the practice were discontinued in Japan, reference to it in the United States virtually disappeared, and signs of tension between Nichiren Shoshu and the larger culture have diminished almost to a point of nonexistence. While a small organization of former members has been formed to oppose NSA, in the demise of controversy, that organization has been ineffectual in attracting attention or aligning its work to the larger anti-cult movement.

Sources-Primary

Causton, Richard. *Nichiren Shoshu Buddhism*. San Francisco, CA: Harper & Row, 1989. 299 pp.

Ikeda, Daisaku. *Complete Works of Daisaku Ikeda*. Tokyo: Seikyo Press, 1968.

—————. *Guidance Memo*. Tokyo: Seikyo Press, 1966. 297 pp.

Kirimura, Yasuji. *Fundamentals of Buddhism*. Tokyo: Nichiren Shoshu International Center, 1977. 180 pp.

The Sokagakkai. Tokyo: Seikyo Press, 1962. 172 pp.

Williams, George M. *The Gosho Reference*. Los Angeles: World Tribune Press, 1976. 294 pp.

—————. *NSA Seminars: An Introduction to Buddhism*. Santa Monica, CA: World Tribune Press, 1982. 76 pp.

—————. *Victory in Faith: Experiences of NSA Members*. Santa Monica, CA: World Tribune Press, 1985. 180 pp.

Sources-Secondary

Anesaki, Masaharu. *Nichiren, the Buddhist Prophet*. Cambridge: Harvard University Press, 1949. 160 pp.

Brannen, Noah S. *Soka Gakkai*. Richmond, VA: John Knox Press, 1968. 181 pp.

Montgomery, Daniel B. *Fire in the Lotus: The Dynamic Buddhism of Nichiren.* London: Mandala, 1991. 322 pp.

Murata, Kiyoaki. *Japan's New Buddhism.* New York: Walker/Weatherhill, 1969. 194 pp.

L. OSHO (RAJNEESH) FOUNDATION INTERNATIONAL

During the early 1980s few Indian teachers had the support and the controversy as had Bhagwan Rajneesh. However, by 1985 his major North American project, the town of Rajneeshpuram, had been dissolved and he had been deported. Back in his former ashram in Poona (now Pune), India, he reorganized his work and in 1989 changed his name to Osho (a Japanese term for a follower of the Bodhidharma, the way of the Buddha or Enlightened One, and a term of respect) and his organization became Osho Commune International. Then in January 19, 1990, he unexpectedly died and left no successor. His movement continues under the collective leadership of some of his close disciples. The course of the development of the Rajneesh movement provides one of the better illustrations of the evolution of a new religious movement.

The Founder

Bhagwan Rajneesh was born Rajneesh Chandra Mohan at Kuchwada, Madhya Pradesh, India, on December 11, 1931, to a family of the Jain faith. He attended the University of Jabalpur where he received his B. A. degree in 1951. He attained his master's degree in philosophy at the University of Saugar in 1957. Concurrently with his graduate work, he began to teach at Raipur's Sanskrit College and later at the University of Jabalpur.

According to Rajneesh, he first experienced *samadhi* (enlightenment) when he was but seven years old. However, on the evening of March 21, 1953, while still a student at the University of Saugar, he attained complete enlightenment. He describes the event:

That night another reality opened its door, another dimension became available. Suddenly it was there—the other reality, the separate reality, the really real, or whatsoever you want to call it. Call it God, call it truth, call it Dharma, call it Tao or whatever you will.

That night I became empty and became full. I became nonexistential and became existence. That night I died and was reborn.

While continuing with the boundaries of his academic career, Rajneesh began to travel and speak to people about his experience and the teachings which grew out of it. He was both an eloquent speaker and advocate for controversial religious views. Finally in 1966 he resigned his university post and became a full-time spiritual leader. He traveled throughout India from his home in Jabalpur for several years before moving to Bombay in 1969 with a small group of his most dedicated disciples. Around 1970 the first Westerners discovered him and began to come to his Bombay apartment headquarters. Then in 1974 he purchased a site for an ashram in Poona and founded the Rajneesh Foundation (now the Osho Commune International).

During the years in Poona, Rajneesh became one of the most famous nonconventional gurus in all of India. Traditional religionists expressed strong disapproval of his reinterpretation of *sannyas*, the renounced life, and of the public displays of affection shown by his disciples both at the ashram and on the streets of Poona. Meanwhile, his following among Westerners was growing, and centers began to appear in North America, Australia and Europe.

In 1981 events which were to heighten the controversy already surrounding this most controversial religious leader began just as he entered a period of silence. In May 1981 he moved to the United States, first to his center in New Jersey. Two months later, Ma Anand Sheela (Silverman), his secretary, announced the purchase of the 64,000-acre former Big Muddy Ranch near Antelope, Oregon. A small group, which grew to over 200 within a year, moved to the ranch and began to construct Rajneeshpuram, a model community expected to house 4,000-

6,000 by the end of the century. The cafe in Antelope was purchased, turned into a vegetarian restaurant, and renamed "Zorba the Buddha."

The next five years were ones of growing controversy. In December 1981, a group of Oregon environmentalists and local land owners organized to fight the building of Rajneeshpuram. Month by month what became a war between the leadership at Rajneeshpuram (guided by Ma Anand Sheela) and various citizen groups and government structures escalated. Crucial to the downfall of the community was the outbreak of salmonella food poisoning in several restaurants in The Dalles, Oregon, which at a later date some leaders of the commune would be accused of spreading.

In September 1985, Rajneesh accused a number of the leaders of the community, including Ma Anand Sheela, of various crimes and expelled them. One leader, former mayor Krishna Deva (Berry Knapp), quickly established communication with the legal authorities and became the key person in the future investigation of the community. Sheela, who left for Germany, was indicted in October. Rajneesh was arrested in November in North Carolina, after what federal agents charged was an attempt to flee the country. He subsequently pleaded guilty to two felony charges and agreed to leave the country. After a trip which took him to a number of countries, he settled back in Pune, India. The community property was eventually sold.

In India Rajneesh began to reorder the program of the community even as the movement worldwide adjusted to the changes. Several leaders of Rajneeshpuram were indicted and convicted of a variety of charges, while the American movement reorganized and returned to the rather decentralized organization of former years.

Rajneesh developed a new form of meditation called the Mystic Rose, which became the central practice at Pune and slowly was communicated to groups around the world. He then announced his name change to Osho in 1989 a few months before his death.

Teachings

Both his mystical experiences and his philosophical training led Rajneesh beyond the Jainism of his parents. He has attempted to create a new religious synthesis which brings elements of all the major religious traditions together with the new Western techniques of inner transformation and therapy (many borrowed directly from humanistic psychology). This new religion is centered upon Rajneesh as the Enlightened teacher, who was generally referred to by the honorific title "Bhagwan," literally a godman, but now called Osho. Following a widespread Indian belief, Rajneesh taught that it is difficult to grow spiritually without surrender to an enlightened accomplished master.

Rajneesh offers to his followers a number of techniques to move them along a path to enlightenment. Prior to initiation, followers are called *shravakas*, sympathetic listeners, and shravakas are encouraged to become sannyasins. Rajneesh redefined *sannyas*, the renounced life, as the right way to live, to live consciously. Thus rather than renouncing the material life, Rajneesh taught disciples to accept and affirm all of life and to build a synthesis between the spiritual and material.

During the early years of the movement, those who took initiation as a sannyasin, or more properly, a *neo-sannyasin*, agreed to do four things: (1) to dress in red or orange, the colors of the sunrise; (2) to wear a *mala* (a necklace of 108 beads and a picture of the guru) outside the clothes in plain sight; (3) to use the new name given at the time of initiation; and (4) to meditate regularly. In 1985 Rajneesh released followers from any obligation to wear red or orange clothing.

Rajneesh taught a variety of techniques of meditation, the five most important being: dynamic meditation, *kundalini* meditation, *nataraj* meditation, *gourishankar* meditation and *nadabrahma* meditation. These various meditation techniques are integrated into a daily program of activity. The day begins and ends with the chanting of the Buddham Sharanam Gatchchhami:

> Buddham Sharanam Gatchchhami
> Sangham Sharanam Gatchchhami
> Dhammam Sharanam Gatchchhami

which translated means:

> I go to the feet of the Awakened One
> I go to the feet of the commune of the Awakened One
> I go to the feet of the Ultimate Truth of the Awakened One

During Rajneesh's lifetime, those who lived at or visited his ashram attended *satsang*, in the morning, in which they sat in silence spiritually communing with Rajneesh, and listened to music or tapes of him speaking. In the evening, *darshan* was a celebration in which the disciple, through singing and dancing, melts into the essence of the master. While these activities most closely conform to what is traditionally termed worship, Rajneesh taught that worship is basically day-to-day living performed not for gain but out of the abundance of the inner self transforming mere activity into creativity.

In 1983 an attempt was made to codify the basics of the common faith and practice (including the meditation techniques and the process of becoming a sannyasin) of the followers of Rajneesh, and a small book describing the basic steps was issued as *Rajneeshism: An Introduction to Bhagwan Shree Rajneesh and His Religion*. In 1985 Rajneesh renounced the book and the concept of Rajneeshism, though most of the practices enunciated in it were retained.

The Mystic Rose, the new meditation technique has three stages and takes three weeks to complete. For the first week participants engage in three hours (once a day) of laughing for no reason at all. The second week participants cry for three hours a day and in the final week sit in silence for three hours. The process may be repeated any number of times.

Rajneesh emphasized individual freedom within the broad guidelines of the initiate's life. However, initiates are encouraged to refrain from the use of narcotics, to imbibe alcohol only in moderation and at mealtime, and to follow a vegetarian diet.

Disciples of Osho celebrate four special days: March 21, Osho's enlightenment Day; July 6, Master's Day; September 8, honoring all who have died; December 11, Rajneesh's birthday; and Master's Day, a day set aside to celebrate the existence of Osho, usually held in the summer.

Organization

The teachings of Rajneesh were disseminated by the Rajneesh Foundation International, until early 1986 headquartered at Rajneeshpuram, Oregon. Also located at Rajneeshpuram was the Foundation's press which printed many of Rajneesh's books and two periodicals, *The Rajneesh Foundation International Newsletter* and *Bhagwan*. The Foundation was headed by Rajneesh and administered by its president, Ma Anand Sheela. Following Rajneesh's return to India, the administration of the Foundation and its various administrative departments was turned over to a group of close disciples who reorganized it.

The instructional program at Osho Commune International was reorganized as the Osho Multiversity which offers a full range of programs for self-development from martial arts to massage training to various psychotherapeutic techniques, what in the United States would be referred to as a New Age center. The bimonthly *Osho Times International* is issued simultaneously in several languages from twelve countries.

The Foundation recognizes three categories of ministers: *acharyas*, *arihantes*, and *siddhas*. Ministers are characterized by "the particular type of energy he or she possesses: introverted, extroverted, or a synthesis of the two." Arihantes are basically extroverted and reach God through service to others. They are designated to perform marriage and birth ceremonies. Siddhas, the introverted, concentrate on personal transformation and are designated to perform the death ceremony. Acharyas are given authority to perform all the prescribed ceremonies, including the initiation of neo-sannyasins. To be a minister, a person must have been a neo-sannyasin for at least two years and go through a program of meditation and training.

Current Status

Through the 1970s and 1980s, Rajneesh meditation centers had been established throughout North America and around the world. During the years of Rajneeshpuram, most of these centers continued, little affected by the headquarters move from India to the United States. Only a small percentage of Rajneesh's disciples took up residence at Rajneeshpuram, and hence very few were directly affected by the fall of Rajneeshpuram.

In 1991 approximately 250 centers were to be found in 40 countries, of which 37 were in the United States and 6 in Canada. In North America Osho's books are distributed by Chidvilas in Boulder,

Colorado, and the *Osho Times International* is distributed through the
center in Mill Valley, California.

Controversy

Rajneesh has been a controversial figure from the time he began
to assume the role of a spiritual leader while still a teacher at Jabalpur.
His redefinition of traditional Indian religious concepts and the overt
emotional displays which accompanied some of the group's meditational
practices offended many. The open approach to and positive acceptance
of sex by Rajneesh and his neo-sannyasins (in the face of a cultural image
of sannyasins having renounced all sexual activity) became a particular
focus of hostile criticism during the years of the Poona ashram. Shortly
before Rajneesh moved to the United States, a fire swept through the
ashram, thought by many to have been set by arsonists.

Attacks upon Rajneesh and his followers began soon after the
purchase of the Big Muddy Ranch near Antelope, Oregon, and his arrival
in the United States. In the fall of 1981, the Portland district office of the
U.S. Immigration and Naturalization Service began an investigation of
Rajneesh's followers on charges of immigration fraud. Also in the fall of
1981, the Rajneeshees voted to incorporate the ranch as a city named
Rajneeshpuram. In response, the 1000 Friends of Oregon and a group of
nearby landowners filed suit to block the urbanization of the ranch.

Tensions within the community led to a focus of news coverage
as followers of Rajneesh struggled to realize their plans and began to
overcome the obstacles. In July 1982 approximately 7,000 followers
gathered for a lengthy summer festival. In November of that year the
petition for incorporation of Rajneeshpuram was submitted. In the
December election, disciples of Rajneesh won the mayor's office and a
majority of the seats in the city council of Antelope. Finally in February
1984, an initial effort to deport Rajneesh was blocked when papers
revealed his 1936 adoption by Swami Swarupananda (the father of Ma
Anand Sheela) who had become a permanent resident of the United
States in 1973.

Settled in Oregon, Rajneesh was attacked regularly, more for his
show of wealth than for his controversial teachings. His followers had
given him a large fleet of Rolls-Royces (almost 100 by 1985) in which he

took daily rides. Though he did not own the automobiles, they were made available for his use. The Foundation was, however, also involved in the cult controversies due to the unfamiliar nature of Rajneesh's teachings. While no significant charges of brainwashing were leveled, critics held up for ridicule the unfamiliar practices of dynamic meditation. Lying behind the attacks upon Rajneesh was the fear that other nonconventional religious groups would attempt to form similar communities, thus further distorting the social and political fabric at Antelope.

The controversies continued through the fall of 1985 with both sides scoring what each felt were victories. Then suddenly in September 1985, Ma Anand Sheela resigned her position and Rajneesh denounced her, accusing her of crimes against him and the movement. Following the break with Sheela, Rajneesh found himself in a serious situation. On October 23, he was indicted for immigration fraud. Four days later, for reasons unknown, he left Oregon. Believing he was attempting to flee the country, federal agents arrested him in North Carolina. In a plea bargain, on November 14, he confessed to two felonies, paid a $40,000 fine, and agreed to leave the United States and eventually returned to India.

The fall of Rajneesh was followed by an announcement that the ranch would be shut down and the property, including the automobiles, sold. Almost anticlimactic was the announcement several weeks later that a court had ruled the incorporation of Rajneeshpuram violated principles of separation of church and state, as it amounted to religious control of a municipal government. After being tied up in a number of technical problems, the land was finally sold in 1990.

Rajneesh and his followers thus returned to the decentralized state they were in prior to Rajneesh's arrival in the United States. The movement in other countries around the world was only minutely affected by the events of 1985, and followers everywhere voiced their faith in Rajneesh's innocence of charges brought against him. While the most serious charges against Rajneesh personally have been settled, the charges against movement leaders continue to be heard.

Ma Anand Sheela was convicted of several felonies in 1986 and given a 4 1/2 year sentence. She was released in 1988 and deported. Other leaders at Rajneeshpuram were also tried on related charges, including a plot to kill U. S. Attorney Charles H. Turner. Meanwhile, present followers of Osho contend that the government drugged and attempted

to poison him following his arrest in 1985 and that their actions finally
resulted in his early death. As a whole, the movement has put the legal
problems of the Rajneesh period behind them and are moving on to a
new phase of their life, contrary to what many superficial observers of the
movement predicted at the time of the fall of Rajneeshpuram.

Sources-Primary

Forman, Judith. *Bhagwan: Twelve Days That Shook the World.* Cologne,
Germany: Rebel Publishing House, 1989. 518 pp.

Joshi, Vasant. *The Awakened One.* New York: Harper & Row, 1982. 210 pp.

Meredith, George. *Bhagwan: The Most Godless Man Yet the Most Godly Man.*
Poona, India: Rebel Publishing House, 1987. 316 pp.

Rajneesh, Bhagwan Shree. *The Great Challenge.* New York: Grove Press, 1982.
211 pp.

————. *I Am the Gate.* New York: Harper & Row, 1975. 194 pp.

Rajneeshism, An Introduction to Bhagwan Shree Rajneesh and His Religion.
Rajneeshpuram, OR: Rajneesh Foundation International, 1983. 77 pp.

Sources-Secondary

Belfrage, Sally. *Flowers of Emptiness.* New York: Dial Press, 1981. 240 pp.

Gordon, James S. *The Golden Guru: The Strange Journey of Bhagwan Shree
Rajneesh.* Lexington, KY: The Stephen Greene Press, 1987. 248 pp.

McCormack, Win, ed. *The Rajneesh Chronicles.* Portland, OR: New Oregon
Publishers, 1987. 322 pp.

Mehta, Gita. *Karma Cola.* New York: Simon & Schuster, 1979. 201 pp.

Strelley, Kate, with Robert D. San Souci. *The Ultimate Game: The Rise and Fall
of Bhagwan Shree Rajneesh.* San Francisco, CA: Harper & Row, 1987. 381 pp.

Thompson, Judith, and Paul Heelas. *The Way of the Heart: The Rajneesh
Movement.* Wellingborough, UK: Aquarian Press, 1986. 142 pp.

M. SIKH DHARMA (HEALTHY, HAPPY, HOLY ORGANIZATION)

The first people of the Sikh faith to come to America seem to have been a few East Indians who visited New England in the 1790s. No large-scale migrations took place, however, until the early twentieth century when Canadian railroads brought many Punjabis into British Columbia. Some of these began to move southward into Washington, Oregon, and, eventually, California. A new element was added to this somewhat stable Punjabi Sikh community in 1968 in the person of S. Harbhajan Singh Puri (known by his followers as Siri Sahib Bhai Harbhajan Singh Khalsa Yogiji and popularly called Yogi Bhajan), a Sikh teacher newly arrived from India prepared to teach the faith to all.

Founder and Early History

Yogi Bhajan (b. 1929), a well-educated Sikh from Delhi, India, moved to Toronto in 1968. Later that year, in December, he relocated to Los Angeles. In 1969 he founded an ashram and the Healthy, Happy, Holy Organization (3HO) to teach kundalini yoga and meditation. During his classes he also began to share his Sikh faith and gather an interested group of believers. In 1971, accompanied by a group of 84 young Americans he visited the Golden Temple at Amritsar, Punjab, the world headquarters of the Sikh faith, and from the Akal Takhat (the Guru's Throne), the highest spiritual authority in the faith, he was given a sword of honor, ordained a minister, and granted authority to ordain others as Sikh ministers and initiate individuals into the Khalsa, the Sikh Brotherhood. As the Chief Religious and Administrative Authority for the Sikh Dharma in the Western World, he is the first person outside of India to be granted such recognition. With the formal establishment of the Sikh Dharma in the West, the 3HO became its educational arm.

In 1974, Gurcharan Singh Tohra, President of the Shiromani Gurudwara Parabandokh Committee of Amritsar (the chief administrative body of the Sikh Dharma in India), and Giani Mahinder Singh Ji, Secretary of the S.G.P.C., toured the Western centers of the Sikh Dharma. At the Akal Takhat in November, Yogi Bhajan received the honorary title, "Bhai Sahib," in recognition of his work in spreading Sikhism outside of India. And the Sikh Dharma had grown. Over 100 ashrams had been founded in the United States, Canada, and Europe.

The Sikh Dharma is a branch of the orthodox Sikh religion, one of the major faiths of India. While one in belief with Sikhs around the world, it is organizationally separate from the several older Sikh bodies in the United States, such as the Sikh Foundation in Stockton, California, and the International Sikh Federation in Madison Heights, Michigan. These organizations represent most of the Punjabi Sikhs in North America, while most of the members of the Sikh Dharma are non-Indian.

Beliefs and Practices

The Sikh religion was founded by Guru Nanak (1439-1538), who sought to reconcile the religious differences and social conflicts between the Hindus and Muslims. The new faith drew elements from both religions. He emphasized that there was One God, the Creator, and that His Name transcended the barriers of race, caste, and creed. He taught his followers to earn an honest living by the sweat of their brow but always to share their possessions with those in need. Guru Nanak was the first of ten gurus recognized by Sikhs. After the death of Guru Gobind Singh, the *Siri Guru Granth Sahib*, the writings of Guru Nanak, became the guru for the movement. Members are encouraged to learn Gurmukhi, the language in which the *Granth Sahib* was originally written.

For Sikhs, God is self-existent, immortal, immanent, transcendent, omnipotent, omnipresent, and omniscient. He is experienced through chanting of the Name of God, which in the original language is "Sat Nam" (God's name is Truth) or "Wahe Guru" (Experience of Infinite Wisdom). Chanting God's name is frequently done by repeating the mantra, "Ek Ong Kar Nam Siri Wha Guru" ("There is One Creator and one creation. Truth is His name. He is all Great. He is all Wisdom.") Members normally rise before sunrise each day to chant God's name and meditate.

While not required to do so, individuals associated with the Sikh Dharma are encouraged to seek formal initiation and join the Khalsa, the Brotherhood of the Pure Ones, a fellowship begun by Guru Gobind Singh. New members are baptized with sweetened water stirred with a sword. Members of the Sikh Dharma are then required to keep the traditional practices introduced by Guru Gobind Singh that became the distinguishing marks of the Sikh community, known popularly as the five "k's." All hair, including the beard is kept uncut (*kesh*) and tied on top of the head in a turban. The hair is kept neat with a comb (*kangha*). Sikhs wear special underwear (*kachera*) originally designed to allow freedom of movement in battle; a steel bracelet (*kara*) symbolic of an inseparable bond with God; and a dagger (*kirpan*) symbolic of a commitment to defend truth, righteousness, and those people who cannot defend themselves.

Ministers in the Sikh Dharma also normally wear a long hemmed knee-length skirt (*kurta*) and special pants which are loose at the waist and tight around the legs (*chudidas*). Both are solid white as is the turban.

Health is of prime concern within the Sikh Dharma. Natural foods are preferred and fish, meat, alcohol, and drugs prohibited. A number of members have opened health food restaurants and groceries. Members also prefer natural methods of healing.

The Sikh Dharma observes the traditional holidays of Sikhism, especially Balsakhi Day, the birthday of the Khalsa (April); the Martyrdom days of Guru Tegh Bhadus (November) and Guru Arjun Dev (May); and the birthdays of the ten gurus.

Beyond what is normally considered orthodox Sikhism, Yogi Bhajan also teaches kundalini, laya, and tantric yoga, the techniques of which he had mastered prior to his coming to the United States. Kundalini yoga consists of exercises which stimulate and control the energy within man which expands the capacity of the self. Laya yoga is the technique of altering consciousness by sound and rhythm. Tantric yoga is practiced by couples who share energies and consciousness. It must be done in the presence of a master or Mahan Tantric (Yogi Bhajan).

Organization

The Sikh Dharma is organized into numerous congregations each headed by a minister approved by Yogi Bhajan and appointed by the Khalsa Council. Ministers are entitled "Singh Sahib" (men) or "Sardarni Sahiba" (women). Regional, national, and international oversight and administration of the Sikh Dharma are in the hands of the Khalsa Council. The Regional and Administrative ministers who constitute this council are entitled "Mukhia Singh Sahib" or "Mukhia Sardarni Sahiba." Ultimate authority rests in Yogi Bhajan. Headquarters of the Sikh Dharma, located in Los Angeles, was transferred in stages to Santa Cruz, New Mexico, in the 1980s.

In 1988 the Sikh Dharma reported 139 ashrams/teaching centers in the United States and 11 in Canada. Of approximately 250,000 Sikhs in the United States, some 5,000 to 10,000 are associated with the Sikh Dharma. Foreign centers were reported in 22 countries. 3HO publishes two magazines, *Beads of Truth*, its own quarterly, and the *Journal of Science and Consciousness*, the journal of Kundalini Research Institute.

The Healthy, Happy, Holy Organization is incorporated separately but shares space in the Sikh Dharma headquarters building. As the Sikh Dharma's educational arm, it carries out an extensive program. It operates a number of ashrams, each headed by a spiritual director appointed by Yogi Bhajan. In most cases the ashram director is a Sikh Dharma minister and the local congregations use the ashram for meetings. 3HO sponsors Yogi Bhajan's workshops and seminars on kundalini and tantric yoga, which he periodically gives around the United States, as well as a variety of different programs on yoga, diet, and health for the general public.

Under the control of 3HO is the Kundalini Research Foundation headquartered in Pomona, California. Founded in 1973, KRI was established to verify, scientifically, the effects of kundalini yoga. It publishes a number of instructional manuals in yoga and meditation and reports of its research.

Each June 3HO holds its annual Summer Soltice Sadhana which includes classes, lectures by Yogi Bhajan, and business meetings. The event is held near Espanola, New Mexico, where Yogi Bhajan resides.

Yogi Bhajan has been one of the most ecumenical of the Eastern teachers in the United States. He has given strong support to the annual Human Unity Conferences originally begun by Kirpal Singh, a Sant Mat master, and aligned himself with the larger community of Eastern and mystical teachers, generally referred to as the New Age Movement. Associated with the Sikh Dharma through the 1980s was Spiritual Community Publications of Berkeley, California. Spiritual Community periodically published *The New Consciousness Sourcebook* (formerly the *Spiritual Community Guide*), a guide to New Age groups in North America, and put out one edition of *A Pilgrim's Guide to Planet Earth*, an international New Age directory. For several years it published *New Directions*, a monthly New Age magazine. It published several important books for the Sikh Dharma, *Guru for the Aquarian Age*, a volume on the life and teachings of Guru Nanak, and *Peace Lagoon*, an English translation of selections from the *Granth Guru*.

Controversy

The first issue to confront the Sikh was its relationship to the older Punjabi Sikh community. Tension developed during the mid-1970s as members of the Sikh Dharma complained that the Punjabi Sikhs had become lax in their discipline, especially in their adherence to the five "k's." The tension led to an attack on Yogi Bhajan and his followers by Dr. Narinder Singh Kapany, editor of the influential *Sikh Sangar*, the magazine of the Sikh Foundation. Kapany condemned Bhajan's emphasis upon yoga and his strictures on diet. Kapany's criticisms have been echoed by other Sikh leaders in both the United States and India. The issues have never been resolved, and the two communities have remained separate. The continuing tension between the two communities arose to prominence in 1984 when a number of high ranking leaders in the Sikh Dharma left the organization complaining of the intense discipline and being cut off both from the Sikh community as a whole and middle American culture.

Compared to some of the other new religious groups, the Sikh Dharma has received relatively little attention from the anti-cult movement. There were a few deprogramming attempts in the early 1980s, however, the militant Sikhs announced a policy of actively opposing any attempts by deprogrammers to attack their organization and no further attempts have been reported. One ex-member left and accused Yogi

Bhajan of sexual involvement with several of his staff members, but there was no verification of the charges. Controversy has primarily been focused in other areas.

Sikh Dharma members have experienced a series of conflicts over their dress, especially the turbans. As early as 1971, Thomas C. Costello faced a military court-martial for refusing to either cut his hair or remove his turban. His case led to a change in Army regulations granting permission for Sikhs to wear turbans. However, in 1983 Gurusant Singh Khalsa was not allowed to enlist in the Army because he was a Sikh. As recently as 1984, Karta Kaur Khalsa was threatened with loss of her teaching certificate because she refused to take off her turban during classes. In 1985 the Oregon Court of Appeals declared the law under which she was suspended to be unconstitutional. (The law was originally passed during a wave of anti-Catholicism to keep nuns out of the classroom.)

While these tensions remain, the Sikh Dharma has been praised highly for its drug rehabilitation program, and Akal Security, a security guard business formed by a group of members in New Mexico, created in no small part out of the image of the fierce Sikh warrior, has been highly sought for its services.

Sources-Primary

Bhajan, Yogi. *The Experience of Consciousness.* Pomona, CA: KRI Publications, 1977. 138 pp.

―――. *Furmaan Khalsa: Poems to Live By.* Columbus, OH: Furmaan Khalsa Publishing Co., 1987. 301 pp.

―――. *The Teachings of Yogi Bhajan.* New York: Hawthorn Books, 1977. 193 pp.

Kaur, Sardarni Premka. *Guru for the Aquarian Age.* San Rafael, CA: Spiritual Community, 1972. 131 pp.

Kundalini Yoga/Sadhana Guidelines. Pomona, CA: Kundalini Research Institute, 1978. 107 pp.

Liberation. Los Angeles: "The Source," n.d. [1970s]. 136 pp.

Sources-Secondary

Cole, W. Owen, and Piara Singh Sambhi. *The Sikhs.* London: Routledge and Kegan Paul, 1978. 210 pp.

Meyer, Nancy. "Meet the Sikhs." *Los Angeles* 29, 3 (March 1984): 174-80, 241-45.

N. TRANSCENDENTAL MEDITATION
AND THE
WORLD PLAN EXECUTIVE COUNCIL

From a mass movement which introduced hundreds of thousands of Westerners to the practice of meditation, the Transcendental Meditation movement has settled down to the hard task of testing its numerous claims and through its international organization, the World Plan Executive Council, actualizing its leader's plan for global transformation.

In the United States, a crucial juncture in that process was reached in 1978 when a New Jersey court ruled that the practice of Transcendental Meditation was a religious activity. That ruling effectively thwarted the Council's plans to introduce TM to mass audiences through a number of public institutions (the public schools, the Armed Forces, etc.). Thus the Council was sent back to the marketplace to compete with the hundreds of other new religions and meditation groups and to make the case that its form of meditation was superior. During the 1980s, TM faded from the public eye but has continued to mobilize people to carry out the World Plan of enlightening humanity.

Founder and Early History

Biographical sketches of Maharishi Mehesh Yogi, the teacher of TM to the world and the founder of the World Plan Executive Council, almost always begin with a reflection of the lack of facts about his early life. It is a common practice of Hindu monks, once they have reached a certain stage in their life, to refrain from any mention of their prior life. Maharishi has followed that example. Some who claim to have known him in India say that he was born Mehesh Prasad Varma in Utter Kashi, October 18, 1911 (other sources say "1918"), the son of a local tax official (some sources say "forest ranger"), of the Kshatriyas (warrior) caste. His confirmed biography begins, however, in 1940, when he graduated with a degree in physics from Allahabad University.

Instead of pursuing a career in science, he left everything to go to Joytir Math (monastery) in Badarinath to study with Swami Krishanand Saraswati, popularly known as Guru Dev. A recluse for many years, Guru Dev had become famous and was finally persuaded to become the spiritual leader of the Math. Maharishi became his favored student and stayed with him until his death in 1953. Guru Dev taught a form of meditation which he had rediscovered by reading the various Hindu holy books. Three years after Guru Dev's death, Maharishi emerged from a period of seclusion and began to teach what has become known as transcendental meditation. Beginning in southern India in 1956, he toured India speaking and lecturing, and he organized the Spiritual Development Movement. The Council dates the beginning of Maharishi's worldwide movement from 1957, in December of which Maharishi held a large meditation conference at Madras. On January 1, 1958, at a celebration of Guru Dev's eighty-ninth birthday, he announced the launching of a "spiritual regeneration" movement to spread the teachings of his guru around the world.

He left soon after the celebration, traveling first to Burma, Singapore, and Hong Kong before arriving in Hawaii in the spring of 1959. He traveled on to San Francisco, Los Angeles, and London. He also established an international organization from those who accepted his teachings, the International Meditation Society, and developed a three-year plan to spread Transcendental Meditation around the world. Returning to India, he decided to concentrate on teacher training. The first class of teachers, who graduated in 1961, included Beulah Smith, the first teacher in America.

Maharishi made a world tour, which included the United States, annually for the next several years. He visited followers and centers throughout the West. Among his significant students was Jerome Jarvis. Jarvis convinced Maharishi to begin speaking on university campuses, out of which the Student International Meditation Society was born, for several years the most successful branch of the work.

The movement received a significant boost in 1967, when the Beatles, the popular rock group, became followers of Maharishi and publicly endorsed TM. George Harrison, the Beatle later connected with the Hare Krishna movement, had been taking lessons from Indian musician Ravi Shankar. Harrison learned of Maharishi's presence in London and persuaded the other Beatles to attend. Together they then went on a retreat Maharishi conducted. In January 1968, along with actress Mia Farrow, they went to Maharishi's center in India. They were the first of a number of celebrities from Efrem Zimbalist, Jr., to Joe Namath who became meditators and who helped make Maharishi a celebrity and turn TM into a 1970s fad among older teens and young adults. The movement grew dramatically in the United States and Europe during the early 1970s. By the end of the decade, almost a million people had taken the basic TM course.

On January 8, 1972, Maharishi announced the World Plan, the overall strategy that has guided the movement since that time. The goal of the World Plan is to share the Science of Creative Intelligence, the movement's comprehensive understanding of life and knowledge, of which Transcendental Meditation is the practical aspect, with the whole world. The goal has been to establish 3,600 World Plan centers, one for each million people on earth. Each center is to have 1,000 teachers, thus establishing a constant ratio of one teacher per 1,000 persons in the general population.

The World Plan, the program guiding the course of the movement, suffered several major reverses in the mid-1970s. Around 1976 the number of new people taking the basic TM course in North America dropped dramatically. Faced with the decline, the Council announced an advanced *siddha* program, which included as its claim teaching meditators to levitate. The program was immediately attacked and in the face of insufficient evidence to substantiate the claims, the organization suffered a credibility gap. The reaction to the siddha program was soon followed by the 1978 federal ruling that TM was a religious practice. Previously, the basic TM course had been taught in a variety of public institutions with teachers supported by public funds. The ruling denied access to that market, and progress slowed dramatically in the United States, though growth proceeded in other areas of the world.

Through the 1980s the movement introduced several new programs, the most visible one being the Ayurvedic Medical program, touted as a comprehensive science of natural health care. As part of the program the organization is sponsoring the distribution of Maharishi Amrit Kalash, a herbal compound, designed to balance the body and protect it from harmful influences. Plans have also been announced to build the Maharishi Center for Perfect Health and World Peace in Fairfield, Iowa.

Beliefs and Practice

Transcendental Meditation is the basic practice taught through the World Plan Executive Council. It was offered as a simple system of meditation, basically consisting of daily meditation using a *mantra*, a word which is repeated over and over again as one sits in silence. Meditation by the use of mantras is an old and honored Hindu technique. Maharishi, however, advocated the use of a single mantra which was given to each student at the time of their taking the basic TM course. According to an early introductory flyer,

> The method of meditation is imparted at a short, private ceremony after preparatory lectures and an interview with the teacher. The object of meditation is a sound, specially chosen to suit the nature of the way of life of the particular man or woman. Further, students are told not to divulge the mantra that they are given.

Two observations on the description of the TM method are important. First, the nature of the ceremony was revealed to be a simple Hindu devotional service, called a *puja*, venerating the lineage of gurus from which Maharishi claimed his authority and an invocation of various Hindu deities. The mantras are given out only at these puja ceremonies. Second, the mantra given to any individual is determined by their sex and age at the time of their puja. Several former meditators have compiled and published the list of mantras.

The Council has made extraordinary claims for the effects of the practice of TM. Scientists who were among the hundreds of thousands who took the basic TM course were encouraged to test these claims. Their findings have been published in a variety of scientific journals and summarized in several Council publications such as *Fundamentals in Progress* (1975). TM has claimed that its regular practice can produce changes in the body which, in turn, lead to, for example, increased intelligence, improved academic performance, higher job productivity, improved resistance to disease, and better psychological health. TM can totally transform a person's life.

The scientific findings concerning the effects of Transcendental Meditation provide the basis for the proposal of a total world view, the Science of Creative Intelligence, defined as including the experience and knowledge of the nature, range, growth, and application of creative intelligence. Creative intelligence is the single and branching flow of energy and directedness in the universe, a concept approaching what others have called the Absolute, in common parlance, the Divine.

The World Plan spreads the knowledge and experience of creative intelligence through attacking problems in the seven basic areas of human life: individual, governmental, educational, social, environmental, economic, and spiritual. In each area it has a specific objective: to develop the full potential of the individual; to improve government achievements; to realize the highest ideal of education; to eliminate the age-old problem of crime and all behavior that brings unhappiness to the family of man; to maximize the intelligent use of the environment; to bring fulfillment to the economic aspirations of individuals and society; and to achieve the spiritual goals of mankind in this generation.

The basic avenue for achieving these goals is the spread of Transcendental Meditation in the population. However, Maharishi has also taken additional steps in developing the World Plan. For example, he declared the presence of the World Government of the Age of Enlightenment, a government which has sovereignty over the domain of consciousness. In the name of the World Government, in 1978 he inaugurated a world peace campaign by sending over 100 "World Governors" (adept meditators) to each of five sites of major global tension: Iran, Lebanon, Zimbabwe, Central America, and Thailand. In 1983 he announced the readiness of the World Government to solve the problems of any existing government and invited government leaders to make contact. From December 17, 1983, to January 6, 1984, he brought 7,000 TM siddhas to join the several thousand students at Maharishi International University in Iowa for a two-week period of peace. The collective meditation of the 7,000-plus adepts was to purify world consciousness.

During court hearings in a case brought by an ex-member, advanced teaching material was presented which suggested that underlying the practice of TM was a belief that during this practice the body produced a particular substance referred to in the Vedas, the Hindu holy books, as soma. This substance is thought of as the food of the Gods and the production of soma nourishes the Gods in this dark age. The coming age of Enlightenment depends upon the reviving of the sleeping deities.

Organization

The original spiritual regeneration movement begun by Maharishi in 1958 is now in the hands of the World Plan Executive Council whose international headquarters are at the World Plan Administrative Center in Seelisberg, Switzerland. The work of the Council in spreading the World Plan and its practical element, Transcendental Meditation, is carried through five task-oriented structures. The International Meditation Society has the main task of introducing the general public to TM. The Spiritual Regeneration Movement concentrates upon that segment of the population over thirty. The Student International Meditation Society functions with campus populations. The American Foundation for the Science of Creative Intelligence is in charge of applying TM within the business community.

Maharishi International University is a regular four-year liberal arts college which offers both bachelor's and master's degrees. MIU was given a specific role in implementing the World Plan. It offers a special set of courses on the seven objectives, including teacher training courses. MIU is also developing Global Television, a program to make TM available in every country through modern audiovisual technology.

Current Status

International headquarters of the Council are in Switzerland. American headquarters are in Washington, D.C. MIU, established at

Santa Barbara, California, moved to the former Parsons College campus in Fairfield, Iowa, in 1974. In 1987 the University began a scholarly journal, *Modern Science and Vedic Science*, to focus the dialogue between Maharishi's teachings (Vedic science) and modern Western science. The American Foundation for the Science of Creative Intelligence has headquarters in Washington, D.C., and has centers in Chicago, Atlanta, Boston, Los Angeles, New York City, and San Francisco.

There are over 300 World Plan Centers in the United States. Over 1,000,000 individuals have taken the basic TM course, however, only a small fraction of those who took the course remain meditators or in any way connected to the World Plan Executive Council. The active meditators, also still connected with the Council, are estimated to number in the tens of thousands.

Controversy

The success which Maharishi (and TM) enjoyed in the 1970s made his name a household word. It also brought criticism and controversy, which centered on three issues. First, TM's claims to scientific substantiation have been challenged on several levels. Among the early findings of psychologists were those related to the physical effects of TM, particularly those which relax the body. Psychologists studying yoga and meditation noted that similar results could be produced from a wide variety of practices, of which TM was but one. Other scientists have challenged the findings of their colleagues, pointing out that positive results could only be obtained from special samples of meditators. Social works, such as the sending of the World Governors to the several trouble spots, have had no visible results.

Second, critics, primarily those interested in the separation of church and state, boosted by evangelical Christians who opposed TM as a non-Christian religion, challenged the use of state funds to spread the practice. They argued successfully that the World Plan Executive Council was in fact a Hindu religious organization and TM a practice essentially religious in nature. The major elements of their case were the puja ceremony, the pattern of Maharishi's life and its essential Hindu religious roots through Guru Dev, the existence of the Spiritual Regeneration Movement (with its obvious religious overtones), and Maharishi's own religious writings which coincide with the World Plan, particularly *The Science of Being and Art of Living.*

Finally, TM critics have charged the movement with an element of deception. They claim (with good evidence) that Maharishi brought TM to America but soon discovered that it did not appeal to the masses he hoped to reach. Therefore, he created a new image, in part based upon the early scientific papers, and began to deny the religious elements. By this method, arguing that the practice of TM led to reduced dependence on drugs, TM spread through the school system and into the U. S. Army. [It should be noted that, in spite of the 1978 court decision, the Council still insists upon its nonreligious nature, though it does acknowledge a primary "spiritual" goal.]

During the 1970s, TM came under attack because of the siddha program. A former international leader in the movement, Bob Kropinski, took the organization to court charging fraud and psychological damage from the practice of the siddha program. He claimed that while the advertisements promised to teach students the ability to levitate, in fact they taught only a form of hopping while sitting in a cross-legged position. The jury awarded him $138,000 dollars. TM proponents have answered Kropinski with testimonies of TM's healthful effect upon their life. Meanwhile, the organization has yet to produce generally verifiable evidence of the siddha program being able to produce anyone who can do any of the extraordinary feats its advertising promises (the ability to levitate, walk through walls, or become invisible).

Sources-Primary

Alliance for Knowledge. Seelisberg, Switz.: MIU Press, 1973. 98 pp.

Benson, Herbert. *The Relaxation Response.* New York: Avon, 1975. 222 pp.

Denniston, Denise, and Peter McWilliams. *The TM Book.* Allen Park, MI: Versemonger Press, 1975. 224 pp.

Forem, Jack. *Transcendental Meditation.* New York: E. P. Dutton, 1974. 274 pp.

Fundamentals of Progress. Fairfield, IA: Maharishi International University, 1975. 55 pp.

His Holiness Maharishi Mehesh Yogi, Thirty Years Around the World: Dawn of the Age of Enlightenment. Vol. I. The Netherlands: MIU Press, 1986. 600 pp.

Maharishi Mehesh Yogi. *Life Supported by Natural Law.* Washington, DC: Age of Enlightenment Press, 1986. 210 pp.

————. *The Science of Being and the Art of Living.* London: International SRM Publications, 1966. 335 pp.

Sources-Secondary

Chapman, A. H. *What TM Can and Cannot Do for You.* New York: Berkeley Publishing Corporation, 1976. 208 pp.

Ebon, Martin, ed. *Maharishi the Guru.* New York: New American Library, 1968. 144 pp.

Patton, John E. *The Case Against TM in the Schools.* Grand Rapids, MI: Baker Book House, 1976. 100 pp.

Richards, Steve. *Levitation.* Wellingborough, UK: Aquarian Press, 1980. 160 pp.

TM in the Court. Berkeley, CA: Spiritual Counterfeits Project, 1978. 75 pp.

White, John. *Everything You Want to Know about TM—Including How to Do It.* New York: Pocket Books, 1976. 141 pp.

O. THE UNIFICATION CHURCH

The single most controversial new religion during the 1970s and 1980s was the Unification Church (officially the Holy Spirit Association for the Unification of World Christianity) founded by Korean minister Sun Myung Moon. Though never very large in North America, it has become a worldwide movement in the years since World War II and became the focus of the anti-cult movement who saw in it all that was evil in the cults.

The Founder

The Unification Church was founded by the Rev. Sun Myung Moon, born Young Myung Moon in Pyungan Buk-do, a rural town in what is now North Korea, on January 6, 1920. When he was ten his parents converted to Christianity, and the family joined the Presbyterian Church. On Easter morning 1936, according to his later reports, the sixteen-year-old Moon had a revelation in which Jesus appeared to him and revealed that he had been chosen to complete Jesus' unfulfilled mission. The vision launched a period of inner searching and struggle during which time Moon finished high school and went to Japan to study electrical engineering at Waseda University. He remained in Japan during World War II but returned to Pyongyang in northern Korea in 1948 and began a career as an independent preacher.

Shortly before his return to Korea, he had an intense spiritual experience which he described as having entered the spirit world and having won a great victory over the Satanic forces. Following this experience, he changed his name to Sun Myung Moon (i.e., Shining Sun and Moon).

His preaching activity led to his arrest in February 1948. He was sent to a prison camp where he remained until October 14, 1959, when United Nations forces liberated the camp. He fled to Pusan where he commenced preaching again and wrote the first draft of the *Divine Principle*, the book which contains the essence of his revelation. It was first published in 1957. In 1954 he organized those who had responded to his preaching into the Holy Spirit Association for the Unification of World Christianity, the official name of what is popularly called the Unification Church. The movement grew slowly but was able to send out its first missionary to Japan in 1958. Eventually a very strong branch of the Church would be built there.

In 1960 Moon married Han Ja Han (his second marriage, the first having ended in divorce) and began the task of completing that part of Christ's unfulfilled mission that included marriage and a family. Over the next two decades, culminating in 1981, Mrs. Moon bore twelve children.

Moon made several visits to the United States in the 1960s, including one in 1964 during which Spiritualist medium Arthur Ford conducted a seance that Moon attended. At the seance, Ford's spirit guide Fletcher called Moon a New Age teacher/revealer who bears the endtime message. In his talks on this trip, Moon also spoke frequently of his own familiarity with the spirit world.

While the Church was growing and spreading in the 1960s, Moon became a successful businessman with concerns in ginseng, titanium, manufacturing, and pharmaceuticals. He also expressed his intense emotional and philosophical rejection of Communism by launching in the mid-1960s a campaign against Communism, an activity that brought him the favorable attention of South Korean President Park Chung Hee.

On New Year's Day 1972 Moon received a revelation to move to the United States. He signaled this move by launching the One World Crusade and conducting a series of "Day of Hope" rallies in major American cities. Having settled in the United States, he directed the development of a multifaceted program for the Unification Church. He also became the center of several controversies, some created by his support of unpopular causes, others revolving around a growing number of accusations by opponents of the Church. Moon supported Nixon during the Watergate crisis, was investigated by a Congressional committee probing South Korean attempts to buy influence on Capitol Hill, and in 1982 was convicted on tax evasion charges brought by the Internal Revenue Service.

Moon has attempted to project his ideas into all areas of American society. He has founded two major daily newspapers in New York City and Washington, D.C. He financed a Hollywood film, *Inchon*. He has courted the scientific and scholarly world and organized numerous conferences, a peace academy, and a Washington think tank.

One question both within the movement and to outside observers concerns the role Moon has assumed in the history of salvation as part of the task he was assigned at the time of his vision of Jesus. It is generally conceded that Moon has completed the unfinished task of Jesus and that he is rightly understood as the "Lord of the Second Advent." However, both Moon and the Church have hedged on public declarations of that fact and have shown a willingness to allow a range of opinion as to the exact role of Rev. Moon in cosmic history. Speaking before the Church-sponsored Assembly of the World's Religions 1990, Moon described his position as follows:

> . . . The world needs to find the true Parent who can liberate it from Satan's love, life and lineage, this person is the Messiah. . . . To help fulfil this purpose, I have been called upon by God. For this objective I have dedicated all.

Within the movement, Rev. Moon is generally called "Father," and he and his wife are seen as the True Parents who have come to restore the world to God's original purpose.

The Unification Church in the United States

The Unification Church came to the United States in January 1959 in the person of three Korean missionaries—Young Oom Kim, David S. C. Kim, and Colonel Bo Hi Pak. The Kims settled in Eugene, Oregon, where Ms. Kim attended school and where the two worked together for several years. In January 1961 Ms. Kim moved to Berkeley,

California, and established a branch of the Church adjacent to the University of California campus. Col. Pak, a diplomatic aide at the South Korean embassy, settled in Washington, D.C.

In 1962 Ms. Kim sent the members of the Church in Berkeley to other campus locations in California and the next year dispersed them to cities around the United States. During the 1960s the Church grew slowly, operating under the name the United Family. A periodical, *New Age Frontiers*, was begun in 1964.

The growth of the Church was spurred in 1972 by Rev. Moon's move to the United States. During the years 1972-1976 it grew from a few hundred members to around 6,000. International headquarters were established in New York City and missions initiated around the world. Church centers were opened in most states (though most were quite small), and members began intense fund-raising efforts to give the Church a firm financial footing and money to launch its many programs. In 1975 the Unification Theological Seminary was established to train future Church leaders.

By the mid-1970s, the Unification Church had become the major focus of the anti-cult movement and its every action became the object of media attention. It became well known for its various efforts to mobilize the professionals and academics in support of its various causes. The most successful program has been the annual International Conference on the Unity of the Sciences, but a variety of conferences on subjects as varied as minority concerns, the role of the media in culture, and new religions filled an agenda. He also invested large sums of money in structures aimed at influencing cultural elites and public opinion.

Belief and Practice

Within the Unification Church a pluralistic theological atmosphere exists around a core of belief and practice. When the Church first arrived in America, it was infused with a hope for great change in the very near future. By the end of the 1970s, under the pressure of unrealized prophetic expectations and the growing theological sophistication spreading through the Church from the Seminary, the belief structures changed radically. The early apocalyptic hope of the visible inauguration of the kingdom of God, prophesied for 1957, 1976, and 1981, gave way to a long-term perspective in which the work of building the kingdom initiated by the Lord of the Second Advent would be accomplished over many years. Thus Church members settled down to the hard task of changing the world slowly.

The core of theological affirmations within the Unification Church centers upon the three principles of Creation, Fall and Restoration.

The Principle of Creation is that God created the world and through the visible world the invisible God can be known. The world is divided into two expressions, the Sung Sang (inner, invisible, feminine) and the Hyung Sang (outer, visible, masculine). God created the world out of his inner nature, his heart, his impulse to love, and to be united in love. The purpose of creation was to experience the joy that comes in loving.

The Principle of the Fall is that Adam and Eve did not realize God's purpose. They fell away from God by the misuse of love (adultery) and subsequent failure to constitute a perfect family. They placed Satan in control of this world. History is the story of God's attempts to restore the original creation and overthrow the rule of Satan.

The Principle of Restoration is that in order to accomplish the task of restoring the world, since God cannot override humanity's free nature but must deal with its immersion in sin, a Messiah is required. The Messiah must meet several requirements. He must be born fully human, must conquer sin, and manifest God's masculine nature. He must also marry a woman who will manifest God's feminine nature. Jesus accomplished only half of his Messianic mission, as he failed to marry. Thus Jesus offers his followers only a spiritual salvation. By completing that mission, Rev. Moon now offers a complete physical salvation as well.

Humans participate in the restoration by aligning themselves with the Messiah. They accomplish this alignment through a process of indemnity and preparation for entering the restored kingdom. The period of indemnity and preparation is spent in sacrificial work and absolute celibacy. At the end of the period, members are matched by Rev. Moon with a suitable mate and married in a ceremony conducted by the True Parents. The consummation of the marriage, which involves a ritual in which the process of indemnity and restoration is dramatically reenacted, gave rise previously in Korea to rumors of sexual improprieties on Rev. Moon's part, a practice that would be diametrically opposed to the Church's stance on sexual purity.

The work of the Unification Church through its members who have been blessed (i.e., married) is the establishment of the Kingdom of God on earth. In the establishment of the Kingdom, the physical salvation initiated by Rev. Moon becomes manifest through the children born to blessed couples and the spread of the Kingdom ideal of one human family transcending race and nationality. (Typically Unification Church members marry across racial and national boundaries.)

Organization

The Unification Church is headed by Rev. Moon who has complete authority. He is assisted in the task of administering the affairs of the Church by a Board of Church Elders, most of whom reside in the United States, and all of whom are Korean by birth. The Board appoints the national president for each country or region. In the United States, the Church is further divided into missions, one or two for each state.

Also operating under the Board are the many departments and missions which have been created to carry out the work of the Church. As the Church has created institutions and organizations they have primarily been placed under the direct care of three persons: Col. Bo Hi Pak, who is in charge of most cultural and political programs; Chung Hwan Kwak, who oversees evangelical thrusts; and David Kim, president of the Unification Theological Seminary. The Board also appoints the presidents of the Church in each country who have direct oversight of local congregations.

Through the years the Unification Church has created numerous structures which have two principal goals: the evangelization of the world (i.e., the recruitment and training of church members) and the infusion of the world with the ideals of the Kingdom of God (with all its cultural, religious and political implications) as perceived by Moon. The cultural, charitable, religious and political organizations created by the Church bring members and nonmembers together for the promotion of a limited set of shared ideals from religious liberty to the search for a unity of science and religion in the realm of values. The cultural and political organizations usually serve a secondary goal of acquainting nonmember participants with the Church in a favorable context and offering opportunities to learn of its theology, program, and internal life. It is this secondary goal which has led many critics, not without some justification, to call these organizations fronts for the Church. On the other hand, the Church has endeavored to separate its teaching of theology and recruitment of members from its other programs and has continued to invite people who are personally antagonistic to the Church and its ideals but who share a particular concern (be it religious liberty, interfaith dialogue, anti-Communism, or international relations in the Pacific Basin) to its conferences.

The Church's activities aimed at cultural revitalization have recently been reorganized under the International Cultural Foundation, founded in 1982, which seeks to bring people together across national boundaries in activities to promote international understanding, global morality, and civic understanding. Its most famous and successful activity has been the annual International Conference on the Unity of the Sciences, which has brought together scientists and other scholars to discuss the implications of science for moral and religious values. Equally important on the international level has been the Professors World Peace Academy, which deals with issues of world peace. Out of these two organizations in America has come the Washington Institute for Values in Public Policy, a Washington, D.C., think tank. Each of these organizations has been able to attract some of the country's leading scholars. The ICF also became the seedbed for the new scholarly publishing venture Paragon Press.

Three structures have been among the prominent charitable programs of the Church. Project Volunteer and the National Council for the Church and Social Action have had a major impact on the distribution of food and surplus materials to the poor and needy in a number of urban centers. Between 1977 and 1982 over $6,000,000 in food and other needed supplies were given out in Harlem, Washington, D.C., and Philadelphia. The International Relief Friendship Foundation provides emergency and long-term assistance in over 50 countries through the distribution of food, materials, and medical care.

During the 1970s, the leading institution advocating the Church's political goal of defeating world Communism was the Freedom Leadership Foundation. In the 1980s FLF's thrust has largely been taken over by CAUSA, an anti-Communist group which has found its major support among Spanish-speaking peoples, including the leaders of some South American countries.

The Unification Theological Seminary, located at Barrytown, New York, is the major educational arm of the Church. It offers a two-year theological curriculum. Most of the faculty are non-Unification Church members, but many are very active in initiating and building several church-related programs. The New Ecumenical Research Association, which annually sponsors a variety of academic seminars and conferences, was nurtured by the seminary faculty in its early days. More recently its work has been subsumed under a new umbrella, the International Religious Foundation. The Seminary also assisted in the creation of the Global Congress of the World's Religions. The Seminary initiated a scholarly publishing program through Rose of Sharon Press, though most of that endeavor has now been turned over to Paragon.

Evangelistically the Church has made its presence felt through a variety of programs. The mobile fund-raising teams, usually coordinated under the International One World Crusade, regularly saturate the United States to both raise operating funds for the Church and recruit new members. The Home Church program, established wherever the Church has a center, divides the surrounding community into districts. Each district is assigned a member whose task is to visit each residence and offer the Church's resources (usually in the form of community services) to each and every person residing in the area. Possibly the most important evangelistic structure is the Collegiate Association for the Research of Principles (CARP). CARP, one of the oldest UC activities, maintains chapters on many university campuses. It has been one of the Church's most controversial organizations, as it has continually been accused of deceptive recruiting and hiding its connection with the Church. A similar but less active organization directs its activities toward high schools. A publications department oversees a large number of periodicals for the various departments, the most important being *Unification News* (widely distributed), *Today's World* (restricted to Church members), and the *CARP Monthly*. The Church also publishes two additional publications for members only: *Principle Life* and *Blessing Quarterly*, both concerned with married life in the Church.

The national headquarters of the American branch of the Unification Church are in New York City, a few blocks from the mission center which houses most of the international Church's departments discussed above. The national Church oversees the state Churches. Local centers of the Church are headed by a director who is in charge of worship, recruitment, teaching, and training programs of the Church.

Current Status

As the 1980s began, the Unification Church had approximately 5,000 members in the United States with much larger memberships in Japan and Korea, and Church centers and missionaries in 120 countries. Its intercultural and scholarly programs also involve several thousand academicians, pastors (from a wide variety of denominations), businessmen, professionals, and scientists.

The continuing activity of the Church's opponents and accompanying controversy, while hindering the Church in some areas, has kept its programs before the public and continues to attract individuals to investigate the claims of its enemies. Many so attracted stay to participate in its programs.

The Unification Church, like most first-generation religions, is in the midst of a high degree of change. A major transition occurred in 1982 when over half the American Church members were married in the several mass wedding ceremonies. Much of the future of the Church depends upon the role of the new leadership being created at the Seminary, the quality of life of the now predominantly married membership, the persistent opposition to the church, and the acceptance of the Church by the academic and religious community.

Controversy

It almost seems redundant to include a special section on controversy concerning the Unification Church, as it has been the one major focus of the anti-cult movement since the mid-1970s.

One major controversy peculiar to itself consumed the life of the Church in the early 1980s—the conviction of Rev. Moon on tax evasion charges. In 1982 Rev. Moon stood trial for not paying income tax on interest earned in the early 1970s in a savings account in his name. The issue was complicated by one Church official who recreated records for transactions during the period under question and did not reveal that they were recreations until that fact was uncovered by the Treasury Department investigators. Moon argued that the money was Church money even though in an account in his name. The state argued that it was his personal money. He was convicted and the Supreme Court refused to hear his appeal. He spent 13 months during 1984-85 in jail.

The anti-cult forces welcomed his conviction as a victory. The Church fought unsuccessfully to keep Moon from jail. However, during the period the case was under appeal, and afterward while Moon was in jail, many people heretofore neutral or hostile to the Church rallied behind it on grounds of religious freedom. Political, academic, and church leaders wrote numerous briefs for the case in the Church's support. The period in jail was seen as further persecution for the cause and by the end of the decade its effects were largely in the past. Apart from the personal inconvenience, the Church seems not to have experienced any losses as a result of the affair.

Of lesser news, but possibly greater long-term significance, has been the Church's continued effort to make a place for itself within the American media. It has initiated newspapers and magazines, paid for a major motion picture which flopped at the box office, and most recently purchased the defunct *Washington Star* which has reappeared as the *Washington Times*, which in turn has given birth to a national weekly news magazine, *Insight*, and a book-length monthly (600+ pages per issue) *The World and I.* None of these ventures has as yet been able to become independent financially.

The future of the Church depends upon its ability to continue to quell the hostility toward it in the general culture, a hostility which waned but little through the 1980s and appears to be dropping as the 1990s begin. While Moon and the Church are still the target of much negative media coverage, the amount has noticeably lessened, partially a result of the overall loss of steam over the cult controversy.

Sources-Primary

Chull, Pail, Lee Hang Nyong, Sheen Doh Sung, and Yoon Se Won. *Sun Myung Moon: the Man and His Ideal.* Seoul, Korea: Future Civilization Press, 1981. 186 pp.

Divine Principle. Washington, DC: Holy Spirit Association for the Unification of World Christianity, 1973. 536 pp.

Moon, Sun Myung. *God's Warning to the World.* 2 vols. New York: HSA-UWC, 1985.

————. *God's Will and the World.* New York: Holy Spirit Association for the Unification of World Christianity, 1985. 677 pp.

————. *The New Future of Christianity.* Washington, DC: Unification Church International, 1974. 144 pp.

————. *Science and Absolute Values.* New York: ICF Press, 1982. 112 pp.

Outline of the Principle, Level 4. New York: Holy Spirit Association for the Unification of World Christianity, 1980. 316 pp.

Sources-Secondary

Barker, Eileen. *The Making of a Moonie.* Oxford: Basil Blackwell, 1984. 305 pp.

Bryant, M. Darrol, and Herbert W. Richardson, eds. *A Time for Consideration.* New York: Edwin Mellen Press, 1978. 317 pp.

Lofland, John. *Doomsday Cult.* New York: Irvington Publishers, 1977. 362 pp.

Mickler, Michael. *The Unification Church in America: A Bibliography and Research Guide.* New York: Garland Publishing, 1987. 227 pp.

Richardson, Herbert, ed. *Constitutional Issues in the Case of Rev. Moon.* New York: Edwin Mellen Press, 1984. 699 pp.

Sherwood, Carlton. *Inquisition: The Persecution and Prosecution of the Reverend Sun Myung Moon.* Washington, DC: Regnery Gateway, 1891. 705 pp.

Sontag, Frederick. *Sun Myung Moon.* Nashville: Abingdon, 1977. 224 pp.

P. VAJRADHATU (TIBETAN BUDDHISM)

During the 1970s many representatives of the various schools of Tibetan Buddhism established movements in the United States. By far the largest of the several movements was founded by Chogyam Trungpa, Rinpoche, who built a national organization with local centers (called Dharmadatus) across the country. Vajradhatu has spearheaded the growth of Tibetan Buddhism in the United States.

The Kargyupa Sect

Tibetan Buddhism, as is true of most major religious traditions, has split into many sects and subsects. Among these, the Kargyupa was founded in the late eleventh century by Lama Marpa of Lhabrag. Its most famous teacher is Milarepa, Marpa's successor, whose 100,000 songs are classics of Tibetan literature. During the 12th century the Kargyupa sect split into several subsects, the largest of which was the Karmapa.

Among the centers of the Karmapa Kargyupa was the Surmang monastery complex. The abbot of the monastery was believed to be a *tulku*, an emanation of a Bodhisattva who decides to work on earth for others and who takes birth over a period of time in a series of bodies. Upon the death of a tulku, those around him would begin a search for the child in whose body he had taken fresh incarnation. The story of Vajradhatu begins with the death of the tenth Trungpa tulku in 1938.

Guided by two visions of the head of the Kargyupas, the monks set out in search of the tulku in his new infant's body. They soon located the child. He was tested and he was able to pick out the former possessions of the tenth Trungpa tulku. Accepted, he was enthroned by His Holiness Gyalwa Karmapa, the head of the sect. This baby became known as Chogyam Trungpa, Rinpoche.

The Founder

Chogyam Trungpa, Rinpoche, the founder of Vajradhatu, was born in February 1939 in the village of Geje in northeast Tibet. After being identified as the reborn tenth Trungpa tulku, he was taken to Düdtsi-til Monastery to be trained. While still in his teens he received his degrees (equivalent to a master's and a doctorate) but had no time to use either. In 1959 the Chinese invaded Tibet, and the newly ordained monk fled with a small group of his supporters to India. While in India he learned English and was allowed to go to the West. In 1963 he went to Oxford to study art, psychology, and comparative religion.

While at Oxford he discovered Johnstone House, a Buddhist contemplative center in Scotland and in 1967 it was turned over to Trungpa and became Samye-ling Monastery. In 1969 he was severely injured in an automobile accident. While recuperating, he decided to take off his monk's robes and become a layman in order to better communicate with the Western people among whom he had decided to work. He stayed at the new monastery only a brief period, and after a disagreement with some of the leaders, he immigrated to the United States where a group of his students had purchased some land in Vermont upon which they built Tail of the Tiger Monastery. Just before arriving in America, in January 1970 he married Diana Judith Pybus.

During the next few years Trungpa traveled around the country lecturing and teaching and establishing the local centers (Dharmadatus). In 1971 he opened the Rocky Mountain Dharma Center at Ft. Collins, Colorado, and the next year organized the Karma Dzong at Boulder. Then in 1973 his national organization, Vajradhatu, was created and all of his work placed under it. From that point the work began to expand. Seeing the need for a more systematic and advanced training opportunity for his more dedicated students, he held the first seminary class which led to the formation of Naropa Institute in 1974.

1974 became a spiritual landmark for Trungpa and Vajradhatu as Gyalwa Karmapa, the international leader of the Kargyupa Buddhists, made his first pilgrimage to America. He visited the Tail of the Tiger which he renamed Karme-Choling and for the first time in the Western Hemisphere performed the famous black hat ceremony. He recognized Trungpa as a Vajracarya, a spiritual master. Since this initial visit, he has returned on several occasions.

Manifesting the maturity of the American work, in 1976 Trungpa named an American as his Dharma successor. Thomas Rich, a former disciple of Integral Yoga teacher Swami Satchidananda known as Narayana, met Trungpa in 1971 and became his close disciple. He took the name Ösel Tendzin and was eventually appointed Vajra Regent to become head of Vajradhatu upon Trungpa's death or retirement.

Trungpa died in 1987 amid hopes for his son's rebirth. Ösel Tendzin assumed administrative leadership of the community. His reign was to be a brief one, and two years later it was discovered he had a fatal disease. He died in 1990. He was succeeded by the Sawang Ösel Rangdrol Mukpo, Trungpa's eldest son.

Organization

The work built around Trungpa has been organized into two separate corporations. Vajradhatu, the more inwardly directed of the two, recruits, trains, and nurtures the disciples of Trungpa and Tibetan Buddhism. Through the Nalanda Foundation, Trungpa reaches out to the world and demonstrates the value of Buddhism in various otherwise secular realms.

Vajradhatu, literally "the realm of the indestructible," coordinates all the other activities and is headquartered in Boulder, Colorado, in a facility named Dorje Dzong. Under Vajradhatu are: Karme-Choling, the original community located near Barnet, Vermont, on a 530-acre farm. Resident members follow a year-round program of meditation and study and sponsor seminars, retreats, and training sessions led by Trungpa and other staff persons. Karma Dzong, founded in 1972, was modeled on Karme-Choling and for most of the 1970s Trungpa moved regularly between the two. Associated with Karma Dzong is the Rocky Mountain Dharma Center, a small facility high in the mountains used primarily for meditative retreats and other short-term programs. Dorje Khyung Dzong is an isolated center located in the mountains of southern Colorado used primarily for private individual retreats.

Vajradhatu Seminary is not a place so much as an event. Each fall for eighty days the senior staff offer an advanced course in Tibetan Buddhism including its esoteric aspects. This course is a must for all serious students in Vajradhatu.

Vajradhatu also has an editorial and recording department. Most of Trungpa's books have been published by Shambhala Publications, a firm that existed prior to Trungpa's coming to America but, while remaining an independent company, has become closely associated with his movement and moved its facilities from Berkeley, California, to Boulder after Trungpa established his headquarters there. They are currently headquartered in Boston, Massachusetts. Vajradhatu's editorial department oversees the two periodicals of the organization, *Garuda* and *Vajradhatu Sun*. The recording department has begun issuing tapes of Trungpa's lectures and seminars.

The Dharmadatus, the local centers established across the United States by Trungpa, are also under Vajradhatu and their directors are appointed from the Boulder headquarters.

Nalanda Foundation was established by Trungpa as a channel for the permeation of society with Buddhism. The main structure under Nalanda is the Naropa Institute, an alternative school grounded in Buddhism. The Institute nurtures an environment within which Eastern and Western traditions can interact and the standard approach to education can be complemented by an intuitive approach that grows out of a spiritual discipline. College-level courses at Naropa concentrate upon Buddhist studies, exploration of the self and the world, and the arts.

There are still other aspects of Nalanda. The Maitri Therapeutic Community uses Buddhist practices to confront the issues of personal neurosis. The Mudra Theater Group is a dramatic group whose main presentation is a play by Trungpa, *Prajna*, based upon Trungpa's interpretation of the *Heart-Sutra*, a famous Buddhist work. Alaya Preschool is a preschool educational unit.

The newest addition to the Nalanda program is Shambhala Training, a Buddhist version of the weekend growth seminars made popular by Erhard Seminars Training (est) and now conducted by a variety of alternative religious and New Age groups.

Beliefs and Practice

Trungpa brought the teachings of the Kargyupa sect of Buddhism from Tibet. However, after his decision to become a teacher in the West, he developed a modern Western vocabulary, primarily that of humanistic and growth-centered psychology, to express the complicated and sophisticated Tibetan tradition. As is characteristic of the Kargyupa tradition, a secret esoteric aspect of the teachings is taught only to advanced students via oral presentation by Vajradhatu's spiritual leader.

Trungpa emphasized Buddhism as a practice to awaken the mind. The path to the awakened state has three aspects or "wheels": meditation, study, and work. Meditation is the state of being in the present moment and consists of training the mind to exist in the here and now. Study sharpens the understanding of the experience of meditation and the communication of the experience to others. Work allows the meditator to share what has been learned with others.

A major theme of Trungpa's teaching in the Western context was *Cutting Through Spiritual Materialism*, also the title of an early book. He believed that the major error of Westerners who follow a spiritual discipline was their conversion of what they had learned to egotistical uses, thus negating its value.

In his role as guru, Trungpa presented a mixed (some would say contradictory) image. He carried many of the trappings of a Buddhist lama, who is not only a religious but a political ruler in a royal priesthood. On the other hand he divested himself of many Tibetan manners and dressed in Western clothes. He was heavily criticized for his personal habits, which include eating meat and using both alcohol and tobacco. He described his role as providing a context within which individuals can find enlightenment. His job was to prod and keep the seeker honest.

Current Status

Vajradhatu has grown slowly but consistently since its formation. By 1980 there were 37 centers including the major communities in Vermont and Colorado. In 1981 the administration and supervision of these centers was transferred to the Vajra Regent Ösel Tendzin. Approximately 2,000 students of Trungpa have membership in these centers. It is not yet evident what losses have been sustained by the unrest during the last months of Ösel Tendzin's leadership.

Naropa Institute has grown steadily and received the support of Buddhist leaders and scholars throughout North America. It offers both B.A. and M.A. degrees and has applied for full accreditation as an institution of higher learning. Vajradhatu plans to build Naropa into a full university.

Vajradhatu publishes a bimonthly newspaper *Vajradhatu Sun* (which replaced the *Sangha Newsletter*). *Garuda* continues to appear irregularly.

Vajradhatu has made substantive improvements in its program and developed new programs each year during the first two decades of its existence. There is little reason to doubt that this growth will continue into the future.

Controversy

Prior to 1989, the only hint of controversy experienced by Vajradhatu in its growth toward legitimacy as a major center of Buddhism in the West occurred in the fall of 1975. One outstanding poet who had participated in the summer poetry school sponsored by Naropa Institute was allowed to attend the classes for advanced students to follow. Being a pacifist, the poet had been disturbed by the bloody images in some of the Tibetan material covered during the sessions. However, the crucial incident occurred during a Halloween party at Naropa which he and a friend had left early in the evening. During the course of the evening, Trungpa ordered them to return. An argument ensued and the two were stripped of their clothes. The incident sent shock waves through America's poetry community and became the subject of an article in a national magazine and a book.

In 1989 the *Los Angeles Times* broke the story that Ösel Tendzin had AIDS. That in itself would not have been such bad news, however, it was also reported that for three years he had known of his infection and had continued to have sexual relations with others without telling them of the risk. Vajradhatu's board, upon learning of the situation, asked him to take a permanent leave of absence. Refusing to, in effect resign, he did extend his temporary leave until his physical health prevented him from assuming any further ritual leadership role. The ethical questions raised by his not telling his sexual partners of his illness, and in one case passing the infection along, raised enough questions that some of the leadership resigned. Rick Fields, the prominent editor of *Vajradhatu Sun* was ordered not to write about the story. He resigned in protest.

The Sawang Ösel Mukpo assumed leadership immediately upon Tendzin's death and has returned some stability to the organization. It is yet to be seen if Trungpa's intense popularity can carry the organization through the scandal and his son's leadership dissolve any remaining issues. As of the end of 1991, the organization appears to have put the problem behind it.

Sources-Primary

Guenther, Herbert V., and Chogyam Trungpa. *The Dawn of Tantra.* Berkeley, CA: Shambhala, 1975. 92 pp.

Lauf, Detlef Ingo. *Secret Doctrines of the Tibetan Books of the Dead.* Boulder, CO: Shambhala, 1977. 254 pp.

Trungpa, Chogyam. *Born in Tibet.* Boulder: Shambhala, 1977. 280 pp.

————. *Cutting Through Spiritual Materialism.* Berkeley, CA: Shambhala, 1973. 250 pp.

————. *The Myth of Freedom.* Berkeley, CA: Shambhala, 1976. 176 pp.

Sources-Secondary

Clark, Tom. *The Great Naropa Poetry Wars.* Santa Barbara: Cadmus Editions, 1980. 87 pp.

Dasgupta, Shashi Bhushan. *An Introduction to Tibetan Buddhism.* Berkeley, CA: Shambhala, 1974. 211 pp.

Fields, Rick. *How the Swans Came to the Lake.* Boulder, CO: Shambhala, 1986. 445 pp.

Hoffman, Helmut. *The Religions of Tibet.* New York: Macmillan Company, 1961. 199 pp.

Waddell, L. A. *The Buddhism of Tibet or Lamaism.* Hoshiarpur, India: Vishveshvaranand Vedic Research Institute, 1959. 598 pp.

Q. THE WAY INTERNATIONAL, INC.

The Way International, Inc., was founded in 1942 as "Vesper Chimes," a radio ministry initiated by Victor Paul Wierwille, then pastor of the Evangelical and Reformed Church of Paine, Ohio. Its name was changed to the Chimes Hour in 1944 and incorporated as the Chimes Hour Youth Caravan in 1947. In 1955 the name The Way, Inc. was adopted and finally in 1974, the present name was assumed.

The Founder

Victor Paul Wierwille (1916-1985) decided to enter the ministry while a student at Mission House College (now Lakeland College of Sheboygan, Wisconsin). He attended Mission House Seminary (now United Theological Seminary, Minneapolis, Minnesota) where he earned his B.D. He did graduate work at the University of Chicago and Princeton Theological Seminary which awarded him a M.Th. in 1941. In 1942 he was ordained and became the pastor of the Church at Paine. Two years later he moved to Van Wert, Ohio, as pastor of St. Peter's E. & R. (now United Church of Christ) Church.

During the years at Van Wert, Wierwille began the intense personal reading and research on the Bible that would lead to the present teachings of The Way International. He concentrated upon the doctrine of the Holy Spirit, and in 1951 he spoke in tongues for the first time. His research led to his being awarded a Ph.D. in 1948 by the Pikes Peak Bible College and Seminary, an unaccredited correspondence school head-quartered in Manitou Springs, Colorado, that is no longer in existence.

The initial results of his research were incorporated into the first "Power for Abundant Living" class given in 1953. However, Wierwille had not stopped his research. The next year he began to study Aramaic and made the acquaintance of George Lamsa, who had attained some notoriety for his translation of the Aramaic Biblical texts. Wierwille's research led to his accepting a view of Biblical doctrine increasingly distinct from that of his Church and in 1957 he resigned his ministry in Van Wert and left the Evangelical and Reformed Church. He led The Way until his retirement in 1983.

The Development of The Way

The Way began as a radio ministry some years before Wierwille resigned from the Evangelical and Reformed Church. It grew during the 1950s by the initiation of the PFAL classes (1953) and *The Way Magazine* (1954). In 1957 Wierwille took control of the family farm outside of New Knoxville, Ohio, and deeded it to The Way. There he established his headquarters and for a decade watched the work grow. The slow but steady growth was interrupted in the late 1960s when the ministry suddenly burgeoned at the time of the national Jesus People revival. In the wake of the expansion, Wierwille established The Way Corps, a four-year leadership training program. In 1974 The Way purchased the former Emporia College in Emporia, Kansas. It became The Way College, the home of the Corps.

In 1971 Wierwille initiated the Word Over the World Ambassador program which sent young people affiliated with The Way around the United States for a year of witnessing activity. The first Ambassadors were commissioned at the Rock of Ages Festival, an annual gathering of Way members, the first of which was also held in 1971.

In 1983 L. Craig Martindale (b. 1948) succeeded Wierwille as the president of The Way, the occasion of his installation being the 40th anniversary of its founding. Martindale, a former football player at the University of Kansas and president of the Fellowship of Christian Athletes, joined The Way while in college. Following graduation, he became involved in the work full time serving as The Way state coordinator for Oklahoma (1973-74), international director of The Way Corps (1975-77), and president of The Way College (1977-80).

Beliefs

The Way International may be characterized as a Pentecostal ultradispensational Christian group. Its beliefs are summarized in an eleven-point statement:

1. We believe the scriptures of the Old and New Testaments were *Theopneustos*, "God Breathed," and perfect as originally given; that the Scriptures or the Word of God is of supreme, absolute and final authority for believing, for all life and godliness.
2. We believe in one God, the creator of the heavens and earth; in Jesus Christ, God's only begotten Son and our Lord and Savior, whom God raised from the dead; and we believe in the working of the holy Spirit.
3. We believe that the Virgin Mary conceived by the Holy Spirit, that God was in Christ, and that the one mediator between God and men is the man Christ Jesus.
4. We believe that man was created in the image of God, spiritually, that he sinned and thereby brought upon himself immediate spiritual death, which is separation from God and physical death also which is the consequence of sin, and that all human beings are born with a sinful nature.
5. We believe that Jesus Christ died for our sins according to the Scriptures, as a representative and substitute for us; and that all who believe that God raised him from the dead are justified and made righteous, born again by the spirit of God, receiving eternal life on the grounds of his eternal redemption, and thereby are the sons of God.
6. We believe in the resurrection of the crucified body of our Lord Jesus Christ, his ascension into heaven and his seating at the right hand of God.
7. We believe in the blessed hope of Christ's return, the personal return of our living lord and savior Jesus Christ and our gathering unto him.
8. We believe in the bodily resurrection of the just and unjust.
9. We believe in the receiving of the fullness of the holy spirit, the power from on high, plus the corresponding nine manifestations of the holy spirit, for all born again believers.
10. We believe it is available to receive all that God

promises us in His Word according to our believing faith. We believe we are free in Christ Jesus to receive all that he accomplished for us by his substitution.

11. We believe the early Church flourished rapidly because they operated within a Root, Trunk, Limb, Branch, and Twig set up (decently and in order).

The Way International departs from traditional orthodox Christianity at a number of points. Wierwille denies the doctrine of the Trinity and the divinity of Jesus Christ, a point emphasized in one of his books *Jesus Christ Is Not God* (1975). He also denies the personality of the Holy Spirit, which he believes to be the power of God. This view, generally termed Arianism, was popularized by Arius, a second-century presbyter of the Church in Alexandria. Since the condemnation of Arius by the Council of Nicea in 325 C.E., Arianism has been considered a heretical theology by the mainline Christian Church.

Wierwille also taught ultradispensationalism, an approach to Scripture which views the Bible books as products of progressive "dispensations" or periods of different administrations of God's relationship to humanity. Dispensationalism first emerged as a perspective on Biblical history in the nineteenth century within a British group, the Plymouth Brethren, but became a popular theology in the twentieth century through its adoption by leaders such as evangelist Dwight L. Moody and teacher C. I. Scofield, editor of the *Scofield Reference Bible* (1909). Dispensationalism divides the Bible story into seven dispensations (Innocence, Conscience, Government, Promise, Law, Grace, and the Personal Reign of Christ), and believers hold that the Church presently exists in the dispensation of grace which began at Easter, a dispensation that will continue until Christ's Second Coming.

Ultra-Dispensationalism teaches that there was another dispensation, or a period of transition between Easter and the New Testament Church as seen in Paul's later epistles. This period of transition is characterized by John's water baptism and its story is told primarily in the Book of Acts. This view was first expressed by Brethren leader Richard Holden in 1870 but became well known after its adoption by Anglican Biblical scholar Ethelbert Bullinger, editor of *The Companion Bible*. Ultra-Dispensationalism sees Paul's later epistles (Ephesians, Colossians, Philippians and Galatians, but especially Ephesians) as the prime documents of the dispensation or administration of grace.

Following Ephesians 4:5-6, they believe in one baptism, that of the holy spirit, and hence reject water baptism.

Wierwille has also stressed the role of Aramaic as the language spoken by Jesus and believes that the New Testament was written originally in Aramaic (most scholars believe it was written in Greek). The Way emphasizes the work of George M. Lamsa and uses his *The Holy Bible from Ancient Eastern Manuscripts* (1959) and, in the same vein, has reprinted the books of independent Indian Bishop K. C. Pillai, *The Orientalisms of the Bible* and *Light through an Eastern Window.*

Organization

The Way International's structure follows the Biblical mandate for decency and order and is modelled on the pattern of a tree. Five educational and administrative centers that serve the organization internationally are termed the "root" locations. They are the International Headquarters at New Knoxville, Ohio; The Way College of Emporia at Emporia, Kansas; The Way College of Biblical Research, Indiana Campus, at Rome, Indiana; Camp Gunnison—The Way Family Ranch at Gunnison, Colorado; and Lead Outdoor Academy at Tinnie, New Mexico.

Countries are termed "trunk" areas. States are called "limbs" and counties and large cities "branches." The basic units of The Way are the numerous local community fellowships, called "twigs." The Way has not moved to purchase church buildings and organize congregations in the traditional sense, hence their membership, which regularly gathered in the home of a member, tends to be largely invisible in the various communities in which it operates.

Administratively, a three-person board of trustees made up of a president, vice-president, and secretary-treasurer head The Way International and make all policy decisions. The trustees appoint a Trustee's Cabinet that oversees the various departments at the International Headquarters and the staff of the other root locations. Each trunk, limb, branch, and twig is led by a resident coordinator.

Individuals usually begin their affiliation with The Way by taking its basic course, called "Power for Abundant Living." It presents the basic

Biblical perspective developed by Wierwille and is presented through 33 hours of tape or film presentation. After completion of the course, for which pupils pay a tuition, they are encouraged to take a variety of advanced courses, to become involved in such various programs as The Way Corps, or to become a Word over the World Ambassador. Eventually most will become a member of a local twig.

Current Status

In 1983 The Way International reported 2,657 twigs in the United States with an average of ten members per twig. Over 17,000 attended the 1983 Rock of Ages Festival. Foreign work has been initiated in Zaire, Chile, Argentina, Venezuela, and Colombia. Approximately 14,000 took the basic PFAL course during the year. Advanced courses were offered as Intermediate PFAL, Christian Family and Sex, Renewed Mind, Witnessing and Undershepherding, Spiritual Contest, and Rise and Expansion.

The American Christian Press, located within the International Headquarters complex at New Knoxville, publishes bimonthly *The Way Magazine*. It also publishes the many books of Wierwille including *The New Dynamic Church* (1971), *Receiving the Holy Spirit Today* (1972), *God's Magnified Word* (1977), and *Jesus Christ: Our Promised Seed* (1982).

The basic programs of The Way International are built around The Way Corps, The Way Family Corps, and the Sunset Corps through which members are given a thorough training in The Way's perspective on the Bible and its application to daily life. The Way Corps is headquartered at The Way College of Emporia, and The Way Family Corps and Sunset Corps (for older members) are headquartered at The Way College of Biblical Research, Indiana Campus. Those programs are designed for people (such as entire families) who cannot take a full four-year curriculum.

Way Productions, based at The Way International's Cultural Center at New Bremen, Ohio, provides leadership in developing the arts along Biblical principles. Out of its work have come several professional-quality musical groups including "Take a Stand Caravan" and "Branded" (a country and western group). The Way International Fine Arts and

Historical Center at Sidney, Ohio, houses the historical records of the organization.

Controversy

The Way International, one of the largest of the groups which have been labeled "cult," has also been the target of deprogramming. During the early 1980s it replaced the Unification Church as the group reporting the most deprogramming attempts among its members.

In addition to the standard anti-cult accusations of brainwashing and mind control, opponents of The Way have leveled two serious charges. First, during the 1970s, anti-cultists accused The Way of training members in the use of deadly weapons for possible future use against The Way's enemies. This charge derived from the adoption at the College at Emporia of a State of Kansas program in gun safety (primarily for hunters). All the students at the College were allowed, but not required, to enroll. The charges died as no violent activity arose to substantiate them.

Through the 1980s, Christian anti-cultists have picked up the attack on The Way for its radical departure from orthodox Christianity and its adoption of Arianism. Wierwille's denial of the divinity of Jesus and the Trinity has been a constant barrier to The Way's ability to align itself with other Christian bodies. John P. Juedes, the major Evangelical writer on The Way, has challenged what he sees as historical inaccuracies and incompetence in handling the texts of scriptures which call into question the validity of Wierwille's scholarship.

Following Wierwille's death, The Way experienced a period of inner turmoil. Several of the leaders left amid charges of improprieties by Wierwille and several of his close associates. A few established rival groups. Support for The Way dropped noticeably, a reality visibly demonstrated by the attendance at the annual Rock of Ages festival. By 1990, however, the organization was recovering and attendance at the festival began to return to its former level.

Through the 1980s, The Way came under scrutiny by the Internal Revenue Service which questioned both its alleged partisan political involvement and the business aspects of its activities at New Knoxville.

In 1985 its tax-exempt status had been revoked, but that ruling was reversed in a 1990 decision of the Supreme Court.

Sources-Primary

Whiteside, Elena S. *The Way: Living in Love*. New Knoxville, OH: American Christian Press, 1972. 284 pp.

Wierwille, Victor Paul. *Jesus Christ: Our Promised Seed*. New Knoxville, OH: American Christian Press, 1982. 306 pp.

———. *The New Dynamic Church: Studies in Abundant Living*. New Knoxville, OH: American Christian Press, 1971. 242 pp.

———. *Power for Abundant Living*. New Knoxville, OH: American Christian Press, 1971. 370 pp.

———. *Receiving the Holy Spirit Today*. New Knoxville, OH: American Christian Press, 1972. 360 pp.

Sources-Secondary

Juedes, John P. *Trinitarianism—A Pagan Creation?* Milwaukee: C.A.R.I.S., 1981. 16 pp.

———, and Douglas V. Morton. *From "Vesper Chimes" to "The Way International:" The Founder, History and Activities of The Way Ministry*. Milwaukee, WI: C.A.R.I.S., [1983]. 78 pp.

Morton, Douglas V., and John P. Juedes. *The Integrity and Accuracy of The Way's Word*. St. Louis, MO: Personal Freedom Outreach, 1980. 48 pp.

Williams, J. L. *Victor Paul Wierwille and The Way International*. Chicago: Moody Press, 1979. 158 pp.

R. WITCHCRAFT AND NEOPAGANISM

Magic (often spelled "magick" to distinguish it from stage illusionism) experienced a revival during the twentieth century, especially during the last generation. Of the several groups which include magic as an important aspect of their structures, Witchcraft claimed the most adherents and emerged as a popular movement, far outstripping most other groups labeled as "cults."

Definition

The term "witchcraft" is used to describe a wide variety of phenomena (both secular and sacred), and very distinct groups can be easily confused. In the Bible, the Hebrew word *ob* is sometimes translated witch, as the famous *ob* of Endor (I Samuel 28). We do not exactly know what the ancient *obs* did, but we do know that they specialized in herbs, poisons, and mediumship. The shamans and priests in many preindustrial societies are popularly called "witch doctors" and their practice "witchcraft." The medieval Church equated witchcraft with Satanism, the worship of the devil (Satanism is discussed elsewhere in this volume). Finally witchcraft is synonymous with malevolent sorcery, the attempt to do evil by occult or supernatural means. In this context, voodoo is also equated with witchcraft.

While North America is home to a growing voodoo community, a few Satanists, and even several witch doctors or shamans, the great majority of people who call themselves Witches fit none of the categories described above. Rather most modern Witches are followers of a polytheistic faith centered upon the worship of the Great Mother Goddess, usually called Diana, Isis, or Demeter, though many different names are used. When a contemporary Westerner describes herself or himself as a Witch, it is this form of Witchcraft to which they refer.

Founder

Contemporary Wicca or Witchcraft was founded by Gerald B. Gardner (1884-1964), British civil servant and amateur archeologist. Gardner spent most of his working years in Southern Asia where he absorbed a knowledge of magic. He wrote the definitive book on the Malaysian magical knife, *Kris and Other Malay Weapons* (1936), joined the Masons, and quickly involved himself in the occult scene.

According to Gardner's own account, after his return to England just prior to World War II, he joined a Theosophical group, the Fellowship of Crotona. At one of the group's meetings, he met some Witches who eventually introduced him to their priestess, a woman known only as "Old Dorothy." After Old Dorothy's death, Gardner was allowed to publish a novel about Witchcraft, *High Magic's Aid* (1949) under his Wiccan name "Scire," and then a nonfiction descriptive volume, *Witchcraft Today* (1954), which he wrote after the repeal of the British witchcraft laws in 1951. *Witchcraft Today* maintained that Witchcraft was a dying religion and that Gardner wanted to record what witches actually did for posterity.

Contemporary research, as well as the writings of Doreen Valiente, Gardner's priestess, suggests that rather than discovering a pre-existing Witchcraft group, Gardner created modern Wicca during the 1940s. Gardner's own magical workbook, which has become available to scholars in recent years, indicates that Gardner took the magical resources he acquired in Asia, added selections from Western literature and several magical texts, and created a new religion centered upon the worship of the Mother Goddess. Once the original rituals were constructed, he continued to revise them for much of the rest of his life. Gardner also developed a "coven," a group with which he worked his magical system, and out of the coven's life a set of "laws" emerged. New "Gardnerian" covens were started by his initiates, and eventually several people such as Alexander Sanders and Sybil Leek broke with Gardner and began independent covens with slightly revised Gardnerian texts.

Witchcraft in America

Both Gardnerian and Alexandrian Witchcraft were brought to North America beginning in 1962, and covens were established across the continent by the end of the decade. Sybil Leek came to the United States in 1966 and established covens in Ohio and Massachusetts. In addition, new variations of Wicca developed as early initiates, rejecting the emphasis upon nudity and the lineage of priestesses of Gardnerian covens, created what were termed traditionalist covens. Such independent covens, while often claiming pre-Gardnerian roots, usually took Gardner's rituals and simply added material to them which emphasized a particular ancient tradition (Welsh, Celtic, Strega, etc.). Then in the mid-1970s, some Witches, who had a strong emphasis upon feminism, developed a militant feminist Witchcraft which spoke of it as "Wimmin's Religion."

The presence of Gardnerian Witchcraft brought into the open a group of people who wished to worship the Goddess but who did not accept the designation "Witch." They called themselves "Pagans" and several—Fred Adams, Donna Cole, and Ed Fitch—wrote new rituals that followed broad Gardnerian patterns but introduced a new degree of variety into Goddess-worshipping and, by example, encouraged the development of many new ritual formats. Tim Zell, founder of the Church of All Worlds, dubbed the non-Wiccan Goddess worshippers "NeoPagans."

By 1980 most Witchcraft and NeoPagan groups were eclectic in that they followed some basic ritual guidelines developed by Gardner while drawing upon a rich variety of materials and newly written rituals for their group work and training procedures. While the Gardnerians have survived as a recognizable body of covens tied together by a common ritual and the lineage of priestesses, other Wiccan and Neo-Pagan organizations are associations of independent covens that allow an extreme latitude in ritual and practice.

Among NeoPagans, the diversity of practice has been limited somewhat by the relatively small number of individuals who have produced sets of rituals for distribution throughout the community. The original set of NeoPagan rituals written by Ed Fitch, published as a *Book of Pagan Rituals* (1974, 1975), remains the most popular. Some Neo-Pagan groups have adopted a particular cultural heritage such as Norse, Egyptian, or Druidic and have limited their work to that single tradition.

Beliefs and Practice

Witches and NeoPagans worship the Great Mother Goddess, usually seen in her triple aspect as maiden (Kore), Mother (Diana), and Crone (Hecate), thus representing the basic stages of life. Beside her is the Horned God (Pan), her consort, and together they represent the male and female principle basic to life. They also acknowledge a pantheon of deities who come to the fore at the various seasonal festivals. Many witches see these deities as merely projected aspirations of the individual or Jungian archetypes.

Witches and NeoPagans practice "magic," the art of causing change through the use of the cosmic power that is believed to underlay the universe. Magic is of two basic varieties. Low magic seeks change in the mundane world and is most frequently employed for healing or improvement of one's immediate condition (a new job, love, or relationship). High magic is worked for the transformation of the individual. Meetings of Witches combine the worship of the deities with the invocation of magic.

Ethically, Witches value freedom and harmlessness as expressed in the Wiccan Rede, "Lest ye harm none, do what you will." They also believe that the effects of magic will be returned threefold upon the person working it, a belief that severely limits the pronouncing of curses. A basic love of nature and natural things pervades the Pagan community and leads many to espouse ecology, natural foods, and compassion toward animals.

Witchcraft and NeoPaganism is organized in small autonomous groups called "covens" (variously, "groves," "nests," and "circles"). Covens will have from four to twenty-six people. They meet semimonthly at the new and full moons for regular meetings called "esbats." There are eight major solar festivals, "sabbats," beginning with Samhain, often referred to as Halloween (October 31), and continuing with Yule (December 31), Oimelc, sometimes called Candlemas (February 2), Spring Equinox (March 21), Beltane (April 30), Summer Soltice (June 21), Lammas (August 1), and Fall Equinox (September 21). Sabbats are frequently occasions for several covens to come together.

Individuals generally pass through three degrees of initiation in a Pagan or Wiccan group (though some traditions recognize more). Once a neophyte has passed through the first degree, he or she becomes a full member of the coven. Once the member has mastered a set of basic knowledge, he or she is given the second degree as an accomplished Witch. The third degree admits one to priesthood. Admission to the third degree usually involves the Great Rite (ritual sexual intercourse) between the new priest/ess and the officiating priest/ess of the opposite sex. The Great Rite is usually performed symbolically by the plunging of the ritual knife (the athame) into a chalice of wine. It should also be noted that there are many solitary Witches who practice apart from a coven though they may join in on major festivals.

Current Status

There are, by best estimates, over 40,000 Witches and NeoPagans in North America, a slight majority of whom are female. Most are found in totally independent covens and keep a very low profile as a means of protection from what they perceive as a hostile public. A number of covens (though a minority) have attached themselves to one of the major national Witchcraft or NeoPagan organizations which are discussed below.

Church of Circle Wicca

By far the largest Witchcraft-Pagan organization is the Church of Circle Wicca, headquartered in Mt. Horeb, Wisconsin. It was founded around 1975 by Selena Fox and Jim Alan who have spent many years building a national network of Goddess Worshippers. Circle publishes *Circle Network News*, the largest circulating Pagan periodical and holds annually a series of public Pagan festivals, the largest of which is the Pagan Spirit Gathering every summer. They also publish the annual *Circle Guide to Wicca and Pagan Resources*, a national directory of Pagans and Pagan organizations.

Gardnerian Wicca

Oldest of the several Witchcraft groups in the United States, Gardnerian Wicca was brought to North America in 1962 by Rosemary and Raymond Buckland who established a Witchcraft Museum in Long Island. They built a series of covens across the United States. Gardnerian Wicca is distinguished by its worshipping "skyclad" (in the nude) and its lineage of priestesses. New Gardnerian covens are formed by a priestess leaving the coven in which she was initiated and beginning a new group. She acknowledges her initiating priestess as a Witch Queen. While a Gardnerian coven can meet and conduct worship without a priest, it cannot operate without a priestess present.

Following a divorce, Raymond Buckland turned the leadership of the Gardnerians over to Theos and Phoenix, a couple who live on Long Island. He has moved on to develop other systems and remains a prominent leader in the NeoPagan community. Theos and Phoenix have now turned the work over to Lady Rhiannon and Theseus (also known to those outside the movement by their religious names). Gardnerians support several periodicals which are available only to members and, *The Hidden Path*, which circulates more widely to interested outsiders.

Covenant of the Goddess

Second in size only to Circle, the Covenant of the Goddess was formed in 1975 as an association of autonomous covens on the West Coast. It has since expanded into a national organization. Unlike Circle, membership in the Covenant of the Goddess is open only to groups which define themselves as Witches, but member covens represent the wide variety of Wiccan tradition and diversity.

The Covenant of the Goddess holds an annual festival at which a Grand Council (consisting of all the member covens) conducts Covenant business. Each Coven is allowed one vote. The Covenant also grants ministerial credentials. The headquarters and the publication site of its periodical move frequently as new officers are selected. The *Covenant of the Goddess Newsletter* is published eight times annually.

Feminist Wicca

Around 1974, several women began to combine Witchcraft with a strong feminist position. They not only included lesbian separatists such as Zsuzsanna Budapest of the Susan B. Anthony Coven #1 then in Venice, California, who saw Witchcraft as "Wimmin's Religion" and advocated all-female covens, but more moderate voices who saw in Witchcraft a religion that recognized the equality of women and the need for social justice. Initially as sources of controversy as older Wiccan leaders complained of their missing the female/male balance inherent in the religion, through the 1980s they have been fully accepted and now form a key element of the community. The feminists have also taken the lead in integrating the community into the larger debates concerning women's status and role in society.

Many of the most vocal feminists have become active in the Covenant of the Goddess (Zsuzsanna Budapest, Margot Adler, Starhawk, Allison Harlow, Deborah Bender), but others continue to remain independent. Prominent among the latter is Ann Forfreedom, priestess of the Temple of the Goddess Within of Oakland, California, and editor of a quarterly, *The Wise Woman*. Ann Forfreedom was the coordinator of the 1982 Goddess Is Rising Conference, one of the largest Witchcraft-Pagan events ever held.

NeoPagan Organizations

Prior to 1976, the largest Pagan organization was the Church of All Worlds, a NeoPagan group headed by Tim Zell, who also published and edited *The Green Egg*, which for many years was the prime periodical linking Pagan and Wiccan groups together. However, in 1976 Zell moved from St. Louis to California and dropped his role as editor of *The Green Egg* and leader of the Church. The magazine soon ceased publication and within a few years the national organization disappeared, though several "nests" remain.

Away from the responsibilities of running the Church, Zell, who changed his name to Otter G'Zell, devoted his time to a number of research projects upon which he had long desired to work. The most famous of these projects was an experiment with goats in the hopes of producing a unicorn. Zell had contended that the picture of unicorns in traditional visual art indicated a variation on a goat rather than a horse (which has neither beard or horns). The result of his work has been the appearance of several "unicorns" which have been widely exhibited around the United States.

Some NeoPagans have adopted a single national ethnic tradition, the Norse, Druidic, and Egyptian being the most popular. The principal Norse Group through the 1980s was the Asatru Free Assembly (formerly known as the Viking Brotherhood). However, it disbanded in 1989 and has been replaced by several smaller groups made up of former members. The oldest Egyptian NeoPagan group is the Church of the Eternal Source, headquartered in Burbank, California. Druids have had an up-and-down existence ever since a group of students at Carleton College in Northfield, Minnesota, created what they termed Reformed Druidism out of several anthropological textbooks. Reformed Druidism found some support around the country and has had its most effective exponent in Isaac Bonewits, author of a popular magical text, *Real Magic.* Bonewits currently heads Ar ndraíocht Féin and edits *The Druid's Progress,* one of the most substantive Pagan periodicals.

Possibly the most substantive advance in the 1980s within the NeoPagan community has come in the organization and formal recognition of the Covenant of Unitarian Universalist Pagans (CUUPS). CUUPS has found significant support within the highly intellectual Unitarian-Universalist community and is spearheading the emergence of a seminary-trained leadership for NeoPagans. Through the last half of the decade, CUUPS chapters have been established across the United States and NeoPagan Unitarian-Universalist ministers have completed their seminary education and become professionals and pastors within the church. CUUPS has provided NeoPagans with an avenue into mainstream society for those who wish to pursue it.

Sources-Primary

Cunningham, Scott. *The Truth about Witchcraft Today.* St. Paul, MN: Llewellyn Publications, 1988. 185 pp.

Gardner, Gerald B. *Witchcraft Today.* London: Rider, 1954. 192 pp.

Farrar, Janet, and Stewart Farrar. *The Life and Times of a Modern Witch.* Custer, WA: Phoenix Publishing Co., 1987. 208 pp.

————. *The Witch's Way.* London: Robert Hale, 1984. 349 pp.

Martello, Leo Louis. *Witchcraft, the Old Religion.* Secaucus, NJ: University Books, 1973. 287 pp.

Starhawk. *The Spiral Dance*. New York: Harper and Row, 1979. 218 pp. Rev. ed.: 1989. 288 pp.

Sources-Secondary

Adler, Margot. *Drawing Down The Moon*. New York: Viking, 1979. Rev. ed.: Boston, MA: Beacon Press, 1987. 608 pp.

Drury, Nevill. *The Occult Experience: Magic in the New Age*. Garden City Park, NY: Avery Press, 1989. 161 pp.

Kelly, Aidan A. *Crafting the Art of Magic. Book I. A History of Modern Witchcraft, 1939-1964*. St. Paul, MN: Llewellyn Publications, 1991. 190 pp.

Marron, Kevin. *Witches, Pagans and Magic in the New Age*. Toronto: Seal Books, 1989. 230 pp.

Melton, J. Gordon. *Magic, Witchcraft and Paganism in America: A Bibliography*. New York: Garland Publishing, 1982. 231 pp. Rev. ed.: 1991. 339 pp.

V.

Counter-Cult Groups

A. EVANGELICAL CHRISTIANITY AND THE CULTS

Evangelical Christianity has been the mainstream of religion in America. In its attempts to be true to traditional Protestant Christian affirmations, it has been among the most conservative of religious forces and has commanded the largest segment of the religious public. It has also been the most attentive to the increasing number of religious options vying for acceptance in America's religious marketplace. Evangelical leaders were the first to recognize that the Christian Church faced a growing number of challenges to its religious hegemony of America and the West.

In 1917, William C. Irvine published his *Timely Warnings*, the first of the modern counter-cult books. Irvine warned Christians of groups and philosophies that denied the essential doctrines of Christianity. The denial of these key doctrines—incarnation, atonement, the divinity of Jesus, the Trinity, the authority of the Bible—cut the heart out of the Gospel message and turned Christianity into a shadow of itself. Under its new title, *Heresies Exposed*, Irvine's book went through twenty-nine printings by 1955 and remains in print at present.

Irvine's survey of the heresies faced by orthodoxy stood alone for two decades though specialized polemical texts of single groups such as the Jehovah's Witnesses or Spiritualism appeared. Then, in 1938, Jan Karel Van Baalen's *Chaos of the Cults* set the tone for much future Evangelical interpretation of the cult question. Van Baalen singled out approximately a dozen alternative religions and analyzed them in terms of their denial of central Christian truths. He then explained that the appeal of these new (for the West) religions was due to their central focus upon a single Christian truth which had been largely neglected in the modern church. For example, he concludes his critical analysis of Spiritualism (which he calls "Spiritism") by noting that, "Spiritism has again called attention to the existence of a spiritual world, to a life hereafter, to future retribution in a time of gross materialism, we can appreciate." He then concludes that in spite of Spiritualism's accomplishment, it is incompatible with Christianity.

Only after World War II did the initial work done by Irvine and Van Baalen call widespread attention to the threat to the Church posed by the growing number of cults, and during the 1950s numerous items of counter-cult literature were published. Louis T. Talbot and Walter R. Martin emerged as prominent Christian apologists on cult issues. Talbot, a Congregational minister and a teacher at the Bible Institute of Los Angeles, published a series of popular booklets on several prominent new religions such as the Unity School of Christianity, Christian Science, Seventh-Day Adventism, and Anglo-Israelism. However, it was Martin who was most effective in alerting a resurgent Evangelicalism of the danger posed by the cults. He authored three important counter-cult books in the 1950s—*Jehovah of the Watchtower* (1955, co-authored with Norman Klann), *The Rise of the Cults* (1955), and *The Christian Science Myth* (1956, co-authored with Norman Klann). He went on to become a popular radio Bible teacher and founder of one of the most important counter-cult ministries, the Christian Research Institute. During the 1960s he wrote his most important text, the *Kingdom of the Cults* (1965), the book which became a standard reference for the numerous counter-cult ministries which arose in the 1970s and 1980s.

As the explosion of new religions became a public issue in the 1970s, the amount of Christian counter-cult literature proliferated exponentially. James Bjornstad, Harold L. Bussell, Edmond C. Gruss, Dave Hunt, Bob Larson, Gordon R. Lewis, William J. Petersen, Jack Sparks, and M. Thomas Stakes and J. Stafford Wright are among the most prominent writers. Special mention belongs to Ronald Enroth who by the end of the decade had become the single most widely read of the Evangelical Christian counter-cult writers. A professor of sociology (that in itself is unusual as most Christian counter-cultists tend to specialize in either the Bible or theology), Enroth authored two popular early texts, *Youth, Brainwashing, and the Extremist Cults* (1977) and *The Lure of the Cults* (1979). In addition he has written numerous articles in Christian periodicals, the lead chapter in Inter-Varsity Press' *A Guide to the Cults* (1983), and more recently edited a second collection, *Evangelizing the Cults* (1990).

With the proliferation of counter-cult literature in the 1970s came a parallel multiplication of the number of independent organizations formed primarily to engage in counter-cult apologetics. A few such organizations, with a specialization in evangelism to a particular group, had been formed by converts from those groups. The first organizations led by former Mormons and by Jews were founded in the nineteenth century, and many new ones were added through this century. After World War I, efforts directed toward Jehovah's Witnesses were begun. After World War II, a few organizations, such as the Religious Analysis Service (founded in 1946), which dealt with the broad spectrum of cults, emerged. Besides Martin's Christian Research Institute, among the more prominent of the Christian counter-cult organizations which appeared in the 1970s are: The Spiritual Counterfeits Project, which grew out of the Jesus People revival in Berkeley, California; the Institute of Contemporary Christianity, headed by James Bjornstad; Christian Apologetics: Research and Information Service (popularly known as C.A.R.I.S.), headed by Michael Van Buskirk and Robert Passantino; and Personal Freedom Outreach, headquartered in St. Louis, Missouri.

Beyond the hundred or more independent counter-cult organizations, several evangelical denominations have created counter-cult offices, most important being the Lutheran Church-Missouri Synod and the Southern Baptist Convention. While most denominations have had little to say concerning the cults, these two churches have published an impressive array of material that has steadily improved in quality.

During the 1980s the number of counter-cult ministries (over 500 by the end of the decade) continued to increase. Most were small and, rather than producing their own literature, have been content to circulate that produced by the larger organizations. The whole world of cult ministries was deeply affected in the middle of the decade by the libel suit brought against the Spiritual Counterfeits Project by the Local Church. The Church claimed that it had been greatly harmed by SCP telling malicious untruths about it and its leaders and won an $11 million judgment, which forced SCP into bankruptcy and reorganization. It also showed the vulnerability of the cult ministries in leveling unfounded allegations against the new religions.

The suit seems also to have supported the noticeable change of emphasis by the counter-cult ministries to a primary focus upon the New Age Movement. Whatever the cause, the New Age has joined the continuing interest in Mormonism and Jehovah's Witnesses as a primary concern of counter-cult ministries. If the number of new books produced during the last years of the decade is used an indicator, the New Age would be ranked as the single most important concern.

Evangelical Understanding of Cult Phenomena

In general, though the line dividing them is by no means clear, the Christian counter-cult ministries can and should be distinguished from the secular militant anti-cult movement discussed in the next chapter. While like the anti-cult movement, the Christian counter-cult ministries seek to convince people to leave the cults, they also tend to view a person's leaving a cult as merely a step along the way. The ultimate goal is the commitment of the former cultist to an orthodox faith in Jesus Christ.

What defines a new religious group as a "cult" in the eyes of Evangelical counter-cultists? In general, Evangelicals understand a cult to be a heretical group. Josh McDowell and Don Stewart began their best-selling volume, *Understanding the Cults*, by asserting, "A cult is a perversion, a distortion of biblical Christianity, and as such, rejects the historic teachings of the Christian Church." Walter Martin succinctly defines his field, "By cultism we mean the adherence to doctrines which are pointedly contradictory to orthodox Christianity and which yet claim the distinction of either tracing their origin to orthodox sources or of being in essential harmony with those sources."

Most recently, some writers have tried to face the contradiction inherent in the traditional definition of cult: most of the groups generally described as cults are Eastern religions which claim no relationship to traditional Christianity. By Martin's definition, many of the groups considered in his books—Transcendental Meditation, the International Society for Krishna Consciousness, and the Sikh Dharma—would not be cults. Thus most counter-cultists began to distinguish between the Eastern, occult, and metaphysical religions on the one hand and the Christian groups which dissent from traditional doctrinal orthodoxy on the other hand. Enroth, for example, reserves the term cult exclusively for the Eastern and occult groups, while speaking of "aberrant" Christian groups when describing Christian groups which deny an essential doctrine of orthodox Christianity. Gordon R. Lewis, counter-cult writer and professor at Denver Conservative Baptist Seminary, makes the same distinction but assumes the exact opposite stance, keeping the term cult for deviating Christian groups (Jehovah's Witnesses, Christian Science, the Unification Church) while setting aside Eastern religions as a distinctly different category.

However, whatever the definition, Evangelicals have followed a basic format in their consideration of the nonconventional religions. Each group is examined and judged according to its allegiance to doctrines and practices which deviate from the doctrines of orthodox Christian faith. The orthodox Christian tradition is expressed in the ancient creeds of the church (such as the Apostles and Nicean) and explicated in the writings of the early church fathers who defined and rejected the classic heresies, and in more recent statements such as the early twentieth century definition of *The Fundamentals*. Using the variety of documents, to which Christians have traditionally looked for the correct presentation of faith, Evangelicals examine any questionable Christian group on its position on key doctrines, the most important being the Trinity, the person and work of Christ, the authority of the Bible, and the nature of sin and salvation.

With groups which are, in fact, variations on Christianity and which accept the basic ideas and structure of Western orthodoxy while denying one or more traditionally important beliefs, the doctrinal approach can be extremely illuminating. Evangelicals have specialized in criticism of those new religions which see themselves as biblically based Christians but have either (1) reached different conclusions on basic doctrinal issues or (2) have received an additional revelation which adds to (and thus alters) the Biblical message. With such groups, a doctrine-by-doctrine comparison quickly highlights the areas in which differences are manifest. More complex problems are caused by those groups which not only have taken a variant approach to several key Christian doctrines but which have adopted a radically different metaphysical approach to the world. Both the Church of Christ, Scientist, and the Unification Church, although they use biblical language and Christian symbols, give such distinct meanings to certain words and symbols that they raise significant questions as to how they might be seen to fit into Christian tradition, if in fact they do.

When considering those groups which fall completely outside of the Christian tradition, the counter-cult approach has been not so much the comparison of beliefs, doctrine by doctrine (though a few have tried such a methodology), but a comparison of the total belief system of, for example, Zen Buddhism or Transcendental Meditation with the Christian gospel in an attempt to show the superiority of the latter. Such efforts vary considerably in quality. Many Eastern and occult systems place great emphasis upon experience and the mastering of techniques for spiritual growth, and, hence, do not yield easily to doctrinal analysis (if in fact a coherent doctrinal system can be identified). An approach which emphasizes ideas frequently misses the essence and appeal of a group.

Underlying all Christian counter-cult literature is a strong belief that cults are Satanic, not that they worship Satan, but that, as Dave Hunt affirms, "Satan is the author of every cult and false religion, and his imprint is clearly seen on them all." The rise of cults constitutes a direct sign of Satan's activity in the world, for Satan himself has, in his opposition to God, established rival faiths, and lured Christians into false doctrinal positions. The efforts made to counter cults are for the Christian much more than natural competition against a rival. This is a cosmic battle, a war against the principalities and powers (Eph. 6:12). This opposition to Satanic activity largely guides and motivates the Christian counter-cult ministries.

The Work of the Ministries

Christian counter-cult ministries have, in practice, two essential thrusts. However, the ministries devote the overwhelming part of their efforts (time, energy, and production of literature) to fellow believers. Almost all of the material produced by the various ministries is purchased and read by Church members. The effect of such materials is to inform church members of the heretical and false ideas and unChristian practices of the new religions in hopes of strengthening members in the true faith and preventing them from being attracted to a cult.

A small portion of the counter-cult church literature engages members and leaders in a process of self-reflection. The success of different cult groups often highlights the areas in which churches have failed to provide adequate programming. Some cults have succeeded because of their particular attention to evangelism, spiritual nurture and growth, lay leadership, vital worship, or their youth program. Harold L. Bussell of Gordon College suggests that Evangelical churches and cults have much in common and that additional material for reflection will arise from looking at that commonality. Militant anti-cultists have also recognized that commonality and have on occasion treated Evangelical churches like a "cult" and targeted them for deprogrammings along with those groups that both they and the Christian counter-cultists would agree are "cults."

Finally, a few Evangelical ministries also witness directly to members of cult groups. To assist their witnessing work, they regularly distribute literature, primarily tracts and booklets, that delineates errors in a particular cult, to which is added an invitation to accept Jesus as Lord and Savior. The literature is distributed to members of the alternative religious groups in a variety of means though most effectively as an aspect of a direct witnessing program. Witnessing activity varies from distribution of literature in spots where cult members might pick it up and read it, to low-key, long-term contact, to confrontation on the street, to more controversial attempts to invade a group's home territory with an exposé message which questions the integrity of the group, its teachings, or its leadership. Some counter-cultists have made it a practice to visit worship centers (for example, various Mormon temples or the Brooklyn headquarters of the Jehovah's Witnesses) and pass out counter-cult literature to all who would take it.

The Future of Cult Ministries

Cult ministries arose in the nineteenth century as the recognition slowly dawned that the Church was being forced to compete with an ever-growing variety of religious alternatives in the free environment of the modern world. As the number and appeal of these alternatives have increased, so have the number and work of the cult ministries. They have defined a long-term task of apologetics and, to a lesser extent, witnessing, the importance of which to the Evangelical church community can only grow.

Though a few Christian counter-cult ministries have been around for several generations, their expansion and development occurred concurrently with the flowering of Asian religion after 1965. In large measure, the ministries are just now moving into their second generation and are still discovering means of coping with the new pluralism. Their future seems dependent upon their ability to mature in their knowledge and appreciation of other religious systems. Most of the contemporary writers of counter-cult literature show a lack of training in comparative religions with a resultant inability to enter into the world of a Buddhist or a Theosophist and thus appear lost in trying to understand the dynamics and appeal of a foreign faith. This inability to appreciate other religions leads to the proliferation of errors and a constant misunderstanding of the different alternative religions discussed in Christian literature, and is the source of the many complaints that Christian literature slanders different cult groups by substantively misrepresenting their teachings.

The basic distortion of the teachings of various new religions, especially the Eastern and occult ones, derives in large measure from the subservience of the cult ministries to the apologetic task and their rejection of the experience gained in interreligious dialogue. The failure to engage members of other religions in dialogue almost guarantees that errors in comprehension of the targeted faith community will occur, be passed along in the literature, and never be corrected. Such dialogue is imperative when the object of concern is a first-generation religion such as Scientology or the Unification Church, which typically undergoes a process of rapid change during its first decades as it develops and institutionalizes its original vision. The accelerated changes in the newer religions over the past decade have rendered obsolete most of the descriptive literature produced in the 1970s.

Like the cults, the counter-cult ministries, almost all of which are also in their first generation, have changed during the last decade. They had had a significant amount of trouble in moving into a radically pluralistic situation in which religious ideas have been relativized and the number of religious options are continually growing. Their ability to be of service in a pluralistic world will greatly depend upon their ability to handle the increasingly complex situation of American religion.

Sources

This list is a sample of the most prominent books on cults representative of the Evangelical Christian counter-cult perspective as described above. In addition, throughout this text, titles produced by Evangelical Christian polemicists against specific individual new religions are listed in the chapters on those groups.

Enroth, Ron, ed. *Evangelizing the Cults.* Ann Arbor, MI: Servant Publications, n.d.[1990]. 195 pp.

————. *The Lure of the Cults.* Chappaqua, NY: Christian Herald Books, 1979. 139 pp. Rev. ed.: Downers Grove, IL: InterVarsity Press, 1987. 140 pp

————. *Youth, Brainwashing, and Extremist Cults.* Grand Rapids, MI: Zondervan Publishing House, 1977. 221 pp.

Larson, Bob. *Larson's Book of Cults.* Wheaton, IL: Tyndale House Publishers, 1982. Rev. ed. as: Larson's New Book of Cults. Wheaton: Tyndale House Publishers, 1989.

Lewis, Gordon R. *Confronting the Cults.* Grand Rapids, MI: Baker Book House, 1966. 198 pp.

McDowell, Josh, and Don Stewart. *Understanding the Cults.* San Bernadino, CA: Here's Life Publishers, 1982. 199 pp.

Martin, Walter. *Kingdom of the Cults.* Minneapolis, MN: Bethany Fellowship Publishers, 1965. 443 pp.

————. *The New Cults.* Santa Ana, CA: Vision House, 1980. 419 pp.

Schipper, Earl. *Cults in North America.* Grand Rapids, MI: Baker Book House, 1982. 173 pp.

Tucker, Ruth. *Another Gospel.* Grand Rapids, MI: Zondervan Publishing House, 1989. 462 pp.

Van Baalen, Jan K. *The Chaos of Cults.* 1938. 4th ed.: Grand Rapids, MI: William B. Eerdmans Publishing House, 1962. 414 pp. 27th printing, 1975.

B. THE ANTI-CULT MOVEMENT

The Problem of Religion

During the last generation several trends in American religion came together. Throughout the twentieth century, church membership has increased dramatically as an ever-larger percentage of the growing population found an organized religious affiliation. At the same time, the number of denominations also steadily increased. By 1985 over 800 different Christian denominations competed for the allegiance of the Christian public. Also growing, both in number of organizations and in number of people involved, were the many different varieties of unorthodox and nonconventional religious and spiritual groups—occult, metaphysical, mystical, and Eastern. While most Americans found their spiritual home in a Christian church, a smaller, but nevertheless significant number, became Spiritualists, Theosophists, Rosicrucians, Buddhists, and Hindus. These alternative religious perspectives had received a boost in 1965 by the rescission of the Asian Exclusion Acts. Since that time, a steady stream of Oriental teachers have migrated to America to launch new movements and to pump new life into those previously founded by pioneering bands of disciples.

Observers first noticed the increase in the number of nonconventional religions on the West Coast. Coincidental to the arrival of the first wave of Eastern teachers was the emergence of the world of the street people, an outgrowth of the post-hippie subculture. At the end of the 1960s, evangelical Christians had begun work among the street people, and by 1970 the "Jesus people" revival was visibly shaking the community from San Diego to Seattle. In California, the Children of

God, the Christian Foundation (headed by Tony and Susan Alamo), the Jews for Jesus, the World Christian Liberation Front, and Jesus People International were organized.

As the Jesus People revival gained momentum, other groups began to actively recruit among the street people. Rev. Sun Myung Moon made his first visit to the United States in 1965 and took up permanent residence in 1972. Swami Bhaktivedanta founded the International Society for Krishna Consciousness in New York in 1965. Yogi Bhajan brought the Sikh Dharma to Los Angeles in 1968. Kirpal Singh, a leader of one branch of the Sant Mat tradition, made the first of several visits in 1965. Maharaj Ji, the teenage guru, made his first visit in 1971, a prelude to his eventual movement to America in 1973. In the beginning, however, these movements were less important than the Jesus People groups.

The street people culture set the environment for the emergence of the anti-cult controversy. Each summer the number of street people greatly increased as college students finished the school year and headed to Berkeley and Hollywood to participate in the street people life during summer vacation. At the end of the summer, a small percentage of these summer dropouts chose to remain in California and failed to return to college. Some already out of contact with their family did not reestablish contact with them as fall classes were due to begin. They did reappear at a later date, sometimes at Thanksgiving or Christmas, to confront their families with the fact that they had joined a new, unknown, and most unconventional religion.

Parents of the new converts were understandably upset. Their sons and daughters, young people from well-to-do, educated, and mainline religious backgrounds had dropped out of schools and left jobs only to reappear as members of a heretofore-unheard-of group which made a high demand upon their time, boasted unusual ideas, and vocalized a very low opinion of many established societal structures. The changes in their child's behavior—adoption of strange religious apparel, vegetarian diets, chanting and meditation, the rejection of any career orientation, and the assumption of an austere lifestyle—upset the parents even more. Converts of these new religions had, it seemed, moved quickly from the nominal attention to religion characteristic of much of Western society to a position in which religion was the dominant reality of their life, infusing every moment, restructuring social relationships, and demanding almost all of their time.

Too often, membership in the new religion coincided with an outward break in family relations. Parents blamed the religions for alienating their sons and daughters. All they saw was the radical change in their offspring who rejected all their parents saw as good and right—a college degree, marriage, a career, and a home in the suburbs—all that they as parents had worked to provide. Among the first to express his concern, William Rambur of Chula Vista, California, learned that his 22-year-old daughter, who had just begun her career as a nurse, had left her job and her fiance to join the Children of God. After a frantic search, he located her on the ranch at Thurber, Texas. Through his middle-class suburban eyes, the ranch seemed primitive, appalling. Unable to convince his daughter to leave, he denounced the group to the press and began a personal campaign to warn other parents of what he had discovered. After he returned to California, he met Theodore Patrick, Jr., an employee of the State of California, who had also had a negative encounter with the Children of God through his son and nephew. Together with several other like-minded parents, they formed the first anti-cult association, the Parents Committee to Free Our Children from the Children of God (later shortened to "Free the Children of God," and popularly called "FREE-COG." Thus began the anti-cult movement.

The Spread of the Anti-cult Movement

As FREECOG became known, parents whose children had joined other demanding and unconventional religions contacted Rambur and Patrick. Although it initially resisted the temptation to diversify, FREECOG eventually acceded to requests and reorganized as the Volunteer Parents of America. It accepted membership from parents of all cult members though it remained largely a southern California organization.

VPA grew, and similar groups appeared in other parts of the country and in Canada. By 1974 Rambur and other leaders of the burgeoning movement, seeing the need for a national organization, formed the Citizen's Freedom Foundation (CFF). By 1975 membership reached 1,500 though it was merely the largest of several parent's associations then in existence.

1976 was a crucial year for the movement. By that time the Unification Church had become the major symbol of all that was considered evil in cult life, and the anti-cult movement increasingly targeted its efforts to it. A major sign of the shift was that the leaders of the movement convinced Senator Robert Dole to hold hearings in Washington, D.C., as a forum for parental and other complaints against the cults in general and the Unification Church, in particular. CFF published the proceedings.

The hearings became the catalyst for the formation of what many hoped would be a successful national umbrella organization. The National Ad Hoc Committee Engaged in Freeing Minds was headquartered in the home of George M. Slaughter, III, of Grand Prairie, Texas. Slaughter's daughter Cynthia, recently deprogrammed from the Unification Church, appeared as a star witness at the hearings. The CEFM, however, soon ran into problems and was unable to obtain a tax-exempt status. It was replaced by the Pennsylvania-based Individual Freedom Foundation Educational Trust (IFFET). However, IFFET succeeded in holding the diverse movement together only for a matter of months before it, too, fell apart as a result of various internal disputes. The failure of IFFET returned the focus of the movement to the numerous local groups, only a few of which reached beyond a single metropolitan area. Typically, these organizations published a newsletter (which allowed them to keep in touch nationally), sponsored regular programs for the public, and facilitated parents' efforts to contact deprogrammers.

The failure of IFFET seemed to portend the decline and demise of the whole anti-cult movement. Then the events of November 1978 in Jonestown, Guyana, gave it a fresh start. Seizing the occasion, the movement's leaders mobilized new support, and Senator Robert Dole of Kansas responded by creating a new anti-cult forum in the form of hearings on the Guyana tragedy. The rebirth of interest in the cult problem served as a catalyst to the formation of another national organization (which did not replace the many local ones), the American Family Foundation. AFF became important immediately as its leaders included several psychological professionals, most notably psychiatrist Dr. John R. Clark, an adjunct professor at Harvard University. It began publishing the most substantive periodical produced by the movement to date and later began a quarterly journal.

Through the 1980s AFF and the Citizen's Freedom Foundation, more recently renamed the Cult Awareness Network (CAN), have been the foci of the continuing anti-cult movement. From its offices in Chicago, CAN's leaders are often quoted by the media in stories on questionable religious groups.

The Anti-cult Action Program

From its beginning, the anti-cult movement focused upon a single problem, the distress of parents whose young adult sons and daughters (to whom the literature typically refers as "children" regardless of age) had abandoned home, career, college, and a "normal" future for membership in a demanding nonconventional religion (i.e., a cult). This single concern determines the shape of the movement's program and most of the organizations within the movement exist solely to serve parents who want their son or daughter removed from a particular religious group. In their effort to provide more than just personal support for parents grieving over the "loss" of a child to a cult, the movement developed an action program. The program had three main components: deprogramming, legislative procedures, and lawsuits.

Deprogramming. Deprogramming, as developed by Ted Patrick in the early 1970s, was a coercive technique designed to force cult members to break their ties to the group which they had joined. It included the forced detention of the cultist and the application of a variety of intense psychological pressures (interrogation, loss of privacy, profanation of the sacred, and parental and peer group pressure), with the goal of having the member renounce his or her religious affiliation and adopt a life and faith more acceptable to the parents. Deprogramming had only a 50 percent success rate, primarily among cultists who had been with the group less than two years. However, the successes were important in giving hope to those parents who could afford the deprogrammer's services. Successfully deprogrammed former cultists became important spokespersons for the movement, adding the authority of their experience in the cult to the charges of the movement. Once deprogrammed, many ex-cultists became deprogrammers themselves.

Deprogramming came under attack by civil libertarians almost immediately. As early as 1974, church leaders passed a strong resolution against it, through the National Council of Churches. Several organizations, such as the Alliance for the Preservation of Religious Liberties, largely backed by the Church of Scientology, brought together church leaders, religious liberty activists, and cult leaders to defend the rights of those groups whose members were being subjected to deprogramming. Such groups publicized the accounts of people who had experienced deprogramming but had remained members of the cult. They placed emphasis upon the incidents of violence and the personal abuse they suffered. While unable to stop the practice, opposition did inhibit the legitimization of deprogramming in law and in the courts.

During the 1980s, additional criticism of deprogramming emerged. First, ex-cultists who had been deprogrammed began to speak out against unnecessary coercion and manipulation involved in the practice. Secondly, and possibly more important, led by Ronald Enroth, Christian counter-cultists who had informally supported the anti-cult groups began to speak out against deprogramming. As Walter Martin, possibly the most prolific Christian writer on the subject of cults, wrote in 1980, "I cannot stand behind such practices. It is true that cultists have been blinded by the 'god of this age,' but it is also true that they have the right to make up their own minds, and we should not stoop to unChristian tactics to accomplish God's ends."

The added attack from former allies forced some anti-cult groups to revise their stance. In 1981 the Citizen's Freedom Foundation issued a new statement on deprogramming in which it abandoned support for the practice as it existed in the 1970s: "CFF does not support, condone, or recommend kidnapping or holding a person against his will." It gave its verbal support to what has since become generally known as "exit counseling," a directed counseling procedure aimed at encouraging a cult member to leave the cult. Other anti-cult groups as well as individual members of CAN continue to promote and facilitate deprogrammings, though the practice declined markedly in North America during the mid-1980s.

Influencing Legislation. As soon as the anti-cult movement widened its initial focus upon the Children of God to include all of the new cults, it also sought assistance from legislators. As early as 1974, concerned parents were able to convince State Senator Mervyn M. Dymally, Chairman of the California Senate's Subcommittee on Children and Youth, to convene a hearing on the "Impact of Cults on Today's Youth." As with the later Dole hearings, no legislative action followed, but during the 1970s and early 1980s legislators, persuaded by the arguments of anti-cult constituents, introduced numerous bills to curb cult activities. Some bills would have granted parents and families of cult members a conservatorship during which time a deprogramming could proceed. Others sought to regulate "non-traditional" religions by forcing them to give prospective members a full disclosure of practices and beliefs before allowing anyone to join. Still others wanted to place cults (as opposed to genuine religions) under the regulations guiding public trusts and non-religious charities.

A decade of attempts to legislate against cults proved both expensive and unproductive. The various bills were overwhelmingly defeated, most never being reported out of committee. Only one, the Lasher Bill (which would have granted conservatorships) passed a legislative vote and was placed on a governor's desk for approval. It was vetoed on two occasions by the governor of New York.

The last attempt to gain some kind of legislative favor occurred in 1988 on the tenth anniversary of Jonestown. During that year, anti-cultists lobbied for the passing of a bill which would have designated the week of the anniversary as national cult awareness week. The bill was gaining support until legislators who were members of several groups which had been targeted as "cults" over the years (primarily Mormons) killed the bill and substituted a religious freedom celebration in its stead. This action effectively killed further legislative initiatives against new and unconventional religions.

In the Courts. The Courts were a final place of redress of parental grievances against cults. Parents explored the possibility of obtaining court-ordered conservatorships over their children who had joined cults. While a few of these were granted, most courts refused such requests as outside the intent of conservatorship laws (designed to protect incapacitated or elderly people). The courts' refusal to act led directly to the legislative attempts to broaden the conservatorship laws. However, even as the anti-cult movement sought remedies in court, so did the cults. Cult members who had gone through a deprogramming attempt filed criminal charges against their abductors. Generally, they too, found the court unwilling to take sides in what was considered a family dispute.

Initially rebuffed, both sides turned to the civil courts. Cult members have had some success. Synanon, for example, won a major libel suit against the Hearst newspapers. In 1977, a class action suit closed the deprogramming center in Tucson, Arizona, and forced the retirement of several deprogrammers. In several lesser suits, brought by individuals against their deprogrammers, courts have awarded damages, though most have ended without any substantial settlement.

The anti-cult movement has had little success in the civil court suits it has brought. In most cases where a lower court did grant damages, the decision was reversed on appeal. Such was the fate of the highly publicized award of $2,000,000 to a former member of the Church of Scientology. (As this volume goes to press, a multimillion dollar judgment against the International Society for Krishna Consciousness continues through a laborious appeal process.) In the final analysis, the drain of time and financial resources in so many legal actions has slowed the movement's attempts to vindicate its cause in the courts. Legal fees have drained the treasuries of the movement and increased the price of deprogramming beyond the reach of most parents. Without a substantive victory in court, this thrust of anti-cult activity may soon be abandoned.

Further attempts by parents to use the courts in their fight against the new religions was given what some see as a fatal blow in 1987 by the American Psychological Association. The primary weapon in the various court cases had been some controversial testimony by psychologists and psychiatrists. The leading psychologist in these cases was Margaret Singer. In the mid-1980s, she was invited to form a task force and submit a report on her conclusions concerning the processes used in cults to recruit and indoctrinate. The report of the "Task Force on Deceptive and Indirect Methods of Persuasion and Control" was submitted for review in 1987. It was rejected because it lacked "the scientific rigor and evenhanded critical approach necessary for APA imprimatur." The rejection of the report left Singer and the others who were testifying in the various court cases without the necessary consensus of the scholarly community to present their opinions in court. As a result of making public the APA's rejection, Singer and University of California professor Richard Ofshe have been denied their status as expert witnesses. Without their testimony, the essence has been cut out of the anti-cult court cases.

Dissemination of Information. While its action programs initiated in the 1970s have flagged, the anti-cult movement can point to one clear success. In its first decade of activity it impressed upon the popular consciousness a negative image of cults, the full effect of which only history will be able to discern. Articulate spokespersons of the movement have presented the anti-cult rationale and program in numerous books, pamphlets, and articles for popular periodicals. Persistently cultivating the media the anti-cult movement has received widespread coverage in both magazines and newspapers, which have featured accounts of life in and out of the cults by former members. Alerted to the cult issue, the media have been quick to seize upon stories of improprieties of cults and their leaders. Thus, the movement has created both directly and indirectly a vast body of literature that will haunt the new religions for many years.

This massive attack through the media has alerted several government agencies, particularly the Internal Revenue Service, to the existence of nonconventional religions. Spurred in part by the negative image of cults, the IRS has investigated several newer religions. Prosecutions have led to the denial of tax-exempt status to several groups and the conviction (in a highly controversial case) of Rev. Sun Myung Moon, leader of the Unification Church, for tax evasion. The anti-cult movement has claimed partial credit, and rightfully so, for government actions against cult groups and has welcomed each success as a step in its overall goals.

The change of name by the Citizen's Freedom Foundation also signaled a change of public image. The Cult Awareness Network has in recent years modeled itself as a consumer advocate group. It has established an office in Chicago and made itself available to the media to speak on any new religious movement which wanders into the public spotlight. While it has lost credibility with most religion editors, it is still frequently quoted in stories which originate on the news desks of daily newspapers.

The Rationale of the Anti-cult Movement

The program of the anti-cult movement required a means of transforming the purely familial and religious concerns of the parent groups into a secular public issue and turning the personal hurt felt by families into the aura of potential harm threatening all of society from the cults. Only by accomplishing such a transformation, the parent groups quickly learned, could they hope to influence either courts or legislatures, both of whom tended to dismiss their petitions as strictly family concerns and to reject suggested actions against the cults on grounds of religious freedom. In the crucible of controversy, the groups experimented with various approaches and by the late 1970s produced the dominant rationale to which the movement could adhere.

In the early 1970s, parents reported significant and unexpected changes in the behavior patterns and attitudes of sons and daughters who joined the cults. They concluded that the cults had somehow changed their otherwise normal son or daughter into a different person, one who would follow a weird, idiotic, foreign religion. Often unaware of or choosing to ignore their offspring's internal turmoil or period of religious experimentation prior to encountering the cult, they searched for a mechanism to explain what they saw as a sudden change. They toyed with hypnotism and talked of the pressures of adolescence. Nothing proved satisfactory until the "brainwashing" rationale emerged.

According to this hypothesis, cult groups and leaders are seen as entirely manipulative toward their members. Cults recruit impressionable youth through deceit, typically by inviting them to a harmless-looking event which is actually a carefully staged recruiting event for the group. Once involved, the prospective member is subjected to a number of mind-control techniques designed to destroy his/her rational faculties and subtly manipulate the person into ever-greater involvement in the group program. These techniques include the application of intense peer pressure, the frequent repetition of group beliefs, low-protein diets, sleep deprivation, denial of privacy, control of the immediate environment, the manipulation of language (jargon), the use of rituals to induce mystical trance-like states, and the wholesale condemnation of established structures (family, school, church, etc.). With their critical abilities reduced, victims are psychologically coerced into converting to the cult.

Having joined, the person continues to suffer the brainwashing techniques until completely united with the group and is unable to act or think apart from the leader's will. Prolonged existence in the cult environment, in a state of mental control, is believed by many anti-cultists to cause mental and emotional disorders, and a few theorists have suggested that permanent brain or nervous system damage will result from prolonged membership.

The discovery of brainwashing, or thought reform, in the literature on former Chinese prisoners of war of the 1950s facilitated the necessary transformation of the familial concerns into a public issue. Parental concern became a threat to public health, and a radical solution was necessary if further damage to individuals was to be prevented. The public threat demands government action while the harm being done to individuals requires immediate psychological treatment (i.e., deprogramming).

Deprogramming has been understood by anti-cultists to be a means of reversing the effects of brainwashing. During the deprogramming process, the individual is bombarded with all the reasons to disaffiliate from the group and at some point snaps back, i.e., regains the ability to think for him/herself apart from the constant pressure of the group. When that event occurs, the cultist immediately sees the mistake in joining the group, comprehends the process of brainwashing and mind control through which s/he went, decides to leave the group, and expresses gratitude to all involved in the deprogramming for their rescue.

Even as the techniques employed by deprogrammers were being refined, parents discovered that their deprogrammed children suffered from varying degrees of emotional distress. At first given the popular label "information disease" by anti-cult writers Conway and Siegelman, the symptoms were eventually identified as those of the very common traumatic stress syndrome. Psychiatrists such as Margaret Singer, who worked closely with the anti-cult movement and counseled many deprogrammed ex-cultists, attributed the syndrome to membership in the cult group. More recent studies have pointed out that the syndrome is largely confined to those cult members who withdraw as the result of a deprogramming. It does not show up among the far larger number who leave voluntarily. Such evidence suggests that the trauma of deprogramming, not membership in the cult, produces emotional distress among former cult members.

The testimonies of successfully deprogrammed cultists became the prime piece of evidence which could be presented to both the public and the movement to demonstrate the truth of the anti-cult position. Having accepted the deprogrammers' redefinition of life in the cult, new ex-cultists frequently joined the anti-cult movement and regularly testified publicly about their experience. Critics of the anti-cult movement quickly attacked the testimonies of the ex-cultists noting the distortion which had entered into their accounts due to the deprogramming process and the infusion of the anti-cult rhetoric into the ex-member's story. The sameness of stories told by public apostates derives in part from the ex-member's molding the account of the actual experience in the group into conformity with a pre-existing script. The distortion caused by the traumatic withdrawal from a cult through deprogramming has been clearly demonstrated under examination during legal proceedings.

The Future of the Anti-cult Movement

After a decade of activity, the anti-cult movement had one significant accomplishment to its credit. It had succeeded in creating a pervasive negative image of the new religions and spreading a popular public prejudice against several groups which had become well known as "cults." However, it proved incapable of implementing any of its major program goals, which sought to severely regulate, inhibit the growth of, and eventually eliminate the cults altogether. Several factors now seem most relevant in predicting the future of the movement.

First, it must be noted that in spite of its success in creating a negative image of cults among both the media and the general public, the movement has been totally unable to stop or even to slow the growth of the so-called cults. While the membership in various groups fluctuates year by year, the number of alternative religions and of people involved in them continues steadily to grow. Many former members retain a positive appraisal of the group(s) with which they were affiliated and form a base of positive support in the larger culture. In fact, the anti-cult movement seems to have doomed itself to failure in that it set itself the task of reversing a major trend in American society toward radical religious diversity.

Second, while it is difficult to access the overall effect of anti-cult efforts on individual groups, it is possible that it has inhibited the growth of some of the more vulnerable groups such as the Children of God (which has largely withdrawn its members from the United States) and those groups which have suffered successful prosecution by the government on various criminal or tax charges (Unification Church, Church of Scientology, Synanon). On the other hand, the anti-cult movement has given many obscure groups the publicity they needed to reach a large audience of potential members. The movement has done as much to spur the growth of cults as inhibit them.

Third, the vast amount of time and energy expended to pass anti-cult legislation has completely failed, and with its loss of this area, the movement has also lost a prime instrument in mobilizing public support and media attention.

Fourth, the growing critique of deprogramming forced most of its exponents to adopt less coercive (and hence less effective) methods of forcing cult members to disaffiliate. While deprogrammings will continue to be attempted, the withdrawal of support (as well as the increased cost due to legal complications) will further weaken the movement's ability to attract and hold their main support, distressed parents of cult members. The anti-cult groups, especially CAN, in spite of public denials, continues to be the main organization facilitating deprogramming by placing parents in contact with the several deprogrammers still in the business.

Fifth, while both sides in the cult wars have won and lost battles in the courts, the anti-cult movement has been unable to win any significant victories. What appeared to be major wins came in lower courts where juries have tended to support parents and have been persuaded by the testimonies of deprogrammed ex-cultists. However, on appeal, judgments have tended to be reversed on Constitutional grounds. The reversal of the Christofferson decision in Oregon (in which an ex-member had been awarded a large sum from the Church of Scientology) and the similar Robin George decision (Hare Krishna) were severe losses. The Movement suffered when a federal court reversed the Peterson decision. In this case, a Minnesota court had ruled that when a person undergoing deprogramming begins to cooperate with the deprogramming, they release the deprogrammers from any liability.

While also unable to win decisive victories, cult members have brought suits which have measurably hurt the anti-cult movement. Court victories have (1) forced the closing of anti-cult facilities (such as the Freedom of Thought Foundation in Tucson, Arizona), (2) yielded court orders against further active participation in deprogramming and other anti-cult activities by various anti-cult leaders, (3) exempted specific groups from further deprogrammings through class action decisions, and (4) driven individual deprogrammers (including Ted Patrick) from the field by depleting their financial resources in civil suits. The disavowal of psychological testimony on brainwashing has probably brought the era of civil court battles concerning cults to an end.

Thus the anti-cult movement seem destined to become the domain of a small number of anti-cult activists who will be limited to fighting their battles verbally in the press to an increasingly disinterested audience. There is little doubt that it will continue active in some form for the foreseeable future. It is headed by a core of dedicated individuals, many of whom are either the deprogrammed ex-cultists themselves or their parents. They possess an extreme dedication to the cause. The only question, given the movement's failures, its loss of media attention, and the steady growth and acceptance of alternative religions, is the level at which it will be able to function. It is not unlikely that by the end of the decade the movement will be reduced to a number of small isolated groups whose major activity will be the circulation of anti-cult propaganda.

Sources

Two significant and complementary studies of the anti-cult movement have been made by sociologists David Bromley and Anson Shupe. Shupe has also published a large collection of rare documents of the early years of the movement.

Shupe, Anson D., Jr., and David G. Bromley. *A Documentary History of the Anti-Cult Movement*. Arlington, TX: Center for Social Research, University of Texas at Arlington, 1985. Unpaged.

————. *The New Vigilantes*. Beverly Hills, CA: Sage Publications, 1980. 267 pp.

————, and Donna L. Oliver. *The Anti-Cult Movement in America: A Bibliography and Historical Survey*. New York: Garland Publishing, 1984. 169 pp.

Listed below are the major sources representative of the secular anti-cult position. Not included in this list are many items directed toward a single cult, many of which may be found listed in the appropriate chapter elsewhere in this text.

Appel, Willa. *Cults in America*. New York: Holt, Rinehart and Winston, 1983. 204 pp.

Conway, Flo, and Jim Siegelman. *Snapping*. Philadelphia: Lippencott, 1978. 254 pp.

MacCollam, Joel. *Carnival of Souls*. New York: Seabury Press, 1979. 188 pp.

Patrick, Ted. *Let Our Children Go!* New York: E. P. Dutton, 1976. 188 pp.

Rudin, James, and Marcia Rudin. *Prison or Paradise.* Philadelphia: Fortress Press, 1980. 164 pp.

Verdier, Paul A. *Brainwashing and the Cults.* No. Hollywood, CA: Wilshire Book Company, 1977. 118 pp.

VI.

Violence and the Cults

VIOLENCE AND THE CULTS

[*Note*: This chapter was originally written as the report of a specific study conducted by the Institute for the Study of American Religion in 1983-84. Rather than attempt a revision of it, an addenda has been added at the end of the chapter with reflections on its conclusions six years later.]

The most serious charges leveled at new and unconventional religions concern their great potential for violence or the additional denunciation that such religions in fact have been and are the source of an inordinate amount of violence. As evidence, cult critics have pointed to the incidents of violent activity associated with nonconventional religious groups: the murder/suicides at Jonestown, the Manson Family killings, the takeover of three buildings in Washington, D.C., by the Hanafi Muslims, and the beating death of a child in the Michigan-based House of Judah.

This chapter broadly examines cult-related violence in order to isolate substantive issues concerning the potential for violence within the nonconventional religions, some five to six hundred of which currently dot the American landscape. Unfortunately, prior attention to the question has almost entirely focused on the People's Temple, a group so different from typical American cults as to offer little insight on the problem. In contrast, this chapter is based on a survey of cult-related violence conducted in 1983-1984 by the Institute for the Study of American Religion. The survey led to the compilation of a file of reported incidents of violence regarding cult groups. Both newspapers and magazines, especially those published by anti-cult groups, were scanned and knowledgeable people were solicited for accounts of violent incidents. Some stories of cult violence that had received attention in the media were examined at greater depth and the groups involved asked to comment upon them. The results of that survey appear below.

The issue of cult-related violence is fraught with emotion and requires great care in the use of data. In merely cataloging the reported incidents, as was done in the early stages of this survey, one could easily come to the false conclusion suggested by many cult critics that cult life is inherently dangerous and threatening. The evidence, however, fails to support such a conclusion. Overwhelmingly, nonconventional religious groups have been free of reported incidents atypical of their day-to-day life. Those few nonconventional religious groups which have suffered a history of violent interaction with society are very much the exceptions of those groups which have been labeled "cult."

Most of the groups which have shown a long-term tendency for violent interaction with society have received little or no attention from the anti-cult media. This lack of attention is due, in part, to the primary focus of anti-cult groups upon those cults that concentrate their energy in the recruitment of young adults. The more violent groups have been either predominantly black in membership (anti-cult groups tend to be upper-middle-class white) or older in membership.

However, certain groups do have a reported history of violence and, as a result, are a matter of legitimate concern. Groups which show a confirmed and continuing pattern of violence need the attention of religious scholars, psychologists and social scientists, the legal authorities, and the general public.

Some Preliminary Considerations

The survey established some necessary guidelines for evaluating the reports of violence. First, previous definitions of cult-related violence need to be considerably broadened. Levi, in his introduction to the only book-length treatment of the subject, defines it as "intentional homicide and intentional suicide initiated within a religious group."[1] That definition should be broadened to include (1) violent actions short of homicide which result in significant bodily injury or unintentional death. Violent acts reportedly perpetrated by cults include rape, beatings, and child abuse. Further it should also include (2) practices that in themselves might not be considered violent but which may nevertheless lead to injury or death of innocent bystanders or members of the group. Such practices might include, for example, unusual diet restrictions or the denial of necessary medical attention.

Inadvertently, Levi's definition also assumes a conclusion very much contradicted by the evidence, that all cult-related violence is initiated from within nonconventional religions. The survey has shown that violence directed toward nonconventional religions by outsiders is equally important and equally extensive though the object of only distant attention by the media. Thus the definition must also be enlarged to include (3) the very real violent activity directed against groups labeled cults. Anti-cult actions include the assassination of leaders, the bombing and burning of buildings, assaults upon groups by night riders, and the abduction of group members for coercive deconversion (i.e., deprogramming). Only one step from actual violence is (4) the threat of violence and terrorism against groups which are isolated either in a rural center or by public prejudice in an urban center. The effects of threats of violence are multiplied when reports of such threats are disregarded by legal authorities and groups are left on their own to face the possibility that threats foreshadow violent actions. It should be noted that the experience of threatened violence had led many rural religious groups, especially those isolated from efficient law enforcement structures, to initially develop an internal security system. Such systems, which often include a modest cache of weapons, are almost the sole basis of the frequently heard charges of religious groups stockpiling weapons. In like manner, the necessary training of security officers is transformed into an image of preparation for urban warfare upon society.

In this report, cult-related violence shall be defined as *violent behavior which leads to bodily harm or death (homicide and suicide) of individuals or the significant destruction of property due to actions initiated within a nonconventional religion against either members or the general public and also actions by the public against nonconventional religions' members and property.*

Second, the treatment of cult-related violence must attempt to filter the many unconfirmed reports and even malicious rumors from verified accosts of violent activity. Within the hostile climate that has pervaded the public consideration of cults, numerous false reports and rumors have been circulated. That problem was vividly illustrated in the midst of compiling the data for this report. Based upon the accusation of excessive child abuse made by ex-member Roland Church against the Northeast Community Church, the State of Vermont conducted a massive raid and took all of the children of the group into custody. Though a judge had ruled the raid illegal and dismissed most of the cases, two months after the June 4, 1954, raid, Church confessed that he had lied in making the charges in order to justify his defection from the group.[2] Similar distortions have been regularly uncovered in the accounts of ex-members who left with a grudge against the group or who have gone through the experience of deprogramming. Hostile reports of the defectors from nonconventional religions must be double checked against independent sources, and unverified claims either rejected or, at best, put aside for possible future verification.

The most pervasive unverified reports have concerned the stockpiling of weapons and the training for guerrilla warfare. For example, in 1978 reports began to appear in the press that the Hare Krishnas were stockpiling weapons at their farm community in West Virginia. Not reported were the several attacks upon the community by armed intruders or the fact that the entire stockpile consisted of several .22-caliber rifles which have to date (1984) never been used. Then in 1980, a cache of weapons was found in a car parked at the Krishna farm in California. News accounts heralded the discovery of a stockpile of Krishna-owned weapons, the arrest of Srila Hansadutta Swami (one of the organization's initiating gurus), and plans to search other California properties of the group. Again, not widely reported, were other facts: the guns found in the car were not owned by the Krishnas, rather, they were owned by several members who had purchased them in spite of the groups belief in nonviolence. Hansadutta was released by the authorities when it was discovered that there was no substance to the charges of possession of illegal weapons. Most importantly, no coverage was given to the disciplining and removal from positions of authority of Hansadutta and those deviating from the nonviolent stance of the Krishnas.

Unfortunately, in the case of Hansadutta, the problem continued after his reinstatement, and in 1983 he was excommunicated from the organization. He took the former Berkeley, California, temple of the International Society for Krishna Consciousness and formed the Vedic Cultural Society. In his own publications he has advocated the right to bear arms in self-defense and use them to protect members of his community. Subsequent to his establishment of an independent center, he was arrested as the result of a shooting incident in Berkeley.

The media coverage of the Krishnas' problems, which has wedded images of Krishnas and guns in much media treatment of ISKCON, fades beside the space devoted to reports of military training supposedly accorded members of the Way International at the Way College in Emporia, Kansas. For three years in the late 1970s the College was one of several institutions of higher learning which offered a course in hunting safety initiated by the State of Kansas. This program, which used state money in its implementation, was carried out under state guidelines and did not include any military tactical training or the familiarization of pupils with military weapons. It did, however, generate numerous rumors of The Way training members for urban guerilla warfare, rumors which have continued to be repeated, even in the major news media, in spite of the lack of evidence to verify them.[3]

But as shall become obvious here, even the removal of such unverified and demonstrably false reports from the catalog of violent incidents leaves a substantial list. The existence of these several widely reported stories concerning violent activity, however, should serve as a warning against the confusion of mere charges of violent activity (which are far too numerous to present individually) with verified accounts. It is to the harm of all that some have crusaded against nonconventional religions with unverified stories of weapons stockpiling and child abuse. Their actions, which amount to a sophisticated form of crying wolf, distract attention from those individuals and individual groups which might in fact, be stockpiling weapons, conducting military training, or abusing children.

Third, cult-related violence must be placed in the larger context of violence in American religion. While no attempt was made to survey violence in mainline churches, the survey of cult violence led to reports from mainline denominations concerning child abuse, mistreatment of residents of church-run homes for the elderly, shootings, and sexual mistreatment of members. No attempt to catalog these reports, which cover the range from Catholic to Protestant to Free Church congregations and structures, has been made, but such incidents, some equally as spectacular as those involving cults, rarely received national news coverage. There was one exception, of course.

Jim Jones' Peoples' Temple, labeled a cult after the deaths in Jonestown, was in fact a congregation within mainline Christianity. It was a full member of the Christian Church (Disciples of Christ), which in turn is a member of the National Council of Churches. Liberal Protestants heralded it for its social action program, and during the mid-1970s, several denominations such as the United Methodist Church devoted an entire adult church school lesson to extolling its virtues. The People's Temple was not a cult in any traditional sense; it was a representative of an unnoticed class—the mainline church which has degenerated into something not recognizable by reference to its parent body. As shall be noted below, the Peoples' Temple is not the only recent representative.

Fourth, different nonconventional religions can and should be separated according to the differing levels of violence associated with them. Most cults have had no serious charges of violence leveled against them. Some have had some violent interaction with society. Only a very few have passed through a period in which violence was a real factor in the group's life (the Church of the Lamb of God, the Black Muslims, Faith Assembly, etc.). These groups should be sharply distinguished from the rest.

Cult critics, when discussing the issue of violence, continually yield to the very attractive temptation to lump all cults together and brand all with the guilt of any one. Such guilt by association, which unfortunately has been integral to the media treatment of cult issues, is no less deplorable than the racism and anti-Semitism from which it has been copied. Such a tactic is, however, especially disheartening when adopted by an individual or organization otherwise publicly identified with the fight against group prejudices.

Violence Against Cults

Early one morning in 1978 the devotees at the Hare Krishna Community, New Vrindaban, in rural West Virginia, gathered for the worship which begins each day. Suddenly, the barrels of several shotguns appeared in the window and the sound of chanting was interrupted by buckshot tearing through the air. The gunmen entered the temple. One forced the leader of the group to walk up a nearby hill and ordered him to begin digging his own grave. Others forced devotees to destroy statues of the deities. Fortunately no one was killed, and eventually the intruders left. Shaken by the events, leaders finally agreed that a minimum of security must be established and so they purchased several .22-caliber rifles.

The incident did not go unnoticed by the press, but in the resulting coverage emphasis was shifted. It became a story of the purchase of the weapons by the Krishnas and rumors of reprisals on the local community. The coverage of the incident illustrates the lost element in discussions of cult-related violence: violence inflicted upon cults.

In its most aggressive form, violence against cults has led to the assassinations of cult leaders. Most are aware of the shootings of Mormon leaders Joseph Smith (by a mob) and James Jesse Strang (by several assassins). Less well known are the murders of Eric Jansson (the Bishop Hill commune) and Krishna Venta (W.F.L.K Fountain of the World) by angry ex-members of their groups. In the past two decades the list of assassinated nonconventional religious leaders would include:

> Malcolm X
> the family of Hamaas Abdul Khaalis
> Joel LeBaron
> Rulon C. Allred
> Swami Nityananda

This set of deaths most clearly illustrates a major distinction among nonconventional religious groups in relation to violence, i.e., the distinction between those few groups whose members seem willing to resort to violence to further the group's goals and the overwhelming number of nonconventional religions which avoid violence except in self-defense. In each case cited above, the assassin of the cult leader was a member of a rival cult group. Malcolm X and the family of Hamaas Abdul Khaalis were both killed by men later identified as members of the Nation of Islam headed by Elijah Muhammad. Followers of Ervil LeBaron, leader of the Church of the Lamb of God, killed both Joel LeBaron and Rulon Allred. A member of the Ananda Marga lured Swami Nityananda to his death. With the exception of the Hanafi Muslims led by Khaalis, whose case is considered below, none of the afflicted cults took violent action against the rival group beyond demanding the prompt response of law enforcement agencies.

Slightly different in kind was the shooting of San Diego Sikh Dharma leader Jagat Singh Khalsa by a man who broke into the San Diego Temple brandishing a carbine. This isolated 1978 incident ended fortunately without anyone being killed but served to heighten the fear among groups which had been subjected to lesser forms of violence.

More numerous than the assassination of leaders, of course, have been attacks by individuals and small groups upon cult members and property. While contemporary groups seem to have been relatively free of the kind of mob violence such as that which in the last century was directed against Roman Catholic convents and/or monasteries and against the Mormons, there have been repeated incidents of attacks upon members (simple assault) and buildings (arson, shootings, bombings). Few of the assault cases have been reported in the media, unless coincidental with a deprogramming attempt, but several attacks by armed night riders have become known. For example, once the people in and around Dimmitt, Texas, became aware of the presence of the Coven of Arianhu, a Witchcraft group associated with the national Church and School of Wicca, teenagers selected the isolated farm of leaders Louise and Loy Stone as a popular spot for visits after dark. On several occasions the Stones reported harassment by truckloads of young people driving around their property, trespassing and shouting their disapproval of the Stone's religion, which many confused with Satanism. On Halloween 1977, a truck full of youths appeared. A short time later a shotgun appeared. Shots were fired. One youth was killed and another was wounded. (The death may have been partially due to the delay in getting the wounded girl to the nearby hospital. For some reason the driver of the truck took over an hour to drive the short distance). Loy Stone, arrested for the shooting, was found not guilty in the trial.

Less ambiguous was the burning of a building at Camp New Hope owned by the Unification Church in Ulster County, New York. Prior to the burning, the camp was a target of numerous rock-throwing and several shooting incidents. The Metropolitan Community Church, a church whose members are predominantly homosexual, has had several of its church structures destroyed by arson. A pipe bomb was exploded in the campus of The Way College in January 1981. The San Diego Temple of the Hare Krishnas was bombed in 1979. These violent actions against property seem to be an extension of the frequent incidents in which rocks, along with the occasional threatening note, are thrown through windows, a common complaint of owners of occult bookstores and supply houses.

Of the several reported bombings of nonconventional religious centers, none have shown more vicious intent than the incident in 1984 at the Philadelphia temple of the Hare Krishnas. Early one morning, a bomb exploded. A few minutes later, a second bomb exploded in the same location. The first bomb, the weaker of the two, had been meant to attract people to the site. The second, larger bomb was timed to kill or seriously injure any assembled Krishnas. Fortunately, the temple residents were slow to respond to the first bomb, and no one was injured.

These more or less sporadic acts against cults are the most extreme form of violence against nonconventional religious groups. The seemingly random pattern of their occurrence radically contrasts with the most prevalent form of violence against nonconventional religions: deprogramming. This practice of abducting and physically detaining members of cults began in the early 1970s. Though the number of incidents peaked around 1980, deprogramming continues as a popular practice (The Way International reported approximately 100 attempts in 1983) and has spawned a core of professional deprogrammers. The number of total deprogrammings and deprogramming attempts during the past decade run into the thousands.

Each case of deprogramming, it should be noted, involves the abduction and forced detention of the adult member, and, in most cases, the physical violence is limited to those two actions, though the process of deprogramming involves a massive assault upon the psyche and value system of the victim, as traumatic for some as a physical rape. On occasion, however, the deprogramming has become even more violent. If the deprogramming victim attempts resistance and escape, s/he will almost surely be physically assaulted and often restrained with ropes and/or handcuffs. On several occasions deprogramming of female victims has led to sexual assault. In one case the husband of a woman undergoing deprogramming was severely cut with a razor while trying to free his wife from her abductors.

It should be noted that the number of violent assaults on nonconventional religious groups and their members has been as under reported as the number of violent incidents initiated by cult members has been exaggerated. Most incidents, especially incidents of threats, minor assaults, and property damage, go unnoticed until they have been compounded and erupt into a violent confrontation or even homicide.

Cult Against Cult

Review of the list of cult-related violence clearly exposes the location of the single most violent activity initiated by nonconventional religious bodies: where two or more closely related groups allow intense religious polemics (a very common characteristic of groups undergoing a process of splintering) to escalate into open warfare. Such incidents form a transition in the discussion of cult-related violence as such conflict finds a cult inflicting violence, but equally a cult as a victim of that violence. Two prominent examples from recent decades immediately stand out—the Mormon polygamy-practicing groups of the Southwest and the Black Muslims.

During the 1970s, Ervil LeBaron left the polygamy-practicing Church of the First Born of the Fullness of Times, founded and led by his brother Joel. With his followers he organized the Church of the Lamb of God. He then declared himself leader of all of the polygamy-practicing groups and demanded that the other leaders acknowledge his new role. When they ignored him, he threatened violence. They still refused to accept him. He ordered executions. Joel was murdered in 1972. In 1973 Ervil ordered a raid on the town of Los Molinos where many of Joel's followers and family lived. The raiders set fire to several buildings and killed two people. In 1977 Ervil ordered several members to execute Dr. Rulon Allred, the leader of one of the largest polygamy groups. Allred died in his office of multiple gunshot wounds. The violence ended in 1979 with the arrest and conviction of Ervil Le Baron.[4]

Even more violent was the case of the Black Muslims. The Nation of Islam, which had been founded in the 1930s, grew rapidly in the years after World War II (during which time its leader Elijah Muhammad had been in prison for encouraging draft evasion). Then in the mid-1960s it began to splinter. Malcolm X, one of the Nation's most charismatic leaders, defected, organized a rival Muslim Mosque, and criticized his former leader for his departure from orthodox Islam. In 1965 Malcolm X was assassinated by members of the Nation of Islam. The murder of Malcolm X signaled the beginning of a decade of violence that left bodies lying on the streets from Brooklyn to Pasadena. The blood bath even touched Elijah Muhammad's family when his son-in-law Raymond Sharieff was shot as he left the offices of the Nation's periodical.

Most deaths in the Islamic wars occurred in fighting between the Nation and the Hanafis. On January 19, 1973, several men, later identified as members of the Nation of Islam, broke into the home of Hanafi Muslim leader Hamaas Abdul Khaalis, a friend of Malcolm X and former Nation official. Several weeks earlier Khaalis had circulated an open letter in which he called Elijah Muhammad a "lying deceiver." Not finding Khaalis at home, the invaders took their toll among other residents. Four were shot and killed. Khaalis' wife survived but is paralyzed for life. His three children were drowned. The men convicted of the crimes were given what many, including Khaalis, considered a relatively light sentence. In 1977, partially in response to his anger and frustration over the incident, Khaalis demanded, among other terms, that authorities produce the men convicted of the 1973 murders. Presumably he would have killed them if given the opportunity.[5]

Violence Initiated by Cults

In spite of the attention given to cult-initiated violence, little systematic effort has been made to analyze the data and to address the substantive questions they raise. Commentators have been content merely to list reported incidents in the attempt to support a prior conclusion that the level of cult violence is sufficient to warrant suppression of nonconventional religions by society and the government. The cataloging of reported acts of violence now allows examination apart from anti-cult polemic which has treated all violence as symptoms of a single cult phenomenon. Such previous amalgamations of data, gathered only as ammunition with which to assault the cults, have provided no useful assistance in, for example, locating potential pockets of future violence or preventing their occurrence.

The specter of cult violence centers upon the possibility of a cult, motivated by some "religious" ideal peculiar to itself, randomly attacking innocent people. Occasionally, the specter grows into an image of violent revolution and urban warfare. Of course, the Manson Family and extremist groups (from the Ku Klux Klan to the Symbionese Liberation Army) have supplied some verification of such possibilities. One less heralded case of a nonconventional religion also supplies material to ponder: the "Zebra" killing involving the Nation of Islam in the San Francisco Bay Area.[6]

During 1973 and 1974 a series of random shootings occurred in San Francisco. The perpetrators turned out to be members of an informal group which had been organized within the Nation of Islam. Though the members of this small group kept their activities secret from the rest of the Temple, they assumed that they had been brought together on directives from the highest level of Muslim leadership in Chicago. Their mission: translate the violent anti-white rhetoric of the Nation of Islam into action by killing selected white victims. While there is no evidence that Elijah Muhammad and/or the formal leadership of the Nation of Islam either authorized or knew of the group, there is no doubt that the anti-white theology articulated by the Muslims provided the fertile ideological ground out of which the group could emerge. That is to say, the Nation of Islam created a group organized around their hatred of white oppression of blacks and a religious doctrine of divine disapproval of whites which justifies action against them. While the Zebra killers found their roots in the history of Black oppression in the United States, they have their precedents in those groups throughout recorded history who have called down divine sanctions to justify their anti-social actions. Historically, quite apart from warfare between rival religions, radical religious groups have committed robbery, rape, torture and even murder against non-members whom they define as evil, outside of God's chosen people or realm of law, or otherwise deserving of the violence inflicted upon them.

While some call upon the divine to sanctify anti-social action, others revel in what society calls evil which they redefine as their "good." They take the Lord of Evil as their God, and what society calls sin is their path. Such Satanic groups, though rare, small in membership, and short-lived, do nevertheless exist. Much of the growing fear surrounding Satanic groups originates in their secretive nature and in the descriptions of what they do.

Possibly the first actual Satanic group, a group who took the Christian devil as their deity, was the seventeenth-century cult built around La Voison, a figure in the court of Louis XIV of France. With the aid of defrocked priests, La Voison led black masses and dispensed potions to keep followers in their positions of power and influence. When discovered, the group, by the extent of its infiltration to high places close to the king, threatened to topple his government. While it is not known if the number of Satanic groups has increased in recent decades, certainly the reports of their existence have.[7]

Satanic groups, at least in the past two decades, have been of two distinct varieties. The milder Satanic groups which have grown out of the work of Anton La Vey have propagated a rather mild form of allegiance to His Infernal Majesty. His Satanic church and other groups such as the Temple of Set have had a high profile and have been careful to conduct their rituals and other activities within the law. La Vey and other leaders have frequently cooperated with the police on cases involving an occult angle. The second type of Satanist group is a small, closed group consisting primarily of either (1) young teenagers experimenting with the occult and/or drugs, or (2) sociopaths and psychopaths. Illegal and violent activity arose from this latter type of group.

Even in milder forms, Satanic rituals may use two hard-to-obtain items—the bones of the dead and the consecrated hosts from a Roman Catholic Eucharist. Satan is perceived by his worshippers to be the ruler of dead souls and the archenemy of what Christians would consider most sacred. Roman Catholics believe the Eucharistic host to have been transubstantiated into the very body of Christ. Most Satanic groups, particularly those consisting of young occultists, thus signal their presence by (and limit their anti-social activities to) the desecration (vandalism) of religious buildings and theft of objects from churches and graveyards.

Most Satanic groups come and go very quickly as they release whatever psychopathic or sociopathic urges that led to the formation of the group in the first place. Occasionally, however, the pathology goes much deeper, and the activity of the group can lead to the torture and sacrifice of an animal (usually a cat or a dog) or to the ritual murder of an individual. If a human victim is chosen, it will usually be an ex-member of the group, a personal enemy of the leader(s), or an attractive young female. A recently discovered group in New York, for example, targeted German Shepherds for ritual death and mutilation.

While an encounter with a Satanic group can be extremely traumatic, if not fatal, to an individual, their small number has, with one exception, limited their larger social impact to the fear they engender. Since the early 1970s, the rural west has been plagued by a series of cattle mutilations. Researchers dismissed one early hypothesis which blamed the mutilations on Satanists as few signs of ritual behavior were associated with the dead cattle. More important in discounting the Satanic cult theory was the massive number of cultists which would have to exist to accomplish the large number of reported mutilations. However, more recent thorough examinations of the cattle mutilation reports have found that the overwhelming number of reported cattle mutilations were attributable to natural causes (primarily to predator damage on cattle killed by such hazards as lightning, snake bites, poison weeds, disease, and simple accidents). The modest number of cases which emerged as attributable to human causes were those associated with ritual activity: their number was small enough as to be readily assigned to the activity of the few known and hypothesized Satanic groups.[8]

The warfare between two groups touches a relatively confined sphere, and even the real incidents of assaults or death from Satanic groups seem remote. And yet, on several occasions, a large, stable, and relatively visible group becomes involved in an intensely hostile situation which over a period of time yields to violence. Such situations become the focus of legitimate concern by the public and law enforcement agencies. But in each of the several prominent cases which have emerged during the 1970s, violence was preceded by a decade or more of antagonism, heightened rhetoric, and hostile actions (just short of violence) by both members and non-members which created a climate of distrust, misinformation, and latent hostility, all of which worked against more peaceful resolutions to problems.

The Synanon Foundation, now the Synanon Church, moved into Marin County, California, in 1964. Almost from the beginning, hostile attitudes began to be expressed within the community. As it acquired more land and expanded several times the size of its original 65-acre purchase, complaints were voiced that it was taking an increasing amount of land off the county tax rolls. Adding fuel to the controversy were complaints that the county was lax in enforcing zoning laws (which would have slowed construction) and ignoring environmental impact. New buildings were supposedly being constructed without the issuance of required permits. On occasion, problems with neighbors, especially one through whose property Synanon had an easement, led to arguments. Stories circulated of children left by parents in Synanon's care running away and complaining of cruel treatment. Several negative media articles critical of Synanon had been met with lawsuits, at least one of which had been won for a sizable amount. The growing tension between the community and Synanon erupted into a series of increasingly violent incidents in 1978.

As community hostility grew, the Synanon community, which was somewhat isolated in the most rural section of Marin County, began to experience some direct violence in the form of night riders. Shots were fired into buildings on several occasions. By the time the sheriff's office could respond, the perpetrators were far from the scene. To protect itself, early in 1978, Synanon purchased a supply of guns and ammunition for the use, if necessary, of its security force. Several weeks after the announced purchase, with their concurrent rumors of weapons stockpiles, a county grand jury issued a report criticizing (1) officials for not making Synanon abide by the county regulations, and (2) Synanon for disregarding the regulations and doing little to correct the problem with the children in its care. In the midst of these events, an ex-member was awarded $300,000 in a lawsuit against Synanon.

The increased anger against Synanon, about which the residents of the county were choosing sides with most opposing, and Synanon's own beleaguered condition set the stage for events to follow. Someone, and it may never be known exactly who, placed a rattlesnake in the mailbox of the attorney of the former member who had won the $300,000. Synanon founder Charles Dederich and two residents were arrested. Before the case could go to trial, Dederich suffered three strokes. The three defendants decided to plead no contest. Not only was Dederich's health a consideration, but significant public feelings, generated by media reports, called the possibility of a fair trial into question. The two residents were sentenced to a term in prison, and Dederich was ordered to cease any active role in the running of the community. Soon after, the Synanon Church sold its Marin County property and moved its offices and community to Badger, California.

Since the move, no further incidents of violence have been reported, however, the fallout from the rattlesnake incident has been enormous. Over forty people associated with Synanon received widely publicized grand jury indictments; then all of them were quietly dropped before going to trial. As a result of the attention, Synanon became involved in a series of litigations which, it appears, will be some years in the adjudication process. It is the opinion of Synanon that it has been the victim in the whole process, and it has sought vindication by initiating lawsuits against the people it feels were responsible for damaging its program and image.[9]

Another group which developed an image permeated with violence is the Ananda Marga Yoga Society, though almost all of the violent incidents, including the death of 17 Ananda Margis at the hands of a Calcutta mob in 1982, occurred outside of the United States. Trouble began in 1971 when Anandamurtiji, the leader of Ananda Marga, was arrested in India for murder. Anandamurtiji, who was also a political theorist and founder of a political party, had previously accused Indian Prime Minister Indira Gandhi of corruption. His trial was denounced by international human rights groups as purely political, and in 1978 his sentence was reversed and he was released. Meanwhile accusations of violence piled up and were lent credence by the conviction of two members in Australia for murdering a politician and the presence of numerous documents in law enforcement agency files linking Ananda Marga members to a variety of violent crimes. (It should be noted that Ananda Marga has denied the many accusations against it and attributes their proliferation to the same persecution that originally sent their leader to jail; and apart from the Australian case none of the accusations have led to arrests and/or convictions).[10]

Though not reaching a level of violence of such as either the Nation of Islam or Ananda Marga, the history of the Church of Scientology follows a parallel path. Soon after its founding, the Church began to experience problems. In 1958 the Internal Revenue Service withdrew its tax-exempt status. In 1963 the Food and Drug Administration seized a mass of books, tapes, and E-Meters used in the Church's counseling procedure called auditing. As the United States government moved against Scientology trouble spread. Based upon information supplied by U.S. government officials, inquiries began in Australia which led to Scientology's banning in 1965. In response to these actions, the Church, in 1966, established the Guardian's Office, to which it assigned the task, among others, of safeguarding Scientology and its organizations. Almost immediately, the Guardian's Office was forced to devote a major portion of its time to the continuing government attack and a new assault from several expose-type books which the Church considered libelous. It countered with lawsuits to force the books off the market.

By the mid-1970s the Church charged that a coalition of government agencies, ex-members, and individuals who simply disliked the Church were combining to destroy it. They spent much of the decade in legal battles. They attempted to obtain government documents on the Church through the Freedom of Information Act and were frequently met with denials of the existence of the requested documents, only to have the said documents appear elsewhere. In the process both sides developed a war-like attitude, and both eventually sent spies and even *agents provocateurs* into the others' camp. In the midst of this war, charges surfaced that the Church had turned violent, that Scientologists had harassed, beaten, and even murdered some ex-members and individuals defined as "enemies,' though no Scientologist was ever formally charged or tried. People involved in lawsuits against the Church accused Church members of breaking in and stealing files. Finally, members of the Church associated with the Guardian's Office were arrested and convicted on charges of stealing government documents from the Federal Bureau of Investigation and the Internal Revenue Service.

In the period since the conviction of top-level Scientology officials, the Church has taken significant steps to reorganize and to alter its polemic stance vis-à-vis society, but, as with Synanon, it will be many years before fully disposing of the problems created during the 1970s. Major steps in changing the past history occurred in 1983 when the High Court of Australia reversed all of that country's anti-Scientology acts. However, that was followed by a United States tax court ruling against the Church and a civil court decision against the Church involving a multimillion dollar case brought by an ex-member.[11]

One cannot leave the accounts of groups with a history of violence without some mention of the Children of God (now called the Family of Love). While there have been no reports of violence toward the general public, ex-members have made repeated charges of member-on-member violence. Almost all of the reports originate within the circle of members in relatively close contact with David Berg, the leader. Very early in the life of the Children of God, a sex ethic which varied considerably from that generally accepted in society emerged. Most of the charges of violence, some well-documented, relate to sexual abuse and rape. The charges seem to have been a by-product of Berg's attempts to manipulate the social bonding within the higher echelons of the Family and to use sex as a proselytizing tool. The latter practice, called "flirty fishing," brought large-scale public reaction as well as an outbreak of venereal disease and has been discontinued in many places. The charges against Berg and his associates were largely responsible for their abandoning the United States in the mid-1970s. Charges of problems at the top of the organization, though not the violence of the early 1970s, have continued in the 1980s, most recently being confirmed by Berg's own daughter who left the group after many years.[12]

Again, lest the image be left that nonconventional religious groups are somehow unique in becoming associated with violent events, there is the case of a Santa Ana, California, parish—a case frightening in its parallels to the Peoples' Temple. During the 1950s the Church of the Way was a small congregation in the Free Methodist Church. Then several years after a new pastor came to the Church, denominational officials charged the pastor with deviation from Church doctrine. The congregation stood with the pastor and in 1959 withdrew from the denomination. It continued to grow through the 1960s, but slowly word began to spread that all was not well at the little church down the street, by now renamed Madeley Trinity Methodist Church.

Some have traced the trouble to the early 1970s when lay members began to speak out during the Sunday services. The "exhortations" took the form of accusations against other Church members. Such verbal intimidation became the first step in leading the Church into a separatist stance, and, as separation from other Christians grew, a number of bizarre and not a few violent practices were introduced. Most of the conflict was expressed in an extreme form of the belief in "demon possession." First, pet animals were singled out as "possessed" and beaten to death. Then spouses were ordered to shun their mates identified as possessed. Eventually several members were physically assaulted as a part of an attempted exorcism. In 1977 two members who had been beaten sued and won substantial out-of-court settlements.

Then, suddenly, in the winter of 1979-1980, the Church abandoned Santa Ana and moved to Springfield, Missouri (over 100 members). It held one service in March 1980 in a rented building and then simply disappeared. Members scattered and have kept in touch by way of a set of postal boxes. (At the time of this writing, the Madeley Trinity Methodist Church remains in hiding, even to family members left behind at the time of the sudden move.)

The case of the Madeley Trinity Methodist Church, like the Peoples' Temple before it, manifests that other aforementioned potential for violence—the mainline Church gone bad. The reports of beatings at that Church also lead directly into the last remaining issue which has received substantive concern with regard to cult violence—child abuse.

During the last decade cases linking child abuse to a religious group appeared with a somewhat regular frequency. Thus, given the growing concern about child abuse as a national issue, it was only a matter of time before a substantive case would surface. That occurred in 1982 when a child died as a result of a beating by a parent. The mother,

later convicted of involuntary manslaughter, was a member of the House
of Judah, a small Black Jewish group headquartered in Allegan County,
Michigan. William A. Lewis, the leader of the group, believed in strong
discipline for children and advocated corporal punishment in response to
childish disobedience.

In the wake of the House of Judah case, other reports of child
abuse were quickly assembled as further evidence of the violent tendencies
present in cults. Yet, upon close examination, the child abuse charges did
not come from the major nonconventional religions (i.e., those most
identified as cults in the public mind) but from conservative Evangelical
Christian church groups which took Biblical admonitions (Hebrews 12:6)
about chastising children as literal fact. These included the Gideons
(Ocala, FL), the River of Life Tabernacle (Montana), the Stonegate
Christian Community (West Virginia), the Northeast Kingdom
Community (Vermont), the Covenant Community Fellowship
(Rennselaer, Indiana), the Church of Bible Understanding (New York
and Pennsylvania), and the Church of God in Christ through the Holy
Spirit (not to be confused with the large Pentecostal denomination the
Church of God in Christ).

The strict adherence to literal Biblical admonitions has also led
to other problems beside child abuse. Throughout the twentieth century,
some conservative Protestant sectarian groups have turned against
doctors and the medical profession, frequently as part of a general
adoption of an emphasis on faith healing, a belief that if a member's faith
is strong God will restore that member to health from all diseases and
keep them in a perpetual state of health. During the 1970s, the Faith
Assembly, led by Pentecostal minister Hobart Freeman, emerged as a
strong new sect group with congregations across the Midwest and into the
South. Members followed Freeman in denouncing medicine as a
derivative of Pagan religion and refrained from the use of medical service.
Home childbirth became standard, but leaders frowned upon attendance
at natural childbirth classes. As a result, the Faith Assembly has
experienced a large number of deaths which could have been prevented
by a minimal amount of proper medical care. Deaths have resulted from
diabetics discontinuing their insulin intake, mothers giving birth at home,
and infants being denied medical care. In the wake of the exposure of the
problem, the state of Indiana moved against the Assembly. Several
members whose children had died were convicted. Leader Hobart
Freeman, also indicted, died before his case could come to trial.

Finally, a discussion of the major incidents of violence initiated from within a "cult" body leaves a residue of isolated cases. Some relate to an individual's religious pathology. Individuals on occasion adopt a religious format to express their violent and aggressive urges. Such is the case of Lindberg Sanders, a black man and former mental patient. He gathered a small group around him and preached that police (mostly white) were Satan. In Memphis in 1983, he took a police officer hostage and killed him. In a raid on the house where the hostage was held, Sanders and his small band were killed. Similar is the case of Keith and Kate Haigler who intercepted a Continental Trailways bus in rural Arkansas. At the end of the hijacking incident, the pair asked state troopers to kill them—they believed they would be resurrected in three days. The troopers only wounded them, so the two shot each other.

Of course, a few incidents related to the major cults do appear. For example, a violent incident involving members of the Divine Light Mission of Guru Maharaj Ji was occasioned by a young man who disliked the guru and tossed a pie in his face. While the Guru asked that no retaliation occur, a week later the pie-thrower was severely beaten. The case of Walter Wallace who joined the Kripalu Yoga Ashram of Yogi Amrit Desai is similar. Desai teaches vegetarianism and advocates occasional fasts. Wallace starved to death, seemingly as the result of an extended private fast. While one of the ashram's physicians had warned Wallace not to fast, no one seemed to recognize that he was slowly starving to death.

The Church of Armageddon, also known as the Love Family, is one of several groups that emerged out of the drug culture of the 1960s. At one time in its life its practices included the ritual sniffing of the chemical toluene. In 1972 two members of the group died as a result of their use of the substance. The fact that they had used it in contradiction to group practice, i.e., unsupervised, and that one had been specifically ordered not to use the substance, does little to lessen the responsibility of the leadership of the Church for their deaths. The Church did, however, discontinue the practice after the incident and no other reports of violence from that group emerged, though charges of corruption against the leader led to the group's disruption.[13]

A Note About Suicide

Within the reports of violence are a small number of suicides. For example, on August 5, 1974, Robert J. Williams shot himself in the parking lot of the Law Enforcement Center at Wichita, Kansas. The previous November, Williams had confided to a newspaper reporter that he was a practicing Witch. The reporter, in return for an account of contemporary Witchcraft, agreed to keep Williams' name and identity confidential. He broke his promise, and Williams' story, complete with name and picture, appeared on the front page of the newspaper. Williams was fired from his job as a psychologist at the state reformatory. Though later reinstated, he remained in a tense situation.

Like child abuse, suicide is a national issue. Unlike child abuse, the actual number of cases is miniscule. However, even with the case of Williams, where much more information has been made available than in most cases, the causes of an individual suicide remain difficult to discern under the best of circumstances and impossible from a few newspaper clippings. Unless more cases should emerge, we must judge that no pattern of cult-related suicide exists and dismiss suicide from our discussion as it constitutes no present discernible danger relative to religious groups.

Conclusions

The Correlates of Cult-Related Violence. The causes of cult-related violence discussed above are very complex. They cannot be separated from the generally high level of violence within American society as a whole and the continuing theme of seeking violent solutions to social problems.[14] As one researcher noted, social violence ". . . is highly complex, involving the deep-seated tendencies in the personality with processes in the immediate situation, in the face-to-face group or organization, and in the large society."[15] Much more work is needed before the final appraisal of the origins of cult-related violence can be fully disclosed. This chapter can only offer some tentative observations concerning potential areas of future cult-related situations and some immediate steps which could be taken to reduce or eliminate possible violence. First, it is to be expected in spite of all measures to the contrary, that some cult-related violence will continue into the foreseeable future. Cults participate in the general theme of religious violence. Religion has, in the past, been the cause of wars and innumerable acts of violence upon individuals. Only with the greatest difficulty have populations learned to fight their religious battles with words instead of guns and instruments of torture. Just as religion has been used to sanction slavery and the sexual exploitation of women, there is every sign that it will continue to be used to rationalize the impulses of religious leaders.

Religious people also inherit the violence transmitted by families from generation to generation. Given the high level of family violence in the United States (from child abuse to neglect), it is unlikely that cults will be able to exclude people who carry those deep-seated tendencies to violence from joining them and even rising to positions of leadership, just as they do within mainline religious groups. Further, given the high level of tension in society under which some nonconventional religious groups have been forced to operate, it is not surprising that the violent tendencies of some cult leaders have emerged. What is possibly more surprising has been the relative infrequency of such violent outbursts.

However, violence does occur, and even relatively few incidents cannot be condoned. Does the review of the prior cases of cult-related violence suggest (1) new ways to understand it and (2) actions that could be taken to lessen its occurrence? In answer to that question, four correlates to cult-related violence have been discerned and several suggestions for long-term action proposed. The correlates of violent activity can be seen as indicators of potential for future violence.

First, *some cults have given and continue to give direct sanction to violent activity.* Both the Black Muslims and the Church of the Lamb of God called upon the tradition of holy war to legitimize the killing of the group's (i.e., God's) enemies. The belief that certain times and situations not only allow but demand the faithful to take up arms was articulated powerfully in the Old Testament and from there was transmitted to Jews, Christians, and Muslims alike. It has been used in this century to justify full-scale military operations, the assassination of political leaders, and the killing of random enemies of the faith.

Great potential for future violence can be found in the several conservative Christian groups who have adopted a militaristic program along with pro-Caucasian policy undergirded with anti-Black and anti-Semitic rhetoric. Some of these groups (which include the Christian Conservative Church of America; the Church of Jesus Christ Christian of Aryan Nations; the Covenant, the Sword, the Arm of the Lord; the Mountain Church; and the New Christian Crusade Church) have strong ties to the Ku Klux Klan. The Covenant, the Sword, the Arm of the Lord, the members of which live together in a community at Zaraphath-Horeb, Arkansas, for example, describes itself as a "peaceful people" who "live with guns." It offers training to both members and others of like mind in urban warfare, "Christian" martial arts, and "the use of firearms for military purposes." This group actually puts into practice what others, such as The Way International, have merely been accused of doing.[16]

Less publicized during the 1970s, but possibly the source of more real damage to individuals, have been the numerous cases of child abuse. Occurring most frequently in conservative evangelical Christian groups, the practice has found its sanction in Biblical passages such as Hebrews 12. Violent tendencies within parents who were themselves abused children can be nurtured by a group's belief in strict discipline and an advocacy of corporal punishment as proper means of controlling behavior.

Second, while some groups and group leaders have given direct sanction to violence, *more cult-related violence grows out of the indirect sanction of violence from belief systems which intellectually undergird group members' violent tendencies.* For example, beliefs held by one group which stereotype another group and hence dehumanize its members are easily adopted by individuals as a rationale for action against members of the despised group. The Church of Scientology, for many years, designated people as "enemies," "potential trouble sources," or "suppressive." It went so far as to suggest someone could be considered "fair game." Within the Church and certainly in the literature, these terms are part of a vast body of technical language with specific meanings and correlative action guidelines. However, they are also highly emotive words which in the heart of controversy can convey, and undoubtedly have conveyed, their emotive charge in spite of the precise technical usage.

Such terms as "enemy," "Satanic," "gentile" (as used by Mormons), "counterfeit" (as used by evangelical Christian counter-cult ministries), "heretic," and other terms used by one group to express their contempt of others and to assign them a status outside the realm of God's chosen, and hence of lesser worth, is the religious equivalent of secular terms such as "nigger," "kike," or "wop." Each serves to direct group prejudice against various minorities in a community. They denigrate the member of the group and give tacit legitimation to the flogging of a black man, the defacement of a synagogue, the telling of ethnic jokes, and the deprogramming of a religious believer.

The sanctioning of violence, both directly and indirectly, in a cult-related situation is vividly illustrated in the philosophy of the militant secular anti-cult movement. In its promotion of deprogramming, it has given direct encouragement to the necessary violence connected with each incident (in which a person is forcefully detained and physically confined for a period of days or weeks). It has lightly dismissed, thus indicating the unimportance in its eyes, of the very real cases of physical abuse heaped upon people who strongly resisted their captors. Further, underlying the whole anti-cult movement and providing the intellectual sanction for deprogramming, both to those who practice it and those who merely promote it, the brainwashing hypothesis has been used to create a pervasive negative image of nonconventional religions by stereotyping them as manipulative, destructive cults. Drawing upon the traditional tactics of group prejudice, the movement has pictured leaders as wealthy, selfish, and exercising undue control on members, and attacked groups as threats to the social order. Individual members have been assigned the role of "helpless victim" and referred to as "zombies" and "puppets" to imply their position as the robot-like tools of cult leaders. Ted Patrick, who developed deprogramming, claimed cult members were so changed by their life in the group as to be incapable of independent thought and thus not suitable objects of civil rights. More recently, anti-cultists have spoken of the need of "repersonalization" of cult members, implying, at least partially, the loss of personhood. Patrick, in what is obviously an extreme statement for the movement, drew the logical conclusion that any act is justifiable in efforts to extricate a person caught in a cult.

The secular anti-cult movement has drawn strength from the popular prejudices which have historically been directed against groups holding nonconventional opinions and following unpopular practices. In prior generations such prejudice brought America waves of anti-Masonry, anti-Catholicism, and anti-Semitism and raised the specter of the Yellow Peril, the Turbaned Tornado, and the Red Scare. In each case, the attempt was made to mobilize the public and the legislative machinery to squelch a rising threat by an "un-American" and "leprous" social group.

In response to the sanctions of violence, it should be noted that *the denial of any sanction to violence by people concerned with a cycle of violent activity can short circuit it.* Among the Black Muslims, no such denial existed, as all sides accepted the legitimacy of violence in given situations. However, when attacked by the Church of the Lamb of God, leaders of both the Church of the First Born and the Apostolic United Brethren, brought strong sanctions to bear against any retaliation. Little doubt remains that they had joined in the hostilities initiated by Ervil LeBaron, the death toll could have been much higher and, like the Hatfield-McCoy feud, gone on for decades.

Third, *much cult-related violence must be traced to the youthfulness of the leadership.* Typically, first-generation movements draw leadership from among the early talented followers of the founder(s). If the organization spreads rapidly, young adults still in their twenties can find themselves the managers of a large national movement. Should that movement come under attack by elements in a society or face severe tensions from within, they must guide the believers often without any assistance from older individuals who have expertise in conflict resolution, public relations, or legislative lobbying. Youthful leaders require time to learn the seriousness and consequences of violent outbursts. That learning process may have to proceed concurrently with a period of violence surrounding the group in which they have assumed leadership. The inexperience of youth seems to be a contributing factor in the occasional incidents of violence such as that illustrated in the conviction of the Divine Light Mission leader in Winterthur, Switzerland, for attempted murder, and in the various actions planned and executed by the Guardian's Office of the Church of Scientology in the 1970s.

Fourth, *violence erupts, in most cases, only after a period of heightened conflict between either different factions of a religion or a nonconventional religion and the community.* In such cases, both sides must bear responsibility when and if verbal violence turns to physical violence as both sides will have inflicted damage upon the other and each will have had multiple opportunities either to withdraw and refuse to perpetuate the conflict or seek a satisfactory alternative solution.

The presence of a long-standing conflict, either in the form of heightened rhetoric of one religion against another or community criticism of a particular religious group, should alert observers to a situation in which a potential for violence exists. Such rhetoric and/or criticism is by no means a sure indicator, as almost every group goes through one or more periods of conflict, and very few allow conflict to erupt into violence. If, however, strong violent tendencies appear within some members and if a group sanction for violence is present, the potential is markedly increased. Most groups choose to respond to conflict by seeking nonviolent solutions—through secular legal alternatives—or, in most cases, simply and patiently waiting out the conflict. For example, most cults have reacted and continue to react to the anticult pressures either (1) by seeking redress in the courts (an offensive action) or (2) blocking anti-cult legislation and building aggressive public relations programs (both defensive actions), or (3) nothing (an often effective passive solution). They have with few exceptions, refrained from physically attacking deprogrammers and other leaders in the organized anti-cult movement.

Towards a Reduction of Violence

The People's Temple alerted the public to the potential for violence surrounding religious conflict. While the Jonestown situation is a unique case in many ways, both in the situation of the groups (a Black American group isolated on a rural farm in a foreign country) and in the aura of secrecy which surrounds it (most of the papers collected in the investigation committee have not been released under the Freedom of Information Act due to matters of national security), it points to other occasions of violence. Also, while yet reluctant to pinpoint the causes of religious violence, whether it be the more elusive incident of the Peoples' Temple or other cases closer to home, the discernment of the several correlates of cult-related violence leaves, in the meantime, considerable room for remedial action.

First, *the necessary role played by groups and their leaders in sanctioning violence suggests that efforts to counter such sanctions could produce marked results.* Such an effort has already begun to stop child abuse by exposing family dilemmas which allow it to exist and bringing legal structures to bear on traditional sanctions to its continuance. An additional effort by evangelical Christian ministers to disavow interpretations of Scripture that sanction child abuse could add weight to secular initiatives. In like measure, a rejection by public leaders of such coercive measures as deprogramming coupled with the advocacy of nonviolent alternatives for families disturbed by the membership of one person in a nonconventional religion could hasten the adoption of family counseling measures which could in turn alleviate the single most controllable area of cult-related violence.

Second, *the general commitment to eradicate the structures of religious group prejudice could be strengthened.* The common practice of generalizing about nonconventional religions could be replaced with the more accurate and profitable alternative of discriminating between the various groups and judging each on its individual merits and weaknesses. Toward this end, the promotion of dialogue between members of nonconventional religions, church leaders, and the public could create situations in which cult-based stereotypes held by non-members could be confronted and eliminated. Certainly such attempts at dialogue, especially with groups that have separatist tendencies, would be difficult, but hardly more so than those initial dialogues that began the process of eliminating derogatory stereotypes of Blacks, Jews, or the poor. In each case the value received by culture has been more than amply rewarded for the effort.

Third, *processes of intervention in potentially violent situations could be developed and improved.* Some violence-prone religious groups do exist and others will most likely emerge in the future. The proper agencies of the society should be prepared to mobilize at the first signs of potential violence. However, emphasis should be placed upon the prevention of violence as opposed to dealing with its consequences after the fact. Situations with a violent potential, especially those which involve a nonconventional religious group, do not always respond best to pressures of law-enforcing agencies.

More adequate responses come through community pressures: the full exposure of the potentially violent situation to public scrutiny and the active intervention of knowledgeable individuals who can assist opposing parties to seek nonviolent solutions are more likely to defuse potentially violent conditions than the application of an outside force.

Fourth, *the recognition of the increasingly pluralistic religious environment of the West and the movement to include the so-called "cults" into the larger religious community should proceed with all due haste.* The cults, most of whom are representatives of the massive wave of Eastern and Middle Eastern religious groups, which migrated to the United States during the past two decades, have become permanent residents of the United States, indeed of all the Western world. Their presence can be seen as but one aspect of the shift in American Society from a predominantly Protestant Christian country to a religiously pluralistic society in which the Roman Catholic Church is the single largest religious body and in which Islam has grown larger than Judaism.

The religious diversification of America will be met with dialogue and attempts to understand, or a steadily increasing level of religious conflict can be expected. Given the precedence of several generations of Jewish-Christian dialogue, the amount to be gained from a general shift of perception of the so-called cults seems enormous. The values to be gained from dismantling the structures of hostility and building bridges of insight and discernment could be highly educational to both sides, and, while conserving the energy now put into polemics, result in the creative solution to some common problems. Given the present trends, the development of higher levels of acceptance and understanding of people with different, even radically different, religious outlooks is fast becoming a necessity of cultural survival.

Violence and Religion in the 1980s

During the 1980s, as the various attacks on the new religions by the anti-cult movement were blunted one by one, and the general tension level between the cults and the environment lessened, so the reports of violent activity has noticeably dropped. This decrease has been for both violence aimed at the cults and violence perpetrated by them. The overall trend appears to be a healthy one, as the number of new religions continue to grow at a steady pace.

Among the more visible factors contributing to the decline of violence was the public withdrawal of support for deprogramming by the Cult Awareness Network. While some deprogrammings still occur, and informally CAN still assists in that process, its public backing of non-coercive exit counseling facilitated the removal of deprogramming as a major issue. In like measure, the greater acceptance of the new religions and the maturing of the leadership of the more controversial ones has led to a rejection by them of any violent alternative. The most graphic example has been the development of the Black Muslims who moved steadily toward orthodox Islam and have merged into the larger Muslim community. In the process they, like the Mormons, have left their violent history behind. Unfortunately, the other single most violent American religious group in recent years, the Church of the Lamb of God, was involved in further killings both of rival leaders and disgruntled former members.

While violence as a whole has decreased, two new forms of violence have taken center stage. First, amid the broad concern of clergy misuse of their position, have come increasing charges against the leaders of new religions of sexual assaults on members. Rumblings of the victims of such assaults first emerged in the larger Buddhist community as it was maturing as a uniquely American religious community. Female members began to complain of Zen masters and Buddhist priests taking liberties with unsuspecting students. In at least one well-known case, Richard Baker Roshi was asked to leave the Zen Center of San Francisco. In other cases, members let it be known that such activity was unacceptable.

A similar situation arose in the Hindu community. While rumors had spread quietly through the 1970s that some supposedly celibate gurus were not following their own behavioral norms, beginning with the publication of accounts of Swami Muktananda in the early 1980s, other stories began to surface. Several gurus quietly faded from the scene while others faced with similar sets of accusations, such as Swami Rama of the Himalayan Institute and Swami Satchidananda of the Integral Yoga Institute, have denied the charges and continue to lead their organizations.

Those attempting to understand such failings have pointed to a number of factors, not the least being the celebrity status ascribed Eastern religious teachers coupled with the almost worshipful attitudes of many followers. However, for the purpose of the topic under consideration, the number of serious accusations of sexual abuse against the leaders of new religions is far lower than those against mainline priests and ministers. The Roman Catholic Church has for several decades wrestled with the problems created by priests who have abused both adults and children in their parishes. For many years it paid out hundreds of thousands of dollars to victims to keep the situation out of the papers, but during the last decade has had to consider the problem in the light of widespread media coverage.

The second and more troublesome issue is that of Satanism. During the 1980s numerous reports of Satanic activity and accompanying violence against females associated with Satanic covens have been reported in the media. Collectively, the stories have generated a whole new, hitherto unreported, "myth" concerning the nature of Satanism. The basic account is reported by women in their thirties who claim that as children or teenagers they were forced by their parents to participate in Satanic rituals in which they were physically beaten and sexually assaulted. Most of those who report teenage involvement also claim that they bore one or more children which were immediately taken and used in a sacrificial ritual. These "survivors" have often been referred to as "breeders." This activity was said to have occurred at a time when to all outward appearances they were leading a normal teenage life, attending school, and participating in various social activities. Such accounts now number in the hundreds

A variation on the basic story is the contemporary reports of children who claim (or whose parents claim for them) that they have been sexually abused in a Satanic ritual in the immediate past, usually at the hands of a divorced parent or preschool center teacher. The most famous such case was the McMartin School case in Manhattan Beach, California, in which the entire staff (most members of one family) were accused of regularly engaging the children in ritual and abusive situations over a period of years. The case led to a lengthy trial, but no convictions.

The Satanism cases have been likened to the other cases of adult sexual abuse. However, they stand out as unique in several respects. First, we have not been able to independently corroborate the stories, and, as a whole, the women who report the stories have been unwilling to assist in locating the evidence. For example, in cases where they claim that the Satanist group still exists and that they know its location, they have been unwilling to lead authorities in apprehending them.

The Satanist stories present the outside observer with a particularly hard set of problems. First, with very few exceptions, the women who report the stories are not lying and show obvious signs of trauma. One can quickly discard explanations which involve hoaxing and simple fantasies. But at the same time, the women tell an extraordinary tale centered upon their being involved in the group, coming to know its members and secrets, and then being released. The group seemed content to risk their never divulging the story. In fact, the women seemed to have forgotten it until it was recalled bit by bit under the guidance of a counselor.

If each individual story presents its own problems, the stories taken collectively provide an additional set. Since each story tells of a different coven operating twenty to thirty years ago, together they document a large network of thousands of people involved in Satanic practice, all doing roughly the same thing and reportedly tied together for various nefarious purposes such as stealing and purchasing babies for ritual sacrifice. In the meantime, these covens were able to operate through the 1950s, 1960s, and 1970s without a hint of their existence, even in the rumor mill. Even people who claimed to be former Satanists who converted to Christianity at a later date knew nothing of them. Meanwhile, they were able to kill and dispose of thousands of bodies without any trace (an extremely difficult task).

Thus, while the survivors tell convincing stories, for these and other reasons, their stories have been called into serious doubt, and alternative explanations have been sought. In many cases, it has been suggested that some childhood trauma, most likely incest or sexual abuse by a friend of the family, might have been the starting point. In other cases, guilt over an abortion may be partially to blame. In many cases, increasingly so as time goes on, the Satanic element is counselor generated.

Whatever the final explanation turns out to be, the hardest obstacle to overcome in accepting the stories at face value is lack of any independent evidence that the events occurred. In this regard, the Satanist survivor stories are very much like the account of UFO abductions. A number of people, mostly women, also tell of being captured by UFO entities and having various kinds of "experiments" done on them. The stories are quite convincingly told, but there is the same lack of corroboration that the events ever occurred. In this respect, the stories differ markedly from those of the average accusation of rape. In a large percentage of rape cases there is little question that the event of sexual intercourse occurred or that the male involved actually existed. What is in question is the element of force involved and the intentions of the two people. In both the Satanist and UFO cases, the very existence of a perpetrator is in question.

Given the serious questions which have been raised concerning Satanic abuse cases, we must put them aside until they either go away or the needed evidence substantiating them emerges. It seems more likely, given present knowledge, that the former will occur.

Conclusion

It is a good sign that at least some sanctions to violent, religiously motivated activity have been removed during the last decade and that the overall tension level between the new religions and society have decreased significantly. In such a climate the hard process of religious dialogue and understanding-building can proceed. Moving among new religious groups for the past twenty-five years has convinced me that I was encountering serious religious communities which were here to stay. Many of their leaders were people of mature spiritual insight who were in turn producing a new generation of mature, if very different, spiritual leaders. As they have now become our neighbors, it is time to concentrate our energies on creating together the world we want to leave to our children.

Endnotes:

1. Ken Levi, ed., *Violence and Religious Commitment* (University Park, PA: Pennsylvania State University Press, 1982).

2. Don Nori, "Persecution at Island Pond." *Charisma* 10, 4 (November 1984): 68-78.

3. Cf. Alan M. Schwartz, "The Way International." *ADL Research Report* (Spring 1982): 1-17.

4. For a more detailed account of the Church of the Lamb of God, see Ben Bradlee, Jr., and Dale Van Atta, *Prophet of Blood* (New York: G. P. Putnam's Sons, 1981) and Verlan M. LeBaron, *The LeBaron Story* (Lubbock, TX: The Author, 1981).

5. On the Black Muslim incidents, see C. Eric Lincoln, *The Black Muslims in America* (Boston, MA: Beacon Press, 1961) and George Breitman, Iterman Porter, and Baxter Smith, *The Assassination of Malcolm X* (New York: Pathfinder Press, 1976).

6. Clark Howard, *Zebra* (New York: Berkley Books, 1980).

7. Cf. H. T. F. Rhodes, *The Satanic Mass* (New York: Citadel Press, 1955) and Arthur Lyons, Jr., *The Second Coming: Satanism in America* (New York: Dodd,

Mead, 1970).

8. Daniel Kagan and Ian Summers, *Mute Evidence* (New York: Bantam Books, 1984).

9. I am grateful to members of Synanon's staff for their response to accusations of violence at Synanon made in such books as Dave Mitchell, Cathy Mitchell, and Richard Ofshe, *The Light on Synanon* (New York: Seaview Books, 1980).

10. N. K. Singh, "Ananda Marg's Lust for Blood." *The Illustrated Weekly of India* (October 10, 1977): 8-14.

11. For a detailed listing of Scientology's litigation, see *What Is Scientology?* (Los Angeles: Church of Scientology of California, 1978).

12. Deborah (Linda Berg) Davis, *The Children of God* (Grand Rapids, MI: Zondervan Publishing House, 1984).

13. See the discussion of the Church of Armageddon in Steve Allen, *Beloved Son* (Indianapolis, IN: Bobbs-Merrill, 1982).

14. Richard Hofstadter and Michael Wallace, eds. *American Violence: A Documentary History* (New York: Alfred A. Knopf, 1970).

15. Nevitt Sanford, "Going Beyond Prevention." In Nevitt Sanford and Craig Comstock, eds., *Sanctions for Evil* (San Francisco: Josey-Bass, 1971).

16. *Hate Groups in America* (New York: Anti-Defamation League of B'nai B'rith, 1982).

INDEX